HISTORY OF THE

MOVIES

Bison Books

First published in 1983 by
Bison Books Corp.
17 Sherwood Place
Greenwich, CT 06830
USA

ISBN 0 86124 119 3

Printed in Hong Kong

WARNER BROS. SUPREME TRIUMPH
AL JOLSON
IN
"The JAZZ SINGER"

CONTENTS

PREVIEWS OF

COMING ATTRACTIONS

It emerged from Thomas A Edison's Menlo Park, New Jersey, laboratories in the 1890s, this marvel of lights and shadows we call the motion picture. One more entry in the catalogue of scientific and engineering achievements that had changed the world in the 19th century – the electric light, the telegraph, the telephone, the steamship and the steam locomotive – it was the follow-up to Edison's phonograph and, in his words, was to 'do for the eye what the phonograph did for the ear.' What it actually did was far surpass the impact of the phonograph and become, in time, joined by radio and television, the world's great provider of mass entertainment, molder of public opinion and setter of fashions, trends and modes of behavior.

Oddly, for a man with an almost unerring instinct for what the public needed and would appreciate, Edison showed little interest in his latest brainchild and was slow to recognize its potential. From the start, its development was left in the hands of his brilliant assistant, William K L Dickson, and once it was in its first working order in 1891, Edison regarded it as little more than a toy and was content to let it remain so. And indeed, it seemed a mere toy, with its pictures photographed on Eastman celluloid film inside a box-like camera called the Kinetograph and then viewed, one person at a time, by peering through the window of another box-like contraption, the Kinetoscope, while turning a hand crank. Looking at it all, Edison shrugged off the advice of his colleagues that the invention be developed to the point where the pictures could be projected on a screen and seen by entire audiences rather than single individuals.

Despite the great man's indifference, the laboratories continued to work towards screened projection. Quite soon, thanks to the public enchantment with the Kinetoscope and all the coins that were flooding into the penny arcades where it had been installed, Edison himself came to realize the profits to be had from audience showings. In the mid-1890s he bought the rights to a primitive Charles Jenkins-Thomas Armat projector, made improvements on it, and on 23 April 1896, at the Koster and Bials Music Hall in New York City, presented the first public showing of a screened motion picture. On that day, the motion picture industry as we now know it was born.

But even then the invention continued to be treated as a toy. Both in the Kinetoscope and on the screen, whether the productions came from Edison's company or the first of his competitors – the Mutoscope and Biograph Company – audiences were treated only to snippets of film, none of which bothered to tell a story. Rather, the menu of the day consisted of what were called 'novelties' and 'topical views.' They ranged from rural views, news clips, and scenes of trains rushing past to pantomimed Shakespearean bits and such risque fare – filmed sex was already profitably rearing its head – as Little Egypt's naughty dance at the 1896 Chicago World's Fair and a little item fetchingly titled 'How Brigit Served the Salad Undressed.'

But only American audiences were restricted to the filmed snippets. Matters were different in Europe. In France, the Lumière brothers – Louis and Auguste – became interested in picture making, as did an ex-stage magician named Georges Méliès. They started experimentally with the snippets but were soon turning out attractions that told a story, with the Lumières credited as being the first ever to do so, with a one-reel comedy titled *L'Arroseur Arrosé* (1895), which involved a mischievous youngster putting a kink in a garden hose and then releasing it just as the bewildered user is investigating the nozzle.

By 1898 the Lumières had done more than 1000 films, among them such ambitious dramatizations as *Faust* and *The Life and Passion of Jesus Christ*. As for Méliès, one of the most imaginative and creative figures in motion picture history, he was performing such cinema tricks as having his characters suddenly disappear (done simply by stopping the camera, removing the actor and then advancing the film again) and turning out such films as the 20-scene *Cinderella* (1899) and the ambitious *Jeanne d'Arc* (1900) with its 12 scenes and 500 extras. Two years later he did the screen's first science fiction story, the charming and memorable *Le Voyage dans la Lune/A Trip to the Moon*.

Nor were the French alone in using the screen to tell a story. In 1900, the Italians joined with them to do a filmed version of a passion play. Five years later, Italy produced *La Presa di Roma,* an historical spectacle. Within the next few years, other spectacles – the hallmark of Italy's early work – took shape, among them *Othello* (1907), *Romeo and Juliet* (1908), *Gli Ultimi di Pompeii/The Last Days of Pompeii* (1908) and *El Cid* (1910).

The United States was to become the world's leading producer of motion pictures, but no one would have prophesied such a future as the 20th century dawned. The filmed snippets remained the order of the day. But audiences were tired of them and attendance was drop-

Previous page: In D W Griffith's epic film, *The Birth of a Nation* (1915), the Southern troops were idealized. Here the Confederates hold off a Union charge. Allowing for rising costs, this picture has been said to be the biggest money-maker of all time, but it has also been an embarrassment to Hollywood because of its anti-Black bias.

Right: 'The Abominable Giant of the Snows' – Georges Méliès' creation for *The Conquest of the Pole* (1912). Although this monster was the hero of the film, he had the unpleasant habit of eating the members of a polar expedition.

ping fast. The infant film industry was on the point of dying, dying simply because it did not have what pictures needed then and have continued to need to this day – stories. Fortunately, due to the efforts of a few pioneer movie-makers, the death was averted.

A central figure here was Edwin S Porter, said to be the most imaginative and innovative of America's early directors. In 1903 he turned out a one-reel film with a definite plot, *The Life of an American Fireman*. It opened with a view of the fire chief in his station office, switched abruptly to a close-up of a hand activating an alarm box somewhere in town and returned immediately to the station, after which it followed a horse-drawn engine through the streets to a burning house, where the firemen rescued a mother and her child. In switching from the station office to the alarm box, Porter gave the US one of its earliest examples of a now-familiar screen technique, intercutting (the abrupt shift from one scene to another to provide the impression of simultaneous action). Porter then spent the remainder of 1903 doing an ambitious production of *Uncle Tom's Cabin* and his best remembered and most influential work, *The Great Train Robbery*. A simply told and exciting little western, *The Great Train Robbery* proved to be such a box office success that it breathed

Top: In *The Great Train Robbery* (1903), the villains are about to make their escape with their ill-gotten gains. This movie helped set the formula for countless Westerns to follow.

Above: There have been very few sports films that have been box office successes. Charlton Heston appeared as a quarterback in one of them – Number One (1969).

Opposite: Many critics acclaim *Citizen Kane* as the finest picture of all time. The film paralleled the career of William Randolph Hearst, the newspaper tycoon. Orson Welles, at the time the boy wonder of American radio (at the time of the release of the movie in 1941 he was only 26 years old), produced, directed and starred in *Kane*. Here Welles (left) and Joseph Cotton are surrounded by stacks of Kane's first newspaper – the *Inquirer*.

Right: A celebration at Kane's house on the success of the newspaper.

life into the dying motion picture industry and is credited with establishing the industry as one that was here to stay.

On the day that stories replaced the film snippets, motion pictures began to come of age. Since then, world-wide, they have found story material in virtually any subject that can be mentioned. They have done a seemingly endless number of character studies, some of their best representatives being *All About Eve* (1950 USA), *Darling* (1965 UK), and *Dersu Azala* (1975 USSR/Japan), and perhaps the very best ever being Orson Welles' *Citizen Kane* (1941, USA). Obviously taking its inspiration from William Randolph Hearst, *Kane* infuriated the publisher's newspaper chain, claimed four US academy Award nominations (Best Picture, Best Director and Best Actor for Welles, and Best Black-and-White Cinematography for Gregg Toland), and won for young Welles and Herman Mankiewicz the Best Original Screenplay Award. *The New York Times* critic Bosley Crowther, reviewing the film on the day following its 4 May opening, commented that *Kane* came close to being the most sensational picture ever to emerge from Hollywood. In the years since, countless moviegoers have done him one better. They see it as the finest film ever made.

But character studies mark just one area that has been explored. The motion picture has looked at medicine in such fare as *The Citadel* (1938 UK) and *The Hospital* (1971 USA). Sports have come under their scrutiny in *This Sporting Life* (1963 UK) and *Number One* (1969 USA). Biography has been seen in *The Life of Emile Zola* (1937 USA); *Reach for the Sky* (1956 UK) – the story of

England's double amputee flying ace of World War II, Douglas Bader – and *Gandhi* (1982 UK - India). Politics have been the source of *Fame is the Spur* (1947 UK), *All the King's Men* (1949 USA), and *All the President's Men* (1976 USA). And history (with the producers sometimes sticking to the facts and sometimes seeming to make everything up out of whole cloth) has been the source of *The Charge of the Light Brigade* (1936 USA), *Fifty-Five Days at Peking* (1963 USA), *Zulu* (1964 UK), *Battle of Britain* (1969 UK), and two of the most splendid and ambitious of the industry's early offerings – David Wark Griffith's *The Birth of a Nation* (1915 USA) and Abel Gance's *Napoleon vu par/Napoleon* (1927 France).

Some subjects have proven so popular over the years and have been given so much attention that they have developed into genre. The principal representatives of their number have been ten:

- The Western
- Fantasy (represented chiefly by science fiction and horror films)
- The Musical
- Comedy
- Crime
- Disaster
- Mystery-Suspense
- Romance
- Social Comment
- War

Of the ten, the first four – the western, fantasy in the form of science fiction and then horror, the musical, and comedy – are considered, by virtue of the massive amount of work done in them, to be the major genre. The remainder – from crime through war – are regarded as secondary genre, not because their fea-

tures are less important or less significant, but simply because they have been, in total production, less fertile.

The purpose of this book, quite simply, is to tell the story of motion picture history by studying the development of the genre, structuring the book so that a chapter is given to each of the major categories and one chapter to the secondary representatives. In the development of each of the genre can be seen the growth of industry production into, at the least, a finely honed craft and, at the best, an art form; and in the development of each can be seen the manner in which this great purveyor of mass entertainment, public opinion, and public manners has guided or responded to the tastes and needs of its vast, sometimes-worshipful, sometimes-derisive but always fickle audience through the so-varied times since the day of Edison's Kinetoscope.

And so it's time to consider a host of films, some of which have been masterworks, some of which have been beguiling or simply passing entertainments, and some of which, frankly, have been wastes of time to make. They've done everything from move the spirit and lift the mind to send us home wondering why we ever paid the price of admission to see them. But, no matter how good or bad any of their number have been, they've had one effect on us all: they and the people who make them have unfailingly fascinated us – and likely always will.

Shall we have the house lights down, please.

THE
WESTERN

Produced by the Edison Company, it was a one-reeler with a running time of about 12 minutes. It cast little more than flickering shadows on the screen and boasted a plot that no one, not even the most backward and backwater of audiences, could ever call mentally taxing. Yet this relic from 1903 stands as one of the most influential films ever made.

It is, of course, *The Great Train Robbery* and its influence can be felt on two levels. A smash hit at the Nickelodeon box office, it breathed life into a dying infant and started the American movie business on its way to becoming an industry that, within three decades, would be taking in 110 million admissions a week. Culturally, and of even greater consequence, *Robbery* gave birth to one of the most enduring of film genre – the western or, if you must, the horse opera, the oater, the cowboy picture.

The western, though certainly not the oldest of the film categories, is, hands down, the most distinctly American of the lot. Science fiction can be set on the red planet Mars or in a polar outpost visited by a 'Thing'; the musical in the South Pacific or Professor Higgins' London townhouse; and the horror film in Transylvania or a Japanese town being stepped on by Godzilla. It all makes no difference. But the gunfighter on horseback – Gregory Peck or Clint Eastwood riding silently through the mesquite to a meeting with destiny in a board and tarpaper town – has to be on American soil (or just yonder over the border in Mexico), regardless of whether the camera belongs to Rome's Cinecitta Studios and all the Indian extras answer to such names as Luigi and Alfredo. He's an American. He has to be. Otherwise, aside from such rarities as Marlon Brando's *Viva Zapata,* the picture just won't work. For 80 years now, he's represented a very basic American type, something deep within the American character, and the blunt American way of handling a problem. For better or worse, audiences the world over identify Americans through him.

They've been a hectic 80 years for the horseman and this most American of film categories. It's a genre that, with periodic lapses in popularity, has advanced from herky-jerky one-reelers to such spectaculars as *The Covered Wagon* (1923), *Union Pacific* (1939), and *How the West Was Won* (1962). Along the way, it has fascinated moviegoers across the world, enchanting millions with its action and sweep while rousing the contempt of millions more as a vehicle for violent and shopworn plots, cardboard characterizations and simplistic black-white moralities. It's produced stars of the dazzling magnitude of a John Wayne on the the one hand, and the anemic glimmer of a whip-toting Lash La Rue on the other. It's given us the best and the worst of cinematic fare – from the classic *Stagecoach* (1939) and the allegorical *3:10 to Yuma* (1957) to the soap operaish *Duel in the Sun* (1947) and the unintentionally hilarious *Westward Bound*. Ah, *Westward Bound!* Breathes there a denizen of the Saturday matinee, circa 1944, who can forget it? It's the quickie epic that, without the funds for such niceties as retakes, permitted a stick of dynamite thrown by Hoot Gibson to land in front of the camera and be recorded lying there while a special effects charge blew up in great style a few yards away.

In a nutshell, then, the western has been all that any genre can hope to be in the care of mere mortals – splendid, good, bad and downright atrocious, but rarely, if ever, dull.

Previous page: The wagon train in John Wayne's film *Red River* (1948).

Above: The posse pursues the thieves through a forest in *The Great Train Robbery* (1903).

ancestor of such white man-red man social treatises as *The Vanishing American* (1925), Jeff Chandler's *Broken Arrow* (1950) and Robert Redford's *Tell Them Willie Boy is Here* (1970).

Finally, the picture was a 'first' for three figures of lasting significance to the film industry. *The Squaw Man* was the first directorial assignment for Cecil B DeMille, who would set the standard for Hollywood action 'spectaculars' for the next four decades. And it was the first production of Jesse L Lasky's Feature Play Company. Owned by Lasky, DeMille and a former glove salesman who had yet to change his name from Samuel Goldfish to Samuel Goldwyn, the company was well launched with *The Squaw Man*'s commercial and artistic success and eventually evolved into Paramount Pictures. As for the one-time glove salesman, his name became a part of MGM and he himself, as an independent producer, made the words 'Samuel Goldwyn Presents' synonomous with high-quality entertainment for millions of filmgoers from the mid-1920s through the 1950s.

The Squaw Man was remade twice. Granite-jawed Jack Holt starred in a 1916 version. The lead in a 1931 production went to Warner Baxter. DeMille directed both remakes.

The honor of being the world's first cowboy movie star goes, as mentioned already, to 'Broncho Billy' Anderson. William S Hart was the biggest attraction to come immediately in his wake. Both men made significant contributions to the growth of the genre.

'Billy' was born Max Aronson in Little Rock, Arkansas, in 1882. By the time he was a young man trying for a stage career in New York, he had altered his name to Gilbert M Anderson. That career never got off the ground and he was working as a model when the Edison Company hired him for a Porter one-reeler, *The Messenger Boy's Mistake* (1902). He then went on to play several supporting roles in *Robbery*. From there, taking on his nickname, he started the climb to western stardom.

That Anderson was a popular western player is considered something of an oddity. He simply didn't look the part. He had none of the classic western characteristics – not the 'high pockets' lankiness of a Gary Cooper, not the hawk-like features of a Randolph Scott, and certainly not the proud grace of a John Wayne in the saddle, the fact of the matter being that he fell from his horse during *Robbery*'s first day of shooting. Anderson was a man of medium height, was on the portly side and had a businessman's slightly jowly face. And, though he finally learned to ride, he never, by his own admission, advanced beyond the competent stage.

But one thing has to be said for him. Anderson was ambitious and hard working. After making *Robbery,* he acted in a dozen pictures, did some directing and then, in 1907, joined with George K Spoor in Chicago to form the Essanay Company, deriving the name from the first letters of their surnames, *S* and *A*. Anderson immediately headed west. He set up shop in Niles Canyon across the bay from San Francisco and launched his 'Broncho Billy' series while Spoor managed the Company's Chicago studio.

Beginning with *The Bandit Makes Good,* Anderson starred himself in nearly 400 'Billy' one- and two-reelers between 1907 and 1914 for that startling average of about one a week. It was an amazing record, made all the more so by the fact that Anderson did his filming throughout the West, hauling his company about in a special train. The train carried a film lab so that the day's work could be processed immediately. Produced at a dead run, Anderson's pictures couldn't help but be flawed with imperfections, but they were nevertheless great crowd pleasers. They gave the screen one of its earliest recognizable characters, lifted Anderson to stardom and established him as the first of that new breed – the cowboy star.

Anderson and the Essanay company did not limit themselves to western pictures. The studio was also a major producer of general comedy fare, specializing in farce and slapstick. Its stars included Ben Turpin, Francis X Bushman, and Wallace Beery. Charlie Chaplin spent 1915 on the Essanay lot and perfected his 'little tramp' character while there. The film that is regarded as his first masterpiece – *The Tramp* – was an Essanay product.

Anderson's prodigious output, attracting audiences everywhere, was his obvious contribution to the growth of the western. But when he brought his cameras west for the sunshine that would give him year-around lighting, he made another, a more important and subtler, contribution, as did all the cowboy picture makers who came to California at the same time. The New Jersey scenery had charmed *Robbery*'s audiences. But now Anderson and his fellow producers did their shooting against the rugged and spectacular backdrop of the actual West. As it has done ever since, the scenery itself endowed the pictures, even the worst of them, with an inescapable physical beauty and with a grandeur that gave the characters – and the simplest of their actions – an added dimension and left audiences with the deep impression of men who, as they struggled among themselves, were also struggling to best

a wild and perhaps untamable land. Anderson and his fellow producers didn't know it, but they were opening the way to the stirring epics of the future and to those mood and character pieces that would raise a simple action category to an art form.

William S Hart, though he hailed from Newburgh, New York, was the first genuine westerner to win stardom in a cowboy costume. Born in 1870, he spent his boyhood in the Blackfoot and Sioux lands of Minnesota and Wisconsin. He saw frontier life at first hand, learned the Sioux language by the time he was six, worked as a ranch hand in his teens and developed an understanding of and appreciation for life in the wilds that would be strongly reflected in all his films.

Bitten by the acting bug somewhere along the line, Hart arrived in New York when he was 19 and went on the stage. Touring first with Shakespearean companies, he steadily developed into a popular leading man, eventually scoring one of his greatest triumphs in the staging of *The Virginian*. His fame as a western hero was already being established.

That fame, however, did not become nationwide until 1914 when, at 44, Hart went to work in pictures for his friend, producer Thomas Ince. After debuting as a villain in several two-reelers, he

Gilbert Maxwell 'Broncho Billy' Anderson (1882-1971), an unsuccessful vaudeville performer who drifted into films in *The Great Train Robbery* (1903). He later founded the Essanay company and made nearly 400 one-reel Westerns starring himself. Anderson was given a special Academy Award in 1957 'for his contribution to the development of motion pictures.'

took to directing and starring in his own western vehicles. Looking as if he actually belonged in the saddle, he was soon rivaling 'Broncho Billy' at the box office and far outdoing Anderson in the quality of his production values.

As did Anderson, Hart made two contributions to the genre. The first sprang from his deep contempt for the westerns of the day. With rare exceptions, they were hell-bent-for-leather yarns that put the accent on heroics and he saw them as glamorizing a way of life that he knew from experience to be hard and often cruel. The whole approach struck him as dishonest and silly. He had lived the real thing. It deserved to be put on film and Hart set out to do exactly that.

A look at any of his pictures leaves no doubt that he succeeded. The sets for Hart towns have a drab, ramshackle look to them. Hart saloons are grim places, hot and stuffy in the summer, dank in the winter. Hart players wear workworn, dusty clothes, their faces are leathery and weather-beaten and they give every appearance of having lived brutalizing lives, as well they should because it was Hart's custom to people his films with players who had actually been on the frontier. This realism made the competition seem pale, impressed audiences deeply, and was much responsible for Hart's work being the best

that the genre had to offer at the time.

Hart's second contribution was a character portrayal new to audiences of his day but one that now ranks among the most familiar of western movie types – the good-bad man. He is the man who, perhaps an outlaw, perhaps a gambling 'no-account,' perhaps a drifter with revenge on his mind, starts out with the worst of intentions and then encounters some circumstance – it can be the moral purity of cause, but most often it is the love of a decent woman – that by the final reel transforms him into the redeemed hero who now faces the future afresh or sacrifices his life for his new-found values. How familiar the character is to anyone who remembers Fred MacMurray in *The Texas Rangers* (1936) or Robert Preston in *Union Pacific* (1939).

What Hart did with the good-bad man can be illustrated by one of his earliest films – *The Bargain* (1914). Hart's character Jim Stokes, is wounded while pulling off a stagecoach robbery. Escaping, he takes refuge with Nell Brent and her prospector father, falls in love with Nell as he recuperates, and wants to start a new and straight life with her as man and wife. The two are married, only to have Jim captured by Sheriff Bud Walsh soon after the wedding. Walsh takes Jim and the stagecoach

William S Hart, shown here taking a director's view of one of his own action-packed films, was a creative genius in the Western genre, and one of the most famous performers in the 1920s. His middle initial was reported to have stood for either 'Shakespeare' or 'Surrey.'

money into custody and then proceeds to lose the money in a gambling hall. Now come the sequences that give the picture its name. Jim strikes a bargain with Walsh: he'll win the money back and save the sheriff's hide if Walsh will then free him. The sheriff agrees. Jim keeps his part of the bargain in a climatic gambling scene, after which he and Nell depart for the Mexican border and that new life.

Considering the strict moral climate prevailing in the United States of his day, it is surprising that Hart's good-bad man character attracted the audiences that it did. The deal that is struck in *The Bargain* has a dishonesty to it that shocked not a few reviewers. And, though not on view in this particular film, Hart's good-bad man was an amoral cuss where women were concerned. His arrangement with such temptresses as Louise Glaum, who played dance hall queens in more than a dozen of his pictures, was strictly one of sex and money. When a sweet and virginal heroine came along and touched him with her innocence, he was just as likely to have a go at seduction rather than marriage on his way to redemption. How could Hart be at such odds with the day's accepted moralities and get away with it? The answer seems to be that the frontier was still a living reality to most audiences and they recognized the good-bad man as an honest Western type, a man who could not possess noble qualities because the raw land, the life that it engendered and its law of the gun would not permit him such luxuries.

Though the good-bad man has survived to this day, the sexual side of his nature was sublimated right out of sight by the stars who came in Hart's wake. The villain could still lust after the innocent maiden in the best traditions of time-worn melodrama – but not the hero. With an eye on rapt kiddie audiences and their concerned parents in countless neighborhood and small town theaters, the hero rescued the maiden to save her honor (whatever that meant to the small fry in the front row) and not to claim her sexually. Fearless as he might be when facing down a group of rustlers, he dissolved into an 'aw shucks' confusion in the grateful and perhaps amorous presence of a good woman. It wasn't until Jane Russell leered up at Jack Buetel in *The Outlaw* (1943) and Gregory Peck leered

down at Jennifer Jones in *Duel in the Sun* four years later that the cowpoke got his lust back.

Though their contributions were lasting ones, Anderson and Hart each enjoyed careers that ran for only about ten years. In 1916, while yet a good box office draw, 'Broncho Billy' sold his interest in Essanay and turned to producing Broadway shows. In later years, he returned to Hollywood for a variety of directorial chores. Anderson, who was awarded a special Academy Award Oscar in 1951 for his services to the industry, died in 1971.

Hart's popularity was on the wane when he left pictures in the mid-1920s. Public taste was undergoing one of its routine changes, with his realism falling out of favor along with the slowly developing plots that his emphasis on the good-bad man characterization required. Riding high now were the pure action feature and serial films of such rangehands as Tom Mix and Hoot Gibson. Hart made his last film *Tumbleweeds* – in 1925. On his retirement, he wrote several western novels and an autobiography, *My Life – East and West*. He lived to see the return of the character/mood westerns that he loved so well. But more of them later. Hart died in 1946.

The major action stars who replaced Hart – Mix, Gibson, Ken Maynard,

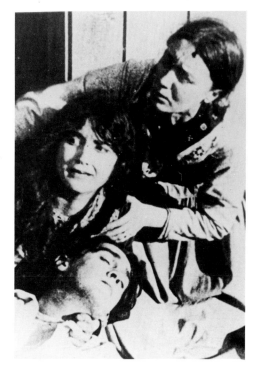

Above: In William S Hart's *Hell's Hinges* (1916), an unruly mob from a saloon kills the town preacher. Following this scene, Hart marches to the saloon, kicks the doors open and shouts, according to the subtitles, 'Hell needs this town, and it's goin' back, and goin' damn quick.'

Below: In another scene from *Hell's Hinges*, Hart meets the beautiful Faith and her minister brother. In the subtitle, she looks at him with 'a different kind of smile, sweet, honest and trustful, and seeming to say, "How do you do, friend!" '

A quartet of cowboy stars of the 1920s and 1930s.

Top left: Hoot Gibson (1892-1962), who had actually been a cowboy. He specialized in good-humored Westerns.

Top right: Tom Mix (1880-1940), a former US Marshal, who later made over 400 low-budget Westerns.

Above: Ken Maynard (1895-1973), who was once a rodeo rider and then worked in films as a stunt man.

Right: Buck Jones (1889-1942), whose real name was Charles Gebhardt. He starred in serials and many Western second features.

Buck Jones and Tim McCoy – were as much the genuine western article as he. Gibson, Mix, Jones, and Maynard each spent pre-Hollywood time stunt riding with Wild West shows and rodeos. After a stint of soldiering, Mix worked for a while as a Texas Ranger. Gibson punched cattle as a teenager in Colorado. McCoy owned a Wyoming ranch, was a recognized authority on Indian customs and history, and was serving as Indian Agent for his territory at the time he took on his first film job – as technical adviser and coordinator of the Indian extras for *The Covered Wagon* (1923).

Like Hart, the men started their Hollywood careers in some minor capacity, often as stuntmen or extras. And, again like Hart, in their best days they made pictures that featured good production values and showed a close attention to the authenticity of detail and locale. And outstanding talent had a habit of cropping up in their efforts. W S (Woody) Van Dyke, who would turn out such diverse MGM hits of the 30s and early 40s as *The Thin Man* (1934) and *Journey for Margaret* (1942), directed McCoy's *Winners of the Wilderness* (1927) and *Wyoming* (1928). A supporting role in *Winners* went to a young woman just beginning what would be a remarkable career – Joan Crawford. Gibson's first major feature, *Action and Sure Fire* (1921), was directed by John Ford.

But, at this point, all similarity to Hart ended. The new stars gave little attention to character. The main thrust was on a breathtaking action that was the antithesis of his slow moving vehicles. Mix, the most famous of the lot, was especially adept at turning out lean films with fast-breaking plots and an almost nonstop action. Though rarely his own director, he always had a strong say in how his pictures were made.

Mix, in fact, can be principally credited with the next major development in the western. While Hart had sought to show frontier life as it had been, Mix now, putting the stress on action, turned the cowboy into a clear-eyed Robin Hood who, chasing bad guys all over the landscape and rescuing poke-bonneted maids, just didn't have time for the true and gritty work of the West – the mending of fences and the rounding up of strays. The result: a neatly (sometimes gaudily) dressed, well combed, stylized hero in an unreal West. Edwin S Porter, in *The Great Train Robbery,* laid out the basic ingredients of the western. Mix, ably assisted by his fellow riders, blended those basic ingredients into a standardized pattern of hero-plot-action that was to serve as the basic format for all but the most unusual westerns to come.

There may have been little connec-

A scene from *Frontier Crusader* with Tim McCoy (second from right). He began his work in films in 1923 when, as an ex-army colonel, he went to Hollywood as an advisor on *The Covered Wagon.*

tion with frontier realities in Mix's films and those of his fellow stars, but audiences loved the action and, with the memory of the real West fading from public consciousness as the years went by, accepted the Never-Never-Land that the cinematic mesas and plains were becoming. And, as something more than just a bonus, they were spellbound by the impressive horsemanship that the action demanded. Experienced and talented riders all, the new action stars did most of their own stunt work, with Mix proving especially daring. Throughout his career, he had the reputation for taking risks that resulted in injury. It was, in fact, the experience of several bad falls while stunting in the early 1930s that prompted the star, by then 52, to retire from the film range.

But all this is not to say that the westerns of the 1920s were completely without character. Hoot Gibson came up with an offbeat hero, the westerner who rarely carried a gun and was as apt to settle his problems by comic means as by action. Buck Jones' work revealed a streak of self-mocking humor that enabled him happily to don ridiculous disguises that could fool a villain but not the youngest kid in the audience. Harry Carey, a major star of the day and a fine character actor in later years, superbly communicated the loneliness of the drif-

ter when he stood apart from the townsfolk, his lined face thoughtful, with one arm characteristically flung across his body to grasp the elbow of the other. And off-screen, Tom Mix, living in a mansion that outdid Pickfair, nightclubbing and hobnobbing with European nobility, developed a flamboyant image that couldn't have been farther removed from his clean-living, straight-shooting screen self but that nevertheless, as did Hart's good-bad man, enchanted his fans.

So Hart's realism was on the way out in the early 1920s and the standard stylized western was here to stay. But there is no such thing as an absolute in history. Realism remained and thrived in one type of western that was born in the 1920s. Just as the decade gave us a new breed of screen cowboy, so did it give us a new breed of western picture – the epic.

If, after having been viewed by millions over the years, it now needs to be defined, the epic tells the story of some

facet of the building of the West, with each yarn fluctuating between sprawling events and personal adventures, trials, and romances. Epics of another nature – such as Italy's *Quo Vadis?* and D W Griffith's *The Birth of a Nation* – were familiar commodities by the 1920s. And we weren't without a western saga by that time; *Tigerman*, the story of a wagon train's westward trek, had come out in 1918. But the epic western can be said to have truly established itself as a part of the genre in 1923.

That was the year that the Famous Players-Lasky company released James Cruze's *The Covered Wagon*. Running more than two hours, it followed, as did *Tigerman*, a wagon train of the mid-1800s westward across deserts, plains, and mountains, enduring hostile Indians, swollen rivers, and blazing heat along the way, until the moment at trail's end when actress Ethel Wales, her face a compound of exhaustion and triumph, could stand holding two clods of rich Oregon soil in her outstretched hands. Among the picture's stars were Ernest Torrence, Tully Marshall, and Alan Hale (Sr), but the greater stars were the rugged Nevada and Utah backgrounds. They gave the picture a scope and, in combination with the players, a hard authenticity – Cruze was always quick to say that the

dust, the Indians, and even the beards in the film were the 'real thing' – that made it a phenomenal box office success and, in time, lifted it to the status of a classic, a deserved status that it continues to occupy to this day.

Its critical acclaim matched its commercial success. Critic Robert Sherwood, apparently forgetting *The Birth of a Nation,* called it 'the one great American epic the screen has produced.' A colleague remarked that it brought a 'breath of fresh air' to an industry whose products had become jaded with the jazz age. Others called it anything from impressive to breathtaking.

But there were some dissenting voices. Several critics teased Cruze for allowing the leading lady to come through the trek with the dual miracle of an unwrinkled dress and an unruffled hairdo. Others thought that her love story got in the way of things. And William S Hart snorted at the picture's much praised authenticity. As he saw it, no sane westerner would have parked the wagon train, as Cruze did, in a box canyon in the heart of hostile Indian country. and no sane westerner, as Cruze did, would have permitted oxen to swim a river with their necks yoked.

Audiences, however, ignored the various jibes. They crowded in to see *The Covered Wagon*. And, with the im-

In *The Covered Wagon* (1923), the wagons form a circle. This big-scale pioneer Western did much to establish the form.

mediacy that always marks imitation, movie makers began exploring other aspects of the winning of the West for story lines. Director John Ford traced the building of the Union Pacific railroad in *The Iron Horse (1924)*. Ricardo Cortez rode through dust storms and a rain of Indian arrows to deliver the mails in *The Pony Express* (1925). Another wagon train – one of so many that the years would see – made its way west in *The Pioneer Scout* (1928). And Richard Dix and Irene Dunne helped to settle Oklahoma in *Cimarron* (1931).

Cimarron must be given special mention here because of its contribution to the genre at the advent of sound. Most western film makers, for a combination of valid and invalid reasons, considered their product a sudden thing of the past with the coming of sound. They thought, quite correctly, that the cumbersome and primitive sound equipment of the day would, both technically and financially, make the recording of outdoor pictures too difficult, if not downright impossible, to deal with. And, mistakenly, many of their number prophesied that audiences would be interested only in the miracle of sound and that, consequently, pictures emphasizing action and requiring only the sparsest and most functional of dialogue would go begging at the box office. It was a view that damaged the standard western throughout the 1930s and sent the careers of such action stars as Buck Jones and Hoot Gibson into a sad decline. But, thanks to *Cimarron*, the epic did not suffer. *Cimarron* proved that the epic, at least, had a place for itself in the era of sound.

Based on Edna Ferber's novel, the picture told the story of the opening of Oklahoma's Cimarron Strip, with the most memorable sequences centering on the wild race of the homesteaders across the desolate countryside to lay claim to open pieces of land. It earned best acting nominations for both Dix and Dunne in the 1930/31 Academy Awards, with Dix losing out to Lionel Barrymore in *A Free Soul,* and Dunne to Marie Dressler in *Min and Bill.* The film itself, however, took the award for Best Picture of the Year and remains the only western ever to win that honor. The National Board of Review ranked *Cimarron* among the ten top pictures of the year, just ahead of Charlie Chaplin's *City Lights.*

Once *Cimarron*'s success had blazed the way, the majority of the expensively mounted and top grossing westerns of the 1930s and 40s turned out to be epics – Wallace Beery's *Viva Villa* (1934), Cecil B DeMille's *The Plainsman* (1936) and *Union Pacific* (1939), Errol Flynn's *Dodge City* (1939) and *They Died with Their Boots On* (1942), *Western Union* (1941) and Joel McCrea's *Buffalo Bill* (1944). Then, when public taste changed through the years and Hart's

Top right: *The Iron Horse* (1924) was directed by John Ford and was one of the earliest movies made exclusively on location. The picture was about the building of the transcontinental railroad and starred George O'Brien. The number of extras was about 6000.

Center right: A scene from *Dodge City* (1939). Errol Flynn (center) and Alan Hale look in on the jailed Guinn 'Big Boy' Williams.

Right: In *They Died With Their Boots On* (1942), Errol Flynn, playing General George Armstrong Custer, lectures Arthur Kennedy, as Joe Sawyer, the sergeant, looks on.

Top: John Wayne and Montgomery Clift in *Red River* (1948), one of the great Westerns and among the finest accomplishments of director Howard Hawks. The love-hate battles of the two stars, as father and surrogate son, told in the context of the first cattle drive on the Chisholm Trail, gave the movie its interesting blend of character conflict and epic sweep.

Above: The second version of Owen Wister's *The Virginian* (1930) starred Gary Cooper and Mary Brian. It had been filmed previously with Dustin Farnum (1914) and later (1945) with Joel McCrea. In 1964 it appeared as a television series with James Drury.

Right: *In Old Arizona* (1929) was an experiment in an all-talking outdoor drama. It was the first sound picture featuring the Cisco Kid, and starred Edmund Lowe.

character/mood western, as perhaps best exemplified by *High Noon* (1952) returned to vogue, the epic continued to do well for itself. Later examples from this branch of the genre include *Red River* (1948), *Fort Apache* (1948), *Across the Wide Missouri* (1951), *The Alamo* (1960), *How the West Was Won* (1963) and *The Way West* (1967). By the late 1960s, along with all other types of western, the epic was in decline.

As was said earlier, the western movie makers, for a combination of reasons, bowed their heads with the advent of sound and agreed that their product was dead. As proved by *Cimarron*, they were dead wrong on this latter point. And, providing more proof to the contrary, were two 1929 releases – *In Old Arizona* and the Gary Cooper-Richard Arlen remake of a 1914 hit, *The Virginian*. Both arrived on the market two years after Al Jolson's historic *The Jazz Singer*. Both were commercial and artistic successes. For his work in *In Old Arizona*, Warner Baxter won the 1928/29 Academy Award for Best Actor of the Year. Yet, unlike *Cimarron*, these two successes went ignored by the studio bosses. The western had been declared dead and that was that.

And so a pattern was set for the 1930s. The epic and, now and again, a grade-A action standard, both richly budgeted and boasting performers highly popular in a variety of other genres, played to the first-run houses in the big cities and raked in the giant profits and the critical praise. As predicted, the run-of-the-mill standard product, with its exclusively western stars, went into a decline. But it did so in a paradoxical fashion. Though no longer a first-run item, it continued to attract thousands of moviegoers who preferred action to dialogue and all that 'love stuff' and who didn't care that their heroes, when outdoors, seemed to be speaking into a barrel. In both its feature-length and Saturday-matinee serial form, the standard western continued to make money in second-run downtown houses, in neighborhood theaters, and in countless small towns. It has been estimated that the averge western played in at least 6000 theaters before it was relegated to the studio archives.

Though the profits were good, they were, by Hollywood standards, small potatoes, a fact that, in combination with the economic headaches of the Great Depression, gave birth to one of the most interesting periods in the western's history – the three-decade age of the 'quickie.' Inexpensive cowboy pictures had always been made, but now a tight budget and fast camera work became the hallmarks of the standard western. Depending on the studio from which it came, it could sport a budget from a low of $12,000 to an average high of around $60,000. As for speed of production, even the best of its number were usually turned out in less than two weeks. Most of the Gene Autry and Roy Rogers 'singing cowboy' pictures of the late 1930s (and, make no mistake, they featured good production values) were shot in an amazing six days each.

The quality of the quickies was broadly varied, from highs established by Republic (considered to be the best second-rank studio in town) in the Autry and Rogers vehicles and in *The Three Mesquiteers* series to lows set by such poverty-row outfits as Victory and Reliable with the likes of *Westward Bound* (remember that stick of dynamite lying there while the special effects charge blew up yards away?). The highest quality was seen when the double feature was born in the mid-1930s to draw depression audiences back into theaters. Within a few years after its introduction, the B picture – the bottom half of the double bill – was being turned out by every major studio in town. The standard western won a place among the Bs, was awarded a higher budget than was possible for the quickie, and showed the benefits of big studio care in such productions as Cesar Romero's Cisco Kid series at Fox. The term, B picture, was soon broadened to embrace all inexpensively-made pictures, even the cheapest.

As for the performers themselves, they formed as much of a study in contrasts as did the production values. Riding the B range, first, were those coming down from the heights; with major studios considering that the western was dead, Buck Jones, Ken Maynard, Hoot Gibson and Tim McCoy were forced into cheaper and cheaper productions, with only Tom Mix retiring while his career was still pretty much intact. They were joined by a host of new heroes – Donald 'Red' Barry, Johnny Mack Brown (a veteran romantic lead from the silents), Bob Steele, William 'Wild Bill' Elliott, Ray 'Crash' Corrigan, Bob Livingston, Tim Holt, William 'Hopalong Cassidy' Boyd and Lash La Rue. Some, such as Boyd, enjoyed a tremendous success and, in time, salted away greater fortunes than many a big studio star. Others, after a time in the saddle, went on to later major-studio successes, as did Tim Holt in Orson Welles' *The Magnificent Ambersons* (1942) and John Huston's *The Treasure of the Sierra Madre* (1947), and as did Barry and Steele, who made late-life careers for themselves as respected character actors. And some – La Rue and Maynard being prime examples here – eventually rode over the horizon and into obscurity.

Left: Gilbert Roland also played the Cisco Kid in *Riding the California Trail* (1948).

Below: Don 'Red' Barry was another popular star of grade 'B' Westerns.

Bottom: Johnny Mack Brown (standing), a Western star who was a former All-American football player.

Above: Roy Rogers, 'The King of the Cowboys,' born Leonard Slye in Cincinnati.

Right: Gene Autry at the end of a fight stares down at his victim in *Sioux City Sue*. Autry, an easy-going Texan, made millions in films from 1934-54 as a singing cowboy, usually with his horse, Champion.

Of course, there were those who stopped by the B bunkhouse while on the trail up to major star status. Robert Mitchum began his screen life as a bit player in a Hopalong Cassidy B, *Hoppy Serves a Writ* (1939). Two years before winning acclaim for his role in *Golden Boy* (1939) and establishing himself as one of the screen's most respected character actors, Lee J Cobb worked as a villain in *North of the Rio Grande* and *Rustler's Valley*. John Wayne spent the 1930s in a string of low budget westerns and serials, sometimes, as in 1933, appearing in as many as 12 a year. In 1938, he replaced Robert Livingston in *The Three Mesquiteers* series and did eight films as the Stony Brooke character. Then came *Stagecoach*.

The greatest successes of the era were recorded by four solid performers – Autry, Rogers, Boyd and Randolph Scott. With *Tumbling Tumbleweeds* (1936), the Texas-born Autry launched the highly popular 'singing cowboy' cycle and, by 1938, was on the list of Hollywood's ten top money earners; he and Rogers were the only exclusively western stars ever to make the list; he remained on it until he left Republic and joined the armed forces in World War II. Rogers, an Ohioan who came to California as a migratory fruit picker in 1929, played a bit role in *Tumbling Tumb-*

leweeds, with his popularity then growing to the point where, on Autry's departure during the war, he could take over the 'King of the Cowboys' crown at Republic. When the 'singing cowboy' cycle had run its course in the early 1950s, the two moved to television with their own production companies, added several years to their careers, and met with a success that enabled them to retire from the screen as wealthy men. Their pictures, whether for the theater or the television screen, were fast-paced and tightly plotted, with the action emphasized as much as the singing. And, more successfully than others, they took advantage of another passing but popular B trend – the combining of elements from the old and new West. Cars and airplanes were as likely as horses to play major roles in the chase sequences. The Rogers' pictures were also responsible for developing the genre's most popular female star – Dale Evans, whom Rogers married in 1947.

Boyd's career dated back to 1920 when he worked as an extra in Cecil B DeMille's *Why Change Your Wife*. He quickly graduated to leading roles, his best silents being *The Volga Boatman* (1926) and *King of Kings* (1927). In the mid-1930s, with his popularity waning, Boyd agreed to play the villain in a minor western, but was handed the lead

instead when the original choice, James Gleason, decided against the assignment. The picture, *Hop-A-Long Cassidy* (1935), made a western star of Boyd and launched him on a second career.

In the next years, Boyd, white-maned and ruggedly handsome, developed Cassidy (the first name was contracted to Hopalong in 1936) into a character distinctive for its mature authority and decisiveness. In all, he starred in 66 Cassidy episodes and eventually purchased the rights to the character that writer Clarence E Mulford had originally created for *The Saturday Evening Post*. To say that the purchase was a wise one would be a gross understatement. When the series began to lose its following in the late 1940s and Boyd's career went into another decline, he transferred his old features to the infant television. They were an instant hit with a new audience of youngsters and Boyd got down to the job of cranking out 52 half-hour segments for the small screen. He ended up with a third career on his hands, one that endured throughout the 1950s and enabled him, like Autry and Rogers, to retire a rich man. Boyd died in 1972.

In the minds of many moviegoers, the greatest artistic success belonged to Randolph Scott. Starting as a bit player in 1929, Scott spent the 1930s as a lead-

ing man in a variety of features – everything from musicals, romances and comedies to action yarns and a string of major westerns, among them *The Texans* (1938), *Frontier Marshal* (1939), *Western Union* (1941) and Gene Tierney's idealized and slightly ridiculous *Belle Starr* (also 1941). With his rugged, hawk-like looks (the more leathery they got, the better he got), Scott emerged as a striking western figure and, in the 1950s, made a lasting contribution to the genre when he played a still-tough but aging and lonely hero in a series of high-quality and generously budgeted Bs made for Ranown, a production company that he owned with producer Harry Joe Brown. The pictures – they included *Seven Men From Now* (1956), *Decision at Sundown* (1957), *Buchanan Rides Alone* (1958), *Ride Lonesome* (1959 and said by many to be the best of the lot) and *Commanche Station* (1960) – were all critical and commercial successes, winning praise for displaying a combination of style, mood, and characterization that made them far superior to many major productions of the day.

Scott, an astute businessman as well as an accomplished performer, retired a wealthy man in the 1960s, with many a western fan contending that his final film – MGM's *Ride the High Country* (1962) – had to be among his best, if not

Top: A scene from *Ride the High Country* (1962), which starred Joel McCrae (left), Mariette Hartley (center) and Randolph Scott (not shown). In the film, two old-time lawmen (Scott and McCrae) sign on to escort gold from the goldfields to the bank, and meet trouble on the way.

Above: In *Ride the High Country* (1962) Randolph Scott (right) and Joel McCrae, in their last performances as Western heroes, were given the best roles of their lives, and they made the most of it. It was a controlled, subtle film and was directed by Sam Peckinpah.

actually his best. Again, the central figure is the lonely and aging cowboy, the weary and last remnant of an all-but-dead Old West. The character is as superbly portrayed by co-star Joel McCrea as by Scott himself. McCrea's death as Scott watches at the film's end, with its dialogue echoing old memories and gently but unsentimentally accepting the close of a life, has to stand among the most touching moments ever filmed and reduces to absurdity the obligatory and nonsensical murmurings in the traditional western death scene.

The era of the Bs stretched from the early 1930s to the late 1950s when television sounded their death knell and, indeed, for a time, threatened the existence of the entire industry. But, by then, a 'new' kind of western had been long on the scene. With the still highly popular epic, it helped the genre to survive a potentially lethal crisis.

This 'new' western was a product that, without sacrificing the epic's scope and the B's action, added a fresh element – an emphasis on character and mood. If it must be given a name, perhaps it can best be called the personalized western.

Fresh though it seemed to audiences, this type of picture was anything but new. It had been around since Day One in the western's history, with mood seen

in the sense of lonely splendor that the outdoors could give to the most inferior of early offerings, and character always shining through the epics. And, of course, character and the distinct mood that it produces had been the hallmark of William S Hart's work. But, once changing public taste had driven him from the scene, they had played anything from a nonexistent to a secondary role in most westerns. It was not until 1939 that they again emerged, fresh and unfamiliar, to rival and even surpass the action and the scenic scope. If not born that year, then the personalized western was reborn.

The picture that brought them back was director John Ford's *Stagecoach,* a richly detailed portrait of eight people traveling east to Lordsburg, Wyoming. At base, it was a *Grand Hotel* or *The High and the Mighty* on wheels, but its quality, the tautness of its script, the expertise of its players, and its uniqueness as a western have made it a classic.

Stagecoach efficiently combined many elements of the epic and the standard western. In the mold of the epic were the breathtaking shots of the coach moving across the windswept wastes of Monument Valley, Utah. From the standard western came John Wayne's showdown with the Plummer brothers in the film's climactic moments. And from both came the memor-

able chase sequence when the stage – with Wayne sprawled on its roof and firing a rifle with deadly accuracy and then climbing down and leaping forward to control the charging horses – sweeps across the sands and outruns an Indian war party.

This was all magnificent stuff. But, above all else, there were the superb character portraits etched by a cast that didn't have a single weak player in its midst. To this day, the memory of the people aboard the stage remains with anyone who saw the film – the nervous and garrulous driver Buck (Andy Devine), the tough but compassionate sheriff (George Bancroft), the hardened yet vulnerable saloon girl Dallas (Claire Trevor), the alcoholic doctor (Thomas Mitchell), the courageous pregnant wife (Louise Platt), the timid whiskey drummer (Donald Meek), the chivalrous gambler (John Carradine), the thieving banker (Berton Churchill) and the Ringo Kid (Wayne), the young outlaw who, boarding the coach at trail-

Below: From left to right: Andy Devine, George Bancroft, John Carradine, Donald Meek, Louise Platt, Claire Trevor and John Wayne in *Stagecoach* (1939). The John Ford Western classic told of a group of assorted passengers on a stage going into Indian territory and their reactions under stress.

side after the death of his horse, is seeking revenge on the Plummers for the murder of his brother.

The personalized western was launched in auspicious fashion by *Stagecoach*'s great commercial success and the immense popularity that John Wayne enjoyed in its wake. After a decade of sound, Hollywood finally awoke to the fact that westerns other than epics could make money – and plenty of it – in big city first-run houses. The personalized western was not to be relegated to the nation's neighborhood and small town theaters. For the next thirty years, it ranked among the most profitable wares offered by major studios.

The fact is that grade-A westerns of all types were triggered by *Stagecoach*'s reception, with the best of them all being the character/mood pieces. In the same year that *Stagecoach* was released, James Stewart came up with a fine comic characterization in *Destry Rides Again* and thereafter punctuated a career of varied roles with western vehicles. Gary Cooper and Walter Brennan followed in 1940 with *The Westerner,* a character study of the infamous Judge Roy Bean, the 'law west of the Pecos.' Dana Andrews starred as the brooding lynch victim in *The Ox-Bow Incident* (1943). Another star of that picture, Henry Fonda, went on to John

Top: Gary Cooper at the end of a fight in *The Westerner* (1940). Behind him, wearing suspenders, is Walter Brennan, who played Judge Roy Bean, who ran things his own way. Brennan received an Oscar for the role.

Above: Cooper confronts Brennan in *The Westerner,* which told the story of a dispute over land rights and the action taken by those who considered themselves in the right.

Top: The lynching scene from *The Ox-Bow Incident* (1943), the low budget film that has taken its place as a movie classic because of its powerful indictment of man's inhumanity to man.

Above: Just before the lynching, a victim (Anthony Quinn) confesses to a sympathetic member of the posse (Chris-Pin Martin) in *The Ox-Bow Incident* (1943).

Ford's starkly moody *My Darling Clementine* (1946) and then, like Stewart, punctuated his remarkable career with western roles. Gregory Peck evened things up for the ridiculous *Duel in the Sun* (1947) with the sensitive portrayal of a weary outlaw in *The Gunfighter* (1950). Humphrey Bogart, Walter Huston, and Alfonso Bedoya (the bandit, 'Gold Tooth') all turned in fine character performances in *Treasure of the Sierra Madre* (1948), a picture that, though not strictly a western, still fitted within the category. Gary Cooper, in *High Noon* (1952) stood alone as the sheriff abandoned by his town in the face of danger. After starting as a dead-eyed criminal and then varying his roles, Alan Ladd emerged as the quiet-spoken, regretful gunman in *Shane* (1953). Glenn Ford and Van Heflin provided an at-times unbearable good-evil tension in *3:10 to Yuma* (1957), with Ford going on to join Henry Fonda in the earthy and comic character study, *The Rounders* (1965). And, beginning with *Red River* and *Rio Grande* (both 1948), John Wayne began to develop a many-faceted, weatherbeaten character that was to come to splendid maturity as the hard-drinking, one-eyed, paunchy marshal in *True Grit* (1969), for which he won an Academy Award, and *Rooster Cogburn* (1975).

Left: In *My Darling Clementine* (1946) Henry Fonda played Wyatt Earp and Linda Darnell played the love interest. The locale of the picture was Tombstone, Arizona, where Earp was marshal, and the film culminated with the oft-photographed gunfight at the OK Corral.

Below, left: Gregory Peck played a gunslinger named Johnny Ringo in *The Gunfighter* (1950). The performance by Peck has been called one of his finest.

Above: Humphrey Bogart (center) talks with his two partners, Walter Huston (second from left) and Tim Holt (far right) in a Mexican village in *The Treasure of the Sierra Madre* (1948). This story of thieves falling out over gold after an arduous search in bandit country won Oscars for Huston and two for his son, John, for screenplay and direction.

Left: In *Rooster Cogburn* (1975), the two stars, John Wayne and Katharine Hepburn, search for the murderer of her father, a minister.

Top: In the classic, *High Noon* (1952), Gary Cooper marries Grace Kelly.

Above: *High Noon* tells the story of one man, the marshal, and his search for support against a gang of revengeful outlaws. He can find no help and takes on the gang single-handedly. Here Gary Cooper fires at a concealed member of the gang.

From that moment on, Kane faces a morning of terrible trials. First, he must decide whether to flee – as urged by his fellow townspeople and his new wife – or to stay and face the outlaw in a gun battle that will assuredly see one of them dead. A proud man who knows that flight is useless and that he would be stalked to the end of his days, Kane decides to remain.

Now he seeks to enlist the help of the townspeople in facing the outlaw and his three cohorts. One by one, for reasons that range from cowardice and physical disability to dislike of Kane, they refuse and leave him to face the noontime train alone; even his bride Amy, because of her religious convictions, turns away from him. Angry and frustrated at the desertions, frightened but nevertheless resolute, Kane faces his enemies in a gun battle that carries them through town, sees the three cohorts killed, and ends when Amy, casting her principles aside, comes angrily to her husband's aid. The picture closes with Kane disgustedly dropping his tin star in the dust of the main street and, with Amy, riding off to a new life.

The story is simplicity itself, as are the moralities and emotions that surface as the picture develops. The plot unfolds with a deadly one-step-at-a-time movement towards the meeting that fate and Kane's nature – and those of the townspeople – have set for him. All the while, director Fred Zinnemann builds an almost intolerable suspense by cutting periodically to the railroad tracks and the face of a clock with its hands moving inexorably to the hour of noon. And all the while, Kane communicates his quiet acceptance of a destiny he cannot escape and strikes a wonderfully human balance between fear and pride. In Kane, so far as most critics were concerned, Cooper, who had charmed audiences with such diverse roles as Mr Deeds, Sergeant York, and baseball's Lou Gehrig, built his finest screen character.

The role won Cooper the 1952 Academy Award for Best Actor. Nominations went to Zinnemann for best direction, and to Carl Foreman for best screenplay. The film itself, which much of the public saw as a commentary on the political horrors of the McCarthy era because of its theme of the man alone in the midst of treachery, was nominated as the year's best picture. It lost to DeMille's *The Greatest Show on Earth*.

Pictorially, *Shane* is the more impressive picture. Photographed in color against the sweep of the Grand Tetons and shown on a wide screen, it tells the time-honored story of homesteaders struggling against a cattle baron out to

Though all the above were excellent productions, two of their number must be singled out for special mention – *High Noon* (1952) and *Shane* (1953). There can be little argument that they represent just about the very best that the character/mood western had to offer. Released within a year of each other, both were critical and financial successes, with *Shane* eventually proving to be the greater dollar winner by grossing $9,000,000 in its lifetime.

Filmed in black and white (which contributed much to its mood), *High Noon* opens with the marriage of Sheriff Will Kane (Cooper) and Amy (Grace Kelly) on the day of his retirement. Immediately following the wedding ceremony, Kane learns that an outlaw whom he sent to prison has been released and, with revenge on his mind, is arriving in town aboard the noon train.

take their lands away. It's a struggle that an ex-gunman drifter named Shane (Alan Ladd) finally wins for them in a shootout with a professional killer (Jack Palance) hired by the cattleman. The scene itself is worth the price of admission, played as it is in a dimly-lighted saloon with the antagonists moving silently, coldly, and professionally through the shadows.

Though the story line is a familiar one, director George Stevens handled it in a fresh and captivating manner by letting the audience see the unfolding events through the eyes of a little boy (Brandon De Wilde). The youngster's innocence, his childish curiosity about Shane's shadowy past, his wonder at Shane's six-gun, and his blend of excitement and fear when he witnesses a fistfight involving his father (Van Heflin) and Shane on one side and a band of the cattleman's thugs on the other – all stand out in sharp contrast to the bloody and savage business of a range war and give the picture a dimension that it might well not have if treated otherwise.

Shane, as did *High Noon,* fared well in the Academy Awards, though, in the end, it captured only one statuette – for Best Color Cinematography. De Wilde and Palance were nominated for best supporting actor, George Stevens for

Above: Van Heflin presides at the funeral of the man who has been killed by a gunfighter in *Shane* (1953).

Left: In *Shane,* Alan Ladd plays the title role, a man who is a good-guy gunfighter who kills the bad-guy gunfighter, Jack Palance. This scene shows Ladd with the hero-worshipping boy, Brandon de Wilde.

For a Few Dollars More (1967), a
Spaghetti Western sequel to *A
Fistful of Dollars* (also 1967),
tells the story of a stranger with
no name, a bounty hunter, and is
filled with violence.

Above: Clint Eastwood as the
stranger, strolls into a Mexican
cantina.

Right: Lee Van Cleef plays
Eastwood's well-armed partner
in the search for Mexican
bandits.

best direction, and the film itself for best
picture. John Ford's *The Quiet Man* won
out over it.

'All things to all people' might be an
apt description of the western of the
1940s and 50s. Still on the scene from
the 1920s and doing well was the epic.
The standard was being turned out for
both major and minor houses. The char-
acter/mood piece was winning critical
acclaim and enjoying a busy box office.
Comedy – which dated back to Essanay's 'Snakeville Village' series of 1911
and had enjoyed success in the 1930s
with *Ruggles of Red Gap* (1935) – was
being handled nicely by Bob Hope in
Paleface (1948) and *Son of Paleface*
(1950). And musicals had been added to
the genre with *Annie Get Your Gun*
(1950) and *Seven Brides for Seven
Brothers* (1954).

As mentioned earlier, television began to take its toll in the 1950s. Hardest
hit by customers who now preferred to
take their screen entertainment at
home was the standard western. By the
end of the decade, it had pretty much
disappeared from theaters. But it was
anything but dead. Led by Autry, Rogers, Boyd, The Lone Ranger and Duncan Renaldo's Cisco Kid, it simply
transferred itself to the small screen
and continued to play on happily
through the 1960s and 70s in such

series fare as *Gunsmoke, Rawhide* and *Bonanza,* and in such made-for-television features as *The Over the Hill Gang* and *Kate Bliss and the Ticker Tape Kid.*

Though not killed by television, the theater western, in common with virtually every other film genre, was badly wounded by the new competition. In the late 1940s, westerns had accounted for about one-quarter of Hollywood's output. By the 1960s, their share of the output was dropping to one-thirteenth. But the theater western managed to survive, doing so with the same strategy used by its fellow genres. The producers spiced the story lines with various 'special somethings' that they thought the public wanted and then advertised them to the hilt. They cashed in, for instance, on that frightening characteristic of the times, violence, with Randolph Scott's *The Tall T* (1957), director Sam Peckinpah's *The Wild Bunch* (1969) and Clint Eastwood's Italian 'spaghetti westerns,' *A Fistful of Dollars* (1964), *For a Few Dollars More* (1965) and *The Good, the Bad and the Ugly* (1966). Parody and wild comedy – *Cat Ballou* (1965) and Mel Brooks' *Blazing Saddles* (1974) – proved just as much of a draw. The sexual frankness of the day was reflected profitably in *McCabe and Mrs Miller*

Above: In *The Wild Bunch* (1969), a cynical band of outlaws fight law, order, and the Mexican army on the Texas-Mexico border in 1913. These members of the gang are (left to right) Ben Johnson, Warren Oates, William Holden, Ernest Borgnine.

Left: *Cat Ballou* (1965) was a spoof Western for which Lee Marvin received an Oscar for a dual role as a gunfighter and (shown here) the town drunk.

(1971) and, with high good humor, in *The Cheyenne Social Club* (1970), in which James Stewart and Henry Fonda shared star billing. The added dimension of Cinerama paid off for the critically debatable epic, *How the West was Won*.

The biggest 'special something' that the producers had to offer were the stars themselves, none of whom were strictly western performers, but all of whom were solid box office draws regardless of the genre in which they elected to work. Paul Newman hit the money-making trail with *The Left-Handed Gun* (1958), went on to the contemporary western, *Hud* (1963), then to *Hombre* (1967) and topped everything off with Robert Redford in *Butch Cassidy and the Sundance Kid* (1969), after which he did *The Life and Times of Judge Roy Bean* (1972). As for Redford, he moved to *Tell Them Willie Boy is Here* (1970), *Little Fauss and Big Halsy* (also 1970) and *The Electric Horseman* (1979) with Jane Fonda. A year earlier, Miss Fonda won acclaim in *Comes a Horseman*. Dustin Hoffman etched a memorable character portrait in *Little Big Man* (1970). Kirk Douglas and Burt Lancaster teamed up for *The Gunfight at the OK Corral* (1957), with Douglas later working in *Lonely are the Brave* (1962) and *There was a Crooked Man* (1970), and Lancaster going to *The Unforgiven* (1960) and *The Hallelujah*

Paul Newman has played in many Westerns in his long and varied movie career.

Top left: In *Hombre* (1967) he played the role of a white man raised by Indians. The screenplay raised some interesting moral issues. Here, Newman, as John Russell, visits a white man's saloon with two Indian friends (Merrill Isbell and Pete Hernandez).

Center left: Newman, in the title role in *The Life and Times of Judge Roy Bean* (1972), stands with his foot on the corpse of his latest victim.

Left: Newman (left) starred with Robert Redford and Katharine Ross in *Butch Cassidy and the Sundance Kid* (1969). The film was based on the lives of two legendary bank and trainrobbers who clowned their way through much of the 1890s before fleeing to South America.

Left: In *Lonely Are the Brave* (1962), Kirk Douglas played a cowboy who escapes from jail and is hunted by a sheriff's posse. The film contains a well portrayed contrast between the old way of life and the modernization of today, with the cowboy as a man out of his time element.

Below left: Dustin Hoffman, in *Little Big Man* (1970), played the part of Jack Crabb, a white who was captured by the Indians as a boy and took on their way of life.

Above: Makeup man Dick Smith created this makeup for Hoffman showing Jack Crabb at the age of 121, retelling the story of his life in *Little Big Man*. Crabb, an army scout, claimed to be the sole white survivor of Custer's Last Stand at the Little Big Horn.

Left: *Gunfight at the OK Corral* (1957) was another rehash of the Wyatt Earp Tombstone story. Here Wyatt (Burt Lancaster, second from left) and his two brothers head for the corral with Doc Holliday (Kirk Douglas, left).

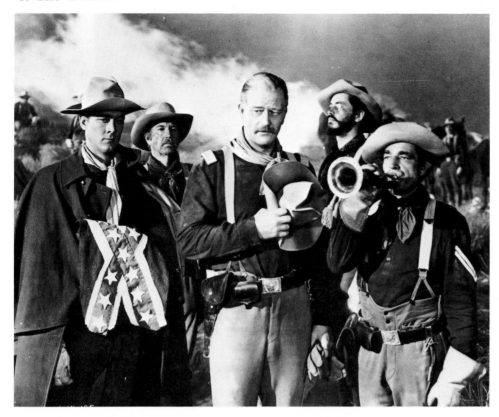

Above: John Wayne played the part of a rugged commander of a cavalry outpost in *She Wore a Yellow Ribbon* (1949). Although undermanned, he is forced to drive invading Indians back north. The director was John Ford – the master of the Western.

Below: One of the stars of John Wayne's film, *The Alamo* (1960) was Laurence Harvey (center). The film ran over three hours and cost some 12 million dollars, but most critics agreed that it was pretty boring, although the siege sequence was outstanding.

Trail (1965). Charlton Heston came up with effective and sombre characterizations in *Major Dundee* (1965) and *Will Penny* (1968).

Of all the stars who periodically rode the filmland range, there can be little argument that John Wayne was the most popular and the most durable. After his ten years in B work and his success in *Stagecoach*, Wayne enjoyed a lasting stardom that saw him develop into the embodiment of the American hero and that, in the end, raised him to the status of a national institution. It was a status that his outspoken super-patriotism placed in jeopardy during the Vietnam era but that was firmly re-established when, in his final days, he endured a terminal illness with the same tough dignity that he brought to his screen characterizations.

Though Wayne played a variety of roles – from football coaches and pilots to enlisted men and officers in every branch of the armed forces – he was most closely identified with the western. His popularity can be seen by looking at a list of the top grossing westerns of the 1950s, 60s and 70s. Of the 30 films listed, 11 are Wayne vehicles, with a 12th being *How the West was Won*, in which he played a brief role, that of Civil War General William T Sherman. In the descending order of their box office take, the pictures are:

Left: *The Searchers* (1956) starred John Wayne. He and Jeffrey Hunter play the searchers looking for a girl (Natalie Wood) who has been kidnapped by Indians many years before. The five-year search is an adventure story encompassing violence, subterfuge and terror. The film is one of the few Westerns that can be labeled a work of art.

Left: Wayne won an Oscar for his role as Rooster Cogburn in *True Grit* (1969). In the picture, Cogburn, an over-the-hill, one-eyed, crotchety US marshal helps a 14-year-old girl track down her father's killer.

Below left: In *True Grit,* Cogburn and the young girl (played by Kim Darby) are, for a time, accompanied by Glen Campbell (left).

Below: John Wayne's last film was *The Shootist* (1976). He played the part of an aging gunfighter who was dying of cancer. In the film, James Stewart played the part of the town doctor who diagnosed the disease.

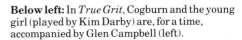

True Grit (1969), $14,250,000
How the West Was Won, $12,150,000
Rooster Cogburn (1975), $8,022,000
The Alamo (1960), $7,910,000
Big Jake (1971), $7,500,000
The Cowboys (1972), $7,500,000
The Sons of Katie Elder (1965),
$6,000,000
The War Wagon (1967), $6,000,000
El Dorado (1967), $6,000,000
Chisum (1970), $6,000,000
The Shootist (1976; Wayne's last film),
$5,987,000
Rio Bravo (1959), $5,750,000

If these achievements are not sufficient proof of Wayne's drawing power, then take a look at his history so far as the annual list of the industry's ten top money-making stars is concerned. Wayne first made the list in 1949. With the exception of one year, 1959, he remained on it until 1974, when his failing health had reduced his appearances to just one a year. In 1950 and 1951, his name topped the list.

In his closing years, Wayne saw his popularity matched by that of Clint Eastwood, who, after starting his film work in the science-fiction monstrosity, *Revenge of the Creature* (1955), was catapulted to international stardom in the Sergio Leone 'spaghetti westerns,' so-called because they were made in Italy. Eastwood joined Wayne on the list in 1968 and remained on it into the 1980s, in the interim turning out such westerns as the comic *Two Mules for Sister Sara* (1970) with Shirley MacLaine, *High Plains Drifter* (1973), *The Outlaw Josey Wales* (1976) and *Bronco Billy* (1980).

As did Wayne, Eastwood has varied his roles and has devoted only a part of his career to the western, making such contemporary pictures as the haunting and moody *Play Misty for Me* (1971) and the violent *Magnum Force* (1973) and

Clint Eastwood eventually graduated from Spaghetti Westerns to Hollywood Westerns.
Top left: As a marshal in *Hang 'Em High*, he escorts Alan Hale Jr to jail. The film is a story of an avenger who sets out to take care of the men who strung him up and left him for dead.

Center, left: In *The Outlaw Josey Wales* (1976) he was the star as well as the director.

Bottom left: Richard Benjamin (left) and James Brolin starred in *Westworld* (1973) as two men who come to a vacation spot which offers the ultimate fantasy – playing in such settings as Medievalworld, Romanworld and Westworld. Each resort is equipped with robots programmed to do the humans' bidding and play out their secret dreams. The two men choose Westworld then the robots suddenly stop obeying orders.

Left: Gunfighter Nate Champion (Christopher Walken) fights for his life in a shootout in front of his cabin in Michael Cimino's *Heaven's Gate* (1980), one of the biggest box office disasters in Western history.

Below: A poster for the film *Tom Horn* (1979), starring Steve McQueen in the title role.

The Enforcer (1976). Since the late 1970s, he has shown a sharp comic talent for 'good ole' boy' characterizations – a sort of modern offshoot of the cowboy – in his highly successful *Every Which Way* films.

The late 1970s saw the western, both in the theater and on television, enter a period of eclipse. Caused in part by an unending parade of TV westerns that couldn't help but exhaust audiences in time, and in part by another of those periodic changes in public taste, the eclipse continues with hardly a new western to be seen, but with the sun breaking through now and again, as it did with Eastwood's $14 million grosser, *Bronco Billy*. But though the genre itself is going ignored, its basic ingredients still thrive. They are on hand to be seen in such fare as Burt Reynolds' *Smokey and the Bandit* films and TV's *The Dukes of Hazard*, with high-powered cars replacing the horses in the chase sequences, and with the good guy-bad guy relationship being carried on by the happily fleeing driver and the bad tempered, always-outwitted sheriff. Perhaps the eclipse won't last too much longer. Public taste being the ever-shifting thing that it is, the whine of engines and the screech of tires may begin to bore all but the most devoted of drive-in fans and the sound of John Wayne's old command, 'Mount up' (though, without him, it may never be quite the same) will be heard again.

See him before he sees you.

McQUEEN IS TOM HORN

Based on the True Story

Distributed By Warner Bros.
A Warner Communications Company

The magnificent spacecraft from *Close Encounters of the Third Kind* (1977).

FANTASY I
SCIENCE FICTION

Because of the visual magic that can be wrought with the motion picture camera, the subject of fantasy has given us much varied entertainment over the years. Watching *The Wizard of Oz* (1939), we traveled with Dorothy down a yellow brick road to a wondrous never-never-land kingdom. We battled a giant octopus in *20,000 Leagues Under the Sea* (1954). We accompanied a team of minuscule scientists through the human body in *A Fantastic Voyage* (1957). We met a virile fellow from the afterlife in *The Ghost and Mrs Muir* (1947), a congenial witch in *Bedknobs and Broomsticks* (1971) and a levitating governess in *Mary Poppins* (1964), not to mention our frightening encounters with eternal youth in *The Picture of Dorian Gray* (1944) and a strife-torn future in *Things to Come* (1936).

Though fantasy is a genre able to cover an almost endless array of topics, it has always been at its busiest in two categories – science fiction and horror. Hundreds of films of these types have been produced over the years, films that range from some of the most splendid cinema fare offered to what must undoubtedly be the worst ever concocted. It is to these two categories that this chapter and the next will devote themselves.

The mention of science fiction and horror in the same breath, however, always presents a problem. If each category is to be discussed, then each must be defined. But the two defy precise definitions. This is because, in theme and approach, they have the bad habit of intruding on each other's territory.

But a definition is necessary if the pictures involved are to be placed in the areas where they belong. So let's say that, in general, science fiction concerns matters that are the work of man or the result of that work, while horror films, putting the accent on everything from a delicious creepy tingle up the spine to outright shock, deal principally with odd phenomena and physical aberrations. Within the science fiction category, then, obviously fall such space films as *Destination Moon* (1950), such futuristic films as *Metropolis* (1926) and such mad-doctor nonsense as *The Captive Wild Woman* (1943). To horror belong the vampire, werewolf, devil and occult films, the blood-bath epics of *The Shining*'s (1980) ilk and such psychological thrillers as Alfred Hitchcock's *Psycho* (1960). But, too often, the lines of demarcation prove difficult to discern with such fare as the Frankenstein series. Though the Monster is the work of man and though the laboratory appropriately abounds with exotic equipment, who can look at Karloff

stalking the fog-shrouded countryside and deny the presence of horror?

And what of *Dr Jekyll and Mr. Hyde*? Which of the two is it? With the emphasis on Hyde's terrible features in Fredric March's 1932 portrayal, it seems to be horror. But when Spencer Tracy, in 1941, places the accent on the evil in Hyde's character, it tends to look more like science fiction.

And so only the loosest and most flexible of definitions are possible. Keeping them in mind, let's now trace the history of the two categories, putting in each those films that distinctly belong there, and those that, by virtue of emphasis, seem best placed there.

Filmed science fiction began in France, with that stage magician turned imaginative filmmaker, Georges Méliès, and with the best remembered of all his many productions – the 14-

Opposite: In *Fantastic Voyage* (1966), a shrunken submarine and its microscopic crew navigate the inner recesses of a human body. A team of surgeons and scientists are in the craft on their way to the man's brain, where a delicate operation will be performed.

Top: The control center in one of the earliest color science-fiction films – *Destination Moon* (1950).

Above: In George Méliès' *A Trip to the Moon* (1902), the rocket ship lands in the right eye of the Man in the Moon.

minute masterpiece of 1902, *A Trip to the Moon/Le Voyage dans la Lune.*

Moon, despite its antiquity, remains today a complete charmer. Laced with clever special effects and mounted with lavish sets, it's full of fantasy, satire, high good humor and Méliès' very astute sense of showmanship. The picture opens with a meeting of a French astronomy society and immediately parodies the academic pomposities of the day as a quite daffy professor discusses his planned voyage to the lunar surface. From there, Méliès takes us to the construction of the projectile in which the scientist's team will travel, and then to the construction of the monster cannon (looking like something out of the Napoleonic Wars) that will fire the thing into space. Next, Méliès deposits us at the launch site, spicing the scene with a group of scantily attired young ladies, all on hand to wave the scientists

farewell. Méliès apparently liked young ladies with a daring amount of flesh showing. They managed to put in an appearance in a number of his pictures.

Then boom! We're fired into space. The moon approaches and, in the best of fairy tale traditions, it turns out to be a huge smiling face. And now comes what is perhaps the film's most memorable sequence: our rocket crashes into the face, smack into the right eye. That done, we step outide for a look at the desolate lunar surface. Suddenly, up jump little dancing moon people. Our scientist friends make them disappear in puffs of smoke by smacking them with umbrellas. Next, we descend to an underground kingdom. Our scientist companions are captured by the creatures there, but manage an escape back to the rocketship, which then departs and tumbles vertically through space, unerringly heading for Earth and plop-

ping down in the Atlantic Ocean. We spend a few bad minutes under the waves before breaking free and making our way to France. There, of course, our scientist friends are much feted by an awestruck public.

Siring not only filmed science fiction but also the French motion picture industry with this magnificent bit of special-effects tomfoolery, Méliès ventured further into the field with *The Impossible Voyage* (1904) and *Tunneling the English Channel* (1907). Other producers, captivated by his fanciful offerings, began trying their hand at similar material. His fellow countryman, Emil Cohl, came up with *The Joyous Microbes* (1909), which featured tiny dots flowing together in dancing patterns to represent the birth of various diseases. In the United States, *The Great Train Robbery*'s Edwin S Porter directed *The Dream of a Rarebit Fiend* (1906). Its big scene featured a brass bed sailing through the night skies while its occupant hung on for dear life.

The trick photography that made these films possible delighted audiences. Fantasy and its science fiction branch were off to a good start. But it was not until the 1920s that science fiction itself really began to come into its own. Here was a decade that saw the release of several feature-length pictures of distinction. Two of them – the USSR's *Aelita* (1924) and Germany's *Metropolis* (1926) – rank as milestones in the genre.

Aelita, based on a Tolstoy novel, tells the story of two young Russians who visit Mars and encounter the beautiful Queen Aelita. One falls in love with Aelita while the other leads the planet's slave population in a revolt against her totalitarian rule. In its depiction of the slave class, *Aelita* marks a pioneer working of a theme that filmed science

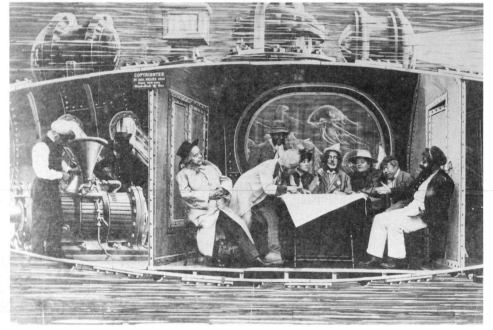

Two scenes from George Méliès' *The Impossible Voyage* (1904).

Above: A train is airborne. Note the submarine in the last car.

Left: An interior view of the submarine.

fiction would use repeatedly through the years in its futuristic productions – the problem of social injustice. Lavishly mounted, the films also stands as one of the first serious efforts to depict interstellar travel.

Social problems and a look to the future are combined in what is still regarded as one of the finest science fiction films ever produced – *Metropolis – Das Schicksal einer Menschheit im Jahre 2000*. Directed by Fritz Lang, who would later make the unforgettable *M* (1931), it has won a lasting acclaim for its theme, photography and special effects.

The picture is set in a magnificent, spired city of the early 21st century, a city controlled by industrialist John Frederson and maintained by gigantic underground machinery that is operated by an army of slave workers. Frederson and his colleagues live on the surface in an Eden-like garden while the workers survive below in deplorable conditions. Beneath the surface, unrest is rife and the workers are on the threshold of revolt but are held in check by the almost saintly Maria. Though she is as upset over their lives as they, she counsels patience, prophesying that help will soon come in the form of a deliverer whom she calls the Mediator.

On hearing of the unrest, Frederson fears that the quiet and charismatic Maria, despite her pleas for patience, will eventually undermine his rule. He turns to Rotwang, a brilliant but insane scientist, and commissions him to build a robot that will be identical in appearance to Maria. Frederson's plan is to have the robot delude the slaves into a revolt that will see them destroy the underground machinery and thus themselves.

The scheme almost works. As intended, the robot incites open rebellion.

Two scenes from the USSR's science-fiction film, *Aelita* (1924).

Above: The beautiful queen, Aelita, strolling through her palace.

Right: Aelita enters the throne room.

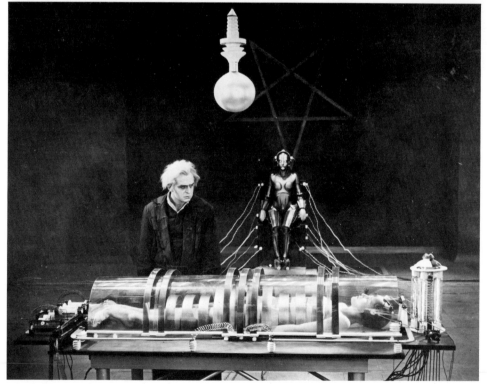

On rising and destroying their machine masters, the workers cause the underground reservoir to burst. Water floods the caverns. Helped by Frederson's son, Maria leads the workers and their children in an escape to safety. In the end, peace is restored. Frederson's son and Maria, who have long been in love, are married. Frederson promises to mend his ways. Capital and labor are united.

Though the basic theme and the imaginative look to the future were much praised, *Metropolis* came in for its share of harsh words. Many critics felt that Frederson's plan was illogical, endangering as it did the machinery on which the city survived. The ultimate harmony achieved – the uniting of capital and labor – struck just as many others as beyond human attainment. But the damnation could never outmatch the praise, with no one denying that, technically, *Metropolis* added up to unforgettable cinema fare. The photography was superb, as were the special effects – the miniatures built to represent the city and the underground machinery. And such sequences as the flood, the bringing to life of the robot in Rotwang's laboratory, and the destruction of the giant machines left audiences gasping.

Two other notable efforts, though they could not measure up to *Metropolis*

Top: A view of the heart of the city, from Fritz Lang's *Metropolis* (1926). Lang is said to have received the inspiration for the film when he first came to New York in 1924 and saw the Manhattan skyline from the deck of his ship.

Above: The evil Rotwang (Rudolph Klein-Rogge) about to transfer Maria's (Brigitte Helm) form and substance to the robot, in *Metropolis*. The film is set in the year 2000, and it is a fantastic, futuristic vision, produced on a huge scale.

in scope, theme and production values, came in its wake. In 1929, Lang turned out *Die Frau im Mond* (English title: *The Girl in the Moon*), which detailed the first landing on the moon and, like *Aelita*, dealt seriously with inter-stellar travel and was as scientifically accurate as the day's space knowledge would allow. In the United States, 1929 saw the release of the Lionel Barrymore vehicle, *Mysterious Island*, a picture with a Lost Atlantis theme. It is chiefly remembered for its fine sets and its use of a primitive Technicolor.

Hollywood welcomed the 1930s with one of the oddest science fiction features ever produced – the musical-drama-comedy *Just Imagine*. For the most part, the picture was set 50 years in the future, in a New York City of 1980 and was graced with miniatures of a future city that were equal – and, some think, superior – to those in *Metropolis*. But the film, with its blend of music and an absurd plot, was dismissed by audiences as just so much silly fluff. They had a point. Late in the picture, the heroes visit Mars and find it inhabited by sets of twins who wear shiny outfits and have a penchant for breaking into dance routines. The best thing about *Just Imagine,* which starred Maureen O'Sullivan, is the fine comic performance by that American-born master of the Swedish dialect, El Brendel.

With the arrival of the 1930s, science fiction began to sprout off into various branches. Some of the branches had been discernible in the 1920s. But, from this point on, they become quite distinct. There are four in all – the mad doctor pictures, the creatures-created-by-nuclear-havoc pictures, the space films and the futuristic films.

Though the mad doctor is principally a product of the 1930s and 40s, it must be said that the 1920s also managed to spawn their fair share of scientists of a peculiar and frightening bent. Germany, for instance, had its Dr Mabuse, just about as evil a power-struck genius as you'd care to meet, and Hollywood, in *The Wizard* (1927), had its Dr Coriolos and the avenging ape creatures of his devising. But, before the mad doctor could truly come into his own, he had to wait until 1931 and that memorable blend of science fiction and horror – Universal's *Frankenstein*. Critically and commercially, the film enjoyed an outstanding success and – though the title role, as played by Colin Clive, was that of an obsessed rather than insane scientist – fathered the dozens of 'mad doctor' productions that crowded the next years.

Based loosely on Mary Shelley's 19th century novel, the picture is set somewhere in Germany – a foggy, gnarled-tree somewhere. In a windmill con-

Top: The rocket ship in Fritz Lang's *Die Frau im Mond (The Girl in the Moon)* released in 1929. The design of spacecraft in the movies did not change much for the next 30 years.

Above: A set showing the city of New York in the year 1980, from *Just Imagine* (1930). New Yorkers of the 1980s all have numbers instead of names and their own airplanes to get around in.

Top: A poster for the re-release of the 1931 version of *Frankenstein*. Boris Karloff (born William Henry Pratt) as the man-made monster wandering across the moors.

Above: The monster visits the bride on her wedding day. The combination of Jack Pierce's fine makeup job and Karloff's sensitive acting make this a film that has held up well.

verted to a laboratory, Dr Frankenstein, assisted by the Dwarf (Dwight Frye), constructs a human-like creature of parts robbed from graves. He then takes advantage of the electrical currents generated by a thunderstorm to infuse his creation – the Monster (Boris Karloff) – with life. Frankenstein's initial pride of achievement is quickly replaced by fear when the mindless brute strangles the Dwarf and escapes to roam the countryside, terrifying the local villagers and, at one point, killing a child. The villagers band together and, with torches flaring in the night, pursue him back to the windmill laboratory. There, Monster and creator confront each other and lock themselves in a death struggle. Frankenstein is badly injured, but survives to marry his fiancee. The Monster dies when the villagers set fire to the windmill.

The picture was applauded for its moody and frightening atmosphere, an atmosphere much created by the use of vaulted, high-windowed sets and director James Whale's technique of aiming his camera upwards. Colin Clive, though his British accent clashed with the German setting, won praise for his

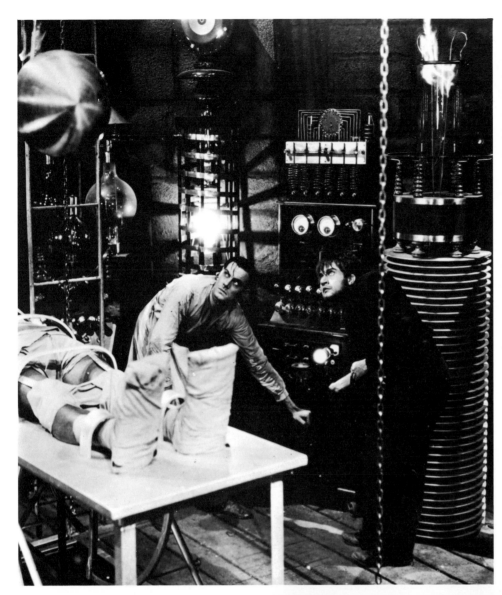

Left: The creation of the monster, from *Frankenstein* (1931). Karloff is wrapped up on the table, Colin Clive, as Dr Frankenstein, is about to throw the switch as Dwight Frye looks on. Mel Brooks used the same equipment in his comedy, *Young Frankenstein* (1974).

Above: A closeup of Jack Pierce's makeup for Boris Karloff.

Below: The Monster just before he drowns the girl. If we remember that he had no sense of right and wrong, his actions are reasonable. The girl was throwing flowers in the water. Flowers are pretty. The little girl is pretty. Therefore, the little girl should be thrown in the water.

driven and then terrified characterization. But the greatest praise was reserved for Karloff's portrayal of the Monster. In an unforgettable and marvellously crafted Jack Pierce makeup, he gave a remarkable performance, communicating a variety of emotions through a grunted, wordless speech. Quite correctly, critic Mordaunt Hall of *The New York Times* commented that he portrayed not a robot but a living creature.

From the very moment that the Monster was introduced in a series of shadowy close-ups, the British-born Karloff secured for himself a position in science fiction and horror films that he would hold to the end of his life in 1974. It mattered not that this mild mannered actor with his slight lisp would play a variety of roles in the years to come – from the demented trooper in *The Lost Patrol* (1934) to television's gentlemanly Colonel March of the 1960s – he would always be most closely associated with science fiction and horror films.

Frankenstein's popularity triggered a series of eight follow-ups from Universal. In the first two – *The Bride of Frankenstein* (1935) and *The Son of*

Right: *Frankenstein* was such a success that the next sequel, *The Bride of Frankenstein* was made in 1935. Left to right: Colin Clive, Elsa Lanchester (as the bride), Boris Karloff, Ernest Thesiger.

Below: Then came *Son of Frankenstein* (1939). Left to right: Basil Rathbone, Bela Lugosi, Karloff. This was the last time that Karloff played the Monster.

Bottom: In *Frankenstein Meets the Wolf Man* (1943), Bela Lugosi finally played the Monster, a role he had turned down in 1931. Lon Chaney Jr was the Wolf Man and wore another makeup job designed by Jack Pierce.

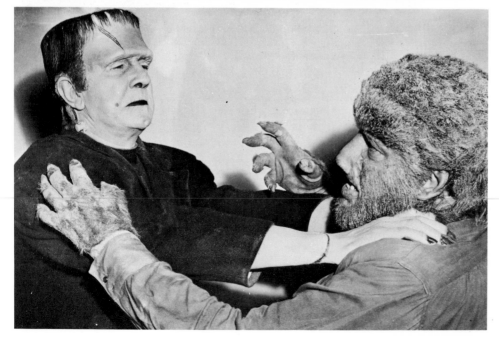

Frankenstein (1939) – Karloff reprised his role as the Monster and quite successfully expanded on aspects of the character. In *Bride,* for instance, he shows a child-like gratitude on being given a cup of water, and an equally child-like pleasure when he tries his first cigar. He is gently comic (and this may be the key to the Karloff characterization: the gentleness of his own personality showing through the Monster's animal brutality) and he delightedly strokes the face of the yet-to-be-animated creature who is being constructed to serve as his mate. At one point, trussed to a cross by the again terrified villagers, he comes starkly across as a Christ-like figure.

The next pictures saw the series begin to go downhill. The role of the Monster went to Lon Chaney, Jr in *The Ghost of Frankenstein* (1942). Chaney was criticized for playing the character as a beast rather than a semi-human. The picture marked Universal's last serious treatment of the Frankenstein theme.

From then on, the pictures took on a 'gimmicky' look, with the studio blending into them other money-making creatures of its invention. Turned out in 1943 was *Frankenstein Meets the Wolf Man,* with Chaney doing his werewolf character and Bela Lugosi performing effectively as the Monster. Glenn Strange (later the bartender in TV's *Gunsmoke*) took over the Monster role for Universal's final three efforts – *The House of Frankenstein* (1945), with Chaney cropping up again as the Wolf Man, John Carradine enjoying a leering field day as Dracula and Karloff stoically suffering the indignity of being demoted to playing the mad Dr Niemann; *The House of Dracula* (1945), with John Carradine once more having a fine time as Dracula; and *Abbott and Costello Meet Frankenstein* (1948), an enterprise that, though it reduced a once chilling concept to outrageous comedy, was well received and won critical pats on the back for its special effects, horror sequences and comic turns.

Once this acknowledged piece of fluff was out of the way, Universal abandoned Dr Frankenstein and the Monster. It remained for others to keep them alive. France turned out *Torticula contre Frankensberg* in 1952 and, a few years later, Britain launched a well mounted series for Peter Cushing – *The Curse of Frankenstein* (1956), *The Revenge of Frankenstein* (1958), *The Evil of Frankenstein* (1963), *Frankenstein Created Woman* (1966) and *Frankenstein Must be Destroyed* (1969).

Without doubt, the biggest science fiction-horror stars of the 1930s were Karloff and the Hungarian-born Bela Lugosi. Both found movie stardom in

Above: Christopher Lee, the British counterpart to Boris Karloff, in *The Curse of Frankenstein*. Universal had a copyright on the Jack Pierce makeup, so a new look was devised.

Above: Frankenstein was made in England for the first time by Hammer Studios. It was retitled *The Curse of Frankenstein* (1956), and starred Christopher Lee as the Monster.

Below: A poster for *The Evil of Frankenstein* (1963), also starring Cushing and Lee.

Below: In *The Curse of Frankenstein*, Peter Cushing, as Dr Frankenstein, prepares to give life to the Monster (Christopher Lee) while Robert Urquhart looks on.

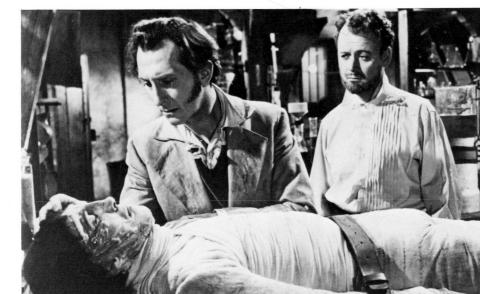

Right: Looking like everybody's two favorite uncles, Lugosi (left) and Karloff smile for the publicity cameraman.

Below: A poster for *The Black Cat* (1934). In this film, oddly enough, Lugosi was on the side of law and order, while Karloff was a practitioner of black rites. The Jacqueline Wells in the film later changed her name to Julie Bishop.

CARL LAEMMLE *presents*

KARLOFF *and* BELA LUGOSI *in*

EDGAR ALLAN POE'S

"The BLACK CAT"

with

DAVID MANNERS • JACQUELINE WELLS
LUCILLE LUND • EGON BRECHER • HARRY CORDING
HENRY ARMETTA • ALBERT CONTI • LOUIS ALBERNI

the same year, 1931, with Karloff's portrayal of the Monster, and Lugosi's film repeat of his Broadway success, *Dracula*. Singly and together, they worked in a string of well-produced, well-acted and highly entertaining mad-doctor features.

Together, they made *The Black Cat* (1934), *The Raven* (1935) and *The Invisible Ray* (1936). Of the three, *The Black Cat* is generally considered the best, with Karloff looking satanically handsome as a scientist practicing the black arts while Lugosi combats him and eventually destroys him in one of the screen's better explosions. Both *Cat* and *The Raven*, with their titles (but nothing else) taken from Edgar Allan Poe works, put much emphasis on a chilling atmosphere and so perhaps should qualify as horror-cum-science fiction pieces. *The Invisible Ray*, however, is distinctly science fiction. In it, Karloff and Lugosi play scientists who track down a meteor that crashed to earth eons ago. They're able to do so because Karloff has invented a device that, capturing light rays from deep space, enables him to see earth in prehistoric times and thus locate the exact spot where the meteor crashed.

Though Karloff and Lugosi were tops in their field, they weren't the only major players to creep into their laboratories for a bit of grisly fun. In *Island of Lost Souls* (1932), a filmed version of the H G Wells novel, *The Island of Dr Moreau*, Charles Laughton conducts experiments that hasten the evolutionary development of animals and then, after bringing his subjects to a condition close to human, holds them as slaves. Though the film's premise is an interesting one, the picture was soundly criticized as being lurid and sensational. A pedestrian remake under the book's original title was turned out in 1977. Burt Lancaster took the Moreau role.

Critically acclaimed, however, was Universal's adaptation of Wells' *The Invisible Man*. With Britisher Claude Rains portraying a scientist who is able to render himself invisible with injections of a drug, the film was hailed for its chilling mood, its sets, its performances and, in particular, its special effects. Even today, in an era when audiences take visual wonders for granted, the scene in which Rains unwraps the bandages from about his head and reveals a nothingness underneath still has the power to seize audiences.

The success of *The Invisible Man* resulted in several follow-ups, none of which matched the original. The *Invisible Man Returns* (1940) came as close as any with its story of a scientist who employs invisibility in tracking down his brother's murderer. But the same can't be said for *The Invisible Woman*

Left: The man in the suit is Boris Karloff in *The Invisible Ray* (1936). He plays a scientist who contracts radiation that gives him a touch of death and a slowly deteriorating mind.

Below: Gloria Stuart looks aghast as she learns that her boy friend, Claude Rains, is invisible, in *The Invisible Man* (1933). The picture made a star of Rains although his face was seen only briefly, in death.

Left center: In *The Raven* (1935) Bela Lugosi played a plastic surgeon who likes the works of Edgar Allan Poe, while Boris Karloff is a gangster on the lam who needs a face lift, which Lugosi botches. Here they are preparing to subject Samuel S Hinds to the torture from 'The Pit and The Pendulum.'

Left: Charles Laughton disciplining his monsters in *The Island of Lost Souls* (1932). The one with the most hair is Bela Lugosi.

Right: David Hedison as *The Fly* (1958). The film was so successful that a sequel was made the very next year – *The Return of the Fly,* with Vincent Price and Brett Halsey. This was followed by the *Curse of the Fly* (1965), with Brian Donlevy and Carole Gray.

Below: Bela Lugosi starred as *The Ape Man* (1943). It was a minor horror effort about a scientist who turned himself into an ape with mysterious injections.

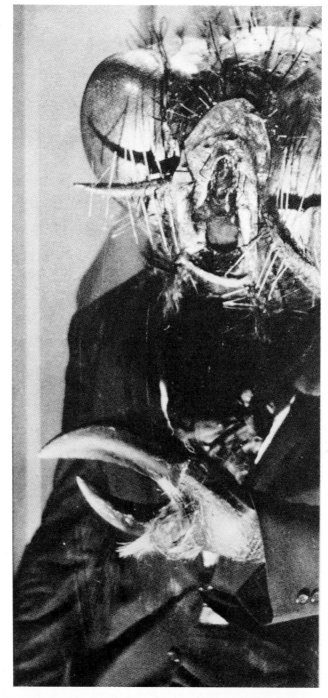

Opposite: *The Beast from 20,000 Fathoms* (1953) was a low-budget thriller that had the distinction of having a screenplay by Ray Bradbury. It also was a rampaging monster film with good special effects.

(1940) and its obvious gimmick of reducing a lady to invisibility, nor for the definitely B-grade *The Invisible Man's Revenge* (1944). Finally, as had happened with Frankenstein, Universal's favorite comedy team got in on the act with *Abbott and Costello Meet the Invisible Man* (1951). The results of having the Invisible Man hire the two as private detectives aren't as bad as might be expected. The comedy is broad and amusing, and the special effects, as usual for Universal, are well done.

In common with all other film categories, science fiction was affected by the era of the B picture, which began in the Depression-ridden mid-30s and continued until the late 1950s when television pretty much killed the market. The era saw the major studios and the independents turn out a flock of inexpensively budgeted mad-doctor films that arched over the spectrum from the good – even excellent – to the poor and downright atrocious.

Among the better efforts, in great part because of the performances by their stars, were: *The Man They Could Not Hang* (1939), with Boris Karloff inventing an artificial heart device; *Dr Cyclops* (1940), an ambitious undertaking that, regardless of Albert Dekker's menacing portrayal of a scientist able to shrink people to doll size, fared poorly with audiences because a bright Technicolor ruined its mood; *Dr Renault's Secret* (1942), which is graced by J Carrol Naish's sensitive work as an ape man; and *The Mad Ghoul* (1943), a picture that, despite its lurid title, is fondly remembered for David Bruce's excellence in the role of a doctor kept in a state of living death. Ranking high on the list of later commendable efforts was *The Fly* (1958). Though its story line is silly – that of a scientist who, in the course of molecular experiments, accidentally swaps heads with a fly – the picture was well received, with several of its sequences having a chilling feel to them, and with Al (later David) Hedison being especially effective in those moments when he communicates the horror to which he is being subjected. The picture prompted a sequel, *Return of the Fly* (1959), in which, predictably, Hedison's son is the man-into-fly victim. The sequel came nowhere near matching the original.

And now the poor to atrocious: Bela Lugosi, his motion picture career faltering badly, uses chemicals to attain the strength of a simian in *The Ape Man* (1943). A female ape is surgically changed into a human in *Captive Wild Woman* (1943). And a gangster, assisted by a demented scientist, uses an 'atomic brain' thingamabob to kill off his enemies in *The Creature with the Atom Brain* (1955). But enough said.

The mad doctor began to fade from popularity in the mid-40s. He lingered on, to be seen in Ray Milland's interesting *The Man with the X-Ray Eyes* (1963) and Gregory Peck's *The Boys from Brazil* (1978), but, in the main, he was doomed with the coming of the atom bomb. The bomb suggested a whole new line of endeavor for science fiction and horror producers. They began to see all the creepy and outsized things – both human and animal – that could emerge from nuclear experimentation or accident. Such inspiration drove the doctor into retirement. He had to move over and make way for the creature.

Frankenstein, of course, qualifies as a creature film, as do *Man Made Monster* (1941) and *King Kong* (1933). The former was a Universal B effort starring Lon Chaney, Jr as the man transformed into a monster by electricity. The latter remains one of the most fondly remembered of all Hollywood films.

Directed by Merian C Cooper for RKO, *King Kong* told the story of the producer of jungle pictures who captures a fifty-foot tall ape and brings the thing back to New York City, with the predictable result that the creature breaks free, wreaks havoc throughout the city as he strolls through Manhattan, stepping on cars, tearing down an elevated railway, and eventually climb-ing to the top of the Empire State Building, where he meets his end by being bombarded with bullets fired by attacking military planes.

The picture featured such durable players of the day as Robert Armstrong, Fay Wray, Bruce Cabot and Frank Reicher, but the true star was Kong himself, a model ape created by special effects wizard Willis H O'Brien. Kong, standing approximately two feet tall, was given animation by photographing him a frame at a time against a background of miniature sets.

O'Brien, whose special effects work in films dated back to 1914, later received an Academy Award for his magic on another creature epic, *Mighty Joe Young* (1949). From *Kong,* he went on to work on such fare as *Son of Kong* (1933), *Black Scorpion* (1957), and *The Giant Behemoth* (1959). His greatest creation was given a handsome remake – *King Kong* – in 1976. The new effort was, of course, more technically perfect than its predecessor but no more entertaining.

The creature born of nuclear experiment or accident did not come along until the 1953 release of *The Beast from 20,000 Fathoms.* In this particular vehicle, he turns out to be an eons-old scaly beast that nuclear tests release from his icy prison in the Arctic. Part tyrannosaurus and part brontosaurus, he im-mediately heads for his ancestral breeding grounds, which happen to be where New York City now stands. En route, he wreaks havoc wherever possible and then, on arrival, runs wild at Coney Island, leveling the place – roller coaster and all. The thing is finally killed by a scientist (Lee Van Cleef) who hits it with a radioactive isotope fired from a rifle.

The whole enterprise was sheer nonsense. But it featured some good special effects (and some poor ones) and audiences liked it, complaining only that the plot moved a bit too slowly. The result: the triggering of imitations by the dozen, with each trying to outdo the other in the unattractiveness of the creatures unleashed.

As was true of the mad doctor films, some of the entries were laudable and some laughable, with the difference much depending on the quality of their special effects. Belonging in the former category is *It Came from Beneath the Sea* (1955). In this one, a giant octopus is disturbed by H-bomb tests in the vicinity of its underwater lair and takes out its pique on the west coast of the United States. The special effects are at their best when the octopus arrives in San Francisco, wraps the Golden Gate Bridge around with a huge bundle of tentacles, and pulls it down.

Above: In *The Creature from the Black Lagoon* (1954), the fish monster (Ricou Browning) creeps up on the white-clad Julie Adams. Browning, a diver and stunt man, later became a specialist in underwater direction for Ivan Tors on the *Flipper* movie and television series.

Right: Grant Williams runs for his life in *The Incredible Shrinking Man* (1957). Masterful special effects made this sci-fi thriller believable and frightening.

On the opposite side of the quality fence are producer Roger Corman's *The Attack of the Crab Monsters* (1957) and Mexico's *The Monster from Piedras Blancas* (1954), with the latter easily qualifying as one of the most brutal pictures ever made. It stars a two-legged crablike charmer that, in one scene, walks along a beach while proudly holding the head of a decapitated victim in his outstretched claw.

Knowing that they had a profitable gimmick on their hands, producers soon began dreaming up creatures loosed by means other than nuclear experimentation. From that point on, a number of frightening oddities are released from their lairs by natural upheavals, as is the case when a volcano erupts and frees the outsized thing known as *Black Scorpion* (1957). Some are discovered in their natural habitat, as happens in *The Creature from the Black Lagoon* (1954) when explorers come upon an amphibious monstrosity while investigating the Amazon River. And some are the products of solar radiation – a case in point being the giant wasps in *The Monster from Green Hell* (1957).

And, of coure, the producers couldn't overlook the grand fun of having nature do dirt to man himself. In *The Cyclops* (1955), an airman grows to gigantic proportions after being forced down in a radioactive field. Britain's *The Creeping Unknown* (1956) brings a spaceman back to earth and finds him possessed of an alien life that gradually turns him into a gargantuan fungus. In one of the best efforts of the period, *The Incredible Shrinking Man* (1957), a scientist, on being exposed to radiation, begins to decrease in size, continually diminishing until he ends as a molecule within a molecule. The picture, featuring at times some tiresome man-and-the-cosmos dialogue, is memorable for special effects that are genuinely frightening in the sequences in which the man, now reduced to doll size, hides from a cat and fights off a gigantic spider.

The creature franchise did not belong exclusively to Hollywood. Great Britain joined the fun in 1959 with *The Giant Behemoth,* a tyrannosaurus-like animal that reduces London to shambles. The British next dreamed up *Konga* (1961), an ape grown to gigantic proportions because of serum injections, and then followed with the well budgeted *Gorgo* (1962), with London again being trampled underfoot, this time by a glaring Godzilla-like thing. And, speaking of Godzilla, who can forget Japan?

The Japanese got their start in the creature business with the armor-plated tyrannosaurus (they call him Gojira) in 1955 and have been happily at it ever since. In his debuting role, *Godzil-*

la, *King of the Monsters,* the great beast rises from his undersea home after being disturbed by H-bomb tests. He destroys several ships, startles American newsman Raymond Burr, enters Tokyo Bay and comes ashore to incinerate the city with his fiery breath. He is finally killed by a little item known as an oxygen destroyer.

The special effects, especially those of Tokyo being destroyed, are excellent, as is to be expected from a people known for their ability with miniatures. The film met with such success in Japan and elsewhere that, like Frankenstein's monster, Godzilla was resurrected for starring duty in 13 sequels through the next years. But unlike the monster, he was transformed into a hero who did battle with an assortment of horrors out to level not only Tokyo (undoubtedly this planet's most endangered city) but also the rest of the world. A sampling of titles gives more than just a hint as to the nature of his adversaries: *Godzilla vs the Sea Monster* (1966), *Godzilla vs the Smog Monster* (1971), and *Godzilla vs Megalon* (1973), with Megalon being a giant clawed creature whose back makes him look as if he's evolved from a lady bug.

Godzilla's money-making ways inspired a variety of other Japanese creature stars. A giant fire-spouting turtle broke into pictures in *Gamera* (1965) and returned in the heroic mold of his tyrannosaurus colleague to battle a starfish in *Gamera vs Virus* (1967), a flying monster in *Gamera vs Gaos* (1968) and a living knife in *Gamera vs Guiron* (1970). The giant bird-like creature that was released from his underground home when a volcano erupted in *Rodan, The Flying Monster* (1957) likewise made amends for destroying Tokyo by turning into a hero for a series of 1960s and 70s features. Then there were *Gappa, The Triphibian Monster* (1968) and the giant walrus *Gorath* (1962). And, in a borrowing from Hollywood, a child survivor of the Hiroshima blast grew to giant proportions and saved the world from a giant lizard in *Frankenstein Conquers the World.* Another Hollywood creation cropped up in *King Kong vs Godzilla* (1963).

By the early 1960s, as indicated by the last title above, the Japanese had taken to co-starring their creatures. In *Godzilla vs The Thing* (1964), made shortly before the tyrannosaurus became a good creature, they have him threaten and then do battle with Mothra, the giant moth that is said to be the most Japanese of all the creatures because, despite her size, she manages always to convey a feminine delicacy in her performances; Godzilla, by the way, suffers the indignity of being dumped into the sea. Moving to the side of vir-

tue, he teams with Rodan in helping a group of aliens save their planet from the ravages of the three-headed, fire-breathing dragon, Ghidrah, in *Monster Zero* (1970); Ghidrah, incidentally, is one of the few creatures destined never to change his evil ways. A year earlier, in what must be the greatest all-star creature epic ever made, *Destroy All Monsters,* the producers dispatch Godzilla, Mothra, Rodan, the giant spider Aspiga, the equally giant snake Mandra and Godzilla's son Minya to do battle against Ghidrah when he assists aliens in an attempted conquest of the world.

Japan happily continued to produce such cinema fare through the 1970s and into the 80s. Years earlier, however, the creature had come upon hard times elsewhere. He was pretty much out of style in Hollywood by 1960, his fate

Some monsters from Japanese films.

Top: The huge flying monster in *Rodan* (1957).

Above: The beginning of a fight in *King Kong vs Godzilla* (1963) with the Japanese helicopters ready to lend a hand. Godzilla has atomic breath. It has been said that the reason why the Japanese went in for monster pictures in which the creature had been created by atomic explosions is because that country is the only country to have been subjected to such an explosion.

Above: Lloyd Bridges (second from left) was the star of *Rocketship XM* (1950). Here the explorers look around at the deserts of atomic-destroyed Mars. They had originally been going to the moon, but were blown off course.

being much the same as that of the mad doctor. Just as he had pushed the doctor aside in the 1940s, so did he in the 50s have to step aside for a new hero. The age of the spaceman had arrived.

Despite the success of *A Trip to the Moon* and *Aelita*, early space films suffered a limited popularity, in the main, it is thought, because audiences found the subject simply too fantastic for their practical tastes. As a result, with one exception, space went ignored through the 1930s and 40s. The exception: the serials. Their space efforts – especially the adventures of Buster Crabbe in *Flash Gordon* (1936), *Flash Gordon's Trip to Mars* (1938) and *Flash Gordon Conquers the World* (1939) – delighted Saturday matinee crowds everywhere. Crabbe also did the serial, *Buck Rogers,* in 1939. It was enjoyable, but not considered up to the standards of *Flash Gordon.*

But space as feature material lay dormant until 1950. In that year, it abruptly came into its own with two solid box office hits – *Rocketship XM* and George Pal's *Destination Moon.*

Of the two, though it featured a strong cast headed by Lloyd Bridges, *Rocketship XM* is the lesser film, its fundamental problem being that its low budget continually shows through. But, in its story of astronauts who depart for the moon and then are thrust off course to Mars by a meteor storm, *XM* earns a

Below: A scene from *Destination Moon* (1950), a story of an American space ship that heads for the moon. This was one of the pioneer science-fiction films, and at the time it was made, the scenery was thought to be remarkably realistic.

WHEN WORLDS COLLIDE

COLOR BY
TECHNICOLOR

PRODUCED BY GEORGE PAL DIRECTED BY RUDOLPH MATE

lasting place in science fiction films because it is the first of the modern pictures to use space travel as a theme. It holds this distinction because it reached the market just ahead of *Destination Moon*.

Destination Moon, which, as its title makes obvious, concerns a lunar space shot, captivated the audiences of its day with its special effects. The spaceship and its hardware may seem a bit on the antique side nowadays, but the other effects, especially those of the moon's surface, remain as impressive as ever.

Both pictures were commercial successes, perhaps because audiences, accustomed to the fantastic realities of the atomic age, were now ready to accept this new fantasy as not so fanciful after all, or perhaps because they were, after a spate of mad doctors and crawly things, ready for something new. Whatever the case, the two films opened the floodgates for a style of picture that, to this day, continues to entice customers in the millions.

For better or worse, the launch pad did duty as one of Hollywood's busiest sets throughout the 1950s and 60s. On the plus side, producer George Pal contrived a string of breathtaking effects for his *When Worlds Collide* (1951), the story of the building of a rocketship in-

tended to take an elite contingent safely away just before a runaway planetoid crashes into Earth and destroys it. There was a degree less quality in Pal's *Conquest of Space* (1955), a tale of the first landing on Mars. But the picture didn't come in for the biting criticism that befell Cameron Mitchell's pedestrian *Flight to Mars* (1951) and Joseph Cotton's *From the Earth to the Moon* (1958), a wooden version of the Jules Verne classic.

On the other hand, *Journey to the Seventh Planet* (1960) was regarded as a little gem in the special effects field. With a plot line reminiscent of those to be seen later in TV's *Star Trek,* the film concerns a landing on Venus, a planet controlled by a giant, illusion-creating brain. In the struggle to resist becoming the slaves of its seductive illusions, the newly arrived astronauts break through the thing's protective barrier of solidified energy and destroy it with liquid oxygen. One word for the picture's special effects: fine.

The US wasn't the only country busy with space when the 1960s arrived. Two especially fine productions, both notable for their special effects, put in an appearance. From Germany came *The First Spaceship on Venus* (1960), followed by the USSR's *Voyage to a Prehis-*

Above: An advertising poster for *When Worlds Collide* (1951) showing the construction of the rocketship that will evacuate a select few from earth just before the planet is destroyed.

Below: One of the passengers braces for the blastoff in *When Worlds Collide.* The special effects, for the time, were considered to be outstanding.

Top: In *Forbidden Planet* (1957) the team of astronauts land on Altair Four. The film was one of the few science-fiction romps to win special acclaim as a lively futuristic comic strip. The tame robot, Robby, in this film later went on to star in *The Invisible Boy* (1957) and the 1960s series on television, *Lost in Space*.

Above: Walter Pigeon as Dr Morbius prepares to meet his doom in *Forbidden Planet* as Leslie Nielsen and Anne Francis prepare to flee.

toric Planet (1964), another tale of a Venus landing. Both contain imaginative special effects, especially of spacecraft, and *Voyage* includes several scenes with English-speaking performers, among them Basil Rathbone and Faith Domergue. In their US release, the two pictures, as good as they are, suffered from poor editing and dubbing.

Of course, comedy was quick to cash in on the space vogue. 1953 gave us *Abbott and Costello go to Mars,* a bit of nonsense that saw the comedy team, now in the twilight of their career, end up surrounded by well-endowed Venusian things who unfailingly manage to look and act like Hollywood starlets. The Three Stooges took off in *Have Rocket Will Travel* (1959), a film with, surprisingly, some good fun in it, plus at least one memorable special effect – a giant fire-spewing spider. 'Fun,' howev-

er, is a word not easily applied to Jerry Lewis' mugging journey through the galaxy in *Way Way Out* (1966).

Possibly the most charming of the space comedy-dramas prior to *ET*'s arrival in the 1980s was the 1964 British adaptation of H G Wells' *First Men in the Moon*. The film, though graced with fine sets (to name just two, the Victorian spacecraft and the moon's glass-like underground caverns), is principally remembered for Lionel Jeffries' top-notch comic portrayal of the English eccentric who, suffering a cold, is trapped into the lunar voyage and then infects the moon's population with his germs.

In the minds of most film critics, there is little doubt that two pictures – *Forbidden Planet* (1957) and *2001: A Space Odyssey* (1968) – stand head and shoulders above all the space efforts of the 1950s and 60s. In fact, there is little doubt that both rank among the very finest science fiction productions ever conceived, with *2001* being called a complete immersion in the cinematic process, and *Planet* matching in the imaginativeness of its theme the most thoughtful offerings of TV's *Star Trek*.

Planet's story, which is drawn from Shakespeare's *The Tempest,* takes a team of astronauts to Altair Four, a galactic speck that, years earlier, had been colonized by earthmen. On arrival, the astronauts learn that all but two of the settlers have died, the survivors being the linguist Morbius and his daughter. Morbius explains that his fellow colonists were killed by some mysterious and invisible force. He cannot understand why he and his daughter alone were spared.

The astronauts and Morbius now find themselves attacked by the force. In the struggle that follows, they discover the

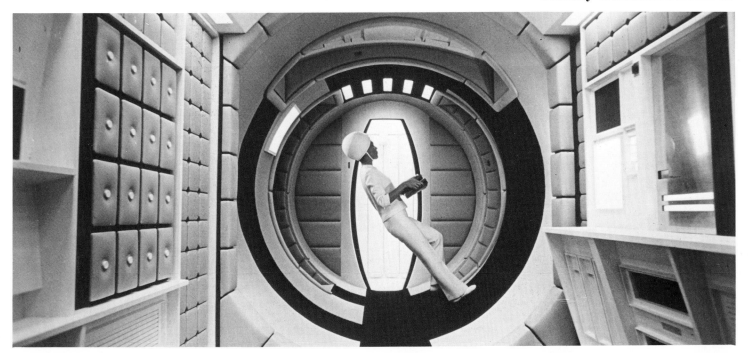

essence of the force – the animal nature in Morbius himself. It is a nature that is given power by machinery built in times past by the now-extinct race that once inhabited Altair Four.

The picture was praised on all levels – for its plot, which admittedly swings from the obvious and frenzied to the philosophically subtle; for its performances, especially the combination of quiet good and menacing evil achieved by Walter Pidgeon as Morbius; and for its special effects, which gave birth to a new screen personality, Robby the Robot. His kin would later be seen in *Star Wars* and in the *Lost in Space* TV series.

All in the same breath, Stanley Kubrick's *2001*, with its script by Arthur Clarke, has been called one of the most masterful and one of the most enigmatic films ever made, tracing man's history from primeval times to a journey to Jupiter, with the major developments in that history triggered by the discoveries of monolithic slabs deposited throughout the galaxy eons ago by a race of aliens. The journey to Jupiter is made by two astronauts (Keir Dullea and Gary Lockwood). It's a journey that sees one of the pair (Lockwood) murdered by the spacecraft's computer HAL and that climaxes when the other, on discovering yet another slab, is transformed from a human to a 'star child,' a super-being who is an amalgamation of man and extra terrestrial,

The picture explains little, if anything, of its characters, its plot, its theme, but simply *shows* what is going on and lets the viewer reach his own conclusions. And it overwhelms the viewer in its visual images, enhancing them with its all-pervasive sound track

Top: The air stewardess, carrying a weightless food tray, enters the cockpit area of the spacecraft *Aries* to serve a meal to the crew on duty. She walks on Velcro-lined shoes which enable her to cling to the Velcro-lined floor in any position even when she appears to be upside down in *2001: A Space Odyssey* (1968).

Above: In *2001: A Space Odyssey,* the crewmen of the Jupiter probe board a smaller spacecraft for a trip into space.

Top: In *Marooned* (1969), the rescue ship approaches the three trapped astronauts. The special effects in this movie won an Academy Award.

Above: *Star Wars* (1977) was the hit of the year. It was described as 'a phantasmagoric space-opera, an intergalactic nine-million-dollar fairy tale . . . and one of the most technically dazzling and enjoyable movies since the art form was invented.' Here Luke Skywalker (Mark Hamill, front seat, left) and Ben (Obi-Wan) Kenobi (Alec Guinness, front seat, right) are stopped for interrogation by enemy troopers. In the back seat are the robots C3PO (See Threepio)(left) and R2D2 (Artoo-Deetoo).

Right: The fierce but lovable Wookie, Chewbacca.

and musical score. The special effects, especially those of the astronauts working outside the spacecraft, were impressive enough to win an Academy Award.

The 1960s ended on both happy and disappointing notes – happily with *Journey to the Far Side of the Sun* (1968) and disappointingly with the all-star *Marooned* (1969). The first of the two adds up to interesting fare in its story of an astronaut (Roy Thinnes) who travels beyond the sun to a planet identical to our own in every detail except a most consequential one – all polarity there is the reverse of ours, with the inhabitants charmingly doing such things as writing and eating backwards. After a series of odd adventures, Thinnes escapes in one of the planet's spacecraft, only to find that its reverse polarity keeps it from landing aboard his orbiting mother ship. He is flung back to earth and crashes into a space center, destroying it. Interesting and as well done as it is, *Sun* didn't attract a wide audience, possibly because it suffers from a script that contains some tiring we-must-understand-people-different-from-ourselves dialogue. But the special effects alone, particularly those detailing the destruction of the space center, may well be worth the price of admission.

Despite a grade-A production treatment and a grade-A cast headed by Gregory Peck and David Jansen, the best that *Marooned* could come up with was a B-picture plot. After breathtaking shots of an Apollo-Saturn launch, the rocket and its crew, in keeping with the film's title, are stranded in space. In a highly criticized plot development, Jansen is sent aloft to pluck them from their capsule prison and bring them home. The whole idea has been harshly panned because it has the smack of Buck Rogers to it – a spare spaceship that just happens to be hanging about and ready for launch in what is little more than a moment's notice. Needless to say, Jansen rescues the crew. And, just to show the international brotherhood that should ideally exist in space experimentation, he is lent a hand by a Russian team that is orbiting the earth.

With this disappointing effort out of the way, audiences moved into the 1970s and were treated to one of the great space epics of all time – director George Lucas' wildly imaginative and splendidly mounted *Star Wars* (1977). Starring Alec Guinness, Mark Hamill, Harrison Ford and Carrie Fisher, the picture has a dazzling, almost comic-strip quality to it that audiences – perhaps weary of the so-called filmed realism then so fashionable and the dreary world events of the recent years – found irresistible. Considering the mil-

Left: Lord Darth Vader, The villain of *Star Wars, The Empire Strikes Back* (1980) and *Return of the Jedi* (1983), played by David Prowse but using the voice of James Earl Jones.

Above: The banquet aboard Darth Vader's ship. Back row, left to right, Lando Carlrissian (Billy Dee Williams) and Chewbacca. Front row, Princess Leia Organa (Carrie Fisher) and Han Solo (Harrison Ford). *The Empire Strikes Back* (1980).

Below left: Luke Skywalker faces the enemy.

Below: The *Star Wars* crew preparing to blast off.

Luke Skywalker, played by Mark Hamill, riding a Tauntaun, one of the creatures on the ice planet Hoth in *The Empire Strikes Back* (1980).

lions who have visited and revisited its joys, all that need be said of the film's plot is that it pits a group of energetic young rebels against a horde of galactic tyrants, involves the rescue of a young princess, and climaxes with one of the most dizzying space battles that anyone could wish for. The picture is simply good fun throughout, with fighter spacecraft and a galactic battle that happily reawaken the awestruck child in all of us, and with special effects explosions in the climatic battle that add up to an unforgettable Fourth-of-July fireworks extravaganza. Along with its sound effects and musical score, *Wars'* special effects took an Academy Award (sharing it with *Close Encounters of the Third Kind*). The picture's success (it earned more than $175 million in three years) prompted two enthusiastically-received sequels — *The Empire Strikes Back* and *Return of the Jedi*.

Late in the 70s came *Star Trek – The Motion Picture* (1979), a film drawn from the television series that, though not especially popular in its US prime-time career, had become a cult symbol in later syndication. Starring the TV cast in their original roles – William Shatner as James (now Admiral) Kirk, Leonard Nimoy as the emotionless Mr Spock, and DeForest Kelley as the irascible Dr McCoy – the picture was a solid commercial success, but its story of a new *Enterprise* going off to face a galactic threat was criticized as being no more than a television episode stretched to a full-length feature. No one, however, could fault the photography, the music and the special effects.

A sequel followed in 1981 – *Star Trek II – The Wrath of Khan*, with Ricardo Montalban effective in the role of the villainous tyrant he created for the TV series.

The 1970s closed with *Alien*, a moody piece that fascinated some audiences and, with its vicious lizard-like creature raising havoc aboard a space vehicle, turned the stomachs of others. Aside from the repulsive intruder, the picture featured the plot twist of having one of the personnel aboard the spacecraft turn out to be a robot.

For more than 30 years now, the venturer into space has enjoyed a profitable and active film career. It must be said, though, that, in number, his exploits diminished with the death of the B market in the late 1950s; since then, except for a now-and-again item cranked out for the drive-in trade, audiences have been pretty much spared the quickie likes of *Catwomen of the Moon* (1953) and *The Angry Red Planet* (1959). And it must also be said that, throughout his three-decade career, the spaceman has been bucking some strong competition from two other science fiction themes. Their popularity has pretty well matched his all along the way. They are, first, the exact reverse of the man-into-space idea – the visitor from space – and, second, the look-to-the-future concept.

We were treated to a visitor from space as early as 1902. When the scientists in Méliès' *Voyage to the Moon* escaped the lunar surface and came tumbling back to earth, they brought with them one of the little, dancing moon creatures. He ended up on display in a Paris museum.

It was not until 1951, however, that he had company. By then, those whirling discs had been sighted above the state of Washington and the term 'flying saucers' had been coined. The world, in a sort of psychological alternating current, was frightened and tickled by the idea that we might be witnessing the arrival of extra terrestrials. And so what was Hollywood, always on the lookout for the profit to be had from a public fancy, to do?

Of course. Producer Howard Hawks and director Christian Nyby turned their cameras on a team of scientists and army personnel studying the Arctic. Hawks has them come upon a flying saucer embedded in the ice. Freeing the ship from its icy tomb with a thermal bomb, they remove from it a block of ice in which its single occupant is locked. And so is introduced to the public the alien creature known as *The Thing from Another World*.

On transporting the creature back to their outpost station, the scientists discover that it is a vegetable in humanoid form. His icy tomb then melts and looses him on a reign of terror within the station. Helpless against his onslaught, the men barricade themselves in a room, then douse him with kerosene and set him afire when he breaks in. A brutal fight ensues, with the creature wreaking havoc before escaping into the Arctic night. He is lured back to the station, where he is at last destroyed.

The Thing is a modestly made film with a modest cast, headed by Kenneth Tobey and with the future Matt Dillon of TV's *Gunsmoke* series, James Arness, playing the towering creature. But it is a memorable picture, acclaimed for its tautness, its slowly building suspense, its implied horror (accomplished principally by Hawks' technique of keeping the creature in shadow and thus letting

Below: In *Alien* (1979), Kane (John Hurt), Dallas (Tom Skerritt) and Ash (Ian Holm) plan their descent on the uncharted planet.

Above: The great spaceship from *The Empire Strikes Back* (1980).

Above: In *Star Trek – the Motion Picture* (1979) Stephen Collins observes a mysterious change in Persis Khambatta.

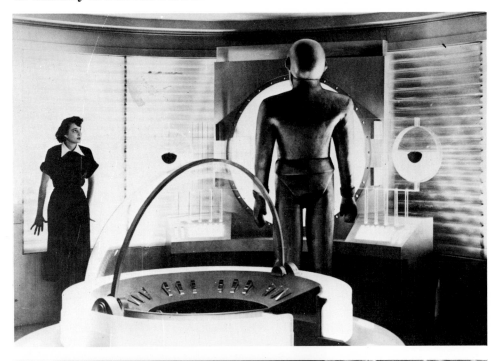

audiences imagine his grotesqueness) and for the underplayed performances of its actors, which give them the look of actual human beings confronting a frightening and bewildering threat.

As had happened to all other science fiction sub-categories on finding a new topic, the floodgates were opened. The visitor to our planet joined all those adventurers who were visiting his planet. At least three of his visits during the decade joined *The Thing* as solidly good and often thoughtful efforts.

Possibly the most thoughtful was *The Day the Earth Stood Still* (1951), which brings the alien Klaatu (Michael Rennie) to Earth for the purpose of warning that further excesses in nuclear power and space work will result in our self-annihilation. Before he can deliver his message, Klaatu is pursued by frightened townspeople and shot, but is then resuscitated by his robot companion. In the closing sequence, just prior to returning to his home, Klaatu stands before his spaceship and eloquently warns the surrounding crowd of the dangerous course along which all earthlings are traveling and begs them to join the other planets in the search for peace. The speech closes with Klaatu saying that the final decision lies with the people.

The film, directed by Robert Wise, is as modestly presented as is *The Thing*. In that modesty lies much of its great impact.

Equaling *Day* in quality and impact but not in the thoughtfulness of its theme is *It Came from Outer Space* (1953). Adapted from the Ray Bradbury fantasy, the film pre-dates by almost three decades the basic idea behind *ET*. We have a group of aliens who, on crash-

Top left: Patricia Neal confronts Klaatu's robot in *The Day the Earth Stood Still* (1951).

Left center: In *It Came From Outer Space* (1953), ectoplasmic forces from the space world materialize in a doorway and eerily confront scientist John Putnam (Richard Carlson).

Left: The Martians invade the earth in *The War of the Worlds* (1953). This fascinating film boasted fantastic trick photography and special effects, and was produced by George Pal, who also made *Destination Moon* (1950) and *When Worlds Collide* (1951).

landing here, want nothing more than to get out and go home. But, without the tools and the materials necessary to repair their craft, they take over the minds and bodies of the local townspeople to get the job done. The picture, starring Richard Carlson and Barbara Rush, was done in the 3-D process to take advantage of a passing early-50s fad.

George Pal made a contribution to the new trend with *War of the Worlds* (1953). The picture, built around a Martian invasion that ends when the intruders are killed off by Earth's myriad germs, was pretty solidly panned as mediocre. But no one had a bad word to say about the special effects used in the scenes depicting the Martian destruction of Los Angeles. They were top-notch.

Masterful suspense is the keynote of *Invasion of the Body Snatchers* (1956), a frightening little tale of how a group of aliens, housed in seed pods, attempt to take over a town – the first step to world conquest – by emerging as duplicates of the townspeople and then taking their places. In the same slowly developing style used in *The Thing,* the picture methodically builds suspense as the town physician (Kevin McCarthy) moves from the vague and uneasy suspicion that something is wrong to the terrible realization of what is actually happening, after which he attempts a desperate escape to warn the outside world of what lies ahead for everyone. The picture was remade in the late 1970s.

Surrounding the foursome – which some science-fiction buffs regard as minor masterpieces – was a string of forgettable efforts. For instance, there was *Killers from Outer Space* (1953), in

Above right: A publicity poster for *Invasion of the Body Snatchers* (1956). This was one of the most subtle of all science-fiction films, despite its terrible title, in that it had no visual horror at all. It was merely the story of a threatened take-over by alien monsters who transplant themselves into human bodies in a small town.

Right: In a late 1970s remake of *The Invasion of the Body Snatchers,* health inspector Dr Matthew Bennell (Donald Sutherland) discovers some strange growth in a friend's garden. One of the gimmicks in this remake was having Kevin McCarthy, the star of the first version, in a walk-on part.

In *The Andromeda Strain* (1971), scientist James Olson quickly gets out of his anti-contamination suit to deal with a lethal organism from outer space as Paula Kelly and George Mitchell watch warily.

which a team of aliens breed an array of giant lizards and insects as a prelude to world conquest. Then, in a pitiful imitation of *The Day the Earth Stood Still*, John Carradine stalks about as a trench-coated visitor in *The Cosmic Man* (1959). He further wastes his considerable talents when he allows himself to be a corpse that is taken over by an alien in *The Invisible Invaders (1959)*. And let us not overlook *Teenagers from Outer Space* (1959), a little bit of pap aimed at adolescents, with the whole idea behind it made obvious in the title.

The forgettables made their way into the 1960s, with the former best represented by *The Navy vs The Night Monsters* (1966). Here we have a variety of aliens posing as man-eating plants down in the Antarctic. They're opposed and eventually defeated by a Navy team and – of all people – Navy nurse Mamie Van Doren. On the other hand, *The Human Duplicators* (1964) is pretty

fair entertainment and so perhaps should be listed as a semi-forgettable. Now we have an alien team who, on arrival here, plan to take charge by replacing key government, scientific and industrial figures with robot duplicates.

Unforgettable, however, is *Five Million Years to Earth* (1967), a superior British production featuring the character, Dr Quatermass, whom audiences had met before in such solid fare as *Enemy from Space* (1957). While excavating a new underground railway route in London, workers come upon a spaceship containing the remains of Martians. The remains, in total looking perhaps a bit too much like grasshoppers, resemble in profile man's idea of the devil, implying of course, that the ship and others like it landed centuries ago and that man's concept of Satan was derived from the visitors.

Investigators discover that the space vehicle is cellularly alive, with its power emanating from the thoughts of the long-dead Martians. That power is accidentally released and destroys great parts of London. The devastation ends when a scientist, braving the ship in its underground lair, grounds the electricity that has released the devastating power. The acting – as is to be expected in all of Britain's better efforts – is fine throughout, and the special

effects, especially those of the withered and dried Martians, are impressive.

Just as the number of space explortion films was diminishing by the 1970s, so was the number of visitation pictures. Yet the decade produced two of the best ever seen – *The Andromeda Strain* (1971) and *Close Encounters of the Third Kind* (1977).

Directed by Robert Wise *(The Day the Earth Stood Still)*, *The Andromeda Strain* is a highly intelligent, thoroughly engrossing adaptation of the Michael Crichton novel. The story centers on a deadly bacterium brought back to the Earth by a space probe that lands in a small western US town. Once the satellite is opened by local officials, all the townspeople die except an infant and a drunk. Immediately the area is sealed off and a team of scientists is assigned the job of unearthing the cause of the deaths. The team soon recognizes the bacterium as the causal agent, after which the search for an antidote to stop its spread begins. At first confounded in their search, the scientists eventually find that the key to the antidote is to be detected in the two survivors. The immunity of the infant and the drunk is established as the lack of oxygen – or, conversely, its excess – in their blood.

The picture is beautifully photographed throughout, chillingly so in the scenes depicting the death-ravaged town. Good, underplayed performances come from Arthur Hill and his male colleagues, all behaving with the professional coolness of laboratory-trained investigators. Running against their bland grain and thus providing a nice emotional balance throughout is Kate Reid's characterization of an abrasive and all-too-humanly upset scientist.

In *Close Encounters of the Third Kind*, we have a film that, like *2001*, offers the viewer one splendid visual image after the other. In a nutshell, the picture tells the story of the visitation, first of a small spaceship and then of its mother ship, and the first communication between earthlings and extraterrestrials. Beginning with the initial sighting of the spaceship by Richard Dreyfuss and then moving to the (at times, confusing) development of a musical language with which to communicate with the aliens, the picture steadily builds suspense and anticipation – the anticipation of the climactic arrival of the mother ship. The anticipation is more than gratified by the landing sequence, a sequence in which the mammoth ship fills the screen and leaves the audience as awestruck as the players.

Though engrossing throughout, the picture reaches a level of pure fascination at this point, with a crashing musical background and deep-throated sound effects combining with strategic intercuts of the ship's surface to give a lasting impression of its immensity. Then, in lovely contrast, come the quietness as the awed earthlings watch the extraterrestrials emerge from the ship, preceded by humans that, so we understand without any explanation, have been taken prisoner by the visitors over the past years. In an exceptionally nice touch, the extraterrestrials are seen only vaguely at all times, the mistiness adding to their mystery and giving the viewer the luxury of imagining for himself what they must look like.

Close Encounters won an Academy Award for its cinematography and shared the Award for sound effects with *Star Wars*. Director Steven Spielberg, along with *Wars'* George Lucas, was nominated for the year's best direction. Both lost to Woody Allen for *Annie Hall*.

Spielberg went on to bring science fiction into the 1980s with what, hands down, has to be the most charming picture ever made within the genre and, possibly, one of the most charming features of any genre – *ET – The Extra Terrestrial* (1982).

Good fun, suspense and a healthy sentimentality are everywhere in this tale of a small alien creature who, during a night-time visit to Earth, wanders away from his spaceship (a globular thing that, with its quaint outside electric lights, looks like something that Jules Verne might have dreamed up) and then is left behind when his friends must depart before being found by approaching law officers. He meets a young boy, with the two of them scaring the wits out of each other before becoming friends, after which he is secreted in the youngster's house, innocently drinks a little too much beer, pines for home, and finally concocts, from the boy's playthings, a device with which he can 'phone home.' Before all is said and done, ET manages the call, falls ill from exposure, dies, revives, and, in a flying bicycle-vs-car chase that would gladden Walt Disney's heart, is spirited away by his young earthling friends to the spot where his spaceship is to land and retrieve him. In a scene that doesn't leave a dry eye in the house, ET and his young protector bid each other a fond farewell, with each vowing never to forget the other as they live their separate lives in separate places.

The picture is a joy throughout, with so much of its impact coming from the fact that the whole adventure is experienced through the eyes of two helpless 'aliens' – a child basically lonely in his own world and an innocent, harmless creature alone in someone else's world. It's a loneliness that, to one degree or another, we all share and the memory of it is made all the more poignant by the separation of the two at the picture's close. Who doesn't remember with a little stab that very special playmate who suddenly moved out of the neighborhood and left behind such an aching void?

Of course, nothing needs be said about *ET*'s star, that whimsical miracle of special effects machinery (actually, there were three mechanical ET figures, plus two costumed dwarfs) that was capable of more than 150 different movements. Somehow, after about five minutes of viewing, it is difficult – and, soon thereafter, virtually impossible – not to think of the little creature as a living thing. There's just too much expression in those eyes, too much intelligence in that face as he sits about reading his young friend's books, too much emotion in the stretch of that neck when frightened, and too much clumsiness in that enchanting waddle for him to be mere machinery.

Filmdom's glimpses into the future began auspiciously in the 1920s with Germany's *Metropolis* and the USSR's *Aelita*. In the US, *Just Imagine* rendered them silly in 1930. Then they came to marvelous fruition with Great Britain's *Things to Come* (1936). In the most practical of show business par-

Above: *ET – The Extra-Terrestrial* (1982) tells the story of a creature from another planet being marooned on earth. The terrified ET peeks out of a closet to see if the coast is clear.

Left: ET's best friend.

lance, here was a hard act to follow. Producers have been trying to beat *Things* ever since. At times, at least in part, their efforts have matched it. But no one has ever truly outshone the Alexander Kordà production in theme and scope.

Based on the H G Wells novel *Things to Come* opens with the outbreak of global war in 1940. Anti-aircraft searchlights probe the night skies above an English city – the symbolically-named Everytown – in an introductory montage that would be often repeated in World War II films, after which the story focuses on the family of scientist John Cabal (Raymond Massey). True to his fears, the hostilities that begin that night rage on for years, at last reducing civilization to bands of warring tribes under brutal and tyrannical leaders, one of whom is played to the hilt by a raggedly-clad Ralph Richardson.

Headed by Cabal, only one group escapes the wholesale destruction. Composed of scientists and intellectuals and their families, the group creates a peaceful, advanced society at Everytown. Then, in the year 2036, Cabal's son Oswald (again Raymond Massey) leads an air attack on the tribes and rids them of their warring instincts with the mind-altering 'peace bombs.' Quiet is restored. But it is short-lived. Everytown itself is struck with unrest, an un-

Opposite: ET showing his magic finger that can cure disease and heal wounds. The special effects from the film won an Oscar.

Above: A little boy leaves his home to join the aliens in *Close Encounters of the Third Kind* (1977).

Below: *Close Encounters'* mother ship.

rest generated by the society's technology rubbing abrasively against the human spirit. A large segment of the population, led by the sculptor Theotocopulous (Cedric Hardwicke), voices that spirit in a demand for a return to a simple life.

The unrest flares into open revolt when Oswald, in his capacity as head of the society, plans to send his daughter and the son of his best friend on Man's first venture into space. Seeing the flight as yet another move away from a simple existence, the sculptor and his followers attack Cabal's launch station and its giant 'space gun.' But the attack comes too late. The gun fires the young couple's spaceship into the black reaches of the night.

The film closes with Cabal's somber comments that the space probe is just one more inexorable step that Man must take to fulfill his destiny. He must, if he is not to be simply an animal snatching at meager happiness for a few years and then dying without consequence, advance from one conquest to another until he has mastered the universe. And even then, Cabal states, man will just be at the beginning.

On all counts, *Things to Come* is an impressive vehicle. As science fiction at the level of pure entertainment, it sports all the magnificent gadgetry that

one could want – everything from the towering space gun and the sprawling, ultra-modern sets of the future Everytown to the space outfit – with its outsized glass helmet – worn by Massey during the air attack that brings peace to the world. As science fiction at the philosophical level, it offers a number of provocative ideas and predictions, though it may be that they are no more than shadows of what author Wells had in mind. Hired by Korda to prepare the screen version of his novel, Wells came up with a massive script that, with the help of Korda and others, had to be edited and re-edited down to a workable size. Wells was reportedly disturbed by all the pruning revisions, but nevertheless the final piece still combines his astute comprehension of past and then-present history with his vision of what that history could bring in the future. It is a vision that proved uncannily accurate – especially in his near-miss dating of the outbreak of war, in his belief that the future lay in science, in his prophecy of space flight, and in his understanding of the human unrest that can be felt when a society invests itself completely in technology. It is an unrest that we have all seen in the decades since World War II.

And, at the technical level, *Things to Come* is a beautifully crafted film. The

Things to Come (1936) was a film based upon the H G Wells fantasy about the destructive world war that wiped out life as we know it, but which paved the way for a better world. Here people gather before a giant TV screen.

photography is sharp, the sets and costumes are excellent, and, of utmost importance, the picture covers a sprawling expanse in event and time with a masterly ease, moving from sequence to sequence with a grace that keeps an admittedly episodic piece from looking too episodic. If the film has a flaw, it's to be seen in the characterizations. They represent human types rather than individuals and, as such, rank always second to theme and vision. Consequently they are not given the opportunity to round themselves out and become truly recognizable and moving human beings.

Despite its impact on both the European and American markets, *Things to Come* did not trigger the flood of imitations that had come in the wake of other influential films. Perhaps, for too many producers, the picture was beyond imitation. Or perhaps imitation promised to be too taxing or too expensive. Whatever the case, except for the Flash Gordon and Buck Rogers serials, the futuristic picture lay dormant throughout the remainder of the 1930s and all of the 40s. Then it stirred again in the 50s. Behind the stirrings was the public concern of what atomic warfare and experimentation could do to the world. The result: the future, as viewed for close to two decades on the motion picture screen, was to be principally one of nuclear devastation.

For example, Arch Oboler's *Five* (1951) told the story of the only people left alive in New York City after an atomic blast. The same idea was explored later in *The World, the Flesh and the Devil* (1959), with Harry Belafonte, Inger Stevens and Mel Ferrer now playing the survivors. Of the two, *Five* has always stood as the more compelling film. Its impact comes from its mature script and the flat simplicity with which it tells its story.

Hollywood immediately sensationalized the devastation theme in several minor efforts, one of the earliest being *Captive Women* (1952) in which mutants from a now generations-old nuclear holocaust do battle with the 'norms' in the year 3000. Cut of the same cloth is *The Day the World Ended* (1955). Now we must deal with the adventures of a handful of atomic survivors, plus one mutant creature. Germany joined in the nonsense and had an exploding missile shower the earth with lethal fragments in the fairly entertaining *The Day the Sky Exploded* (1959).

More solid fare was to be had in *World Without End* (1956). Here, a space flight heads for Mars but somehow breaks through the time barrier and returns to Earth in the year 2508. The astronauts find that the world had destroyed itself 300 years earlier in an atomic war. In a reverse of the living conditions in *Metropolis,* the descendants of the survivors reside beneath the blasted, desolate surface while, above, an army of horribly deformed mutants serve as their slaves.

Stanley Kramer's *On the Beach* (1959), despite some flaws, undoubtedly ranks as the decade's best devastation feature. Adapted from the Nevil Shute novel and set in Australia, the film tells the story of a group of people awaiting death from a radioactive cloud that, in the wake of a nuclear holocaust, has destroyed all life in the northern hemisphere and is now spreading over the rest of the world. The leading players – Gregory Peck, Anthony Perkins, Fred Astaire and Ava Gardner – turn in strong performances and there are excellent moments throughout, among them Astaire's suicide in his beloved racing car and the departure for home of a crewman aboard Peck's submarine during a visit to a now lifeless San Francisco. Memorable, too, is the film's clos-

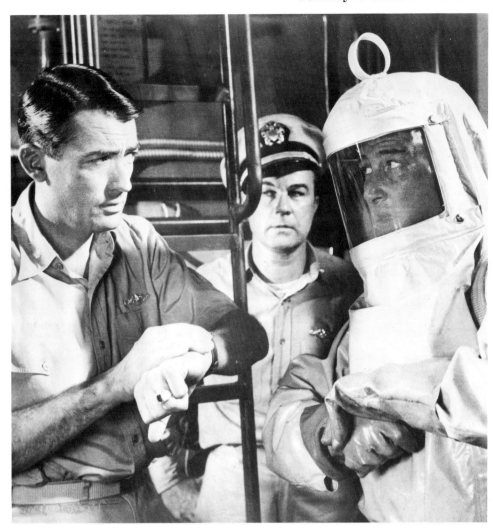

In *On the Beach* (1959) Gregory Peck (left), as the submarine commander, prepares a crew member for the exploration of a radiation-poisoned city.

ing shot – a long view of a street in the world's last surviving city, now as empty and dead as the rest of the planet. Despite these and other pluses, *On the Beach* was criticized as moving too slowly and being too heavily laden with philosophical talk. But, as are all Kramer pictures, it was both thoughtful and thought provoking.

The destruction trend continued into the new decade, first with Hollywood's *Voyage to the Bottom of the Sea* (1961); here, when a meteoritic shower sets the Van Allen radiation belt afire, an atomic submarine embarks to extinguish the blaze with a missile fired from the Arctic Ocean. Britain came up with the especially fine *The Day the Earth Caught Fire* (1961); atomic tests in both the Arctic and Antarctic throw the Earth out of orbit and send it hurtling towards the sun, after which other nuclear explosions are tried in an effort to return it to its proper course. At the picture's end, yet another detonation is in the making and the audience is left to decide for itself as to the ultimate fate of the planet. Both the direction and the acting are excellent as is to be expected from Val Guest behind the camera and Leo McKern, Edward Judd and Janet Munro in front of it. In the US, one-time romantic leading man Ray Milland proved his own directorial talents with

Panic in the Year Zero! (1962); the film has a desperate Milland and family struggling to survive when the country is hit with a nuclear disaster; simply told (but with some perhaps overly drastic plot developments here and there) and modestly acted, the film carries a memorable punch. Not so powerful but still interesting is *Crack in the World* (1965). Predictably, when scientists use undersea explosions in a probe of the Earth's core, they cause a crack to develop in the crust; on schedule – and accompanied by appropriately hairraising geologic upheavals – the fissure circles the globe and threatens to split it into two planets.

Though *On the Beach* was the finest that the 1950s had to offer, hardly anyone will argue that it came anywhere near matching the best of the 60s – Stanley Kubrick's *Dr Strangelove or How I Learned to Stop Worrying and Love the Bomb* (1963), In fact, the consensus is that here we have the best devastation film ever made. Punctuated

Top: Stanley Kubrick had constructed a realistic war room for his production of *Dr Strangelove or How I Learned to Stop Worrying and Love the Bomb* (1963). George C Scott is at top center and Peter Sellers, as President Muffley, is at the right.

In one of his three different character portrayals – that of the title role in *Dr Strangelove* – Peter Sellers enters the room in his wheelchair. The film was the first nuclear comedy, full of black humor about the destruction of the entire earth.

by black comedy throughout, *Strangelove* opens with US bombers being dispatched against Russia by the completely looney General Jack D Ripper (Sterling Hayden) to save mankind and, as he puts it, our 'precious bodily fluids' from the evil designs of Communism. President Mirkin Muffley (Peter Sellers) and his aides desperately attempt to recall the flight, knowing that the attack will trigger Russia's Doomsday Bomb, a neat little indefusible package that, designed as the ultimate nuclear deterrent, will detonate every atom bomb in the world. All but one of the recall efforts succeed – a single bomber, its radio knocked out by a Soviet attack, makes its way to the target area. Its bomb is released and the audience, viewing matters from above the bomb bay, is treated to the spectacle of the empty-headed cowboy pilot (Slim Pickens) sitting astride the thing and riding it happily down to destruction as if it is a bucking bronco, after which the world blows up to the voice-over accompaniment of Britain's Vera Lynn and male chorus blithefully singing 'We'll Meet Again.' Between the film's opening and this fittingly ridiculous close, the audience is treated to some of the most incisive and comic social comment ever put on the screen – comment on everything from man's 20th century alienation, his cynicism and his self-righteousness to his distrust of his fellow man and his powerlessness to control the weapons that, in his quest for power and out of the power of his intellect, he has created.

The cast is impeccable. Peter Sellers superbly portrays three totally different characters, almost certainly the best of which is his President Muffley (no British accent detectable whatsoever). George C Scott is viciously strong as an Air Force General. The actor in Slim Pickens shines through the wily but happy-go-lucky yokel that has always been his principal screen image. And Hayden is superb in his brief, cigar-chewing appearance as Ripper. Along with his characterizations in *The Asphalt Jungle* (1950) and *The Godfather* (1972), this is assuredly his best work, revealing, as none of his romantic and adventure films had ever done, his genuine talents as an actor.

A straight dramatic treatment of the *Strangelove* theme came within months, with *Fail Safe* (1964). Centered about a US training flight that turns into an actual nuclear attack on Russia when the 'fail safe' recall system aboard the bombers malfunctions, the film builds to a climax that sees the American president (Henry Fonda) decide to destroy New York City with an atom bomb in the same instant that Moscow is leveled, this being his only way to prove to the USSR – and thus avoid wholesale war – that the attack is not a deliberate one. The picture, with its predecessor still so fresh in the public's mind, suffered by comparison. Yet it is suspenseful throughout – even nightmarish at times – and features good performances by Fonda, Walter Matthau and Dan O'Herlihy.

Though popular and produced in appreciable number, the devastation films did not hold a franchise on the futuristic market. Ever since the 1950s, they have been accompanied by other cinematic guesses of what is to come. In common with the blown-to-kingdom-come approach, not one guess was a happy one.

For instance, there was *1984* (1955), the ambitious but failed adaptation of the George Orwell novel. Depicted here, if an explanation is necessary in light of the book's widespread popularity, is a totalitarian society that, headed by the omnipresent Big Brother, allows none of its people an iota of privacy. Though interesting, the film proved to be confusing and did not have the same gripping effect as the novel. Fine performances, however, were recorded by Edmond O'Brien, Michael Redgrave and Jan Sterling.

Better by far – and certainly better than its unfortunate title would suggest – was *Creation of the Humanoids* (1962). In this low budgeted and now-acknowledged minor classic, the principal character is angered by his society's complete dependence on the service of robots. In his eyes, the people around him have all but surrendered their humanity. The shocker comes when he discovers that he himself is an android – the R-36, the most advanced android in the world.

The film is memorable much for the straightforward manner in which it tells its story. The same, however, cannot be said for France's *Alphaville, Une Etrange Adventure de Lemmy Caution,* or just *Alphaville* (1965). Now we have a city of the future run by an electronic brain that – a la *1984* – controls the destinies of all people. The picture's hero (Eddie Constantine) finally destroys the thing by feeding it poetry, a commodity that it can neither digest as data nor comprehend. It all sounds pretty pretentious and arty – and it is.

Not to be mentioned in the same breath is the superior *Fahrenheit 451* (1966). The centerpiece here is a society

Fahrenheit 451 (1966) was named after the temperature at which books will burn. Here the secret police are on a raid to collect the outlawed reading matter.

Top: American astronaut Charlton Heston is angered when he discovers that a lobotomy has been performed on his companion, played by Robert Gunner, in *Planet of the Apes* (1968).

Above: The simian high court in *Planet of the Apes*. Maurice Evans played the ape in the center. The splendidly flexible ape-makeup was created by John Chambers.

whose demand for citizen uniformity has driven it to burn all the world's great literature. To keep that literature alive, a rebel segment dedicates itself to memorizing all available books. Thoughtfully scripted from the Ray Bradbury work, the picture is expertly directed, nicely underplayed by an international cast and beautifully photographed.

Nuclear devastation was combined with a clever man-animal reversal to give us the most popular futuristic offering of the 1960s – Franklin Schaffner's beautifully directed *Planet of the Apes* (1968). The picture, which is based loosely (very loosely) on the Pierre Boulle novel, opens as Charlton Heston and two fellow astronauts awaken from suspended animation during an extended space flight. They crash land on an alien planet, learn that it is controlled by a race of literate simians, and find that there are human beings there but that they function as hunted animals and slaves. Heston and his companions are captured by the apes. While one is rendered helpless through brain surgery and another is stuffed and placed on display in a museum, Heston is caged in an underground cavern and put on trial for his life. He manages an escape, however, with the help of two sympathetic chimpanzees (Roddy

McDowall and Kim Hunter). After being relentlessly pursued, Heston stumbles upon a shattered Statue of Liberty and realizes that he is not on an alien planet after all but on Earth in the year 3978, an Earth that centuries earlier had been devastated by nuclear warfare. The warfare, decimating the human population, had opened the way to the development of the apes as the planet's dominant species.

Featuring a vigorous performance by Heston and sensitive (and often humorous) ape portrayals by McDowall, Hunter and Maurice Evans, the picture captivated audiences everywhere, although it was but a shadow of the various themes and philosophies presented in the Boulle novel. Its popularity resulted in four sequels in the early 1970s. In all, they created a cycle that took audiences back in time and showed them how Earth had come to be dominated by the apes.

The first sequel *Beneath the Planet of the Apes* (1970), opens where the original closed. We find that not one but two spacecraft have landed on the planet. The astronauts from the two ships make their separate ways to the taboo area known as the Forbidden Zone. Here, they discover a population of mutants living beneath the ruins of New York City and worshipping the ultimate in nuclear destructive power – the alpha-omega bomb. At the same time, the apes are suffering a famine and invade the Forbidden Zone for food and for some understanding of the legendary evils said to lurk there. They and the mutants become locked in deadly combat. The alpha-omega bomb is triggered and all life on the planet is destroyed.

Escape from the Planet of the Apes (1971) opens in the moments before the alpha-omega blast. Three chimpanzees (McDowall, Hunter and Sal Mineo) escape in one of the visiting spaceships and make their way back in time to the year 1973, landing on the southern California coast. The picture then focuses on the misunderstandings and suspicions that eventually see them killed.

In *Conquest of the Planet of the Apes* (1972), again with the opening dovetailing with the close of the predecessor, the female chimpanzee gives birth to a son shortly before being murdered. The son is raised to young manhood by a circus owner, at which time – the year is now 1990 – a plague kills all the cats and dogs on earth. Apes are then domesticated as pets and, when found to have a superior intelligence, are put to work as janitors and waiters and menial laborers. The son, with his inherited ability to think and speak, mobilizes the apes and leads them in a revolt against their human masters, a revolt that results in

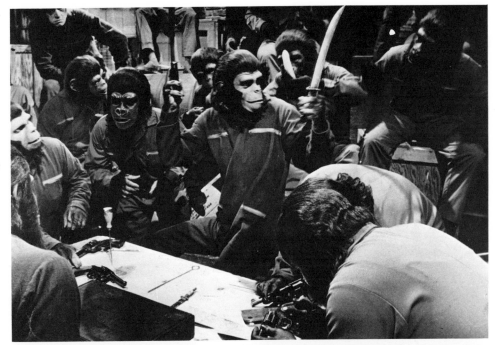

atomic warfare and the beginning simian domination of the planet.

The final picture in the series, *Battle for the Planet of the Apes* (1973), centers on a war that will decide who will finally dominate the planet. Involved are humans, all ape species, and a race of mutants left horribly scarred by the atomic warfare that grew out of *Conquest*'s revolt. The war ends with the apes firmly in control and vowing to live in peace – in a word, the world as Heston found it when he crash-landed there in the original film. The cycle is complete, ironically so because it is Heston's visit that sets in motion the set of circumstances that drives the three chimpanzees to escape back to the California of 1973, where the son is born. Had not that son been born out of his own time, he would never have led the revolt that eventually ended in the planet's simian domination.

After an auspicious introduction to science fiction, Heston went on to make

Top: In the third sequel to *Planet of the Apes*, *Conquest of the Planet of the Apes* (1972), Roddy McDowall passes out the weapons for the rebellion that will put the apes in charge of the earth.

Above: Charlton Heston is seen in the role of Robert Neville, a medical researcher, in *The Omega Man* (1971). Only self-injection with an anti-plague vaccine saved him from death in a global biological holocaust.

Above: A scene from *Soylent Green* (1973). In New York during the year 2022, a food riot brings out control trucks that scoop up people like garbage. The film was made from an adaptation of a novel by Harry Harrison, in which a detective tracking down the assassins of a powerful food company executive uncovers a secret so devastating that no one who knows it can be permitted to live – dying people are made into human food.

Below: From *THX 1138* (1971). The film was directed by George Lucas and was a feature version of a prize-winning short that Lucas had made in college. It is a futuristic tale set in a *1984* vein about a robot-like society where sex is forbidden and everyone looks the same, down to their bald heads. The opening sequence is a film clip from a 1939 Buck Rogers serial.

two more futuristic films – *The Omega Man* (1971) and *Soylent Green* (1973). In the former, he plays the last 'normal' man in a world now populated by the mutant victims of germ warfare. In the latter, he is a policeman in a society so overcrowded that decent air, habitable living quarters, the wonders of nature and all natural foods have all but disappeared. *Soylent Green* is especially memorable because it marked Edward G Robinson's final screen appearance. In light of his failing health, Robinson's death scene is not easily forgotten.

The early 1970s produced a varied crop of futuristic films. In *THX 1138* (1971) director George Lucas came up with a muddled but visually exciting portrayal of a dehumanized society driven underground. Stanley Kubrick's *A Clockwork Orange* (1971), a splendid political allegory that managed to concoct some of the most repellent scenes ever put on film, envisioned a future society ravished by juvenile gangs. *Silent Running* (1972) dealt with a space station that is preserving the last remnants of Earth's plant life. *Westworld* (1973) invented a Disneyland of the future where people can live out their fantasies with the help of Yul Brynner and his fellow androids.

The public taste being the ever-changing thing that it is, the late 1970s and now the early 80s have not proven to be especially fertile ground for futuristic pictures. They continue to be made, but principally, it seems, for the drive-in audiences, chief cases in point here being such admittedly exciting but

nevertheless run-of-the-mill products as *Road Warrior* (1981) and Harrison Ford's *Blade Runner* (1982), the one being a nuclear holocaust survival story and the other a space police yarn. And there has been an increasing tendency to explore if not the future itself then the frontiers of man's experience; *Tron* (1982), for instance, takes us into a computer world while William Hurt's *Altered States* (1980) probes the depths of human consciousness and instinct.

And there has been the tendency not to move far forward in time but to play with it in other ways. Christopher Reeves transports himself from the present back to the beginnings of the century in the sensitively crafted love story, *Somewhere in Time* (1981). Malcolm McDowell, as a youthful H G Wells, pursues Jack the Ripper to present-day San Francisco and meets the whimsically enchanting Mary Steenburgen in *Time After Time* (1979). And the wildest time journey of all drops us back in the prehistoric presence of Ringo Starr's *Caveman* (1982).

In all, though the futuristic film is suffering at least a partial eclipse, the science fiction branch of fantasy is at present in a healthy and profitable state, what with the likes of *ET, Star Wars, Star Trek I* and *II* and *Close Encounters* still attracting audiences everywhere. The same state of health and prosperity is being enjoyed by fantasy's other busiest branch, the horror film. It is to this sometimes genuinely frightening, sometimes too gruesome and sometimes hilarious branch that we now turn.

Above: Malcolm McDowell in *A Clockwork Orange*. He was altogether chilling playing a pathological toughie. After the initial release, Stanley Kubrick, who was the producer, writer and director, re-edited *Clockwork* slightly to make it less violent.

Right: Another Malcolm McDowell film, *Time After Time* (1979). Here he is in his time machine as a young H G Wells, on his way to find Jack the Ripper in San Francisco.

Above: A scene from *A Clockwork Orange* (1971). The film was a shattering political allegory about a loathsome, violent anti-hero in a modern society where young punks run amok and peaceful citizens are imprisoned in their own homes. It was based upon a novel by Antony Burgess which was partially autobiographical, as Burgess' own wife was robbed, raped and severely beaten by three GI deserters during a WW II blackout in London. She later died of her injuries.

FANTASY II
HORROR

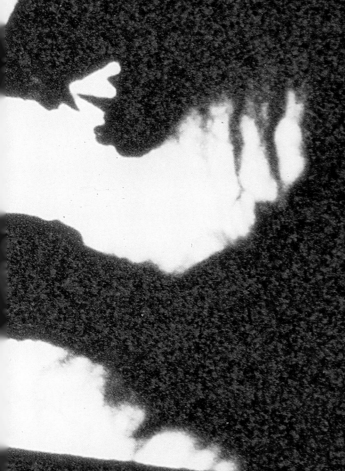

With just two goals on its mind – to scare everybody to death and/or turn every stomach in the house – horror at first seems to be a highly restricted category. In one way, it is; but in another, definitely not. Of necessity, its locales are limited (spooky old manors and fog-shrouded moors are needed, not sunlit streets), with the same holding true for its plot lines (if you've seen one werewolf's problems, you've pretty well seen them all). But, on the other hand, horror has enjoyed a freedom granted to no other genre. Grounded as it is in physical aberration, in the grotesque and in all those creepy phenomena that belong to 'the unknown,' it's been able to develop a sprawling cast of unforgetable characters. The western is forced to stick with the good guy and the bad guy, the romance with the man and the woman.

At horror's disposal, however, is every monstrosity imaginable – everything from vampires, werewolves, monsters, demons, devils, madmen and freaks to that most icy commodity of all, the lurking but unseen presence of evil. They are, all at once, a thoroughly disagreeable and all-appealing lot – appealing because they work on whatever dark and primitive human trait it is that likes to be made revolted and afraid. We may dislike the trait when we see it in ourselves, but it is nevertheless there and it has drawn us to them in the millions over the years, bringing us back time and again for more, in fact, since 1896.

Yes, 1896. Horror is not only one of the most basic film staples but also one of the oldest. It was in 1896 – a scant two years after the motion picture had emerged from Edison's laboratory – that France's ingenious Georges Méliès had a huge bat fly onto the set of a medieval castle and transform itself into Mephistopheles. A courtier entered and produced a crucifix. The devil, unable to withstand the strength of Christianity, threw his hands up and disappeared in a puff of smoke, just as those little moon creatures were to do a few years later on encountering Méliès' umbrella-wielding scientists. The picture that started it all was *Le Manoir Diable,* which was shown in the United States as *The Haunted Castle* and in Great Britain as *The Devil's Castle.*

A look at a comprehensive filmography can give the impression that American producers soon followed Méliès into the horror business. A string of now-forgotten vampire pictures, from one-reelers to full length features, came from US studios between 1909 and the early 20s. But don't be misled. For the most part – as indicated by such titles as

Previous pages: A scene from *The Howling* (1982), a modern day werewolf movie.

Above: Charles Ogle, the first Frankenstein monster on film. He was an actor at the Edison Studios and the movie was made in 1910. In this version the monster was created in a 'cauldron of blazing chemical.' He fell in love and disappeared into thin air.

Was She a Vampire? (1915) and *The Blond Vampire* (1922) – they dealt not with Dracula and his kind but with 'vamps,' those sloe-eyed ladies who were named in honor of the breed because of their captivating ways with men. The first genuine vampire film – *Nosferatu* (1922) – was a European product. America's chief early contributions to the horror field were two workings of a familiar theme that combines horror with science fiction – the Edison Company's *Frankenstein* (1910) with Charles Ogle and the independently produced *Life Without Soul* (1915) with Perry Darrel Standing.

Aside from these productions, little was done in the US until Lon Chaney's splendidly bizarre cripple in *The Miracle Man* (1919). In the meantime, the development of the category was left to Europe where the centuries-old tradition of macabre folk tales, fables and myths – plus a black post-World War I mood – made the ground far more fertile. That the European producers gave the dark sides of their natures free rein can be clearly seen in just a sampling of their works.

Take Denmark's *The Necklace of the Dead* (1910), for example. Playing on old tales and fears of premature burial, it centers on an apparently dead girl who is buried with a valuable necklace about her throat. A thief opens the tomb to steal the necklace and is greeted with the spectacle of the girl stirring and very much alive.

Beginning in 1914, Germany built a series of effective chillers around the Jewish legend of the Golem – the 'body without a soul' – who, so the story goes,

was created from clay by a 16th century rabbi to defend the Prague ghetto against a pogrom. In all, three pictures were made: *Der Golem/The Monster of Fate* (1914), *Der Golem und die Tanzerin/The Golem and the Dancing Girl* (1917) and *Der Golem: Wie er in die Welt kam/The Golem: How He Came into the World* (1920). The hulking, brooding clay creature was played throughout by the distinguished classical actor Paul Wegener, who was best known to American audiences of the period for his work in *The Magician* (1926), shot in France for Metro Goldwyn (before the addition of Mayer's name made it MGM) and directed by Rex Ingram.

Of the lot, the third offering in the series is regarded by film historians as the best. On being given life, the Golem terrorizes the court of the emperor at Prague. His destruction eventually comes at the hands of a child. The youngster innocently offers him an apple and then, just as innocently, pulls the Star of David from the creature's chest. With a life force snatched away, the Golem collapses and dies.

The clay figure, portrayed by other actors, was the subject of a number of additional pictures. In 1936, France and Czechoslovakia released a joint production, *Le Golem/The Legend of Prague.* Directed by Julien Duvivier, the film was based on a novelized version of the legend. Here, a rabbi's young wife discovers the Golem's body in a cellar of the emperor's castle (a symbolic substitute for the ghetto of the legend) and brings him to life to save her husband from execution (symbolically, the pogrom) at the hands of the emperor. The cast, headed by the European favorite Harry Baur (as the Emperor), featured a diminutive actor who would soon win international stardom in Duvivier's *Pepe le Moko* and Jean Renoir's *La Grande Illusion/Grand Illusion* (both 1937) and would then escape Hitler's Europe to become a favorite Hollywood character player, Marcel Dalio.

Czechoslovakia followed in 1951 with a two-part Golem comedy – *Cisaruv pekar/The Emperor's Baker* and *Pekaruv cisar/The Baker's Emperor.* Great Britain, with Jill Haworth clad in lacy pretties as she was carried about by a cone-headed lump of clay, updated the theme and worked it in 1966, titling the effort *It!*

In an interval between the early Golem productions, Germany turned out the memorable *Das Kabinett des Dr Caligari/The Cabinet of Dr Caligari* (1919). Produced by Erich Pommer, who, during the Nazi years, would settle in London and found Mayflower Pictures with Charles Laughton, the film is set in the German town of Holstenwall in the 1830s. At the local fairgrounds, a

Left: Jane (played by Lil Dagover) appears on the scene and looks with fright on Cesare the somnambulist (Conrad Veidt) as Dr Caligari (Werner Krauss) smiles in *The Cabinet of Dr Caligari* (1919).

Below: In *Der Golem/The Monster of Fate* (1914) the golem, played by Paul Wegener. It was a flop in the US despite such advertizing lines as 'If you're tired of the humdrum in photoplay stories you will be interested in *The Monster of Fate*.'

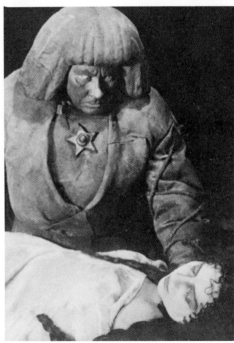

Left: Dr Caligari, who exhibits his somnambulist in a carnival, invites Jane to come into his tent.

Above: In *The Golem: How He Came into the World* (1920), the third golem picture starring Paul Wegener, he gazes at his beloved, Lyda Salmonova.

Lon Chaney Sr in *London After Midnight* (1927). He played the part of a fake vampire. His makeup in the film consisted of a set of thin wires to make his eyes bulge and a set of false animal teeth that he could put up with for only a short time before the pain would get the better of him.

portly but sinister Dr Caligari (Werner Krauss) fascinates the crowds with demonstrations of his hypnotic powers over Cesare (Conrad Veidt). Clueless murders begin to plague the town. The film's young hero, Francis (Friedrich Feher), suspects that Caligari is behind the deaths, a fact that the audience learns for certain when the hypnotist orders Cesare to kill a young woman. Cesare is unable to carry out the murder and instead attempts to kidnap his victim. When the attempt fails, Cesare is pursued by police and townspeople until he dies of exhaustion. Then Caligari himself is pursued, it now being established that he has dispatched Cesare to do the murders while covering his absence by substituting for public view a wax figure of his slave in a coffin-like cabinet. The fleeing Caligari takes refuge in an insane asylum. There, he is unmasked as mad and placed in a strait-jacket. And there, in the closing scene, a plot 'twist' is revealed: the whole story

has been nothing more than the fanciful tale of one of the asylum's inmates. The inmate is the young hero Francis, and the Caligari of his demented imaginings is actually the asylum's quite sane director.

The film was a post World War I effort to satirize the Prussian authoritarianism – symbolized in Caligari's control of Cesare – that had so long shackled Germany and that had led the nation into four terrible years of conflict. Blending old tales and old psychological fears into its over-all theme, *Caligari* impressed audiences as a macabre and thought-provoking vehicle, but there has always been a question as to how well it actually pilloried authoritarianism. The main criticism here has been directed against the 'twist' ending. In the opinion of many critics, it changed the direction of the entire picture and thus destroyed its intended theme. The ending, incidentally, was not in the original screenplay by Carl Mayer (Germany's most noted screen writer of the period) and Hans Janowitz, but was invented and tacked onto the script by Pommer.

No matter whether it did or did not drive home its thematic point, *Caligari* was, visually, the most significant work of its day. Expressionism was a growing art trend in Europe and it was unmistakably transferred to film in the Pom-

mer production. It was there in the surreal backdrops, in the weirdly proportioned furnishings, in the shadowy lighting and even in the pictorial composition, a prime example being the nightmarish quality given to the rooftop chase sequences. In all – the antithesis of the realistic photographic approach used in virtually all films of the time – it reflected the spiritual and intellectual anguish present in postwar Germany and endowed the picture with a particularly deep meaning for the people. And it reflected in at least one producer the sudden burst of creativity and new techniques of visualization that the end of a stultifying war had brought. That burst resulted in what is now called the Golden Age of German films – the period of imaginative and compelling productions that ran from *Caligari*'s 1919 release to Hitler's assumption of power in the early 1930s.

In the vanguard of the new movement, *Caligari* influenced the look of German films throughout the 20s. The *Caligari* 'look' was also to be seen in Hollywood, brought there by German director Paul Leni and imparted to his *The Cat and the Canary* (1927) and *The Man Who Laughs* (1928). It was picked up by American directors and was seen in Rex Ingram's *The Magician* (1926) and Tod Browning's *London After Midnight* (1927), with Lon Chaney. It continued in the 1930s with James Whale's *Frankenstein,* being especially evident in Whale's vaulted sets, elongated windows, curving stairways, eerie contrasts of light and dark and the grotesque angularity at times achieved through his liking for shooting at upward angles.

Considering *Caligari*'s tremendous visual influence of at least two decades (yes, it's still lingering as late as 1939, echoing in that contorted stairway so well recalled by anyone who has seen *The Son of Frankenstein*), it is surprising to learn that the picture was made with a small budget. Running close to two hours in its original length, it was shot in two to three weeks. Most of the backdrop scenery was painted canvas.

The Cabinet of Dr Caligari was 'remade' in 1962. Produced in Cinema-Scope and featuring Dan O'Herlihy and Glynis Johns , it turned out to be a weak psychological drama that had little in common with the original except the title.

NOTE: Filmographies customarily list *Caligari*'s original German title as *Das Kabinett des Dr Caligari*. Author Georges Sadoul, in his *Dictionary of Films* (University of California Press, 1972, translation by Peter Morris), claims this to be a mistake. He writes that Pommer used the word *Cabinet* in the title, doing so to impart a sense of the archaic.

Though it can take advantage of a sprawling cast of bizarre characters, the horror film, by its very nature, has few themes at its disposal. Whenever it has found a good one, it has worked it time and again, varying it as much as the imagination (and, sometimes, a producer's desperation) will permit. Three of the most enduring themes were established by the European films that have been discussed thus far.

The idea of burial while yet alive, as seen in *The Necklace of the Dead,* has served many a picture since. As a deep-rooted fear in one of the characters, it hovered threateningly in the background throughout *Isle of the Dead* (1945) and, though the fear never turned into a reality for the character, it added much to the picture's chill. It was, however, the centerpiece in director Roger Corman's adaptation of Edgar Allan Poe's *The Premature Burial* (1962). That it was brought to grisly heights at the edge of a New England pond in *Ghost Story* (1981), hardly a horror film devotee will deny.

Paul Wegner's Golem series has long been seen as the inspirational antecedent of those classic combinations of science fiction and horror – the Frankenstein tales. On at least two counts, the 1931 *Frankenstein* definitely resembles the Golem rather than Mary Shelley's updating of the similar, and undoubtedly related, Prometheus legend of Greece. First, in the initial Golem offering, 1914's *The Monster of Fate,* the clay creature responds to the gift of life by going on a rampage that ends in his destruction when he falls from a tower; how reminiscent is the fate of Karloff's Monster who, after terrorizing the countryside, meets his creator in brutal combat atop the windmill laboratory and plunges to his death. Second, in all his Golem appearances, Wegener portrays the clay creature as a hulking, brooding, inscrutable brute with a plodding walk. Can anything different be said of the Frankenstein Monster's physical presence as established by Karloff and then faithfully reproduced in subsequent years by Lon Chaney Jr, Glenn Strange and Bela Lugosi?

There can be no denying that the German productions influenced director Whale's approach to Frankenstein and Karloff's approach to his Monster characterization. Since that picture established the atmosphere and the style in which all the follow-ups would be played, it can be said that the Golem's presence can be felt in every Frankenstein feature that has come along.

Caligari, of course, set the stage for the familiar domination-by-evil theme and its many just-as-familiar varia-

tions. In its most basic form, it was seen in *Svengali* (1931), with John Barrymore holding hypnotic sway over Marion Marsh's Trilby, and in England's 1954 remake that cast Donald Wolfit in the title role and Hildegarde Neff as Trilby. It was there, again in its basic form, in Tod Browning's *The Devil Doll* (1936), in which the unjustly imprisoned Lionel Barrymore escapes, employs a secret formula to turn his old enemies into doll-sized creatures, and then has them do his bidding. It was there, full blown, in Bela Lugosi's *Murders in the Rue Morgue* (1932), which, right down to the sets, was a direct imitation of *Caligari.* And it was there in so many of those science fiction/horror 'mad doctor' thrillers of the 1930s and early 40s.

As for the variations, they've mainly been of the 'possession' breed. John

Top: *Premature Burial* (1962) took Edgar Allan Poe's story and packed it with contrivances, clichés and gloomy decors. It was directed by Roger Corman.

Above: *Murders in the Rue Morgue,* from the story by Edgar Allan Poe, has been made in four different versions between 1931 and 1973. The killer is a gorilla.

Barrymore in 1920, Fredric March in 1932 and Spencer Tracy in 1941 all released the evil side of their nature and then were subjugated by it in *Dr Jekyll and Mr Hyde*. On losing his hands in an accident, a famous pianist had those of a murderer grafted on and then became their knife-throwing slave in Austria's *Orlacs Hande* (English: *The Hands of Orlac*) (1925); the improbable story so pleased and repelled audiences that it was remade twice – once in a 1961 combined French-British endeavor and once in the United States; the US production, which starred a bald Peter Lorre as an evil surgeon, was marketed as *Mad Love* (1935). Janet Blair fell under the spell of witchcraft in *Burn Witch Burn* (1962). A demon took possession of a child in *The Exorcist* (1973). The hedonistic spirit of a dead pianist (Curt Jurgens) occupied the body of his protege (Alan Alda) in *The Mephisto Waltz* (1971). And who among horror fans cares to forget those evil spirits that took over a quite ordinary American home in *The Amityville Horror* (1979)?

Out of Europe's early development of the horror film, then, came three of the genre's most basic themes. And out of Germany came yet another theme – one that assuredly must be the most repeated and perhaps, if repetition is a sign of public affection, the most beloved of all. The year was 1922 when the young and brilliant F W Murnau released his *Nosferatu – Eine Symphonie des Grauens,* which is known in its English translation as *Nosferatu the Vampire* and *Nosferatu: A Symphony of Horror.*

Nosferatu was an unabashed filming of Bram Stoker's novel, *Dracula,* and, as such, stands as something of a cinematic oddity. Murnau, though he gave full screen credit to the Stoker work, never obtained permission to use the book. And so, in the screenplay by Henrick Galeem, Stoker's principal setting, aside from Transylvania, is switched from London to the German port of Bremen, and all the characters are rechristened, with Jonathon Harker changed to Hutter, Mina to Nina and Dracula himself to Count Orlock. Further, Galeen and Murnau altered the ending drastically, abandoning the book's stake-through-the-heart climax and substituting an erotic, night-long sequence that became the highlight of the film.

But, no matter the changes, the basic plot was still there, a fact that enabled Stoker's widow to sue Murnau with such success that his film company collapsed. One of the most gifted film makers of his day, Murnau went on to direct Emil Jannings' tour de force *Der Letzte Mann/The Last Laugh* (1924), a silent film so visually perfect that it required

Top: John Barrymore (seated) was the star of the 1920 version of *Dr Jekyll and Mr Hyde*. He turned in a fine performance as a handsome, dashing Jekyll and a horrifying, fanged, taloned Hyde. He was able to appeal to his feminine admirers as Jekyll and do some real emoting as Hyde – altogether an ideal setup for him.

Above: A jolly moment on the set. March is his makeup as Hyde takes tea with Director Rouben Mamoulian and co-star Miriam Hopkins.

Right: Frederic March starred in the *Dr Jekyll and Mr Hyde* remake of 1932. As of now, he is the only person to receive an Oscar for a performance in a horror film. Here he is shown attacking Miriam Hopkins.

no dialogue cards. He then moved to Hollywood, where he did *Sunrise* (1927), *City Girl* (1930) and the South Seas documentary *Tabu* (1931) with Robert Flaherty. Murnau died in a California traffic accident just after *Tabu* was completed. He was 42 at the time of his death.

Nosferatu is set in the 1830s and opens when the real estate clerk Hutter (Gustav von Wangenheim) arrives in the Carpathian mountains to arrange the sale of a property with Count Orlock (Max Schreck). On seeing a small picture of Hutter's young wife (Greta Shroeder), Orlock is immediately attracted to her. He attacks Hutter and makes him his prisoner, after which he departs by ship for Bremen, where the Hutter home is located. As the result of the evil in Orlock, the ship's crew dies during the voyage and, on his arrival in Bremen, a swarm of plague-bearing rats infests the city. Settling into a house across the street from the Hutter residence, the Count begins to make advances on Nina.

In the meantime, Hutter breaks free and returns home. He warns Nina of Orlock's evil powers. Nina decides that she must kill the Count, not only to protect herself and her husband but to safeguard all mankind from the vampire.

She does so in the climactic sequence by keeping Orlock at her bedside throughout a long night and enduring his blood-letting kisses. Captivated by the woman, he fails to see the approach of the dawn, so lethal in vampire legend. Suddenly, a cock crows and the first rays of the sun break through the windows to strike Orlock. Clutching his chest in agony, the vampire slowly disintegrates, at first becoming transparent and then fading from view as he is totally destroyed. Hutter now enters the room. Nina, her heroic victory won, dies in his arms.

Nosferatu was an immediate success in Germany and France. Much of its attraction was due to the grim post-war attitudes still prevailing in Europe four years after the Armistice. Some audiences interpreted the vampire and the plague-bearing rats as symbolic of the 'pestilence' of war. Others saw Orlock as the tyrant who takes a people to war and sucks the blood from them in battle. And others identified Nina's victory as representative of the idea that love and decency can defeat evil.

On top of all else, the picture was an enticing piece of chiller entertainment. It was punctuated with genuinely eerie moments throughout – Orlock staring malevolently down at the Bremen docks from a dead ship, the rats scurrying through the city, Orlock carrying a coffin on his shoulders along a dark

A closeup of Max Schreck as the terrifying Count Orlock in *Nosferatu* (1922). The word schreck means 'terror' in German, and there are those who believe that the actor was really another performer by the name of Alfred Abel.

street, and Orlock's evil visually illustrated at times through the use of negative film. The single most frightening elements of all was Max Schreck's physical presence as the vampire, a presence vastly different from the one that Bela Lugosi would set nine years later in *Dracula* and that would become the vampire's standard embodiment. Lugosi fashioned a character that was sexually potent, physically powerful and satanically handsome. But Schreck's Orlock was a walking skeleton. His head was bald and skull-like, his ears pointed, his nose boney, his face pinched, and his eyes pieces of round, staring glass in sockets outlined with dark makeup. And his hands – they weren't hands at all, but scimitar-shaped talons.

Though the picture attracted wide audiences in Germany and France, it met with a cold reception in Great Britain and the United States. Both countries tended to ridicule it, with many audiences finding the heavily greasepainted Orlock more comic than frightening. Much rejected, too, was the idea that a sane woman, even to save mankind, could bring herself to spend a night abed with that walking nightmare.

But how things were to change in a span of just nine years. The United States may have reacted frigidly to *Nosferatu*. But when Dracula, in his guise as a bat, came flying by in 1931, the country welcomed him and – in common with the rest of the world – has kept the window open for an almost unending series of winged visits ever since.

Prior to *Dracula's* arrival, Hollywood did little with horror films. There were, as mentioned earlier, those two Frankenstein adaptations, one in 1910 and the other in 1915. Producers, even when they could see the profits being reaped in Europe by the Golem features and *Caligari*, were reluctant to experiment with the genre. They felt that the American public – and the reaction to *Nosferatu* must certainly have strengthened their conviction – would not see horror as a fit subject for the nation's children, alone or with their parents. Further, to be effective, horror depended on having audiences accept such elements as the supernatural, the bizarre, the unexplained, the arch fiend, the satanic vil-

Above: One of Lon Chaney's greatest roles was as the hunchback, Quasimodo, in *The Hunchback of Notre Dame* (1924). Based upon Victor Hugo's novel *Notre Dame de Paris*, the film was later remade in 1939 with Charles Laughton and in 1956 with Anthony Quinn.

Right: Undoubtedly Chaney's most memorable role was that of *The Phantom of the Opera* (1925). His nostrils and mouth were said to have been filled with springs and clamps to enhance his makeup. The movie was the story of an embittered disfigured composer who haunts the sewers beneath the Paris Opera House and takes a pretty young singer as his protégée. Chaney was known as 'the man of a thousand faces' because of his elaborate disguises in macabre roles.

lain. As some producers saw things, the streak of practicality that was in the American character would prohibit the necessary acceptance. Either their reading of the public was wrong or the public had changed its outlook by 1931.

If the latter was the case, then it can be said with fairness that one man, more than any other, paved the way to the change – Lon Chaney. A versatile actor, an extraordinary pantomimist (the son of deaf parents, he learned the art early in his efforts to communicate with them), and a performer able to contort his body into seemingly impossible positions, Chaney entered pictures in 1913 and scored his first big hit six years later in the role of a grotesque cripple in *The Miracle Man*. From there, he went on to a string of uninviting but brilliant characterizations – as a legless man in *The Penalty* (1920), as the deformed Quasimodo in *The Hunchback of Notre Dame* (1924), as the mutilated villain in *Phantom of the Opera* (1925), as an ancient Oriental in *Mr Wu* (1927) and as a leering bogus vampire in *London After Midnight* (1927). By the time of his death in 1930, he had played over 150 diverse roles, ranging from the macabre specimens above to the tough sergeant in *Tell it to the Marines* (1927) and the gentle and pathetic figure in *Laugh, Clown, Laugh* (1928).

But Chaney's great audience appeal lay in his talent for creating strange make-up (a fact that prompted his studio publicity department to dub him 'The Man of a Thousand Faces') and for contorting his features and his body. As a result, his films are felt to have accentuated the elements of the grotesque rather than those of true horror.

Aside from Chaney's splendid work, Hollywood in the 1920s flirted with the genre with Paul Leni's Caligari-influenced *The Cat and The Canary* and with *The Bat* and *The Gorilla*. All were taken from popular stage plays of the day. Though replete with such frightening devices as creaking doors, hidden panels, disappearing heroines, lights going out mysteriously and murderous hands emerging from behind curtains and drapes – they were really mystery rather than horror pieces. Further, all the unexplainable, all the supernatural and all the occult elements were given a rational explanation at the end. They were all calculating ploys used by an altogether human villain or hero with a deliberate purpose in mind. They were neither, as they could be in the true horror film, the instinctual nor the evil-for-evil's sake acts of an impossible being such as a Dracula, a Mummy or a Werewolf. Even the vampire creatures in Chaney's *London After Midnight* turn out to be actors who donned their vampire disguises to trap a murderer.

But then that banner year 1931 arrived – and with it Universal's release of *Dracula* in February and *Frankenstein* in December. The US era of the straight horror film and its science fiction/horror brother was at hand.

Dracula was based not on the Stoker novel but on a play that had been made of it. The play was written for the London stage by Hamilton Deane, who then revised it with John L Balderston for a New York presentation in 1927. The Hungarian-born Bela Lugosi, popular in his own country since early in the century but virtually unknown in the US, was assigned the Broadway role in what has long been considered a perfect piece of type casting. Tall (he stood just over six feet), powerfully built and a man of intense manner, Lugosi gave the role the sexual potency and commanding demeanor that Deane and Balderson had written into it. And his thick Hungarian accent, rather than confusing the listener, added just the right touch of the sinister to the character. He was an instant hit and was the natural choice for the film. The play ran for a year on Broadway and then toured the country for two years, breaking attendance records everywhere. On film, it proved to be Universal's biggest moneymaker of 1931. (This fact should not suggest that *Dracula* was a greater hit

than *Frankenstein. Frankenstein,* remember, was released in the closing month of the year. It ranked eighth in the list of top moneymaking films of 1932.)

Directed by Tod Browning and running 84 minutes, *Dracula* opens as Renfield (Dwight Frye), a real estate agent from London, approaches the Count's Transylvanian castle. On his way there to have Dracula sign a lease for Carfax Abbey in England, Renfield is warned by frightened peasants of his host's evil ways. The warnings come true when the Count, after a cordial welcome, attacks Renfield for his blood and makes him his slave.

Dracula, taking the now insane Renfield with him, travels to England by ship, killing all the seamen on board by drinking their blood. On arrival, Renfield is placed in a mental institution. Dracula meets two young women – Lucy and Mina, the latter being Jonathan Harker's fiancee. Dracula first attacks Lucy, drinks her blood, and turns her into a vampire, adding her to the ashen-faced female entourage that has accompanied him from Transylvania. He then turns his evil attentions on Mina (Helen Chandler).

Enter now Professor Van Helsing (Edward Van Sloan), summoned to help diagnose the cause of Mina's declining

Bela Lugosi in *Dracula* (1931) advances on the mesmerized Helen Chandler. He was not the first screen vampire. An unknown actor played a vampire in Georges Méliès' *The Devil's Castle* (1896). That film ended as a man held up a crucifix and the vampire gave up and disappeared, thus establishing a practice that would appear in every vampire film from then on.

health and strange mental state. Van Helsing, an expert on vampirism, quickly ascertains the nature of Mina's problem and suspects Dracula to be the cause. The picture abruptly becomes a duel between the two men, with Van Helsing at one point seeing that Dracula casts no reflection in a mirror, challenging him with a crucifix at another, and finally convincing Jonathan Harker (David Manners) and Mina's father that, if the young woman is to be saved, the three of them must seek out Dracula at Carfax Abbey and drive a stake through his heart while he sleeps the day away.

The final sequences are played in the underground caverns at the Abbey. Van Helsing and his companions locate Dracula lying asleep in a coffin. Nearby is the weak and dazed Mina. Van Helsing stands above Dracula and methodically pounds the stake through the Count's

heart. Immediately, released from Dracula's powers, Mina begins to recover and faces a happy future with Jonathan.

Though the picture was enthusiastically welcomed by the public, *Dracula* did not please many critics and, in the eyes of some film historians, has not worn too well through the years. The script was criticized for being too much like a stage play once the initial chilling scenes of Renfield's coach ride through the mountains to Dracula's castle and then his first encounters with the vampire were out of the way; there was constantly the opportunity in the London and Carfax Abbey sequences for visualizing certain chilling elements, but they went unseen and were only talked about by the characters. Browning's direction was accused of being too static, adding further to the impression of a stage play put on film.

But photographer Karl Freund was universally praised, especially for the chilling atmosphere that his camera evoked in the opening sequences. As for the acting, Lugosi – though his performance, when viewed today, can seem almost comically outdated (and, frankly, a little hammy) at times – was applauded for his Grand Guignol style, with his piercing stare and his rich voice being fertile ground for imitators

ever since, and with his inimitable, almost song-like delivery of the line, 'I am Drac-u-la,' making it a national byword in the 1930s. In the minds of many critics, the verbal duels between Lugosi and Van Sloan provided the film with its best moments.

Oddly, considering its box office appeal, *Dracula* failed to spawn the sequels that Frankenstein did. Universal recognized the bonanaza that it had in Karloff's Monster, but somehow missed seeing that a similar bonanza was at hand in its other horror creations of the day – not only the Count but also *The Mummy* and the unfortunate man-turned-beast in *The Werewolf of London*. It was not until these pictures were re-released and enthusiastically greeted, often on gimmicky 'triple horror feature' bills, that the studio changed its mind and started to plan sequels. The Count's first sequel came in 1943 with the modestly budgeted but slickly produced *Son of Dracula*. The picture was without Lugosi's services. Starring instead was Lon Chaney Jr, playing Count Alucard (Dracula spelled backwards) and traveling from Transylvania to the United States in search of victims.

But the vampire theme itself was kept busy throughout the 1930s. In 1932, France and Germany released the

In *Dracula* (1931), Bela Lugosi confronts the hapless Renfield. Renfield was played by Dwight Frye, who later played the hunchback in *Frankenstein* (1931), *The Bride of Frankenstein* (1935) and *Frankenstein Meets the Wolf Man* (1943).

superbly chilling *Vampyr,* the story of a woman vampire and perhaps the best fare ever offered within the genre. Universal tried a similar theme with *Dracula's Daughter* in 1936, with Gloria Holden in the title role and trying desperately, but unsuccessfully, to overcome her inherited blood lust. Lugosi moved over to MGM in 1935 to be directed by Browning in *Mark of the Vampire,* an expensive remake of Lon Chaney's *London After Midnight,* playing Count Mora to those let's-pretend vampires out to trap a murderer.

Lugosi's screen career, begun so brilliantly with *Dracula,* did well for itself in the 1930s, marked as it was by such fine individual efforts as *Mark of the Vampire* and *Murders in the Rue Morgue* and by his science fiction/horror vehicles with Boris Karloff, *The Black Cat* and *The Raven* chief among them. But, by the 1940s, that career was going rapidly downhill, much because of his willingness – or perhaps financial need – to accept any picture that came along, no matter how inept and cheaply budgeted it might be. And, long addicted to drugs (Lugosi admitted to taking morphine as far back as the filming days of *Dracula* to ease pains in his legs), he was in deplorable health. In 1955, he committed himself to a state institution for treatment of his addiction. Seemingly recovered, Lugosi planned a return to films and intended to be married, but he died in 1956 at age 73. At the time of his death, the man who had earned more than $600,000 in his Hollywood career had only $3000 to his name. He was buried in his red silk-lined Dracula cape, with Hollywood legend having it that he insisted on the cape because he had become so closely identified in his own mind with the vampire characterization.

By the time of Lugosi's death, vampire films had suffered quite as much as his career. Caught in the era of the Bs, with quickie outfits churning them out and with Universal turning from straight sequels to its multiple-monster features – *House of Frankenstein, House of Dracula* and *Abbott and Costello Meet Frankenstein* – they had steadily declined in quality, at last degenerating into the cheapest of forgettables. In all, a once frightening figure was rendered laughable. Further humiliations came in the 1950s with the likes of *The Return of Dracula* (1957), in which John Beal, a genuinely talented actor who deserved better assignments, swallowed a pill that turned him into a bloodsucker. Hardly better was *The Return of The Vampire* (1958), starring another more deserving performer – Francis Lederer – as a Dracula type on the loose in California. The British saw the picture under a title that more aptly suggested its quality – *The Fantastic Disappearing Man*.

Lugosi himself took a hand in two of the worst insults. The first was Great Britain's *Old Mother Riley Meets the Vampire* (1952). In this one, Lugosi came up against Arthur Lucan's impersonation of the vulgar old lady that had long made him a headliner in British music halls. Those who were unfortunate enough to see the film in its American release may remember it as either *My Son the Vampire* or *Vampire over London*. Then, in his final screen appearance, the obviously ill Lugosi portrayed Specter the vampire in *Plan Nine from Outer Space* (released in 1959), a nonsensical nothing about alien zombies. And those unfortunate enough to see it in its British release may remember it as *Grave Robbers from Outer Space*. Again, the British title well indicates the quality.

Happily, though, England's Hammer

Left: As his father had done in *London After Midnight* (1927), Lon Chaney Jr played a vampire in *Son of Dracula* (1943). Here he is about to bite Louise Albritton. There is not much to say about the artistic merits of this film. Chaney was not the suave gentleman that his father was. But he had had so much practice changing into a wolf that the producers let him change into a bat. At the end of the picture his coffin is found and burned and the vampire, Anthony Alucard (Dracula spelled backwards) is killed by the sunrise.

Left: In the splendid ending of *Nosferatu* (1922), Count Orlock gradually disappears – a victim of the rising sun. For the time, the trick photography of his dissolving in the light was exceedingly good.

Films, long-time specialists in things not nice, took over the Count in 1958. His dignity was restored with the first decent screen treatment he had been given in years. Starring a gaunt and fanged Christopher Lee in the title role and a sophisticated Peter Cushing as Van Helsing, *Horror of Dracula* stands as one of the better offerings in the category and sports a chilling ending that combines elements of Lugosi's *Dracula* and Murnau's *Nosferatu*. Van Helsing pursues Dracula back to his mansion at daybreak and, trapping him in a room, yanks aside great draperies to let the sun pour in. Then as the Count desperately tries to remain in the shadows, Van Helsing grabs two giant candlesticks, holds them in the form of a cross, advances on his enemy, and forces him into a shaft of bright light. Experiencing the same agony that Count Orlock had felt 36 years earlier, Dracula disintegrates, screaming, into dust.

With this genuinely chilling piece to its credit, Hammer moved to *The Brides of Dracula* (1960), featuring David Peel in a story of one of the Count's victims, and then to the excellent *Kiss of the Vampire* (1963), a horrid, sensual little tale that follows a honeymooning couple to Bavaria and sees them entrapped by a vampire cult. In 1965, Hammer again contracted Lee and Cushing, this time for *Dracula – Prince of Darkness*. The picture was a direct sequel to *The Horror of Dracula* and began with the ashes to which the Count had been reduced seven years earlier. Blood flowed into the ashes and revived him for a series of films, all starring Lee, that ran well into the 1970s – *Dracula Has Risen from the Grave* (1968), *The Magic Christian* (1969), *Taste the Blood of Dracula* (1970), *The Scars of Dracula* (1970), *Dracula AD 1972* (1972), *The Satanic Rites of Dracula* (1973) and *Count Dracula and His Vampire Bride* (1978).

Well produced and generously budgeted, all were solid box office attractions, with *Dracula Has Risen from the Grave* considered to be the most gruesome of the lot. In it, Lee is pursued to the battlements of a castle, falls, and is impaled on a huge stake. *The Scars of Dracula*, on the other hand, is remembered as the most chilling of the entries. The scenes in which Lee stalks his victims and then forces them to submit to his blood kisses have been singled out as among the most effective ever done in vampire films.

Lee did not limit his Dracula characterization to British efforts. In 1974, he appeared in the French production, *Tendre Dracula*, following two years later with *Dracula Père et Fils*. He appeared in the joint British-Spanish endeavor *Vampir/Count Dracula* (1972)

and went to Sweden for the interesting documentary on vampirism, *In Search of Dracula* (1975). Shot in present-day Romania, the Swedish film deals with Transylvanian folklore and the real-life inspiration behind the Count – the 15th century Wallachian Prince, Vlad Tepes, who devised such awful tortures for his enemies that he went into central and eastern European lore as Vlad the Impaler. Lee narrates the film and appears as Vlad in scenes shot within the Impaler's home, Castle Bran.

It must be noted that Dracula was just one of a series of fine horror characterizations that Lee has molded over the years. He has played the Monster to Peter Cushing's inventive doctor in a series of Frankenstein films and has worked with Cushing in such highly popular fare as *Dr Terror's House of Horrors* (1965), efforts that have made the two of them the most popular horror team of recent years, easily the heirs to the Karloff-Lugosi crown. On his own, Lee has done a version of the Jekyll-Hyde story – *The Two Faces of Dr Jekyll* (1960) and has donned Oriental makeup for Britain's highly successful Fu Manchu series. Proving his versatility, he has escaped the horror genre to do Artemidorus in *Julius Caesar* (1970) and Rochefort in *The Three Musketeers* (1974) and *The Four Musketeers* (1975).

And Britain, for its part, has not limited its vampire efforts to Lee over the recent years. In adaptations of Sheridan Le Fanu's classic novelette 'Carmilla' (on which 1932's *Vampyr* was reportedly based), the ladies were allowed to do the blood kissing in *Lust for a Vampire* and *The Vampire Lovers* (both 1970). Each of these offerings, it must be said, was more concerned with sex, nudity, violence, and lesbianism than horror. In 1970, Britain also came up with *Coun-*

tess Dracula, the story of a female sadist who enjoys nothing better than to bathe in the blood of her victims. Far superior to any of these efforts was France's *El Mourier de Plaisir/Blood and Roses*, released ten years earlier and directed by Roger Vadim; here, in a retelling of the Le Fanu story, we have a young woman who is possessed by a vampire and then made to follow his evil ways. Quite as good is Italy's *Maschera del Demonio* (1961), starring Barbara Steele as a vampire witch. Moodily photographed and adapted from a Gogol story, the film was released in the United States as *Black Sunday*, and in Great Britain as *Revenge of the Vampire*.

Unfortunately, the same quality was not on display in the US vampire films of the 1960s and 70s. In 1966, a caped John Carradine invaded America's Old West, terrorized a frontier town, and got himself done away by – guess who? – in *Billy the Kid vs Dracula*. In 1970 there was *Count Yorga, the Vampire* who decided to conduct a statewide search for blood in California. The picture, starring Robert Quarry (who was to become a minor horror star during the decade), achieved something of a cult status among US college students and was given a sequel *The Return of Count Yorga* (1971). The sequel ended with Yorga's death, but saw one of his followers become a vampire, thus setting the stage for further bat flights – flights that never got off the ground. The 1970s also produced two features with black casts – *Blacula* (1972) and *Scream, Blacula, Scream* (1973). Both concentrated more on spilled blood than vampirism.

Happier notes, however, were sounded as the decade closed and the 1980s dawned. George Hamilton did the clever and lightly comic *Love at First Bite* in 1979 and Frank Langella followed that

A creature from *The Howling* (1982).

same year with the filmed version of his New York staging of *Dracula,* in which he played the Count much as a romantic but driven leading man. Both pictures were enjoyable, with *Love at First Bite* being the greater pleasure, featuring as it did nice tongue-in-cheek performances by Hamilton as a graying but still sexy Dracula and Susan Saint James as the lady who doesn't mind his kisses at all. The picture was a welcome relief from the somber treatments of the past and especially from the 'blood bath' films that had taken over the horror screen in recent years.

Horror and science fiction have walked hand-in-hand ever since they first came into vogue in 1931. Repeatedly – in one mad doctor, creature, space and futuristic film after another – they've been on view in each other's company. They have been so closely entwined in some productions that it has been virtually impossible to tell where the one has left off and the other begun.

There is a good and obvious reason for this mating. Horror has all the awful creatures at its disposal while science fiction has the means – the laboratory experiment, the nuclear disaster, the space visitation – for loosing them on the world. Those means have always been an inviting convenience for pro-

ducers whereas, as stressed earlier, genuine horror themes – themes in which the frightful and the grotesque are aberrations, in which the creepy is part of the 'unknown' and in which evil is played for its own sake by the villain – have always been hard to come by. Yet, beginning with those early ideas advanced in *Caligari* and *The Necklace of the Dead,* the years have seen horror manage to develop themes that, along with vampirism, are distinctly its own.

These themes have been few in number and, on two counts, have been difficult to handle. First, dealing with the likes of werewolves and ghosts, they have not readily lent themselves to the plot variations and the character development needed to keep them fresh for repeated presentations over the years (the same can be said of vampirism, but – perhaps because it is the one theme that speaks most eloquently of the lurking evil that humans see or sense in themselves and their fellows – it has a basic appeal that makes variation and character development unnecessary). Second, some horror characters – zombies and Karloff's Mummy are two cases in point – have been simply such dull fellows at heart that they couldn't hope to have any staying power. The result has been that, contrary to

Dracula's experience, most horror themes have enjoyed only brief moments of popularity or have been used but periodically through the decades since 1931. We turn to them now.

The idea of the living dead has been behind a few individual features that have combined horror and science fiction. A prime example here is Boris Karloff's *The Walking Dead* (1936), which was mentioned in the preceding chapter and which sees Karloff, after being electrocuted for a crime he did not commit, brought back to life by scientist Edmund Gwenn; Karloff, before dying again at the climax, stalks his enemies and triggers their deaths. Ranking with it as examples are Erich von Stroheim's *The Lady and the Monster* (1944) and Lew Ayres' *Donovan's Brain* (1953), both of which concern scientists keeping a vengeful brain alive and then falling under its spell and doing its bidding. The same idea, this time involving a spiteful lady, is on display in *The Brain That Wouldn't Die* (1962).

The living dead theme separates itself from science fiction and becomes distinctly horror when we turn to zombies, those creatures who originate in Haitian folklore and are said to be dead people restored to life by voodoo rites. Depicted on the screen as hulking, plodding, ashen-faced, sightless things, they have been a part of the genre since 1932 when the came stumbling down a night-shrouded hillside in Bela Lugosi's *White Zombie* (1932).

By today's standards, that debut piece – with Lugosi determined to rule a zombie jungle empire – can bring grins or outright laughs in spots. As is evident in *Dracula*, Lugosi's acting is dated and, again, a bit hammy and his lust for Madge Bellamy just a shade too lustful, as was so much of the lust of the times. But the film has its eerie moments, is beautifully photographed, is informative about voodoo practices and treats its zombie creatures seriously. They come across as frightening but still, somehow, sympathetic things – which, in fact, they are in cinema tradition, doing little damage and then usually only at the behest of an evil master.

Because of their helplessness and the impossibility of endowing them with any interesting characteristics – not to mention the fact that the whole zombie concept is one that the practical western mind finds hard to take – the poor souls have generally suffered an unhappy fate over the years since their cinematic debut. They have been used only on occasion and – aside from such rare films as the Val Lewton-produced and Jacques Tourneur-directed B gem, *I Walked With a Zombie* (1943) – have not been treated seriously. Bob Hope and Paulette Goddard romped, the one bug-eyed and the other screaming, through a Haitian castle with a zombie in pursuit in *The Ghost Breakers* (1940), as did Dean Martin and Jerry Lewis in the 1953 remake, *Scared Stiff*. And – certainly enough to send them back to the grave – the creatures have endured being associated with such B fare as *Revolt of the Zombies* (1936), *Zombies on Broadway* (1945), *Zombies of Mora Tau* (1957), *Teenage Zombies* (1968) and Great Britain's (happily above average) *Plague of the Zombies* (1966). They've even suffered the indignity of having a musical something called 'The Zombie Stomp' named in their honor and used in one of the greatest disasters of 1964, *The Horror of Party Beach*.

The living dead theme got one of its most effective workings in 1932 when Universal turned out *The Mummy*. With the picture, the studio intended to take advantage (and successfully did so) of the public's macabre interest in things Egyptian that had been aroused some years earlier by the discovery of King Tutankhamen's tomb. Several members of the discovery team had died shortly thereafter. The press had then happily reported that the deaths resulted from ancient curses bestowed on those who had tampered with the young monarch's final resting place.

Top: Probably the first zombie picture was *White Zombie* (1932). Bela Lugosi was the master of the living dead. Here he has drugged Madge Bellamy so that her husband thinks she is a zombie.

Above: In *I Walked with a Zombie* (1943), Frances Dee, playing a Canadian nurse in the West Indies, leads a planter's wife through the forest and past a Voodoo talisman. The natives have thought that the planter's wife was a zombie and Dee is taking her to a local voodoo priest for treatment.

Left: The end of a monster from *Zombie* (1980).

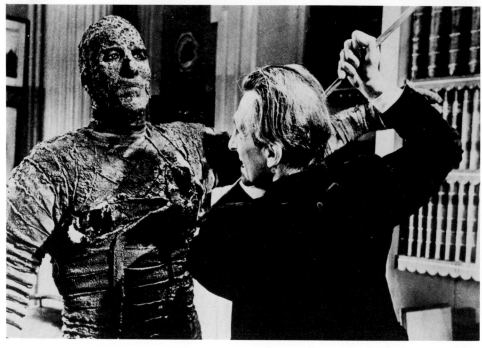

Top: Little does Bramwell Fletcher (left) suspect that Boris Karloff will soon come out of the sarcophagus to pay him a visit in *The Mummy* (1932). The role of the mummy was later recreated in sequels by Tom Tyler and Lon Chaney Jr.

Above: In the British version of *The Mummy* (1959), the creature is played by Christopher Lee. Here he advances on a scientist, played by his long-time co-star, Peter Cushing.

Boris Karloff, his lean frame swathed in bandages and his face done over splendidly by Jack Pierce (who a year before had fashioned the Frankenstein Monster), portrayed a 3000-year-old mummy who, on rising from the dead, takes possession of an ancient scroll containing a secret formula that enables him to be reincarnated in human form. He then dedicates himself to the search for a long-lost love, killing or hypnotizing those who get in his way until at last, as must happen, he himself is destroyed. Much because of Karloff's expert dual playing as the mummy and the reincarnated human, much because of his fine makeup – in its own way, it was quite as good as the Monster creation – and much because of the sense of ancient Egypt that was evoked throughout, the film was an immediate commercial and critical success.

Though it ended up being a success, and though it has always been acknowledged as a classic within the genre, *The Mummy* presented two difficulties as a horror offering. First, with Karloff searching for a lost love, the film seemed to be as much a romance as a horror story. Second, that search aroused an audience sympathy for the character in its reincarnated human form that was not felt as much for Frankenstein's Monster and not at all for Dracula. The opportunities, then, for the introduction of straight horror techniques were limited because they promised to be incongruous when cast against these elements. The result: *The Mummy* is a horror film with very few moments of actual horror in it. In the main, they are limited to closeups – closeups, for instance, of the Mummy's hand as it slowly comes to life and reaches for the scroll, and closeups of Karloff's eyes when he puts to use his strange power to kill or hypnotize from a distance. Throughout, in place of horror, director Karl Freund, who had photographed *Dracula* and was now on his first directing assignment, invested *The Mummy* with a sense of menace and impending disaster. It was an approach that probably saved the picture from looking silly and that won him much critical praise.

Like *Dracula, The Mummy,* as much of a box office draw as it was, failed to prompt a sequel until 1940 when Universal released *The Mummy's Hand.* The studio then followed with *The Mummy's Tomb* (1942), *The Mummy's Ghost* (1944), and *The Mummy's Curse* (1945). Tom Tyler, a second-feature cowboy star of the 1930s, played the bandaged thing in the first of the sequels. The role fell to Lon Chaney Jr in the remaining two. Though competently produced – and graced with the few eerie moments that the camera and Universal's experienced horror specialists could give them – the sequels were all low-budget endeavors and were part of the studio's campaign to turn a profit on its assorted frightful characters.

The Mummy may have been 3000 years old, but his life at Universal proved to be a short one. The studio dropped him after the 1945 *Curse* and – with the exception of *Abbott and Costello Meet the Mummy* ten years later – never used him again. There was a good reason for his dismissal. In the sequels, he was seen always as a bandaged-wrapped creature and, as such, turned out to be a pretty harmless fellow, one hard to find varied plots for, and one hard to make consistently interesting for audiences. As a representative of the walking dead, he was neither bright enough nor energetic enough to dream up his own evil and so had always to have on hand an arch villain who kept

him alive with tanna leaves and sent him on missions of skulduggery – George Zucco, for example, in *The Mummy's Hand* and Turhan Bey of the glossy hair in *The Mummy's Tomb*. Further, zombie-like and hampered by all those wrappings, he proved thoroughly inept whenever assigned an errand that involved chasing someone down. He moved so slowly that all the Universal heroines could easily outrun him. In fact, a look at any of the sequels will show that everyone went to a lot of trouble to have the ladies flee into corners where they could then stand screaming while waiting patiently for him to catch up.

Once his 1955 encounter with Abbott and Costello was done with, the creature was not seen until 1959 when England's Hammer Films took him in hand and did *The Mummy,* a remake of the original that shifted the time locale from the present to the Victorian era. Christopher Lee, supported by Peter Cushing and Yvonne Furneaux, played the title role. Two sequels came in the 60s – *Curse of the Mummy's Tomb* (1964) and *The Mummy's Shroud* (1966). Both, despite Terence Morgan's presence in the first and Andre Morell's in the second, were undistinguished efforts.

Compared to Dracula, Franken-

stein's Monster and the Mummy, the werewolf – the lycanthrope – is a Johnny-come-lately to the horror genre. They were well established figures by the time he arrived in Universal's *The Werewolf of London* (1935). The film starred Henry Hull as a scientist who is bitten by a werewolf while on a Himalayan expedition and then begins to grow hair and behave strangely at the full of the moon. Well mounted and moodily lighted, and with good performances by Hull (though criticized by some for seeming too unsympathetic a character) and Warner Oland as the man who knows his terrible secret, the picture was well received by audiences.

Content with the profits, Universal, as was its custom, let the idea lie fallow. Then in 1941 it developed the Lawrence Talbot character and assigned him to Lon Chaney Jr for *The Wolf Man*. The film proved to be enjoyable throughout, moody in parts, chilling in others, appropriately fog-shrouded in still others, and boasting a cast that made it look like anything but the B feature that it was – Claude Rains, Ralph Bellamy, Warren William, Evelyn Ankers (reputedly, the studio's most accomplished horror-film screamer), and the superb character actress from the Moscow Art Theater, Maria Ouspenskaya. As for Chaney, dismissed over the years

Above: Christopher Lee played the title role in *The Mummy* (1959) both in the present as a mummy and in flashbacks to his previous incarnation in ancient Egypt. Here he is as Prince Kharis.

Below: The great Jack Pierce designed the makeup for Lon Chaney Jr in *The Wolf Man* (1941). It is said that it took five hours each day to apply the makeup and involved the glueing on of yak hairs.

Chaney was not the only one to play a werewolf in films. Under the makeup is the British actor Oliver Reed in *The Curse of the Werewolf* (1961), made by Hammer Studios. This version is probably the most intelligent of all werewolf pictures.

since as an actor of limited range, he fashioned for Talbot a portrayal that was brooding, troubled and sensitive.

The son of Lon Chaney, the actor had been in films since 1932, appearing under his real name – Creighton Chaney – and playing supporting roles. With the studios wanting to take advantage of his late father's box office appeal, he switched to Lon Chaney Jr in 1935. Starting with his 1941 role in *Man Made Monster,* he found a niche for himself in B horror pictures and was much restricted to them and westerns for the remainder of his life (he died in 1973 at age 67). Limited to what was basically inferior fare, Chaney has long been mistakenly regarded as a minor talent. That it is an undeserved regard can be seen in at least two of his portrayals – as the shambling, mindless Lennie in *Of Mice and Men* (1940) and

as the crippled and humiliated lawman in *High Noon*.

Chaney's Lawrence Talbot is a young aristocrat, the heir to an English estate, who is bitten by a werewolf and then doomed to the eternal nightmare of lycanthropy, immune to death unless struck with a silver bullet. Using not the bullet but a silver-headed cane, Claude Rains batters the creature to death at the picture's end. But Universal was not to let Chaney-Talbot rest in peace. He was revived and put to work in that string of multiple-monster offerings that started with *Frankenstein Meets the Wolf Man* in 1943 and ended five years later for him with *Abbott and Costello Meet Frankenstein*. Not one of the pictures came near matching the original piece – nor were they ever intended to.

Despite the popularity of *The Were-*

wolf of London and *The Wolf Man*, the lycanthrope has not been used too often over the years. Like zombies and the Mummy, he presents certain production problems. For one, he is basically a sympathetic character, the helpless victim of a disease, and producers have always found it difficult to invent varied plot lines in which that decency and his evil when the moon is full can be effectively blended. Further, he involves a cost headache. Invariably, the best moments in his films come when he is transformed from man to beast. That transformation only works well when the audience views the change a step at a time, watching the hairs sprout on the face, the nose alter its shape, and the teeth lengthen into fangs. These transformations are difficult and expensive to do right (an audience invariably hollers 'no fair' if he ducks behind a table and then pops up in full hirsute regalia) and they must certainly have discouraged many a tightly-budgeted outfit from ever considering a werewolf film.

On those rare occasions when he has been used, the werewolf has usually been treated shabbily. Granted, Fox in 1942 handled him seriously and well in *The Undying Monster,* as did Oliver Reed in Britain's *Curse of the Werewolf* (1961), but, in the years between, the unfortunate creature was relegated to such low-budgeted sensational tripe as Bela Lugosi's *Return of the Vampire* (1944), Michael Landon's youthful indiscretion, *I Was a Teenage Werewolf* (1957), Mexico's *La Casa del Terror* (1959) and Italy's silly horror/sex mixture, *Werewolf in a Girls' Dormitory* (1961). All are best forgotten, with the same holding true of one of the most recent returns to the theme, *The Legend of the Werewolf* (1974).

On one occasion, however, the werewolf theme has been given a very interesting and chilling variation – in *The Cat People* (1942), which deals with a young woman (Simone Simon) obsessed with the idea that she is the descendant of people able to transform themselves into cats when under emotional stress. Directed by Jacques Tourneur and blessed with atmospheric photography throughout by Nichola Musuraca, the film is regarded as a gem in the horror field, in the main because it sets quite ordinary people against a backdrop of growing menace and never once shows

Above and left: Two types of monsters from *The Howling* (1980).

the always-threatening 'monster,' the Cat Woman. The closest it comes to doing so is in scenes involving a black panther in a zoo. But the unseen presence of the 'monster' is always there, especially in the famous swimming pool sequence and, most subtly and effectively, in the scene in which a frightened woman, fleeing from a sensed menace, hails a bus and then hears its door open with the unmistakable hiss of a giant cat.

The Cat People, which was made for $134,000 and grossed over $4 million, was the first of eleven horror films that Val Lewton produced for RKO in the 1940s. All have achieved the status of minor classics, with the first regarded as the finest of them all. Lewton made an alleged sequel in 1944, *The Curse of the Cat People*. Given that title by RKO (over his objections) to cash in on its

Above: A publicity poster from *Cat People* (1942). It is said that this was the first monster film to refrain from showing its monster.

Below: *The Curse of the Cat People* (1944), also starred Simone Simon. Here she appears with the little girl who is regarded as strange by her friends and parents.

predecessor's appeal, the film turned out to be not a sequel but a psychological study of a child's loneliness. *The Cat People* itself was remade in the early 1980s, but, showing the cat creatures at their hissing worst and playing up a sex angle, it was but a shadow of the original.

Ghosts have been the subject of movie fare for decades now, dating back to some of Méliès' photographic experiments at the turn of the century. But they have spent much of their screen careers in pictures other than horror offerings. Robert Donat, in Britain's *The Ghost Goes West* (1935), played a handsome Scottish rogue of yesteryear who cannot rest in peace until he performs an heroic act, a feat that he finally accomplishes by helping a modern-day family. Gene Tierney moves into a pleasant house on the English coast, meets the shade of its former owner – a salty, bearded sea captain in the person of Rex Harrison – and falls in love with him in *The Ghost and Mrs Muir* (1947). And Marcello Mastroianni heads a group of pleasant spirits occupying an old palace in Italy's *Ghosts of Rome* (1961).

Though ideal material for horror, ghosts were not introduced into the genre until the release of two exceptionally fine films in the mid-1940s. Prior to then, producers usually saw ghosts as entertainments that would upset children (a view, oddly, never extended to the likes of Dracula and

Above: *The Uninvited* (1944) was a story of a young brother and sister who rent a haunted house in England. Left to right: Ruth Hussey (the sister), Alan Napier, Ray Milland (the brother), Cornelia Otis Skinner.

Below: In *The Ghost and Mrs Muir* (1947), Gene Tierney, as Mrs Muir, starred in the bubbly comedy of a woman who has a 'romance' with the ghost of a dead sea captain. With her is George Sanders.

Frankenstein's monster) or as concepts not to be taken seriously by – and, consequently, never to frighten – literal-minded audiences. Any ghost who came along, then, was fashioned into a pretty harmless being. Robert Donat's rogue was a flop. The spirits in *A Christmas Carol* (1938) were given a fairy tale quality. Charles Laughton was a quivering and comic dear when he played *The Canterville Ghost* (1944). And Spencer Tracy, as did his fellow Air Force shades, proved himself a thoroughly nice fellow when he hung about this earth and helped his former girl friend find a new love in *A Guy Named Joe* (1943).

The two films that established ghosts as a serious horror theme were Paramount's *The Uninvited* (1944) and Great Britain's *Dead of Night* (1945). *The Uninvited*, based on the Dorothy Macardle novel, *Uneasy Freehold*, starred Ray Milland and dealt with a young girl (Gail Russell) being possessed by a ghost inhabiting the English house that Milland and his sister rent. In the tradition of *The Cat People*, the picture refrained from showing the spirit, instead making the thing's evil presence felt in chilling breezes and the air gone suddenly clammy. In all, *The Uninvited* is an effective piece of subdued horror, though Milland – who was a year away from making his excellent *The Lost Weekend* – was yet in the minds of audiences so much the strong and capable romantic leading man that his very pre-

Above: In *Poltergeist* (1982), a mother tries to keep her child from being sucked into the closet in which 'The Beast' is hiding.

Right: *The Exorcist* (1974) was a sensational supernatural horror piece about a young girl possessed by the devil. The film was one of the top grossers in the history of the American cinema.

sence tended to reduce the horror. A greater fear might have been communicated to and instilled in the viewer had someone not so rock-steady been faced with the ghost.

Equally effective – even more so in the minds of many critics – was *Dead of Night*. The film concerns a group of people who, spending an evening together in a lonely house, pass the hours by telling each other macabre stories. Five yarns in all are spun, with three concerning ghosts, and a fourth, death. The fifth – and perhaps the one that has proven the most famous of all – is an exercise in fright about a ventriloquist (Michael Redgrave) who comes to think of his dummy as alive and is then driven mad by the figure. Much the same theme was explored by Anthony Hopkins in *Magic* (1978), but, with some unnecessary gore thrown in for good measure, far less effectively.

Other fine pieces in the film include the story of a young girl (Sally Anne Howes) who, while attending a party, hears a child crying in a room. She enters, sees a little boy, and comforts him with stories, only to learn later that he is the ghost of a youngster killed there years earlier. Then there's the tale of the young husband (Ralph Michael) driven to the brink of suicide by the odd reflections that he sees in a mirror, a mirror before which its previous owner

Above: In *The Shining* (1980), Shelley Duvall prepares to defend herself from her crazed husband. As he hacks away at the door with his axe, he cries, 'Here's Johnny!'

Right: Jack Nicholson plays the husband in the film. He and his wife and son are 'house sitting' at a hotel that has closed for the winter. In this scene he is in the bar of the hotel when the ghosts of former guests appear to him.

Above: *Poltergeist* (1982). The film was set in a housing development that had been built over a cemetery. Much of the diabolical action occurred around television sets which were under the control of the ghosts.

Right: *The Swamp Thing* (1982). At best, this is one of the many B pictures of the horror genre, whose main claim to fame was the casting of Adrienne Barbeau as the heartthrob of the beast shown here, who is carried away by him, but later saved from his clutches.

killed himself. And, of course, there's the highly comic vignette about the two golfing friends (Naunton Wayne and Basil Radford). One is tricked by the other into suicide, but then evens the score by coming back to haunt his chum's wedding night.

For audiences who saw the film in its American release, the Sally Anne Howes and Wayne-Radford stories will be unfamiliar. (The golf story was reinstated for American TV.) Both were cut in the interests of time when the picture was sent to the US. The American filmgoer was the loser.

Because they are so restricted in theme (again, there is the problem of finding variations), ghosts have been the centerpieces of but a relatively few horror films since the two pioneering efforts of the mid-40s. Richard Carlson suffered as a husband bedeviled by the seaweed-dragging spirit of a former mistress in *The Tormented* (1960). Deborah Kerr was employed as the governess for two haunted children in *The Innocents* (1961), a superbly creepy US-British adaptation of Henry James' *The Turn of the Screw*. One of her young charges, Pamela Franklin, went on to investigate the terrible secrets behind *The Legend of Hell House* (1973) and was now so grown that she could be seduced by a lecherous spirit there. In the meantime, Julie Harris and Claire Bloom engaged in a good-evil duel in *The Haunting* (1963). In the same year, Vincent Price enjoyed himself thoroughly in *The Haunted Palace,* playing to the hilt his role of a warlock who returns from the dead to take vengeance on the village that allowed him to be burned at the stake centuries earlier.

The later years have brought *The Amityville Horror* (1979) and Steven Spielberg's excellent *Poltergeist* (1982), a film that manages to be chilling and good-humored all at the same time. One of the best offerings in the category is *Ghost Story* (1981). Played against a wintry New England setting, it is tautly told from beginning to end, with its climax (one that could have reduced the whole film to creature silliness had it not been handled correctly) being as close to shattering as you can get. The story centers on four elderly men who are hunted down by the ghost of a young woman whom they had injured as college students. Thinking her dead at the time, they had placed her in a car and then had rolled it into a pond, only to see her rise and stare at them, terrified, as it sank to the depths, not to be retrieved for decades. The girl haunts their memory for the rest of their lives and then returns in their late years to take her revenge on them and theirs.

The film is shot in color – a dangerous

undertaking because the brightness can detract from the somber mood of a horror story. But such is not the case in *Ghost Story*. The color not once gets in the way and, at times, even contributes to the chilling mood. As can be expected when the names of the players are mentioned – Fred Astaire, Melvyn Douglas, John Houseman, and Douglas Fairbanks Jr – the acting is flawless.

At present, horror is one of the busiest of film genre. But – unfortunately, in the minds of many a moviegoer – it is making its money by trading on violence and gore, commodities that, even in the most frightening of tales, were held in check in its earliest years. The trend towards seeing how much blood and brutality audiences can endure began in the 1950s with the likes of French director Georges Franju's grisly *Eyes Without a Face* (1959). Alfred Hitchcock opened the 1960s with the Janet Leigh stabbing in *Psycho* and, a year later, producer William Castle let

Right: In *Carrie* (1976), Sissy Spacek appeared as a girl with telekinetic powers. When she and her date are covered with animal blood in a malicious practical joke at the high school prom, she destroys the gym and part of the town with her powers.

Below: *Exorcist II: The Heretic* (1977) has been called perhaps 'the worst sequel of all time.'

Opposite: In *An American Werewolf in London* (1981), theater patrons were treated to the best transformation from man to werewolf ever put on the screen. The movie starred David Naughton, Griffin Dunne and Jenny Agutter.

Above left: David Naughton, the American werewolf, watches in terror and anguish as the metamorphosis begins when his hands begin to elongate.

Above: A publicity poster for *Halloween* (1978), the first of the 'slaughter of the teenagers' genre and a whopping box office success.

Left: In *The Omen* (1976), Lee Remick protects her young son, little knowing that he is the devil incarnate.

loose with *Homicidal* while a girl named *Carrie* destroyed her school-mates with her telekinetic powers.

Since then, audiences have been treated to a continuing parade of goug-ings, beatings, stranglings, decapita-tions, axings and sundry other stomach-turning fates in such fare as Britain's *Death Line* (1972) and *Theater of Blood* (1973) and America's *Willard* (1970), *Dear Dead Dellah* (1972) and *The Shin-ing* (1979), plus *The Omen* (1976), *Halloween* (1978), *Friday the 13th* (1980) and the sequels they've inspired.

Will the blood ever cease flowing and the sadism finally go out of style? Mo-tion picture entertainment has always run in cycles and, unless tradition here is defied, things must one day change, with horror again being played, not for its shock value, but for the eeriness and the genuine, tingling fright that it once sought to achieve. But, from the look of present-day box office receipts, no one should hope for an altering of course soon. There's no escaping the fact, that, as sickening as they are, violence and gore have a broad mass appeal, espe-cially among today's most avid moviegoers, the young.

THE
MUSICAL

Dependent on sound as it is, the musical, of course, is the latest-born of all the major film genres. The movies were some 30 years old when, on the night of 6 October 1927, a film burst upon the scene with the exuberant voice of Broadway singer, Al Jolson. That night marked the premiere of Warner Brothers' *The Jazz Singer* at their New York theater. The picture not only introduced a new genre but contributed significantly to changing the history of the industry. With it, the days of the silents and the careers of so many of the era's most luminous stars were numbered.

The film that did all this ran for 88 minutes and featured seven songs. It told the story of young Jakie Rabbinowitz (Jolson) who alienates his father (effectively played by that best of all Charlie Chans, Warner Oland) by abandoning a future as a cantor and following a career in jazz singing that eventually takes him to stardom. Using the Vitaphone process (recording discs synchronized with the film), *The Jazz Singer* was primarily a silent, turning to sound only for Jolson's songs and a few lines of dialogue that he reputedly ad-libbed on the set and then were allowed to remain – his patented 'You

ain't heard nothing' yet' and an impassioned speech to his screen mother (Eugenie Besserer).

But those songs – among them such Jolson trademarks as 'Toot, Toot, Tootsie' and 'Mammy,' plus the beautiful Jewish prayer 'Kol Nidre' – and the magic of the singer's voice coming from the screen enchanted the opening night audience. Each number earned an enthusiastic burst of applause, followed by a standing – and, so it was reported, tear-stained – ovation at the picture's end. The result: the birth of a genre and the beginning acceptance by producers that sound, a question mark in their minds throughout its experimental stages because of the technical problems involved, was here to stay. They were right.

The Jazz Singer has long been credited with being the first musical and the first sound motion picture. No matter that it was a landmark film, neither accolade is deserved. The picture was not a musical in the true sense of the word but a melodrama that highlighted seven songs by its young protagonist. The first genuine musical – the first to handle singing and dancing not as simply novel attachments but as integral parts of the story line – did not come until 1929 with MGM's *Broadway*

Previous pages: Seymour Felix won an Oscar for the dance direction of this production number in *The Great Ziegfeld* (1936).

Above: Al Jolson in *The Jazz Singer* (1927). As a story, it was not much, but Jolson's overwhelming stage personality shines through.

Melody, the story of two performers (Bessie Love and Charles King) and their backstage experiences.

As for sound, a few studios, sensing that it was where the future lay and troubled by the growing competition from radio, had been experimenting with it for several years. The young Warner company – it was founded in 1923 – and its production chief, Darryl Zanuck, began working with the Bell Telephone Laboratories' Vitaphone system in 1926. Warner turned out several demonstration sound shorts and then hired the New York Philharmonic to record the background music for John Barrymore's 1926 silent, *Don Juan.* The partially sound *Jazz Singer* was intended as just one more step along the studio's way to a full 'talking picture,' a goal it reached in 1928 with *Lights of New York.* But the Jolson film turned out to be a mighty step.

By the time *Lights of New York,* a crudely done gangster yarn, was in release, the industry was turning itself inside out. Theaters everywhere were converting to sound. Studios were buying microphones and recording equipment, a chief item being a sound-proof – and sweltering – cubicle in which the camera and its clearly audible whir could be housed. Nervous silent stars were hunting up vocal coaches. Producers were looking to the legitimate stage for actors with *voices.* And the musical had become the busiest genre in Hollywood, attacking the market with so many products that it was to wear out its· audience welcome by the early 1930s and come close to dying.

The attack was launched on a number of fronts. First, there were a string of musicals boasting Broadway stars. Warners, of course, produced a series of follow-ups for Jolson – *The Singing Fool* (1928), *Say It With Songs* (1929) and *Mammy* and *Big Boy* (both 1930) – all of which, though popular, never approached the *The Jazz Singer*'s box office take. Then Charles King arrived for *Broadway Melody,* Fanny Brice for *My Man* (1928), Marilyn Miller for a screen version of her 1920 Ziegfeld hit, *Sally* (1929) and Sophie Tucker for *Honky Tonk* (1929). Paramount imported France's Maurice Chevalier and cast him with operetta star Jeanette MacDonald in *The Love Parade* (1929). Paramount also brought in Helen Morgan for what many film historians have called the most interesting musical of the period – *Applause* (1929). Directed by Rouben Mamoulian, the picture, an uncompromising piece throughout, detailed the seamy side of burlesque life.

On another front, a number of silent stars who successfully made the jump to sound were recruited for musical service. Janet Gaynor and Charles Farrell, darlings of the nation after *Seventh Heaven* (1927), worked together in *Sunny Side Up* (1929) and went on to *Delicious* in 1931. Comedian El Brendel joined them in *Sunny Side Up,* graduating then to be the only good thing in the silly science fiction/musical *Just Imagine* (1930). Nancy Carroll, later a successful talent agent and the wife of Alan Ladd, made *Honey* (1931), a film chiefly remembered for Lillian Roth's energetic 'Sing, You Sinners' sequence.

And on yet another front, the studios tried their hand at 'all-star extravaganzas,' sprawling revue-type productions into which they dropped, often haphazardly, all their players. MGM released *The Hollywood Revue* of 1929; its cast featured romantic leading man Conrad Nagel and an ex-vaudevillian about to become a major radio star, Jack Benny, serving as masters of ceremonies; Joan Crawford and Marion Davies doing

Left: A scene from the pitiful remake of *The Jazz Singer* (1980), starring Lucie Arnaz and Neil Diamond.

Below: *The Singing Fool* (1928), starring Al Jolson, was a dismal tear-jerker about a brash entertainer who comes to his senses when his little boy dies. It is best remembered for its featured song, 'Sonny Boy.'

Bottom: The first American film made by the great French entertainer, Maurice Chevalier, was *The Love Parade* (1929). Here the threatening girl is saying 'I'd rather see you dead than in the arms of another woman!'

Above: A production number from *Hollywood Review of 1929* (1929). The film was closer to a vaudeville show performed in front of a camera than to a consistent movie with a plot. It was a mishmash of song, dance, comedy and even Shakespeare, and also had color sequences.

Below: A romantic interlude from *Hollywood Review of 1929* featuring Joan Crawford and Conrad Nagel. Although Crawford (born Lucille le Sueur and known for a time as Billie Cassin) had made her first movie just four years before, this was her 23rd film.

song and dance numbers and Norma Shearer and John Gilbert playing a scene from *Romeo and Juliet*, at first seriously and then for comedy. Other comedy bits came from Buster Keaton, Laurel and Hardy and Marie Dressler. Miss Dressler's sequence, in which, with crown askew, she flounced about as a boisterous monarch and belted out 'For I'm a Queen,' was thought to be the funniest bit in the picture. *Hollywood Revue* produced one of the most popular songs of the day, one that was to see later screen service – 'Singin' in the Rain.' It was performed by Cliff 'Ukelele Ike' Edwards, who later supplied the voice of Jiminy Cricket in *Pinocchio* (1939).

Warners did an all-star turn with *Show of Shows* (1929), assigning to it such diverse talents as Beatrice Lillie, Douglas Fairbanks, Jr, Loretta Young, Winnie Lightner, Chester Morris and Harriette Lake, a sparkling bit player who, in four years, would attain star billing as Ann Sothern. Paramount then contributed *Paramount on Parade* (1930). It provided such fare as dramatic actress Ruth Chatterton singing to Fredric March and Stuart Erwin; Maurice Chevalier dancing with Evelyn Brent and happily singing 'Sweeping the Clouds Away' before a bank of 50-plus chorines; Clara Bow joining Jack Oakie and an array of sailor-suited chorus boys in a Navy song-and-dance routine and a collection of the studio's young players – Jean Arthur, Gary Cooper, Fay Wray (due three years later to suffer the attentions of King Kong), Mary Brian, Phillips Holmes and Virginia Bruce – dutifully making their way through an antebellum sequence.

Finally, on yet another front, the studios turned their cameras on a string of stage operettas and musical comedies. The Technicolor filming in 1929 of the Sigmund Romberg-Oscar Hammerstein II operetta, *The Desert Song*, starred John Boles as the Red Shadow and Myrna Loy as the sultry Azuri. That same year, the Jerome Kern-Oscar Hammerstein hit, *Show Boat*, came chugging into view; the picture starred Laura LaPlante and was the subject of two remakes – in 1936 with Irene Dunne, Allan Jones and, reprising their Broadway roles, Helen Morgan and Paul Robeson, and in 1951 with Kathryn Grayson and Howard Keel. The Ziegfeld production, *Rio Rita*, was transferred to the screen in 1930. And it was the year that saw Jeanette MacDonald and Dennis King do Rudolf Friml's long popular operetta, *The Vagabond King,* the story of France's poet-rebel, Francois Villon.

But there was too much. By the early

Above: Ava Gardner in the 1951 remake of *Show Boat*. She played the tragic Julie, a singer on the show boat who discovers that she is a mulatto. This ruins her life. Her singing of 'My Bill' and 'Can't Help Loving that Man' were dubbed.

Below: The arrival of the show boat from the 1951 production. Marge and Gower Champion, the resident hoofers, are dancing on the pier. To the right of the gangplank is Joe E Brown, who plays Cap'n Andy. Ava Gardner is on the other side of the gangplank.

1930s, the infant genre had over-played its hand. The public was fed to the teeth with one partly or fully Technicolor song-and-dance epic after another. With the Depression hitting its depth, moviegoers, carefully doling out their money a coin at a time, decided to spend no more of what little they had for entertainment on a tiresome, over-exposed product. Grosses plunged. Matters became so desperate by 1932 that some theater owners began making it a point to advertise that their current attractions were not musicals.

The over-exposure itself was bad enough, but there was something more behind the fall from grace. In its first years, the musical had pulled in audiences because sound was such a novelty. Now the novelty had worn off. The days of indiscriminate ticket buying were over. Sound was an established fact of life and, as such, had to be accompanied up there on the screen by those basic ingredients always needed to draw an audience – namely well acted, well told and well produced stories. The musical, tumbling forth in one product after another, simply hadn't filled the bill here, too often sacrificing plot and character for the singing and dancing, too often sacrificing quality in the rush to get to the market and too often – no fault of its own, really, in the primitive days of a new technology – coming up with sound that was unacceptable except as a novelty.

This is not to say, however, that the years between 1927 and 1932 did not produce good, even exceptional, musicals. *The Jazz Singer* itself was solidly entertaining and, when seen today, occasionally has the power to hold an audience's interest as something other than an historic piece. Fine fare, too, was Rouben Mamoulian's uncompromising exploration of burlesque, *Applause*. Director King Vidor did the gripping *Hallelujah!* in 1929 with an all-black cast; a story involving sex, murder, and redemption, the picture was critically acclaimed but criticized for its overly dramatic dialogue. Using anything but grim material, Ernst Lubitsch directed the frivolous and good-fun-all-around *The Love Parade*, starring Jeanette MacDonald and Maurice Chevalier, following it with *Monte Carlo* (1930), which teamed MacDonald with Britain's Jack Buchanan; *The Smiling Lieutenant* (1931), with Maurice Chevalier dividing his time between the charms of Claudette Colbert and Miriam Hopkins and *One Hour with You* (1932), another uniting of Chevalier and MacDonald.

The German-born Lubitsch, a successful stage actor and screen director in Europe before moving to the US to direct Mary Pickford's *Rosita* (1923),

was undoubtedly the most impressive of the early musical directors. The fact is, he was impressive in any assignment he took on, no matter whether it was a musical, a drama or a comedy. It was, however, in comedy – and its musical counterpart – that he earned his greatest fame, displaying both a talent for satire and a deft ability for handling sophisticated themes. Together, they made his comic offerings, from *Lady Windemere's Fan* (1925) to Greta Garbo's *Ninotchka* (1939) and Jennifer Jones' *Cluny Brown* (1945) box office delights. Like most other directors of the 1920s, Lubitsch was not experienced with musicals when he first took them on, but, on brushing them with his very distinct skill – so distinct a skill that it was eventually publicized as 'The Lubitsch Touch' – they emerged as the very best that the early genre had to offer.

Lubitsch musicals, from the first to the last, were delightful, risque puffs of froth. Their main themes were sex and money, with the former being a charming game played by those who had ample of the latter. Involved always were fairy-tale characters – debonair, lavishly uniformed guardsmen with roving eyes who became the love targets of queens and princesses from imaginary little European countries with fanciful names the likes of Flausenthurm. The plots usually concerned marriages that started disastrously but ended happily in (where else?) bed.

That such characters and locales were selected for the plots was no accident. Lubitsch understood that Americans liked sex and money. But he understood just as well that, should his pictures be given a US or some other realistic setting, the bluenose side of the American character might well surface with annoyance and demand a retribution at film's end that simply wouldn't work in a happy musical. He was dead right. Coming out of Hollywood at the time were a stream of sexually accented pictures, plus not a few scandals. They eventually led to a moviegoing revolt and the establishment of the ridiculously strict Hays' Motion Picture Production Code in 1930.

A brief look at the plot of *The Smiling Lieutenant* is all that is needed to see how Lubitsch mingled the above elements. Princess Anna of tiny Flausenthurm, in the person of Miriam Hopkins, visits Austria and falls in love with and wants to marry a dashing young lieutenant in the Imperial Guard. The lieutenant (Chevalier) is a skirt-chasing fellow whose latest love is the very cooperative Franzi (Claudette Colbert), the leader of an all-girl orchestra. Despite his liking for the ladies, the lieutenant simply isn't interested in the

princess and consents to the wedding – only to avoid all sorts of nasty international complications. With such a lack of enthusiasm on his part, the marriage, as anyone can imagine, is in trouble – that is, until Franzi, pretty well over her affair with Chevalier and finding that she likes the princess, teaches the frustrated young woman a few tricks in the womanly art of captivating a man. And what do you know? But of course. They work and everyone lives happily – and, presumably, in sexual contentment – ever after.

Any of the Lubitsch pictures would have worked well without music, but the songs were fitted in neatly and were usually made an integral part of the plot. For instance, playing the eager spinster Queen Louise of Sylvania in *The Love Parade*, Jeanette MacDonald strongly establishes the character as, wearing a quite revealing negligee, she sings 'Dream Lover' on awakening one morning. Then, in *The Smiling Lieutenant*, Colbert and Hopkins gleefully plot Princess Irene's man-baiting campaign with the delightful and risque piano duet, 'Jazz up Your Lingerie.' Lubitsch's most adroit use of music, however, is seen in *Monte Carlo*. Here, MacDonald, as a princess fleeing an unhappy marrige, leans out the window of a train and, singing 'Beyond the Blue Horizon,' anticipates the new and, she hopes, adventurous life that lies ahead. The train's wheels and whistle form the opening of the song, which then is picked up by peasants working in the passing fields and echoed back to MacDonald.

Deservedly, the Lubitsch pictures were successful at the box office. But, aside from their welcome there, the musical was in deep trouble in 1932. With grosses falling, the studios cut back on planned productions. Some went so far as to delete the song-and-dance numbers from musicals already underway so that the pictures could be released as straight features.

Only one Hollywood executive – Darryl Zanuck, head of production at Warners – took a different tack. His instincts told him that the genre was anything but dead, that nothing more was at stake than the end of the musical's first cycle, and that what was needed to restore the infant to favor was a solidly good vehicle. He decided to gamble on an extravagant piece. Casting his planned effort with veterans Warner Baxter, Bebe Daniels, Ginger Rogers (yet to reach the zenith of her career with Fred Astaire but with more than a dozen pictures already behind her) and George Brent, plus two newcomers – Broadway singer-dancer Ruby Keeler and an ex-band vocalist with two screen appearances to his credit, Dick Powell –

Zanuck went into production in the latter half of 1932. When released in March, 1933, his venture more than proved his instincts correct. *42nd Street,* an overwhelming success, gave the genre new life and made it a film staple of the 1930s and 40s.

42nd Street tells the story of the backstage problems, heartbreak and exhausting work involved in mounting a Broadway musical comedy. The central character is Julian Marsh (Baxter), a middle-aged producer who, ill and disillusioned with life, sets out to do what he knows will be his final stage extravaganza. Wanting it to be his masterpiece, Marsh drives his cast with fanatical zeal, only to have his always-troubled star (Daniels) break her leg on the night before the opening. He turns to a talented but inexperienced girl in the chorus line (Keeler), rehearses the fledgling desperately for a day and then, with the words (so dramatic then but so trite now after years of echoing variation in similar films) 'You're going out a youngster, but you've got to come back a star,' sends her onstage. She, of course, does exactly that.

The film's plot was liberally borrowed from an earlier Warners musical, *On with the Show* (1929), a yarn about a hatcheck girl who replaces the hard-to-handle lead in a Broadway offering at the 11th hour and wins instant stardom. For most of its 98 minutes, *42nd Street* doesn't look at all like a musical but rather a backstage melodrama. There are several Harry Warren-Al Rubin songs – including Bebe Daniels' 'You're Getting to Be a Habit with Me' – but for the most part, the singing and dancing are restricted to rehearsal sequences and so seem a logical extension of the story line.

The lid comes off, however, when the curtain opens on Marsh's show. The job of staging the musical numbers in *42nd Street* went to Broadway dance director Busby Berkeley and, at this point, he took over the Warren-Rubin score and provided audiences with the most imaginatively conceived production routines seen to that date and among the most imaginative seen since. First, we're treated to the 'Shuffle off to Buffalo' number, featuring a newlywed couple (Keeler and Clarence Nordstrom) eager to spend their first night together aboard a Niagara Falls-bound train, only to have their Pullman car keep them apart by dividing itself into many berths, all filled with chorus girls who have a thoroughly good time making cynical fun of the two. From there, we move to the 'Young and Healthy' sequence, which begins with Dick Powell singing and evolves into a team

Warner Baxter giving Ruby Keeler a hard time at her rehearsal in *Forty-Second Street* (1933). George E Stone is between them. To Keeler's right is Una Merkel; to Baxter's left is Ginger Rogers.

of chorus girls and boys dancing on a revolving stage and forming what were to become Berkeley trademarks in future films – sensually kaleidoscopic patterns photographed from overhead.

Now comes the finale, the number from which the picture takes its title. Intended to portray New York's high-living and decadent night life, the sequence begins with an evening-gowned Keeler singing '42nd Street', after which she drops her long skirt for a tap dance atop a taxicab. To the song's pulsating rhythm, we immediately move up the crowded street, encounter various Broadway types along the way, witness an attack on a girl, and then a stabbing, remaining with these occurrences only an instant as we fall in with columns of chorus girls tap-dancing along the street. At last, male dancers join the girls and together, with painted boards, form a rising and almost surreal skyline of New York. The number closes with Keeler and Powell looming above the skyline and waving to the audience.

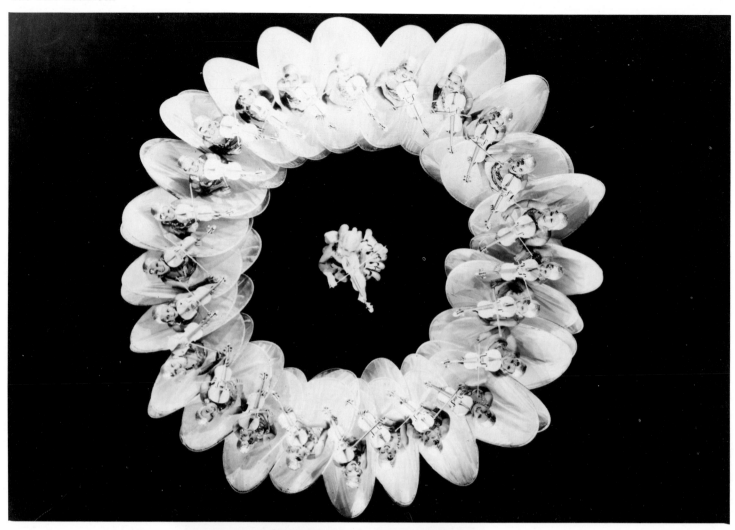

Above: A Busby Berkeley trademark – chorus girls with unusual props photographed from above, from *Gold Diggers of 1933* (1933).

Right: The two stars of *Gold Diggers of 1933* – Ruby Keeler and Dick Powell. This was her second film and his fifth.

Opposite: More Busby Berkeley routines were in *Footlight Parade* (1933). This is the 'By a Waterfall' scene.

The superbly choreographed sequences dazzled audiences and established Busby Berkeley as the premiere dance director of the period. But it would be unfair to say that *42nd Street*'s appeal lay in his efforts alone. Even without its extravagant ending, the picture would have had an attraction for 1930s audiences. It tells a harsh story of struggle and hard work. It tells it with bitter wisecracks and with Baxter's excellent aura of exhaustion and disillusionment – The *New York Times* looked on his Julian Marsh as one of the outstanding characterizations in his career. It plays the story against a tawdry backdrop of chorines' apartments and sweaty rehearsal halls. And, in the midst of the exultation at its close, it sounds a grim note – a hard-faced Baxter looking at the stage and knowing that his life's work is done. In all, the picture deals with tough realities that Depression-era audiences understood and that aroused a definite emotional response in them. When those realities were blended with Berkeley's escapist production numbers, *42nd Street* became a perfectly but eerily balanced Depression product.

Long acknowledged a top Broadway choreographer, Berkeley had first come to Hollywood in 1930 to stage the dance numbers in Samuel Goldwyn's film ver-

sion of Eddie Cantor's stage success, *Whoopee*. With musical production declining, he was on the point of returning to New York when Zanuck called him to Warners. Now, with *42nd Street* breaking attendance records everywhere, he was off and running. Until he left Warners for MGM in 1938, he turned out the production sequences for one Warners musical after another – for Powell and Keeler, *Gold Diggers of 1933* (1933), *Footlight Parade* (1933), *Dames* (1934) and *Flirtation Walk* (1934); for Powell alone, *Twenty Million Sweethearts* (1934), *Gold Diggers of 1935* (1935), *Gold Diggers of 1937* (1936), *The Singing Marine* (1937) and *Variety Show* (1937); and for Al Jolson, *Wonder Bar* (1933), followed by *Go Into Your Dance* (1935), which teamed Jolson with his wife, Keeler.

As inventive as he was in *42nd Street*, Berkeley proved even more so in his later productions. In what many critics regard as the finest example of his work – the 'Lullaby of Broadway' sequence in *Gold Diggers of 1935* – he traced a day and a night in the life of a chorus girl, starting quietly with her face a mere speck on the screen and then, on expanding to full screen, whirling her through a series of experiences that, with their background music ranging from the romantic to the sinister, cul-

Above: *Footlight Parade* (1933) was another in the Powell-Keeler-Broadway mold, but it was important in that it gave James Cagney his first singing and dancing role in the movies. Here he dances on a table top with Keeler.

Below: More of the Berkeley magic in *Dames* (1934). We meet Dick Powell and Ruby Keeler again. The plot is similar to their other outings. But it doesn't matter. The film is an ode to Berkeley's talents.

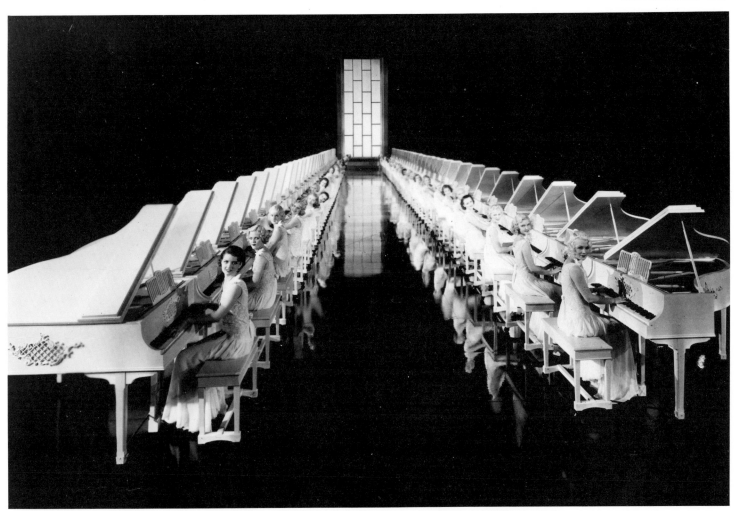

Above: *Gold Diggers of 1935*
(1935) gave Berkeley a chance to
direct an entire movie, not just
the musical parts. Still, he did
not stint when it came to the
songs. He loved to move hordes of
pretty girls around,
individualizing them with a lot of
close-ups, then bringing them
together to form the parts into
one gigantic whole. In this scene,
the girls play separate pianos,
merging finally into one huge
piano.

Left: Ruby Keeler and her
husband, Al Jolson, finally get a
chance to star together in *Go Into
Your Dance* (1935). The
highlight was their singing and
dancing 'About a Quarter to
Nine.'

minate in her accidental death plunge from a balcony as Manhattan's mad and tawdry night life closes chokingly around her; an outgrowth of the '42nd Street' number, it had a far greater sweep and emotional impact than its predecessor. In *Wonder Bar*'s 'Don't Say Goodnight' number, he reflected his dancers into infinity with an octagon of giant mirrors. Free-flowing geometric designs, formed by neon-lighted violins, filled the screen during 'The Shadow Waltz' in *Gold Diggers of 1933*. Berkeley built a 'human fountain' of bathing-suited dancers and reflected them in a pool for 'By a Waterfall' in *Footlight Parade*. Ruby Keeler's image was multiplied endlessly when chorus girls donned masks of her face for 'I Only Have Eyes for You' in *Dames*. And Berkeley, making his stagehands invisible by dressing them in black, had them wheel more than two dozen white pianos and their chorine players through a variety of patterns for 'The Words are in My Heart' in *Gold Diggers of 1935*.

Quite aside from Berkeley's unique stagings, the Warners musicals were an easily identifiable breed. In the *42nd Street* tradition, they usually centered themselves about the birth of a show and all the attendant labor pains. They were fast paced, laced with wisecracking dialogue, and often had a smack of good-humored self mockery to them, in

Above: William Powell, as Florenz Ziegfeld, and Myrna Loy as his wife, Billie Burke, in *The Great Ziegfeld* (1936). The picture won the Academy Award as best film that year. It was a mammoth musical drama for its time, running three hours and recounting the life story of Broadway's great showman.

Below: Dorothy (Judy Garland) and her friends about to enter the haunted forest on their search for *The Wizard of Oz* (1939). To Dorothy's left: The Tin Woodman (Jack Haley), The Cowardly Lion (Bert Lahr), The Scarecrow (Ray Bolger). The film was the most expensive in MGM's first 15 years.

all, brazen pieces into which the master's fanciful and – frankly – sometimes outlandish production numbers fitted perfectly. In a nutshell, the studio found a highly workable and profitable pattern in *42nd Street* and concentrated on it for the rest of the decade.

Warners was not alone in turning out a specific brand of musical product. The same course was being followed at the other Hollywood studios.

MGM spent the 1930s dividing its time between its Nelson Eddy-Jeanette MacDonald operattas and spectaculars featuring production numbers that were obviously Berkeley imitations but that, at times, outdid him in sheer grandeur and that often came across as having less vitality but more sophistication. Along the way, the studio produced two of the decade's most startling efforts – the lavishly mounted musical biography, *The Great Ziegfeld* (1936) and that rapturous flight of fancy, *The Wizard of Oz* (1939).

After first venturing into the musical field with 1929's *Broadway Melody*, MGM backed off when the genre ran into its problems of the early 1930s. But, on seeing *42nd Street*'s cash triumphs, the studio quickly came up with a carbon copy – *Dancing Lady,* an emptiness about a chorus girl (Joan Crawford) being lifted to stardom by a tough dance director (Clark Gable). The picture tried hard at Berkeley-type sequences, but missed the mark. Crawford was panned for her limited song-and-dance talents. The film is chiefly remembered because it marked Fred Astaire's first screen appearance. Playing himself (he was a recognized Broadway performer at the time), he served as Crawford's dancing partner.

The studio did better when it put Paramount's Jeanette MacDonald under contract in 1934 and starred her in the well-received *The Cat and the Fiddle.* That same year, reuniting her with Maurice Chevalier and director Ernst Lubitsch, MGM produced Franz Lehar's *The Merry Widow,* an altogether sparkling film that nevertheless didn't fare as well at the box office as anticipated. Despite that setback, MacDonald was immediately cast in another operetta – the Victor Herbert-Rida Johnson Young perennial, *Naughty Marietta,* the story of a young European princess who travels to pre-Revolutionary America and falls in love with the captain of a troop of mercenary soldiers. For MacDonald, it promised such energetic numbers as 'Italian Street Song'; for her co-star, the rousing 'Tramp, Tramp, Tramp' and for the two of them together, the tender 'I'm Falling in Love With Someone.' To fill the co-star role, MGM selected a young baritone from opera and radio, Nelson Eddy.

Considering *The Merry Widow*'s lukewarm reception and Eddy's lack of screen experience (he'd made brief appearances in three MGM features, among them *Dancing Lady*), the venture was a risky one. But *Naughty Marietta* paid handsome dividends when released in 1935. Somehow, the two disparate singers – MacDonald vivacious and Eddy almost hopelessly wooden (a problem that was to dog him throughout his career) – charmed audiences as a team, perhaps because of their youthful attractiveness, perhaps because their voices, both so genuinely good, blended to close perfection. They were immediately pinned with the sickly-sweet tag, 'the singing sweethearts' and spent much of the next seven years working together.

In rapid succession, they made the operattas *Rose Marie* (1936), *Maytime*

Top: Jeanette MacDonald starred with Maurice Chevalier in *The Merry Widow* (1934). The film featured the grand old Franz Lehar melodies outfitted with new lyrics by Lorenz Hart. MacDonald's career had taken a plunge when musicals went down in the early 1930s. *The Merry Widow* made her a star again.

Above: Left to right: Elsa Lanchester, Frank Morgan and Nelson Eddy in *Naughty Marietta* (1935). This film marked the beginning of the MacDonald-Eddy partnership. The combination of MacDonald's professionalism and Eddy's stiff stoicism made them the darlings of that era's musical films.

(1937), *The Girl of the Golden West* (1938), *New Moon* and *Bitter Sweet* (both 1940), adding to them two filmed versions of popular Broadway musical comedies, *Sweethearts* (1940) and *I Married an Angel* (1942). Individually, MacDonald did the non-musical, *San Francisco* (1936) with Clark Gable, and the Rudolf Friml-Otto Harbach operetta, *The Firefly* (1937) with Allan Jones, while Eddy joined Eleanor Powell in *Rosalie* (1937).

By 1940, the public began to tire of 'the singing sweethearts.' Some of their operettas were going out of date and the stars themselves, looking now a mite too old for their innocent lovemaking and suffering from the fact that their acting abilities never matched their singing skills, were beginning to strike moviegoers as funny. It was the birth of an attitude that, today, has come to re-

Right: Jeanette and Nelson in *Rose Marie* (1936). In this film a young actor, in only his second picture, was tapped as a future star – he played MacDonald's brother and his name was James Stewart. But another young actor, in his fifth picture, was hardly noticed – David Niven.

Below: The singing duo continued with *Maytime* (1937). This schmaltzy film was the biggest money-maker worldwide in 1937. The story was about the romance between a prima donna and a baritone. In the supporting cast was John Barrymore playing a Svengali to MacDonald's operatic Trilby.

gard the MacDonald-Eddy vehicles as high camp. They never worked together again after *I Married an Angel,* though each alone made several films before retiring at the end of the 1940s.

As MacDonald and Eddy were singing love duets, another musical star emerged on the MGM lot – the young, shapely, and exuberant tap dancer, Eleanor Powell. A Broadway performer since age 17, she came to Hollywood to do *George White's 1935 Scandals* at Fox, moving then to MGM for *Broadway Melody of 1936* (1935), which was a sequel in name only to the 1929 *Broadway Melody.* She immediately impressed audiences with her splendid tap routine to the Nacio Herb Brown-Arthur Freed tune, 'Sing Before Breakfast.' Performed at times without music, the number was done on a rooftop with the brother-and-sister dance team of Buddy

and Vilma Ebsen. The loose-limbed Buddy Ebsen, of course, went on to television stardom as a character actor in his later years.

Once established as a star, Powell moved tirelessly from one MGM musical to another, working in 11 over a ten-year period. Her pictures featured lavish production numbers often set against art deco backgrounds – the battleship, for instance, in the 'Swingin' the Jinx Away' sequence in *Born to Dance* (1937), the vast stairway with its curlicue side ornaments used for the major production number in *Rosalie* and the luminous New York skyline against which a top-hatted Powell and chorus performed the finale in *Broadway Melody of 1938* (1939). Her best pictures are considered to be *Born to Dance* and *Rosalie.* Always a pleasure to watch – leggy, vivacious, and superbly talented – Powell slipped from popularity in the mid-40s through no fault of her own. Tap work simply went out of style as audiences switched their affections to the impressionistic dance and ballet being pioneered in such Broadway productions as *Oklahoma!*

Unarguably, MGM's ranking musicals of the decade were *The Great Ziegfeld* and *The Wizard of Oz,* with the latter assuredly among the best produced in any decade. *The Great Ziegfeld* starred William Powell as the flamboyant showman and, in a chiefly fictionalized account, traced his life from carnival sideshows to his Broadway extravaganzas. Hungarian-born Luise Rainer played his first wife, the singer Anna Held, and won an Academy Award for her performance. The role of actress Billie Burke, Ziegfeld's second wife, went to Powell's screen partner in the highly successful *Thin Man* series, Myrna Loy.

The picture itself proved episodic and its story line predictable, but MGM poured all its resources into the musical numbers and they were all breathtaking, at times even awesome. Especially imaginative was the sequence atop the New Amsterdam Theater, a sequence featuring chorus girls dancing atop beds moving in rhythm with them. As for sheer awesomeness, the 'A Pretty Girl is Like a Melody' number has likely never been equaled. Featuring the tuneful principal song, a dash of operatic singing, a spicing of ballet, a pinch of George Gershwin's 'Rhapsody in Blue,' a liberal sprinkling of salt-white and pepper-black costumes, and an icing of honest-to-goodness showgirl spectacle, it was performed on a massive set. The centerpiece was a giant pillar circled by a gracefully winding staircase, its edge girded with pianos for three-quarters of its rising distance. Once seen, the whole number was never easily forgotten. It

earned a dance direction Academy
Award for its creator, Seymour Felix.

As lavish as *Ziegfeld* was, however, it
came nowhere near to matching the
cinema magic wrought by the filming of
L Frank Baum's children's classic, *The
Wizard of Oz*. Starring Judy Garland,
Ray Bolger, Bert Lahr, Jack Haley, the
inimitable Margaret Hamilton and the
equally imimitable Frank Morgan,
here was a combination of sheer beauty,
free-flying imagination, and good fun
that couldn't help but charm audiences.
It did so in 1939 and, in all its encore
showings, has done so to succeeding
generations of filmgoers.

Everything about the film has charm:
the songs by Harold Arlen and E Y Harburg; the special effects – that marvelous yellow brick road, the Wizard's
assorted magical contraptions and the
Witch's skywriting; the musical sequences – Garland singing 'Over the Rainbow,' Bolger dancing at his eccentric
best as the Scarecrow while trying to
keep his straw inside where it belongs,
everyone madly dancing in Munchkin-
land and Lahr's Cowardly Lion plain-
tively growling 'If I Were King of the
Forest' and the characterizations – Jack
Haley's lonely and likable Tin Woodman, Margaret Hamilton's evil,
screeching Wicked Witch and Frank
Morgan's all-stops-out portrayals of various Emerald City residents, among
them the Wizard himself.

It was all the stuff of magic and it
worked commercial and critical magic
for MGM. *The Wizard,* however, had the
misfortune of coming out along with
Gone With the Wind and so did not claim
the Academy Award for the best picture
of 1939, an honor that most likely would
have come to it in any other year. *The
Wizard*'s director, Victor Fleming, received the best direction award, but for
his work on GWTW. The 17-year-old
Judy Garland, however, received a special Oscar for the year's outstanding
performance by a juvenile. An award
went to Herbert Stothart for the picture's musical score, and to Arlen and
Harburg for 'Over the Rainbow.' In all,
The Wizard was an artistic masterpiece
that closed the decade for MGM on a
triumphant note.

The top musical star of the 1930s at
Fox – in fact, *the* top star at the studio –
was a child, Shirley Temple. Starting
professional work at age three in a
series of 'Baby Burlesk' one-reelers in
which she imitated such stars as Marlene Dietrich, the youngster moved to
brief appearances in several features
and then danced onstage during the
'Baby, Take a Bow' production number
to score heavily in *One in a Million*
(1934). Within a year, she was a motion
picture phenomenon and a household
word. From 1935 through 1938, she top-

Above: The great Shirley Temple in *Poor Little
Rich Girl* (1936). Up to that time, Shirley had
usually played the part of an orphan. But in this
film, she has a father and mother. What does she
do but run away from home and is picked up by a
vaudeville team – Alice Fay and Jack Haley. This
is her 'Military Man' number.

Left: Shirley demonstrates her acting talent in
Poor Little Rich Girl. Nobody outdid Shirley. Born
in 1928, she made her first movie in 1934. By 1937
she was making more money than any singer-
actress in Hollywood.

Above: Alice Faye marries Rudy Vallee in *George White's Scandals* (1934). Behind Vallee is Jimmy Durante. Alice Faye had once been a singer with Vallee's band and this was her first film. Its idiotic backstage plot seemed to propel an entertaining, expensive musical. The hit song was 'Oh, You Nasty Man.'

Below: Alice Faye sings to the accompaniment of Tyrone Power and his orchestra in *Alexander's Ragtime Band* (1938). Jack Haley plays the drums while Don Ameche pounds the piano. This was a large-scale musical with many fine Irving Berlin songs – 'Now It Can Be Told,' 'My Walking Stick' and 'I'm Marching Along with Time' among them.

ped the list of Hollywood's ten top money-making stars. A blend of dimpled cuteness and pouting precocity that at times approached brattishness, Temple was a substantially talented performer and such a bright spot in the grim Depression years that she eventually graduated from phenomenon status to that of a national institution. No other child star, neither before nor since, has ever matched her popularity.

Once the youngster had enchanted everyone in *Stand up and Cheer,* Fox kept her continually busy. She made four more films in 1934 and appeared in 15 in the years 1935-1939, after which, outgrowing her cute-little-girl roles, she began to lose her appeal. Temple features did not usually involve lavish production numbers, but all gave her a chance to display her talents, which were as varied as they were substantial. As a dancer, she worked charmingly with Buddy Ebsen against a fishing village backdrop in *Captain January* (1936), attached a doll to her toes for a clever Astaire-Rogers impersonation in *Stowaway* (1936) and made movie legend by tapping up and down a stairway with Bill 'Bojangles' Robinson in *The Little Colonel* (1935). As a singer, she popularized 'On the Good Ship Lollipop' in *Bright Eyes* (1934) and gave entertaining impressions of Al Jolson and Eddie Cantor in *Stowaway*. As a musi-

cal actress, in one tour de force – the 'When I Grow Up' sequence in *Curly Top* (1935) – she went from child to teenager to old woman.

Though the dimpled moppet was Fox's premier draw of the 30s, the studio had a strong adult musical presence in Alice Faye. Faye started her professional singing life at age 14 and, a few years later, joined Rudy Vallee's dance band as a vocalist. She came to Fox with Vallee for a minor part in his *George White's Scandals* (1934) and, in a real-life version of the *42nd Street* format, took over the leading role when the star, Lilian Harvey, walked off the set. On the picture's release, Faye's blond looks, contralto voice and somewhat-tough-but-still-vulnerable image appealed to the public. She became a fixture in Fox musicals for the next ten years.

Often cast at first in Shirley Temple vehicles, Faye was given an assignment in a 1938 production that was to set a pattern the studio's most popular musicals would follow well into the 1940s. The film, *Alexander's Ragtime Band,* covered a span of more than two decades in the lives of three performers – a band leader (Tyrone Power), his pianist (Don Ameche) and a rough-cut-but-eventually-ladylike singer (Faye) – and was built around a variety of highly successful tunes that America's most cherished popular composer, Irving Berlin, had fashioned over the years. Taking the threesome, as well as pals Jack Haley and Ethel Merman, from their first engagements to stardom, the picture gave Americans a passing glimpse of their country's changing musical tastes and tickled their nostalgic sensitivities with its melodies. In so doing, *Alexander's Ragtime Band* played to a splendid box office and inspired the studio to follow with similar vehicles for Faye.

Accordingly, she was sent back to yesteryear for *Rose of Washington Square* (1939), a picture based loosely on the tempestuous Fanny Brice-Nick Arnstein marriage and whose most memorable sequence centered on Faye's fine torch rendition of 'My Man.' Next, there was *Hollywood Cavalcade* (1940), an *Alexander's Ragtime Band* with an early motion picture setting. The singer then revealed her talents as a dramatic actress in *Lillian Russell* (1940), a somewhat saccharine and more-than-somewhat fictionalized account of the famous singer's life; they were talents that were to be very effectively displayed in the non-musical melodrama, *Fallen Angel* (1943). And finally, there was such backward-glancing fare as *Tin Pan Alley* (1940) and *Hello, Frisco, Hello* (1943), the one a music business tale, the other a vaudeville yarn, with the former co-starring Faye's new competi-

That Night in Rio (1941). Left to right: Carmen Miranda, Don Ameche, Alice Faye, Leonid Kinskey. It was the usual musical of mistaken identities and was practically stolen by Miranda, 'The Brazilian Bombshell.'

tion at Fox, Betty Grable.

Starting in 1937, Fox presented the era's most unusual musical star – the Norwegian-born ice skater, Sonja Henie. A skater who set world marks in the 1928, 1932 and 1936 Winter Olympics, Henie was put under contract by Darryl Zanuck after some months spent touring with an ice show. It proved to be a wise move on his part. Henie owned a pert and engaging personality which appealed immediately to audiences, as did the novelty and the excitement of seeing production numbers splendidly performed on ice. The skater began with *One in a Million* (1937) and, in all, made 11 films for Fox, among them *Everything Happens at Night* (1939) and *Sun Valley Serenade* (1941). Her popularity dimmed in the mid-40s and brought about her retirement. She then produced and starred in the highly successful Hollywood Ice Revue extravaganzas staged at New York's Madison Square Garden.

The RKO musicals of the 1930s can be summed up in three words – Astaire and Rogers. The two performers, each so different in looks and personality, blended perfectly as a team and fashioned a series of musicals that were, at times, the essence of elegance and that established dance as a cinematic art that need not be limited to tap shoes and chorus lines.

Their initial teaming in 1933 was, in the main, an accident. Rogers, a former Broadway dancer with some 20 pictures to her credit – films in which she played tough and wisecracking, yet vulnerable young women – was handed a supporting role in a planned RKO musical because, in yet another real-life variation of the *42nd Street* format, the player originally assigned the job, Dorothy Jordan, withdrew on marrying the stu-

dio head. As for Astaire, he had long danced on Broadway with his sister Adele, but their partnership had ended with her retirement when she married an English nobleman. His stage career at loose ends, Astaire moved to Hollywood looking for a career in films, a chancy undertaking because he did not have the handsomeness that the era demanded of its leading men. Signed by RKO, he was lent to Metro for *Dancing Lady* and then brought back for a minor role opposite Rogers in the planned musical.

At the time, RKO was a smallish company struggling to make ends meet in the bottom-of-the-barrel days of the Depression. Its new venture, titled *Flying Down to Rio,* was intended to cash in on Warners' success by outdoing the just released *42nd Street.* The picture was to be set in exotic South America, was to concern a flying bandleader (Gene Raymond) and his romance with a Brazilian beauty (Dolores Del Rio), and was to end with a fantastic production number performed on the wings of airplanes high above Rio de Janeiro. On release, the film turned out to be a rather slow-moving piece, with too much time spent on its love story, but nevertheless a box office success for two reasons. First, that climactic airborne production number (a blend of actual flying sequences and studio shots of the wing-dancing chorines) proved to be as fantastic and as fascinating as the company had hoped. Second, in another

Above: Fred Astaire and Ginger Rogers got their start as a team in *Flying Down to Rio* (1933) and stole the show. The stars of the film were Dolores Del Rio and Gene Raymond, shown here being observed by Astaire.

lively number – 'The Carioca' – Astaire and Rogers danced across the screen for the first time.

Actually, they were anything but the centerpieces of the sequence. Performed in a lavish night club setting, it opened with the orchestra playing a new, highly rhythmic ballroom dance, 'The Carioca,' and then turned to a chorus demonstrating how partners must do the dance with their foreheads touching. Suddenly, Astaire and Rogers ran onstage and presented their own version of the dance. In all, they were seen for just a few moments before the chorus again took over. But those few moments struck audiences – and RKO – as something special. Here were two diverse people – the one tall and (except when dancing) gangly, the other pert and brash – who, when combined, suddenly produced a magic of their own, a magic compounded of grace, intimacy, a seemingly effortless dancing ability and high good humor.

Glowing over their success, RKO gave the couple their first starring vehicle, *The Gay Divorcee* (1934), an adaptation of an earlier Astaire Broadway show, *The Gay Divorce*. The picture had an empty-headed 'mistaken identity' plot, but firmly established Astaire and Rogers as a dance team in the public eye. It, too, cast them in roles far different than the earthy, slangy types they

Below: In *The Gay Divorcee* (1934), the Astaire-Rogers dance team finally were top-billed. In this film they introduced 'The Continental.' The choreographer for the film was the extraordinarily fine dance master, Hermes Pan.

Above: In addition to the Astaire-Rogers dancing, there were fine production numbers in *The Gay Divorcee* (1934).

Left: In 1935 the dazzling duo made *Roberta,* but it was Irene Dunne who had the lead in this Otto Harbach-Jerome Kern stage show. For some reason, Astaire and Rogers were often given strange names in their films. In this one, Fred was Huck Haines and Ginger was Lizzie Gatz.

had played in *Rio.* Now they became the sophisticates that they were to be in the best of their features. It was casting natural for the instinctively elegant Astaire, but that, until she became accomplished in it, Rogers seemed to bear with some ill ease.

And the picture presented them in two extraordinarily good dance numbers – 'The Continental' and 'Night and Day.' The former, reflecting 'The Carioca' in that it likewise involved a new dance step, was a lavish offering that won the first Academy Award ever given for a song. But, for the Astaire-Rogers team and for the development of the musical genre, 'Night and Day' was a far more significant accomplishment. Danced in an art deco ballroom, it established a dramatic story line – the girl reluctantly beginning to dance with an amorous young man and then eventually surrendering herself to him as the music and their partnership in it flow on – that was to be a hallmark of their best numbers. And, allowing very human emotions to show through a dance routine as it did, it was a theme that, with all the variations that reluctance changed into exultation can achieve, has been used time and again by the genre through the years since.

Considering their great audience appeal at the time and how memorable

Opposite: Fred and Ginger appeared in *Top Hat* (1935) in the same year that *Roberta* was released. It was in this film that they danced their memorable 'Cheek to Cheek' routine.

Above left: In *Top Hat,* as usual for an Astaire-Rogers vehicle, everyone seemed to have money pouring from every seam of the sumptuous wardrobe.

Above right: They made *Shall We Dance* in 1937. It included a routine on roller skates to the tune of 'Let's Call the Whole Thing Off,' by the Gershwin brothers.

Below: In *Damsel in Distress* (1937), Fred appeared without Ginger. His partner was Joan Fontaine. George Burns and Gracie Allen also were in the picture.

Top: Bing Crosby's second film was *The Big Broadcast* (1932), a light-hearted entertainment which used a zany story about a radio station to bring in many of the stars of the day. Here Crosby watches romance blossom between Stuart Erwin and Leila Hyams.

Above: One of Crosby's greatest roles was in *High Society* (1956), a musical version of *The Philadelphia Story.* Left to right: Crosby, John Lund, Grace Kelly, Frank Sinatra. Among the great songs in the Cole Porter score was 'True Love.'

films. It featured their 'Cheek to Cheek' number and Astaire's marvelous solo, 'Top Hat, White Tie, and Tails.'

By 1937, the team was in difficulty. Though popular, they were suffering declining box office receipts, as was everyone else, because of the continuing strictures of the Depression. Further, both performers were growing eager to go their separate ways, not because, as the press reported, there was animosity between them but because each was becoming increasingly interested in solo work. Astaire had no wish to be identified simply as one half of a dance team, while Rogers, whose performing abilities had burgeoned in recent years, was looking to a straight acting career. Consequently, they appeared singly in several pictures, Astaire dancing with an awkward Joan Fontaine in *Damsel in Distress* (1937), and Rogers doing a dramatic role in *Stage Door* (1937), and an effective comedic turn in *Having A Wonderful Time* (1938). On completion of the *Castle* picture, a biographical piece about the famous early-century dance team, the couple separated. Astaire – partnered with Vera-Ellen, Paulette Goddard, Cyd Charisse, Rita Hayworth, and Lucille Bremer – moved to his highly successful musicals of the next two decades and then to his fine work as a character actor. Rogers went to a career that saw her win the best acting Academy Award in 1940 for *Kitty Foyle.* The two were later reunited for one picture – MGM's *The Barkleys of Broadway* (1949).

Paramount spent the 1930s concentrating on its *Big Broadcast* musicals and the talents of an amiable singer named Bing Crosby. The *Broadcasts* were slickly-done but nevertheless unpretentious films that, meant to take advantage of the industry's great rival medium, featured a melange of radio and stage personalities in plots that did little more than give them the opportunity to display their entertainment specialities in front of the camera.

The first of the offerings – *The Big Broadcast* – was made in 1932 and featured songs by the Boswell Sisters, Kate Smith, Arthur Tracy and the Mills Brothers, comedy by George Burns and Gracie Allen, and music by Cab Calloway's band. It was followed by three sequels – the *Big Broadcasts* of 1936, 1937 and 1938. Mixed in with Paramount players in these efforts were Jack Benny, Martha Raye, Bob Burns and even opera singer Kirsten Flagstad and symphony conductor Leopold Stokowski.

The *Big Broadcasts* and their glittering assortment of stars were popular at the box office, but Paramount's greatest musical attraction of the decade was, hands down, Bing Crosby. As a member

their combined names yet remain today, it can be surprising to realize that Astaire and Rogers worked together for just six years. From *Divorcee,* they went to supporting roles in Irene Dunne's *Roberta* (1935), then to *Top Hat* (also 1935), *Follow the Fleet* and *Swing Time* (both 1936), *Shall We Dance* (1937), *Carefree* (1938) and finally *The Story of Vernon and Irene Castle* (1939).

In them all, the couple presented superb, seemingly effortless but painstakingly prepared dances – the melancholy 'Let's Face the Music and Dance' and the lovely snow-set 'A Fine Romance' in *Swing Time,* the memorable 'Change Partners' in *Shall We Dance* and the mixture of ballroom steps that sent them happily whirling across a giant US map in *The Story of Vernon and Irene Castle. Top Hat* usually takes the honors as the best of the Astaire-Rogers

of the singing Rhythm Boys, he broke into pictures with Paul Whiteman's orchestra in *King of Jazz* (1930). He then made several musical shorts for Mack Sennett, appeared in Southern California night clubs, began making records and landed a part in *The Big Broadcast*. From that point on, Crosby was a Paramount mainstay, appearing in 18 more pictures during the decade, a smattering of which – among them *Going Hollywood* (1933, MGM) and *Pennies from Heaven* (1936, Columbia) – were made on loan to other studios.

Crosby's musicals of the decade were all-appealing, pleasant affairs (with the exception of *Pennies from Heaven* with its somber plot concerning his care for the orphan daughter of an executed convict), but they were modest efforts when compared to the Warners and MGM spectacles and the elegant Astaire-Rogers vehicles. They now and again sported ambitious production numbers, but more often they limited themselves to plots that enabled him to display his easy-going, even flippant, manner and that invariably placed him in a romantic setting for a quiet but throbbing love song to the heroine. In combination, his casual presence and equally casual voice made him an international favorite for over four decades. .

All this, however, is not to say that his films were without some startlingly good specialty and production numbers. A young Martha Raye, for instance, scored heavily with her 'Mr Paganini' routine in *Rhythm on the Range* (1936) and then did her raucous burlesque stripper bit, 'It's On, It's Off' in *Double or Nothing* (1937). But it was Crosby's singing that usually brought in the customers. Throughout the decade, he turned a parade of songs into international hits – 'The Old Ox Road' (*College Humor*, 1933), 'Temptation' (*Going Hollywood,* 1934), 'It's Easy to Remember' (*Mississippi*, 1935), 'Sweet Leilani' (*Waikiki Wedding,* 1937, and a best song Academy Award winner) and 'Small Fry,' performed with Fred MacMurray and a 13-year-old Donald O'Connor in *Sing You Sinners* (1938).

In all, Crosby provided audiences with a sometimes brash and sometimes sensitive but always refreshing break from the Depression and its problems. But his best work was yet to come – to be seen in his clever *Road* pictures of the 1940s with Bob Hope and Dorothy Lamour and in his fine dramatic characterizations in *Going My Way* (1944) and *The Bells of St Mary's* (1945). *Going My Way* won Academy Awards for itself as best picture of the year, and for its star as best actor. Crosby proceeded to match his triumphs of the 1940s in the succeeding decade, making excellent contributions to *The Country Girl*

Fourteen-year-old Deanna Durbin singing with an orchestra conducted by Leopold Stokowski in *One Hundred Men and a Girl* (1937). She belonged to the operatic tradition of the musical, for she had a classically-trained voice.

(1955) and *High Society* (1956).

Hollywood's musicals of the 1930s came principally from Warners, MGM, Fox, RKO and Paramount. But the other studios were not inactive. Columbia did Crosby's *Pennies from Heaven* and Goldwyn turned out Eddie Cantor's *Whoopee* and *Roman Scandals,* following with the softly colored *Goldwyn Follies* (1938). Universal made a fine version of *Show Boat* with Irene Dunne and Allan Jones. Then, with the release of *Three Smart Girls* (1936) and *100 Men and a Girl* (1937), the studio found that it had a goldmine in young Deanna Durbin and featured her profitably well into the 1940s.

Nor was Hollywood alone in the production of musicals. Great Britain produced a string of highly entertaining light pieces, among them *That's a Good Girl* (1935), starring and directed by Jack Buchanan; *London Melody* (1937), with Anna Neagle; *The Show Goes On* (1937), a Gracie Fields vehicle; and *Sailing Along* (1938) with Jessie Matthews. The 1940s, though they brought J Arthur Rank's ambitious *London Town* (1946) and a fine appearance by Vera Lynn in *We'll Meet Again* (1944), saw little musical activity in the British studios, a situation that continued throughout the 1950s but was changed in the 60s with Cliff Richards' *Espresso*

Above: James Cagney played George M Cohan in *Yankee Doodle Dandy* (1942), and won the Academy Award that year as best actor. Behind him, left to right: Jeanne Cagney, Joan Leslie, Walter Huston, Rosemary DeCamp, the members of his screen family.

Below: One of MGM's top musical teams was Mickey Rooney and Judy Garland, shown here with Tommy Dorsey in *Girl Crazy* (1943). The plot concerned a rich young Easterner whose father exiles him to a small school out west, and the Gershwin score was first rate.

Bongo (1960), The Beatles' *A Hard Day's Night* (1964), Tommy Steele's UK/US adaptation of his stage hit, *Half a Sixpence* (1967) and the Carol Reed-directed *Oliver!* (1968). Britain opened the 1970s with *Scrooge,* starring Albert Finney in the title role, and has pretty well limited itself since to efforts featuring its various rock stars.

The 1930s and 40s together have often been called the 'golden age of the musical,' with the 1930s preparing for the era, and the 40s bringing it to fruition. Helping the age burst into full flower was World War II and the accelerated demand for escapist entertainment that it brought. Every studio turned out its share of musicals, from such ambitious fare as Warners' *Yankee Doodle Dandy* (1942) and MGM's *Girl Crazy* (1943) to such lightweight offerings as the Andrews Sisters' *Swingtime Johnny* (1944) and Republic's modest but well produced *Lake Placid Serenade* (1944), one of its several Sonja Henie imitations with Vera Hruba Ralston doing the skating. Additionally, digging back a dozen years for inspiration, the studios dreamed up a parade of all-star extravaganzas, all actually vaudeville shows on film meant to give any number of stars the chance to do a turn to the delight of entertainment-hungry servicemen and war workers – Paramount's *Star Spangled Rhythm* (1942), MGM's *Thousands Cheer* (1943) and Warners' *Thank Your Lucky Stars* (1943), featuring Bette Davis' hilarious lament concerning her romantic problems with the only men left on the homefront, 'They're Either Too Young or Too Old.'

During the war and after, each studio continued to concoct its own brand of musical. Now and again trying such up-to-date fare as *Down Argentine Way* (1940) and *That Night in Rio* (1941), Fox went on with its light-hearted looks into America's past, turning out *Tin Pan Alley* for Alice Faye and Betty Grable, and then starring Grable in such backward-glances as *Coney Island* (1943), *Sweet Rosie O'Grady* (1943), *The Dolly Sisters* (1945), *The Shocking Miss Pilgrim* and *Mother Wore Tights* (both 1947). Paramount's offerings ranged from the happily inconsequential (Betty Hutton's *The Fleet's In,* 1943) to the little more than modest (*Holiday Inn,* 1942, a clever pairing of Bing Crosby and Fred Astaire that resulted in the now classic Irving Berlin tune, 'White Christmas') to the highly ambitious (*Lady in the Dark,* 1944, with Ginger Rogers impressive in the Gertrude Lawrence stage role). Columbia found a new attraction in Rita Hayworth, successfully featured her with Fred Astaire in *You'll Never Get Rich* (1942), and then moved her to full stardom with *You Were Never Lovelier* (1942), *Cover Girl* (1944) and *Down to Earth (1947),* in the meantime giving her a very juicy dramatic role in the non-musical, *Gilda* (1946).

As had been the case in the 1930s, the most extravagant musicals of the decade came from MGM. Thanks to *The Wizard of Oz,* the studio had in Judy Garland a new but experienced star (she had a half-dozen screen credits by

Top right: In *Down Argentine Way* (1940) Betty Grable and Don Ameche recoil from J Carrol. Naish. Alice Fay had been signed for the film and couldn't make it, so this was Grable's big chance. Making her debut in pictures was Carmen Miranda.

Right center: Grable and John Payne were the romantic ones in *The Dolly Sisters* (1945). The other Dolly sister was June Haver (right). It was the story of the famous vaudeville sister act and contained many old time classic vaudeville songs.

Right: Eddie Bracken and Betty Hutton in *The Fleet's In* (1942). Some of the songs from the film were 'Tangerine,' 'I Remember You' and 'The Fleet's In.'

Above: Gene Kelly danced with Rita Hayworth in *Cover Girl* (1944). The film told the story of a chorus girl (Hayworth) who becomes a top model. The Jerome Kern score contained such fine songs as 'Long Ago and Far Away.'

Below: In this scene from *Cover Girl*, Gene Kelly, Rita Hayworth and Phil Silvers eat at a luncheonette. This was the film that put Hayworth in the motion picture star firmament. The counterman is played by Edward S Brophy.

the time of *Oz*) on its hands. She was immediately cast with the studios other major juvenile talent, 19-year-old Mickey Rooney, in the screen version of the Rodgers-Hart stage show, *Babes in Arms* (1939). The picture, directed and choreographed by Busby Berkeley and featuring the sprawling 'Babes in Arms' and 'God's Country' production numbers, was a financial triumph and was followed by three equally successful Garland-Rooney efforts – *Strike Up the Band* (1940), *Babes on Broadway* (1941) and *Girl Crazy* (1943) with its dizzying Berkeley finale, 'I Got Rhythm.'

Around these efforts, MGM built such lavish spectacles as *Broadway Melody of 1940* (1940), memorable for its 'Begin the Beguine' with Fred Astaire and Eleanor Powell; *Ziegfeld Girl* (1941), with its 'You Stepped Out of a Dream' sequence, featuring Tony Martin singing to Hedy Lamarr and Lana Turner; *Best Foot Forward* (1943), a showcase for the energetic talents of newcomers Gloria De Haven and June Allyson; *Du Barry Was a Lady* (also 1943), adapted from Cole Porter's musical and starring Lucille Ball in the title role opposite Red Skelton's delightfully ridiculous Louis XV; *Bathing Beauty* (1944), an Esther Williams' water spectacle and a string of Judy Garland pleasers – *Meet Me in St Louis* (1944), *The Harvey Girls*

Left: Rooney and Garland teamed up for the first time in *Babes in Arms* (1939). It was one of those 'Hey, kids, let's put on a show!' movies and was based on the 1937 Rodgers and Hart stage musical. But only two of the songs from the play were kept in the picture, one of them being 'Where or When.'

Center: Red Skelton dances with Lucille Ball in *Du Barry Was a Lady* (1943). The Cole Porter score for the film included 'Do I Love You, Do I?' 'Friendship' and 'Katie Went to Haiti.'

Below left: It has been said that her role in *Meet Me in St Louis* (1944) was the best in Judy Garland's career. Certainly it was filled with memorable songs – 'The Trolley Song,' 'The Boy Next Door,' 'Have Yourself a Merry Little Christmas.' Here Judy and young Margaret O'Brien entertain their brother and sisters: Left, standing, Lucille Bremer; sitting, Joan Carroll; right, Henry Daniels Jr.

Below: Another Garland triumph was *The Harvey Girls* (1945). Here she is shown with Angela Lansbury in the film about the restaurant chain that opened the West. Among the songs in the Johnny Mercer-Harry Warren score was the Oscar-winning 'On the Atchison, Topeka and the Santa Fe.'

Right: Gene Kelly and Judy Garland teamed in *For Me and My Gal* (1942), a nostalgic romp down the memory lane of pre-world War I vaudeville life.

Center: *On the Town* (1949) was a huge success because of the music by Leonard Bernstein and the choreography by Jerome Robbins. The film told of a group of three sailors in New York on a 24-hour leave. Left to right: Betty Garrett, Ann Miller, Gene Kelly, Jules Munshin, Frank Sinatra, Alice Pearce.

Below left: *Singin' in the Rain* (1952) made a star of Debbie Reynolds, shown here between Gene Kelly and Donald O'Connor. It was the story of the silents-into-talkies panic in Hollywood during the late 1920s.

Below right: *Singin' in the Rain* had impressive dance routines with Gene Kelly and Cyd Charisse.

and *Till the Clouds Roll By* (both 1946), *Easter Parade* (1948) and *In the Good Old Summertime* (1949).

Fred Astaire, of course, continued his fine work, dancing spectacularly in *Yolanda and the Thief* (1945), *Ziegfeld Follies* (1946) and *The Barkleys of Broadway,* which featured his 'Shoes with Wings On' number, a sequence that saw him as a cobbler bedazzled by an army of dancing shoes. But the premiere dancer of the period turned out to be ex-Broadway choreographer Gene Kelly. At the time of his first film – Judy Garland's *For Me and My Gal* (1942) – the musical, so often the victim of the same story line and the same, however lavishly staged, production numbers – was beginning to lose its freshness. He brought a new vitality to the genre with his imaginative creations – his dance with cartoon characters, Tom and Jerry, in *Anchors Aweigh* (1945); his jazz ballet, 'Slaughter on Tenth Avenue' in *Words and Music* (1948); his combination of ballet and modern dance for 'A Day in New York' in *On the Town* (1949) and, of course, his now-classic dance through a downpour and his climactic 'Broadway Ballet' in *Singin' in the Rain* (1952).

A distinctive feature that could be traced back to the previous decade marked the 1940s – the musical biography. The best offerings of the period were *Yankee Doodle Dandy* in 1942 and *The Jolson Story* four years later. The former, based on the life of showman George M Cohan, won a best acting Academy Award for its star, James Cagney, while the latter made a star of Larry Parks and led to a not too successful sequel, *Jolson Sings Again* (1949). Surrounding the Cagney and Parks efforts were products of varying quality – the pleasing *Rhapsody in Blue* (1945), the story of George Gershwin with

Left: *The Jolson Story* (1947) was the film biography of the popular singer from his boyhood to his success on the stage and in films, and starred Larry Parks. His voice was dubbed by Jolson himself.

Above: Gary Busey and Maria Richwine in *The Buddy Holly Story* (1978), based upon the brief but brilliant career of the young grass roots Texan who became a pioneer in rock 'n' roll.

Below: Mario Lanza starred in *The Great Caruso* (1950). The movie biography of the great tenor had 27 vocal items, including nine opera scenes, and the hit song 'The Loveliest Night of the Year.'

Robert Alda in the title role; the weak *Night and Day* (1946), starring Cary Grant as Cole Porter; the entertaining *Three Little Words* (1950), teaming Fred Astaire and Red Skelton as song writers Bert Kalmar and Harry Warren and the impressive *The Great Caruso* (1950), with the ill-fated Mario Lanza portraying the famous operatic tenor. The musical biography continued into the next decade with Susan Hayward's excellent portrayal of singer Lillian Roth in *I'll Cry Tomorrow*; with Tyrone Power's *The Eddy Duchin Story* (1955), James Stewart's *The Glenn Miller Story* (1954) and Steve Allen's *The Benny Goodman Story* (1956). Among later biographical offerings were two fine but not especially well publicized efforts: Fox's *Star!* (1968), the story of stage star Gertrude Lawrence with Julie Andrews in the title role and Daniel Massey performing effectively as Noel Coward, and Columbia's *The Buddy Holly Story* (1978).

The early 1950s produced their share of well received musicals. Especially popular were Fox's *There's No Business Like Show Business* (1954), Paramount's teaming of Bing Crosby and Danny Kaye in *White Christmas* (1954) and Warners' *Lullabye of Broadway* (1951) with the studio's singing mainstay since 1948, Doris Day. But these successes were exceptions to a growing

Above: Gene Kelly and Van Johnson starred in
Brigadoon (1954). Here they are being pursued by
Eddie Quillan. It was the story of a Scottish
village that came to life every hundred years, and
contained such Allan Jay Lerner-Frederick
Loewe songs as 'The Heather on the Hill,' 'Almost
Like Being in Love,' 'There But for You Go I' and
'Brigadoon.'

Right: *Carmen Jones* (1950) starred Dorothy
Dandridge and Harry Bellafonte. It was an
update of the Bizet opera and contained an
English libretto by Oscar Hammerstein II. Both of
these performers' voices were dubbed.

rule. The genre was again beginning to fall on bad times. There were two reasons for the problem.

First, ever since *42nd Street,* audiences had been treated to an unending (and accelerated during wartime) succession of musicals and were justifiably tiring of them. Second, musicals had always been expensive to produce and were growing costlier by the year. Budget-conscious producers were thinking twice before now investing in efforts that promised a lukewarm box office reception. As a result, the studios, playing it safe, began to depend principally on commodities that had proven themselves Broadway winners. The adapting of stage material was, of course, nothing new. What was new was the fact that the adaptations now became the principal staple offered by Hollywood. Begun was a trend that has continued to the present.

Using MGM's *Annie Get Your Gun* (1950) as a starting point, close to 50 impressive Broadway productions of all stripes have been transferred to the screen. They've engendered new dance concepts, have entwined story line and music with an increasing effectiveness, and have provided splendid screen vehicles for both new and long-established performers – Doris Day, Liza Minnelli, Joel Grey, Julie Andrews, Yul Brynner, Zero Mostel, Fred Astaire, Robert Preston, Barbra Streisand, Howard Keel, Cyd Charisse, Robert Morse, Ben Vereen and Gwen Verdon. The production titles read like a Who's Who of the musical theater:

1951
Show Boat

1953
Call Me Madam
Gentlemen Prefer Blondes
Kiss Me, Kate

Top: Many people were stunned when Marlon Brando sang in *Guys and Dolls* (1955). The film dealt with Damon Runyan's oddball characters and some of the hit songs from the Frank Loesser score were 'A Woman in Love,' 'If I Were a Bell' and 'Take Back Your Mink.' In this crap game scene, Brando sings 'Luck Be a Lady,' Frank Sinatra is in the rear of the row to the right.

Above: *Oklahoma!* (1955) was a hit. It was the first picture filmed in wide-screen Todd-AO and was based on the stage show which had changed the look of Broadway musicals 12 years before. Here Curley, played by Gordon Macrae, sings 'Oh, What a Beautiful Mornin,' while riding through the corn that is 'as high as an elephant's eye.'

Left: Gene Nelson does his 'Everything's Up to Date in Kansas City' song and dance number in *Oklahoma!*

Right: Gordon Macrae starred in yet another Rodgers and Hammerstein musical with Shirley Jones. It was *Carousel* (1956), a tastefully produced musical based on the Ferenc Molnar play *Liliom*. It concerns the marriage of a swaggering carnival barker and a shy girl, and the tragic consequences when he takes drastic steps to provide for their child. Some of the songs from the film were 'If I Loved You,' 'You'll Never Walk Alone' and 'June Is Bustin' Out All Over.'

Below: *The King and I* (1956) starred Yul Brynner as the king and Deborah Kerr as Anna Leonowens, the teacher of his many children. The plot of the 1946 film, *Anna and the King of Siam*, was adapted by Rodgers and Hammerstein, who added such songs as 'Getting to Know You,' 'I Whistle a Happy Tune,' 'Hello Young Lovers' and 'Shall We Dance.' Kerr's singing voice was dubbed by Marni Nixon.

1954
Brigadoon
Carmen Jones
1955
Guys and Dolls
Kismet
Oklahoma!
1956
Carousel
The King and I
1957
Pajama Game
Pal Joey
Silk Stockings
1958
Damn Yankees
South Pacific
1959
Porgy and Bess
1960
Bells are Ringing
Can Can
1961
Flower Drum Song
West Side Story
1962
Billy Rose's Jumbo
Gypsy
The Music Man
1963
Bye Bye Birdie
1964
My Fair Lady
The Unsinkable Molly Brown
1965
The Sound of Music
1966
A Funny Thing Happened on the Way to the Forum
1967
Camelot
How to Succeed in Business Without Really Trying
1968
Finian's Rainbow
Funny Girl
Oliver!
1969
Hello, Dolly!
Paint Your Wagon
Sweet Charity
1970
On a Clear Day You Can See Forever
1971
Fiddler on the Roof
1972
Cabaret
Man of La Mancha
1776
1973
Jesus Christ, Superstar
1974
Mame
1977
A Little Night Music
1978
Grease
The Wiz
1979
Hair
1982
Annie

Left: *The Pajama Game* (1957) starred John Raitt and Doris Day. The plot revolved around a pajama factory union's efforts to get a seven and one-half cent hourly increase. The hit song was 'Hey There.'

Below: *Pal Joey* (1957) featured Frank Sinatra and Rita Hayworth. It was the story of a heel, written by John O'Hara, and had songs by Rodgers and Hart such as 'Bewitched, Bothered and Bewildered,' 'Small Hotel,' 'My Funny Valentine' and 'The Lady Is a Tramp.'

Bottom: Cyd Charisse and Fred Astaire joined forces in *Silk Stockings* (1957). It was a musical remake of Greta Garbo's *Ninotchka* (1939) and the songs were Cole Porter's.

Above: John Kerr, Mitzie Gaynor and Rossano Brazzi in a tense moment in *South Pacific* (1958). The film about the romance between a US Army nurse and a suave French planter in the South Pacific during World War II featured such songs as 'Some Enchanted Evening,' 'There Is Nothing Like a Dame,' 'Bali H'ai,' 'You've Got to be Taught' and 'This Nearly Was Mine.'

Right: Gwenn Verdon tries to seduce Tab Hunter in the 'Whatever Lola Wants' sequence in *Damn Yankees* (1958). One of the few films with a sports theme to make it big at the box office, this story of a modern-day Faust selling his soul to the devil in order to star with the Washington Senators baseball team featured such songs as 'You've Got to Have Heart' and 'Two Lost Souls.'

Bottom: Mitzie Gaynor, as Nellie Forbush, the nurse, entertains the sailors with her 'Honey Bun' routine.

Opposite: *Porgy and Bess* (1959), the film version of the George Gershwin opera starred Sidney Poitier and Dorothy Dandridge in the title roles. It was filled with great songs – 'Summertime,' 'I Got Plenty of Nothin,' 'It Ain't Necessarily So' and 'Bess, You Is My Woman Now' among them.

Right: *Bells Are Ringing* (1960) told the story of a telephone operator (Judy Holliday, in her last film) who falls in love with the voice of a client (Dean Martin). The Jule Styne songs included 'Just in Time' and 'The Party's Over.'

Below: Nancy Kwan leads a street dance in *Flower Drum Song* (1961), the Rodgers and Hammerstein musical set in San Francisco's Chinatown.

Above: A film version of the stage musical retelling the Romeo and Juliet story in a New York slum setting, *West Side Story* (1961) had a score by Leonard Bernstein and Stephen Sondheim. Here, Richard Beymer reacts to the knifing of a member of a rival gang. The film won the Academy Award of 1961 as best picture and George Chakiris and Rita Moreno won Oscars for best supporting actor and actress.

Below: Left to right, Natalie Wood, Rosalind Russell and Karl Malden sing the 'Together' number in *Gypsy* (1962). The musical about the stage mother of all time, Rose Hovick, whose daughters grow up to be Gypsy Rose Lee and June Havoc, boasted a score by Jule Styne and Stephen Sondheim. Some of the other songs were 'Everything's Coming Up Roses,' 'Small World' and 'Let Me Entertain You.'

Above: Robert Preston, as Professor Harold Hill, leads his 'Seventy-Six Trombones' in *The Music Man* (1962). It was a story of a brash, beaming musical-instrument salesman who comes to River City, Iowa in 1912 to sell and skedaddle until charmed by a shy librarian. Meredith Willson's songs include 'Till There Was You,' 'Marian the Librarian' and 'Trouble.'

Right: Rex Harrison as Professor Henry Higgins and Audrey Hepburn as Eliza Doolittle dance 'The Rain in Spain' number from *My Fair Lady* (1964), the Lerner and Loewe adaptation of George Bernard Shaw's *Pygmalion*. Marni Nixon did the dubbing for Hepburn's singing voice. Harrison won an Oscar for his role as the British gentleman who turns the Cockney flower girl into a lady. Some of the songs were 'Just You Wait,' 'On the Street Where You Live' and 'I've Grown Accustomed to Her Face.'

Opposite: Audrey Hepburn ready to go to the races in the 'Ascot Gavotte' number from *My Fair Lady*.

Left: Michele Lee and Robert Morse have a chat in *How To Succeed in Business Without Really Trying* (1967). The film concerned an ambitious window-washer (Morse) who uses his wiles, plus a handbook, to rise to prominence in the Worldwide Wicket Company.

Opposite: Julie Andrews played Maria, soon to become the Baroness von Trapp, in *The Sound of Music* (1965). The Oscar-winning film featured a score by Rodgers and Hammerstein.

Right: *Finian's Rainbow* (1968) combined subtle social commentary with a tuneful Irish musical setting by Burton Lane and E Y Harburg.

Left: Barbra Streisand starred in *Funny Girl* (1968), the musical biography of Fanny Brice, and won the Academy Award for best actress. Probably the most memorable songs from the Jule Styne-Bob Merrill score were 'Don't Rain on My Parade' and 'People.'

Right: 'Please sir, I want some more,' says Oliver Twist (Mark Lester), asking for more food at the orphanage in *Oliver!* (1968), the musical adaptation of Charles Dickens' *Oliver Twist*. It won six Oscars, among them for best film and best direction by Carol Reed. In the score were such songs as 'Pick a Pocket or Two,' 'Consider Yourself' and 'As Long As He Needs Me.'

Below: A dance number from *Hello Dolly* (1969), the musical version of Thornton Wilder's play, *The Matchmaker*.

Left: The 'Hey, Big Spender' routine from *Sweet Charity* (1969), an adaptation of Fellini's film *Nights of Cabiria* (1957). It is the story of a dance hall hostess (Shirley MacLaine) with the proverbial heart of gold. Among the Cy Coleman-Dorothy Fields songs are 'If They Could See Me Now' and 'Rhythm of Life.'

Below: Liza Minnelli won the Academy Award for best actress for *Cabaret* (1972). The film presented a vivid picture of the seamy side of Berlin life in the early 1930s and won a total of seven Oscars.

Below left: A publicity still for *Fiddler on the Roof* (1971), the story of a group of Jewish peasants in the Ukraine in 1905, taken from the writings of Sholem Aleichem. The Sheldon Harnick-Jerry Bock score contained such songs as 'If I were a Rich Man,' 'Tevye's Dream' and 'Matchmaker.' The rooftop violin solo of 'Fiddler on the Roof' was played by Isaac Stern.

Above: The crucifixion scene from *Jesus Christ, Superstar* (1973). Filmed in Israel, the movie told the story of the Passion. Its most popular song was 'I Don't Know How to Love Him.'

Right: Lucille Ball played the title role in *Mame* (1974), based upon the madcap misadventures of Auntie Mame. Here she is in the title song number.

Above: John Travolta (center), fresh from his *Saturday Night Fever* hit, made *Grease* (1978).

Left: *The Wiz* (1978) was a fanciful remake of *The Wizard of Oz* and starred Diana Ross.

Right: *Hair* (1979) was a musical adaptation of the long-running Broadway show about the flower children of the 1960s. It had some fine songs, such as 'The Age of Aquarius' and 'Hair.'

Below: Annie and Sandy in *Annie* (1982). Aileen Quinn played the title role of the musical based upon the cartoon strip. It was director John Huston's first musical.

Bottom: Ann Reinking (left) and a group of orphans cheer the strutting of Albert Finney (Daddy Warbucks) and Aileen Quinn. The hit song from the film was 'Tomorrow.'.

The adaptations have been Hollywood staples over the years, but they have not been the only fare offered by the genre. Throughout the past three decades, enterprising producers have developed material meant especially for the screen and designed for the talents of the leading players. There were those two delightful and sophisticated films for Leslie Caron – *Lili* (1953) and *Gigi* (1958), the latter graced with the splendid singing assistance of Maurice Chevalier – just as debonair as ever in his late years – and England's Hermione Gingold. For Judy Garland in 1954 and for Barbra Streisand in 1974, there were the musical remakes of the 1937 film drama, *A Star is Born*. For the special talk-singing abilities of *My Fair Lady*'s Rex Harrison, there was *Doctor Doolittle* (1967). For Julie Andrews, there were *Mary Poppins* (1964), *Thoroughly Modern Millie* (1967) and her

Right: Leslie Caron and Mel Ferrer starred in *Lili* (1953), the musical about a French orphan girl who joins a carnival and attaches herself to a self-pitying puppeteer. The song 'Hi Lili Hi Lo' won the Academy Award.

Below: Leslie Caron continued to play innocent French girls in *Gigi* (1958). Also in the cast were Maurice Chevalier (standing, left), Hermione Gingold and Louis Jordan. The score was by Lerner and Loewe and contained such hits as 'Gigi' and 'Thank Heaven for Little Girls.'

Top: One of Judy Garland's great roles – as Vicki Lester in *A Star Is Born* (1954), the remake of the non-musical of 1937. Judy was at her pinnacle singing 'Born in a Trunk' and 'The Man That Got Away.'

Above: Barbra Streisand and Kris Kristofferson starred in a 1976 remake of *A Star Is Born*, the third and worst film version of the story. Updating and transposing the story line from the Hollywood movie world to the 1970s rock world was a terrible mistake.

failed but still entertaining *Darling Lili* (1970). For Danny Kaye's frenetic gifts, *Up in Arms* (1944) and *The Court Jester* (1956), and for his gentle side, *Hans Christian Andersen* (1952). For Elvis Presley, a succession of pleasantries from *Love Me Tender* (1956) to *Change of Habit* (1969). For the unique Bette Midler, *The Rose* (1979). And, from the very special musical genius that is Bob Fosse, his brilliant and controversial *All That Jazz* (1979).

The Rose and *All That Jazz* closed the 1970s on a highly imaginative note, with the 80s then being introduced with the high-spirited *Fame* (1980) and the grandiose *Annie*. Though it would be difficult to calculate, the likelihood is that fewer musicals have been made over the past 30 years than in either of the two decades that marked the genre's 'golden age.' But the continuing quality of the productions over those 30 years undeniably indicate that the genre is in sparkling good health. May that health, for the joy that audiences everywhere take from singing and dancing, continue indefinitely.

Far left: Julie Andrews and Dick Van Dyke were the stars of *Mary Poppins* (1964), possibly Walt Disney's most successful film. It was a fantasy based upon the works of P L Travers about a magical nanny who descends on a family in Edwardian London.

Left: Bette Midler as *The Rose* (1979), a hard-rock superstar.

Below: *All That Jazz* (1979), Bob Fosse's semi-autobiographical musical. This is a dream sequence during the hero's (Roy Scheider) heart bypass surgery.

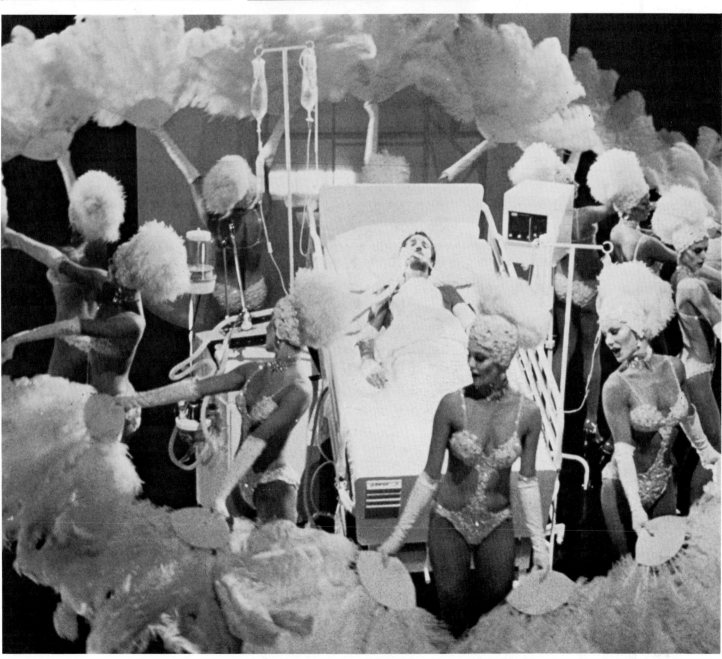

COMEDY

On the basis of existing records, comedy has the right to call itself the oldest film genre. Working at the Edison laboratories at the time the motion picture was being born was a mechanic of comic bent, one Fred Ott, whose specialty seems to have been a sneeze of the raucous kind that Billy Gilbert would make famous in the 1920s and 30s. Early on, the project supervisor, William Dickson, asked Ott to perform his sneeze in front of the camera. The mechanic obliged, at first suffering a few failed takes because of stage fright. Film historians estimate that his eventually successful performance, which lasted just a few seconds, was photographed sometime between 1890 and 1893. *Fred Ott's Sneeze*, as it has long been titled, is the earliest complete film on record in the US Library of Congress.

There is hardly a need to say that, from this primitive beginning, comedy quickly developed into one of the busiest areas in motion pictures and has remained so ever since. Nor is there the need to say that, in time, it transferred to film all of its traditional stage branches – everything from the free-for-all farce staged by the Marx Brothers on the one hand to the satire of a befuddled but yet biting Woody Allen on the other. Without needing to be told, anyone (and there are millions of such 'anyones') who has watched the parade of its various offerings and diverse players over the years knows what it has accomplished.

Its immediate and rapid growth, of course, was to be expected. Providing a momentary escape from life's troubles and an unremitting commentary on human foibles and frustrations, comedy has been steadily drawing customers into theaters for centuries. The motion picture simply gave it a new arena in which to work and please. Further, completely visual in so many of its aspects, it was ideal for use with silent film. As matters turned out, the most outrageously visual of its branches – slapstick – proved the one to be most cherished by early audiences.

Slapstick, if it needs to be defined at this late date, is the branch of farce that assails its performers with every physical mishap and indignity that the mind can devise – the pie in the face, the slip on a banana peel, the tumble down a stairway, the dunk in the ocean, the loss of trousers or skirt. To work, it depends principally on one element: the performers involved in all the frenzied nonsense must never touch the audience as vulnerable, feeling human beings but must come across only as silly, accident-prone machines able to bear every bump and thump without physical injury and with no emotional damage other than a momentarily bruised ego. Cars crash. Bullets fly. People chase each other. They bump into each other. Houses fall down around them. But no one spills a drop of blood. If some player is carted off to the hospital, he's seen in such a ridiculously outsized wrapping of bandages that we know there can be no real pain. When a section of ceiling falls on Oliver Hardy, he winces but is then immediately more concerned with what's been done to his dignity. All that ever suffers, then, is that commodity that we all take delight in seeing punctured – the pompous side of our human nature (so long, naturally, as it's someone else's pomposity that is on the block).

Filmed slapstick can trace its roots back to France and the Lumière brothers' 1895 short, *L'Arroseur Arrosé*, which is the first known picture to tell a story. Here we have a man watering his front lawn. A child sneaks up behind him and cuts off the flow by crimping the hose. Bewildered, the man turns the nozzle towards his face and inspects it. And you guessed it. The child releases the hose, with the obvious result. The little film ends with the victim madly chasing his tormentor about the yard.

Slapstick appeared early in American and British cinema, most often in the haphazard chase and the pratfall. But it remained for Mack Sennett in the US to turn it into the most popular comic fare of the day and to shape it into, if not an art form, then a well-honed craft. Born in Canada in 1880, Sennett (the name was originally spelled Sinnott) aspired to an operatic career but got no further in the theater as a young man than stints in burlesque and Broadway chorus lines. An interest in eating regularly took him in search of a job as an actor at Biograph's Manhattan studio in 1908. Hired on by D W Griffith, he was, within three years, starring in one-reelers for the master, helping him to write scripts (among them Griffith's 1909 success, *The Lonely Villa*), learning all possible about camera techniques and beginning to do some directing. Loving comedy, he left Griffith in 1912 to concentrate fully on it, forming his own company – Keystone – in association with two ex-bookmakers, Charles Bauman and Adam Kessel. Keystone was soon recognized as America's leading producer of slapstick and Sennett was awarded the title, 'The King of Comedy.'

Keystone's success in slapstick was grounded in three basic elements. The first had to do with the performers. Sennett peopled his films with good and experienced knockabout comedians, drawing them from vaudeville, burlesque and the circus. In great part, he picked them for their exaggerated, at times even grotesque, looks, knowing that their very features would add to the unreality and the silliness needed to make slapstick work. Mainstays in his productions included lanky and dour Slim Summerville; obese Fatty Arbuckle and Marie Dressler; pop-eyed and leering Mack Swain, Chester Conklin and Ford Sterling; rubber-faced Polly Moran; cross-eyed Ben Turpin and gangling and gamin-faced Louise Fazenda. They did the basic (and base) comedy while Mabel Normand and the Sennett Bathing Beauties provided a spice that Sennett knew audiences loved – pretty girls with a bit of dainty skin exposed in just the right places.

Second, Keystone took full advantage of a technique that Sennett early learned. He found that, if he shot his pictures at a slow camera speed – at eight to ten frames a second – and then accelerated to sixteen frames per second in the projector, he achieved a frenzied, herky-jerky quality that added to all the inane fun. The technique is most obviously on display in the mad chases staged by Ford Sterling's Chief Teheezal and his Keystone Kops. It not only jerks the action forward at a dizzying pace but adds further to the unreality so required. No matter where they run, no matter how they crash their cars into trees, no matter how they fall, the Kops have the look of those silly little machine people. The audience never once winces at the pain that obviously is being suffered. Little machine people aren't able to suffer like real humans.

Finally, there was Sennett himself. All his films bore the mark of his own love for hectic fun, his ability to improvise (and win inspired improvisation from his players) and his technical expertise, an expertise painstakingly acquired by studying every aspect of picture-making while employed at Biograph. Sennett personally supervised all of Keystone's productions, directing the earliest and often appearing in them. His love of all-out comedy drove him to insist that every picture be choked with visual gags. The need for a keen sense of improvization sprang from his very way of working. Each picture began with no more than the sketchiest of plots, or perhaps an idea on which a string of gags could be draped or even a gag itself that could be given varied treatments. Whatever the case, before moving to the camera, Sennett sat down with his writers (in time, they included such future greats as directors Tay Garnett and Frank Capra) and dreamed up one silly stunt after another for the planned enterprise. The stunts themselves were simply outlined and the players were then free, under

his direction, to play them out as best they saw fit. Further, he allowed the stunts to function as springboards for on-the-spot additions and embellishments during shooting. His technical expertise, though seen on the set, was then put to its fullest use in the cutting room, where he attempted to edit and time all the nonsense to perfection.

Keystone began with split-reelers, quickly graduated to one- and two-reelers, and in 1915 added feature length productions to its output with Marie Dressler's *Tillie's Punctured Romance.* The company eventually came to produce three types of slapstick fare. First, there were the pictures, *Tillie's Punctured Romance* among them, that had plots to them, in *Tillie's* case that of a farm girl's problems with her city slicker boyfriend; the plots were used simply as pegs on which to hang the gags and were usually pushed almost out of sight once the stunts took over. Second there were the parodies of then-current movies, a prime example being *The Shreik of Araby* (1923), with cross-eyed Ben Turpin's implausible but hilarious imitation of Rudolf Valentino. And, most riotous of all, there were the totally plotless pictures, those insane masterpieces that consisted of nothing but a series of gags built around an idea or a setting.

It is unfair to say 'nothing' but gags. An unending succession of ridiculous stunts, with one tumbling forth after the other almost without a hesitation between, is anything but 'nothing.' Take *The Surf Girl* (1916), for example. Running just two reels, it is crammed with every idiot disaster that can befall people spending the day at a seaside amusement park. A giant of a fellow tumbles down the slide and into the park's swimming pool, causing a splash that tosses everyone out of the water (accomplished by running the film backwards). A young man takes a turn swinging on rings above the pool; he's given a helpful push by a young lady, only to have her accidentally snatch his pants away and then tumble into the water with them. Outside, one group of zanies encounters all sorts of havoc aboard a roller coaster, while another finds itself in trouble atop a ferris wheel. Down at the surfside, an ostrich (don't ask how he got in the picture) swallows a young woman's brooch and is madly chased by two lifeguards until he coughs the thing up. Another chase sees a crowd in pursuit of a man suspected of pestering some girls too much. He hides in an amusement booth where balls are thrown at dummies. On posing as one of the dummies, he naturally becomes a favorite target for the passing

Pages 162-3: One of the most famous gag sequences in film history – in *Safety Last* (1923) Harold Lloyd as a 'human fly' hanging from the hand of a clock high on the side of a building, only to have the hand move steadily downward toward six o'clock.

Above: The Keystone Kops. Ford Sterling is the chief in the motorcycle sidecar.

customers. In all, the picture is a perfect example of a basic Sennett rule: all stunts must be introduced, developed and concluded in no more than 100 seconds.

Having no real story line, the plotless pictures simply came to an end when the last gag was pulled. As in the case of *The Surf Girl,* showman Sennett tried to close things off with a 'topper.' In this instance, the Keystone Kops round up a group of miscreants and toss them into a paddy wagon for the ride from the beach to jail. On arriving, the roof of the wagon is torn away as the vehicle passes through the police department entrance. Out pile its bathing-suited occupants. They grab the rooftop and, using it as a shield, make their escape by walking away from the always befuddled Kops. Giving the scene its 'topper' punch is the fact that, with their legs showing beneath the rooftop, they give the impression of some sort of outsize beetle.

Above: Terry-Thomas in *Those Magnificent Men in Their Flying Machines* (1965), a comedy-adventure about an air race from London to Paris during the early days of aviation. Terry-Thomas is one of the most lovable villains the movies have ever served up.

The same sort of 'topper' device was used even in Sennett's plotted pictures. *Tillie's Punctured Romance,* for instance, ends with the Kops and Charlie Chaplin throwing the cast off the end of a pier into the ocean. The sequence, which follows a free-for-all scene, has really nothing to do with the film's story line and, as a climax, certainly does nothing to resolve the problems that heroine Tillie has been enduring.

In common with so many of his contemporaries, Sennett cranked out his early Keystones at a dead run, often at the rate of more than one a week. Some idea of his output can be had by looking at the amount of work done by two of his most gifted principals, Mabel Normand and Roscoe 'Fatty' Arbuckle. In Keystone's first two years, Normand appeared in 73 pictures – 21 in 1912, and 52 in 1913. Arbuckle joined Keystone in 1913 and did 15 of Normand's films, plus 14 of his own. He went on to 45 in 1914. As a result of such speed, the pictures had their shortcomings and were often crude affairs. But, thanks to Sennett's abilities in the cutting room, even the worst of their number were beautifully timed pieces, and all were crowd pleasers. It was acknowledged that Sennett was a master of his particular brand of cinema frenzy.

He was not, of course, the era's only producer of good and popular comic fare. In the five-year span before his death in 1915, the huge and genial John Bunny, usually working with Flora Finch, made more than 200 short comedies in which laughter and pathos were successfully mixed. After launching Essanay with a series of western shorts, Broncho Billy Anderson and George K Spoor in 1911 added comedy to their company's roster of offerings. Essanay turned out two of the most pleasing comedy series of the day, both with rural settings – the *Alkali Ike* and *Snakeville Comedy* pictures. Charlie Chaplin spent 1915 and the first months of 1916 with Essanay's Chicago branch, directing and acting in 14 shorts while there, among them the film that is considered his first masterpiece, *The Tramp* (1915). Two Sennett favorites – Arbuckle and Sterling – eventually formed their own production units. Both did well-received films, with Arbuckle's proving to be especially successful.

Financed by Paramount's Joseph B Schenck, Arbuckle's unit – The Comique Shorts – went into production in 1917, turning out 21 starring vehicles for him in a two-year period. A talented comedian, a graceful man despite his girth and a performer and director able to give his knockabout comedy the look of being choreographed, Arbuckle was highly lauded for the quality of his pictures; in the wake of Comique's first release, *The Butcher Boy,* one critic wrote that, if Arbuckle's future efforts matched its quality, his would be the ranking film work in the country. From that start, Arbuckle moved to feature films in 1920 and reached the zenith of his popularity in 1921, only to have his career abruptly ended by scandal. That year, a young actress, Virginia Rappe, died during a party held in his San Francisco hotel suite. Accused of raping and murdering the woman, Arbuckle was tried three times and finally exonerated. But the incident – seen by large segments of the public as just another example of all the Hollywood debaucheries then being reported in the press – destroyed his reputation (though it must be said that his pictures still continued to be well received in several parts of the country). He spent the remainder of the 1920s directing under an assumed name. In 1932 Warners attempted to bring him back with a half dozen sound shorts. But the comeback went for naught. Arbuckle died in 1933 at age 46.

Once Sennett had launched Keystone, the company grew so quickly that he found himself hiring a fleet of directors, among them Edward Cline, who years later would direct W C Fields' three best films – *My Little Chickadee* (1940), *The Bank Dick* (1940) and *Never Give a Sucker an Even Break* (1941). With help in hand, Sennett was relieved of much directorial work. But he continued to supervise all productions and, with the freedom now to do so, concentrated on improving them and adding to their scope; among the additions of the period: the Sennett Bathing Beauties. In 1915, owning now one of the biggest names in the industry, he placed Keystone under the umbrella of the newly formed Triangle Film Corporation, a move that made him the partner of his former boss, D W Griffith, and Thomas Ince. It was an association that provided him with larger production budgets than before, enabling him to continue polishing his slapstick products and to try his hand at romantic comedies with Gloria Swanson and Bobby Vernon.

Sennett broke with Triangle in 1917 and, forced contractually to leave Keystone behind, formed Mack Sennett Comedies. Concentrating on the usual slapstick shorts and on several feature-length pictures with Mabel Normand, the company operated until 1923. Sennett then joined Pathé for a successful five-year alliance, during which time he launched the career of Harry Langdon. With the coming of sound and its accent on the word as well as the action, Sennett's brand of film-making became passé. His career entered an abrupt decline. He directed a number of two-reelers for a quickie outfit called Educational and then, in the early 1930s, went to Paramount to do some sound shorts for Bing Crosby and W C Fields. Shortly thereafter, Sennett retired to his native Canada. It was a retirement twice interrupted – once in 1939 for a brief stint as technical director on Fox's *Hollywood Cavalcade,* a picture in which he made a 'guest' appearance as himself, and once again in 1949 for a guest appearance in *Down Memory Lane*. Sennett, who received a special 1937 Academy Award for his contributions to filmed comedy, died in 1960 at age 80.

As did its chief purveyor, slapstick went into a decline with the coming of sound. But only something of a decline. The knockabout brand of comedy did not die out altogether and has not done so to this day. Rather, it had to take its place among a growing number of other strains. It was carried on through the decade by Laurel and Hardy, the Marx Brothers, the Ritz Brothers, the Three Stooges, Leon Errol, Edgar Kennedy, Eddie Cantor, Joe E Brown and W C Fields, joined as the 40s dawned by Abbott and Costello. In Britain, too, slapstick made the jump to sound; it had begun in the 1920s with Monty Banks, Lupino Lane and Betty Balfour and was now fostered by such talents as George Formby, Max Miller and Gracie Fields.

The 40s gave the US the sophisticated slapstick of Danny Kaye, seen at its early best in *Up in Arms* (1944) and later in *Knock on Wood* (1954) and *The Court Jester* (1956). The Crazy Gang, featuring a young Peter Sellers, tickled the English, as did Arthur Askey, Sandy Powell and that great dispenser of vulgarity, Frank Randle. France, whose earliest slapstick after the Lumières dated back to Max Linder in 1906, enjoyed the work of Fernandel, Pierre Etaix, Louis de Funes, and the magnificent Jacques Tati. Tati's work would reach its peak much later, in 1953 with *Monsieur Hulot's Holiday*.

As for the US in the 1950s, there was the work of Dean Martin and Jerry Lewis, with Lewis continuing his wild brand of comedy into the 1960s and 70s after the team's break-up. The 1950s also saw one of America's few top female slapstick artists, Lucille Ball, reach her full potential. All the madness worked its way through the 1960s with such pieces as Stanley Kramer's *It's a Mad, Mad, Mad, Mad World* (1963) in the United States and *Those Magnificent Men in Their Flying Machines* (1965) in Great Britain. The 1970s and now the 80s have seen Burt Reynolds, in such fare as *Smokey and the Bandit* (1977), use the automobile in ways that would have set even Sennett's hair on end. And who can forget that the 1970s and 80s have brought all the delightfully insane offerings of Mel Brooks, among them *Blazing Saddles* (1974), *Silent Movie* (1976) and *High Anxiety* (1977).

Keystone practiced the most basic form of slapstick – the knockabout antics of grotesque and completely machine-like little people. But filmed comedy, even in its infancy, was a creative enterprise, and so such crude and rudimentary fare, no matter how ex-

pertly done, could not go for long without refinement by its more gifted performers. The passing years saw the arrival of the talents who were to do the refining. They were to endow the hectic proceedings with fine characterizations, new themes and elements ranging from pathos to satire. In so doing, they were to move filmed comedy out of its boisterous infancy and were to make their names legendary in the process – Arbuckle, Buster Keaton, Harold Lloyd, Laurel and Hardy and the man who is pretty much acknowledged as having been the greatest of the lot, Charlie Chaplin.

The son of music hall performers, Chaplin was born in London in 1889. His childhood was spent on music hall stages and his early youth in London theater productions, playing bit parts in musicals, among them *Peter Pan* in 1902. At 17, Chaplin landed a job that changed the course of his life by setting

Below: A scene from a 'good ol' boy' comedy – *Smokey and the Bandit* (1977). Left to right, Pat McCormick, Paul Williams, Burt Reynolds. Cars are the stars of this race against time as two Texas millionaires commission Reynolds to race from Georgia to Texas in 28 hours with a load of illegal Coors Beer.

him on the path that eventually led to films. He joined Fred Karno's highly successful traveling company and came to the United States twice with the troupe – first in 1910 and again in 1912. The second tour was the important one for Chaplin. It saw him receive and accept a movie offer from Mack Sennett. The tour also held a significance for Chaplin's understudy in the Karno troupe, a thin young Englishman named Arthur Stanley Jefferson. He left the company, struck out on his own in American vaudeville and changed his name to Stan Laurel.

Chaplin joined Sennett in late 1913 and began work in 1914 as a mustachioed villain in *Making a Living.* That year, he made 35 Keystone films, concluding with Marie Dressler's *Tillie's Punctured Romance.* On the one hand, there is little in his first pictures to suggest the greatness that was to come; he performed competently and showed his fine abilities as a pantomimist, but little more. But, on the other hand, there are indications that the character that was to make Chaplin immortal, the little Tramp, was already aborning. The comedian's search for a distinct screen personality, one initially meant to set him apart from his Sennett colleagues, can be detected as early as his second picture, *Kid Auto Races at*

Venice. He is seen wearing baggy trousers and bowler hat, sporting a peculiar mustache and carrying a cane.

Though future greatness may not have been yet evident, those 35 shorts turned Chaplin into a highly popular screen comedian, popular enough for Broncho Billy Anderson's Essanay to hire him on at the start of 1915 for a handsome $1250 a week (he had been making $175 with Sennett), plus a bonus of $10,000. Further, he had become a director. Just three months after starting with Keystone, Chaplin was struck with the urge to direct and was allowed to do so. Beginning with his 12th picture, *Caught in a Cabaret,* he either directed or co-directed all but one of his remaining Sennett pieces, among them *Tillie's Punctured Romance.* As a director he was now better able to control the quality of his pictures and insert his own ideas into them. With that control, which would eventually become absolute, Chaplin started on the way to immortality.

The comedian remained at Essanay for about a year and a half, directing and starring in 14 films, a markedly small number for that day and age and one demonstrating that his box office appeal was now such that the reduced output was more than profitable. Permitted to work slowly, he had the time

One of the greatest comedies in the history of the movies – *The Gold Rush* (1925), with Charlie Chaplin. It pitted The Little Tramp against the Yukon, the affections of a dance-hall girl, the whims of a burly prospector and starvation.

to give his works a quality rarely seen before and to bring his Little Tramp character to full bloom, doing so in *The Tramp* (1915), the picture that is regarded as his first masterwork.

And what a character the little fellow proved to be with his shuffling, toed-out gait, his elegant but so inelegant derby hat, his ill-fitting suit, frayed gloves and cane – a character that managed to be proud, pathetic, graceful, clumsy, noble, conniving, courageous and cowardly. Molded in the hands of a genuine artist and splendid pantomimist, the Tramp was that most cherished of comic rarities – the multi-dimensional and adroitly exaggerated but always fully human character. It was a character that made Chaplin into an international star of a luminosity that would never fade, no matter the personal and political scandals of his later life and the directorial failures of his closing years.

Chaplin left Essanay in mid-1916 to accept a $10,000-a-week offer from Mutual, then contracted for more than

$1 million to make just eight shorts for First National and finally, as the 1920s dawned, established United Artists Corportion with D W Griffith, Mary Pickford and Douglas Fairbanks. Beginning with Mutual, the comedian held full artistic control over his pictures. In his quest for perfection, he went on reducing his output, at last doing only one film every two or three years for United Artists in the 1920s. The result: the years between 1916 and 1936 saw the production of his finest work.

To begin, there were what are called the 'golden dozen' two-reelers for Mutual, all of them displaying Chaplin's abilities to fluctuate between broad, pratfall comedy and pathos. Among the best of the 'goldens' are *The Rink, The Pawnshop* and *The Floorwalker* (all 1916). Next, there was his parody of war, *Shoulder Arms* (1918) and his first starring full-length feature, *The Kid* (1921), with the latter so successful that it trailed only Griffith's *Birth of a Nation* in earnings up to that time. Then came his other full-length triumphs (Chaplin did no further shorts after *The Kid*) – *The Gold Rush* (1925), *City Lights* (1931) and *Modern Times* (1936).

All the films of this period are graced with unforgettable comic moments – in

Above: *City Lights* (1931) was the last of Chaplin's silent films. In it, The Little Tramp falls in love with a blind flower girl and gets money for her to have an operation to restore her sight. Chaplin wrote the script and directed the picture.

Left: Chaplin's next film, *Modern Times* (1936), used sound very sparingly. It is still an up-to-date satire of automation, The Tramp inevitably losing encounters with modern machinery.

The Kid, the scenes of urchin Jackie Coogan deliberately throwing bricks through windows so that his Tramp friend, a glazier, can be hired on for the repair work; in *The Gold Rush,* a starving Tramp eating the sole of his shoe as daintily as if he were at a banquet and, at another point, turning a couple of dinner rolls into little feet by sticking forks into them and then having them execute a tabletop dance and, in *Modern Times,* the Tramp's marvelously choreographed misadventures in the giant 'man-eating' machine.

And, in the closing moments of *City Lights,* there is what may be the single finest scene that Chaplin ever put on film. The picture tells of how the Tramp falls in love with a blind flower girl (Virginia Cherrill) and then helps to have her sight restored. Now, without knowing who he is, the girl sees him for the first time. In her eyes are, in turn, surprise, shock and then comprehension as she comes to realize that this funny little man is the one who so helped her. In sad contrast are the love, the hope, the desperation and the yearning in the Tramp's eyes as he watches her evolving expressions. A superb exercise in facial pantomime, the scene is deservedly one of the most famous in screen history.

Though the sound era had arrived,

both *City Lights* and *Modern Times* were silent features, the result of Chaplin's fear that the Tramp would lose much of his appeal if he were made to talk. Each was so well done and the comedian's appeal was so great that, contrary to dire predictions from all sides, both were financial and critical triumphs. Only with *The Great Dictator* (1940), a film that did not actually feature the Tramp, did Chaplin at last bow to sound. In the film, he played dual roles – a Hitler-like tyrant and a Jewish barber who is somewhat akin to the Tramp character.

From 1916 on, Chaplin did more than present audiences with the most famous and endearing comic figure of the day. He began to explore new themes, themes that increasingly revealed both the emotional and intellectual sides of his nature – sentimentality, satire and social comment. Despite the pathos in the Tramp, Chaplin's earliest films were played for pure and delicious comedy, but sentimentality became a lasting part of his work with *The Kid,* which established such a heart-breaking relationship between an adult and a child. In *Shoulder Arms* he commented satirically on the uselessness of war. *Modern Times* was his outcry against the inhumanity that can come of mechanization. *The Great Dictator* cuttingly paro-

It wasn't until *The Great Dictator* (1940) that Chaplin used a conventional sound track. He played two roles: a little Jewish barber and the megalomaniac dictator Adenoid Hynkel. Chaplin brilliantly used his resemblance to Adolf Hitler in the film, which was a devastating attack on the brutalities of the Nazis.

died Adolph Hitler, with Chaplin achieving one of the best moments in his career when he illustrated the silliness of the dictator and his grand aims by performing a ballet with a balloon globe of the world.

But there was a dark side to Chaplin's nature and he let it be seen in the 1940s and 50s, first in *Monsieur Verdoux* (1947), then in *Limelight* (1952) and finally in *A King in New York* (1957). *Monsieur Verdoux,* a black comedy that is regarded today as having been years ahead of its time, is a sardonic piece, the story of a discharged French bank clerk who marries lonely women for their money and then murders them, all to support his son and crippled wife. The picture is grim throughout, with even its comic moments coming across as chilling. There is Verdoux contentedly trimming his rose garden while, behind him, an incinerator sends up in smoke his latest victims (a scene echoed two years later in Britain's *Kind Hearts and*

Coronets). There is Verdoux desperately trying to dispatch a victim in time to get to the bank before it closes. And there is Verdoux – in the film's one truly hilarious sequence – trying to drown an elusive Martha Raye by pushing her out of a rowboat. The scene, caricatured the famous sequence in the 1931 filmed version of Theodore Dreiser's novel, *An American Tragedy*. The sequence was again played for hard drama by Montgomery Clift and Shelley Winters in a second adaptation of the novel, *A Place in the Sun* (1951).

Monsieur Verdoux dismayed the Tramp's admirers, but there is no doubt that it is a masterwork. The same can be said of *Limelight*, in which Chaplin plays an over-the-hill music hall performer named Calvero. It is a film of sharp contrasts – flashing back at times to the marvelously funny stage bits done by a youthful Calvero and his partner (Buster Keaton in his only role ever done with Chaplin) and then coming forward to deal with the shambles of his present-day life. In all, it can be viewed as a comment by Chaplin on his own life, a statement mingling bittersweet reflections of his theatrical beginnings with bitter echoes of the personal scandals and political problems that marked his later years.

Chaplin's bitterness is especially seen in *A King in New York*. A compilation of problems over the years – ranging from his known predilection for women years his junior to his rumored communist leanings – had outraged conservative elements in the US and had eventually led to him being denied re-entry to the country (unless he submitted to an inquiry into his 'moral worth') during the McCarthy era. In reply, Chaplin remained in Europe and produced the angry *King*. In it, playing a deposed monarch who visits America and runs into the senseless hysteria of the McCarthy years, he unleashed one cutting jibe after another at the nation's life, choosing as targets everything from wide-screen motion pictures and beauty parlors to television interviews and radical students. The result was an interesting and provocative, though highly uneven, political satire.

Chaplin's public life closed on a dichotomous note. On the one hand, there was the failure of his final directorial effort, *A Countess from Hong Kong* (1967), a thoroughly poor film despite the presence of Sophia Loren and Marlon Brando, and Chaplin himself in a cameo role. On the other hand, with the travesty of McCarthyism long in the past, there was his enthusiastic welcome back to the US for the 1972 Academy Awards presentation. Perhaps because of the controversy surrounding him, the Academy had long ignored Chaplin's work, nominating not one of his features, except *The Great Dictator*, for Best Picture honors. (The film lost to *Rebecca*.) But now the Academy presented him with a special award for 'the incalculable effect he has had on making motion pictures the art form of this century.' In his enthusiastic reception by the US and in the award, was complete vindication for the humiliations he had once suffered at the hands of the nation. Five years later, the man who had done so much to lead filmed comedy out of its infancy and whose effect on it had been 'incalculable' was dead at age 88.

Aside from the fact that Chaplin was a genius, there was no secret to his success. He developed and then masterfully portrayed a many-faceted character with whom audiences could identify and for whom they could feel sympathy. It was the element that separated him from most of his Sennett colleagues. And it was the element that accounted for the success of his fellow greats of the period – Buster Keaton, Harold Lloyd and Laurel and Hardy.

Born Joseph Francis Keaton at Piqua, Kansas, in 1895, Buster Keaton spent his childhood doing a knockabout vaudeville act with his parents. Billed as 'The Human Mop' in a spectacular turn that saw his father energetically

One of America's great silent clowns, Buster Keaton, in *Go West*.

sweep the stage floor with him, Keaton was such an accomplished acrobat by age ten that many audiences suspected him to be a midget in disguise. As for the nickname, Buster, it was bestowed on him by Harry Houdini when the magician saw him, then just six months old, tumble down a boarding house stairway and emerge unharmed.

Keaton was a vaudeville headliner when, at age 21, he accepted an offer from Fatty Arbuckle to enter films. Starting with *The Butcher Boy* (1917), he worked with Arbuckle for two years, becoming so popular that a separate production company was established for him. Between 1920 and 1923, Keaton wrote, co-directed (with Edward Cline) and starred in a series of excellent shorts, among the most memorable of which were *One Week* (1920), *The Boat* (1921) and *The Electric House* (1922). From 1928 to 1933, first with his own unit and then with MGM, he concentrated solely on feature-length work, doing, in all, 20 pictures.

Keaton gave audiences a character of two sharply contrasted elements – the dignified young man whose face seemed

frozen in stone but whose body was capable of the most acrobatic of movements. But it must not be thought that Keaton's immobile face was incapable of expression. One of his greatest charms lay in the fact that he could convey the sharpest of emotional reactions with no more than the lift of an eyebrow or the slightest movement at the corner of the mouth. With that face and that elastic body, he created a singular character that couldn't help but fascinate.

Keaton loved knockabout comedy and, in the Sennett tradition, his pictures were laced with pretty girls and wild chases. But, in the tradition being developed by Chaplin and followed by Harold Lloyd, he was also pursuing new comedy themes, themes in which his character and a comic situation and not just a series of visual gags took precedence. For instance, in *One Week* he played a young husband who spends seven frustrating days trying to assemble a portable house from a kit and being thwarted at every step of the way. Working a variation on this theme, he spent his time in *The Boat* trying to launch and then sail a completely uncooperative sailboat.

Keaton's acrobatic skills brought another element to his films that fascinated audiences – his capacity for daredevil stunt work. It was work that he insisted on doing himself, always refusing a double, and at times it proved downright dangerous. For instance, in *The Boat*, he stood in quiet, stubborn dignity on the deck of the uncooperative 'Damfino' while it sank beneath him, taking him with it until only his hat remained floating on the surface of the water. In one of his best feature-length productions, *The General* (1926), he rode a locomotive's cowcatcher while struggling with a railroad tie. And for *Steamboat Bill, Jr* (1928), he designed one of the most suicidal stunts in screen history.

Here, he planned to stand in front of a house and then have the two-ton facade fall forward and crash down on top of him. All that would save him would be a small window opening in the upper story. The stunt required him to be perfectly positioned if he was not to be crushed to death and was so foolhardy in the minds of the director and half the crew that they walked off the set in protest. But Keaton went through with the stunt as planned. It remains today one of the most terrifying sequences ever put on film.

As fascinating as he had been in the 1920s, Keaton faded rapidly from popularity in the early 30s, in great part because of poor vehicles given him when he abandoned his own production unit and went to MGM, where he relinquished the artistic control of his pictures. He spent the remainder of his career in small parts, among them his role in Chaplin's *Limelight*. But respect for his early accomplishments never waned and when, in 1965, just two months before his death, Keaton appeared at the Venice Film Festival, that wonderfully sad face was greeted with the longest and most enthusiastic ovation ever awarded there.

Harold Lloyd, born at Burchard, Nebraska, in 1893, was the first of the era's great comedians to enter films. His debut came in 1912 when he worked as an Indian extra in an Edison western short. He next appeared in several comedies at Keystone and Universal, at the latter studio becoming close friends with a fellow hopeful, Hal Roach. When Roach, financed by a $3000 inheritance, launched his own studio in 1914, he starred Lloyd in a series of one-reelers about a lazy fellow named Willie Work. The character failed with audiences and the two tried another, a Chaplin imitation called Lonesome Luke. Luke's fate proved a happy one. Audiences liked him and he was starred in no fewer than 100 shorts within a year's time.

Despite his success, Luke pleased neither Lloyd nor Roach. In 1917, wanting something unique for his star, Roach came up with an idea for yet another character – a sincere, enthusiastic, noble-hearted young man. The complete antithesis of Chaplin's Tramp, he was to be neatly dressed in suit and tie and – Roach's final inspiration – was to wear a set of outsized, horn-rimmed spectacles. The character, in all, was to represent the ideal young American male, innocent, clean living and ambitious. The fellow was never given a name (Lloyd himself always referred to him as 'the glasses character'), but, painstakingly developed over the years in the hands of a skilled comedian, he became one of the era's most popular figures, with his pictures so appealing that they often outdrew Chaplin's at the box office.

Early on in 'the glasses character's' career, Lloyd and Roach began providing him with story lines similar to those being done by Chaplin, story lines in which the comedy was born not of gags but of character and situation. Lloyd's emphasis on character became so great at one point that Roach complained it was actually over-riding the comedy. If such was the case, audiences didn't seem to mind. A string of Lloyd one- and two-reelers proved so popular that in 1921 he and Roach graduated to full-length features and never returned again to shorts.

In addition to a well-rounded character, Lloyd brought another element to his work. Just as Keaton was a fine acrobat, Lloyd was a superb athlete and his skill here played a major part in his pictures. In common with Keaton's, Lloyd's films were always highlighted by daredevil sequences that demanded the utmost in physical daring and dexterity – the haphazard balancing on a building ledge in *High and Dizzy* (1920); the dash to save the heroine from marrying a bigamist in *Girl Shy* (1924), with Lloyd hopping from car to car in his effort to reach the church in the nick of time; the studio flood sequence that unloosed tons of water on him in *Movie Crazy* (1932) and, of course, that memorable climb up the face of a building and those genuinely hair-raising antics on the face of the building's clock in *Safety Last* (1924).

From 1923 on, having parted amicably with Roach, Lloyd produced his own pictures, at first with Pathé and then Paramount. Contrary to that of so many other stars of the 1920s, his popularity remained high in the early 30s, when his portrayals of innocence, smacking so much of the preceding decade, reminded Depression audiences of a happier day. He was, however, definitely going out of style by 1938 and he retired after making *Professor Beware* that year. He broke his retirement in 1946 for *The Sins of Harold Diddlebock* (reissued in 1950 as *Mad Wednesday*) and, in the 1960s, released two compilations of his early works. Lloyd, who received a special Academy Award in 1952 as 'a master comedian,' died in 1971 at age 77. As the award stated, he was, indeed, a master at his art, challenging and often surpassing Chaplin as the most popular comic figure of his era.

The motion picture has seen its share of comedy teams through the years, but the team acknowledged as the greatest and most beloved ever seen in the industry was Stan Laurel and Oliver Hardy. And, unlike the Marx Brothers of vaudeville and Broadway and Abbott and Costello of burlesque, it was a team created within the industry, with the birth presided over by director Leo McCarey.

Both Laurel and Hardy were in their mid-30s and were experienced solo performers when McCarey, sensing a magic when seeing them together, persuaded them to join forces. Laurel, born Arthur Stanley Jefferson, hailed from Ulverston, England, and, the son of acting parents, had been on stage in music halls and the legitimate theater since age 16. Understudying Charlie Chaplin, he came to the US with Fred Karno in both 1910 and 1912, leaving the troupe during the 1912 visit to strike out on his own in vaudeville. He changed his name to Stan Laurel, eventually made his way into films, worked in comedies (often writing his own material) for Universal, Vitagraph and Metro and at last signed on as a writer with Hal Roach.

Hardy, the son of an attorney, was born in Harlem, Georgia, and, possessing a good singing voice, was allowed to travel for a time as a child with a minstrel show. But his true entry into theatricals came when, managing a Georgia movie house in his late teens, he decided that he could make better pictures than the ones he was showing. Having so decided, he landed a job with a Philadelphia film-maker, went to New York to play villains in a string of one- and two-reelers (all blatant Chaplin imitations) and at last moved to California. He contracted as a performer with Roach in 1926 and soon thereafter met Laurel, with the two of them then taking McCarey's advice.

What was the magic that McCarey saw in the pair and that generations of moviegoers have seen in the years since 1926? It was a magic composed of several elements. First, there was the natur-

Opposite: Many think that the funniest film Keaton ever made was *The General* (1926). It was a Civil War story with Keaton stealing a railroad engine called 'The General.'

Left: Laurel and Hardy in *Babes in Toyland* (1934), an adaptation of the Victor Herbert fairy tale operetta.

Above: A typical Marx Brothers melee, from *Animal Crackers* (1930). Chico (left) and Harpo have it out while Groucho and Margaret Dumont look on.

Below: Groucho is being berated by Sig Rumann, while Chico and Harpo peep out between them in *A Night At The Opera* (1935). Margaret Dumont is stately as ever.

ally funny disparity in their physical appearances, the one stout, pompously graceful and (even in his moments of greatest anger and frustration) cherubic of face. The other was thin, gangingly clumsy and so innocent of face. But of far greater importance was the characterization that was combined in the two – the naivete and the downright stupidity that always managed to get them into no end of trouble and that invariably left audiences feeling superior to, amused by, and sorry for such bumbling specimens of humanity. On top of all else, there was the dignity of that combined characterization, a dignity that was constantly being reduced to a shambles, but a dignity that still somehow flew its proud banners in even the most ignominious of their moments.

Armed with their combined characterization – and spicing it with such, in time, classic gestures as Hardy's coy tie-fiddling and Laurel's stiff-fingered head-scratching – the team made over 100 highly successful shorts (both silent and sound) and 27 features in the years between 1926 and 1950. In their best work, they used not plots but just two basic situations that served as springboards for a mounting series of mishaps that finally ended in chaos. In the first, all the fun started when Laurel pulled some extraordinarily dumb stunt. The second involved a beginning minor incident that triggered a series of increasingly serious incidents that, in their turn, triggered the hilarious chaos that the audience knew full well most inevitably come.

In turn, *County Hospital* (1932) and *Big Business* (1929) serve as perfect examples of the two situations. In the first, the hospitalized Hardy, his broken leg encased in a massive plaster cast and held suspended in traction, is visited by Laurel. With his usual witlessness, Laurel manages to drop the weight controlling the traction cords out the window, with the result that he himself manages to fly through the window and hang, screaming and kicking, high above traffic while Hardy ends up dangling from the ceiling by his cast. In *Big Business,* they arrive as Christmas tree salesmen at the home of Jimmy Finlayson. The trouble begins when the short-tempered Finlayson catches a branch of the tree in his door and scissors the thing free. Ah, what an affront to the dignity of our two salesmen friends. Retaliation is demanded. The two cut Finlayson's tie. And, from there, things go steadily from bad to worse until the irate visitors are taking Finlayson's house apart a brick at a time and he is reducing their delivery car to ruins and the tree to kindling.

Though they were popular in their feature films – especially in such free-for-all pieces as *The Flying Deuces* (1939), which contained sequences that could have been refashioned into self-sustaining shorts – Laurel and Hardy were at their very best in their two-reelers. Those pictures were little gems in which they lovingly choreographed the steps that led to the traditional chaos, performing them with an economy that got the most comedy into the least amount of time. Laurel may have played the dumb (or dumber) one of the pair, but he is credited with being the brains behind their work. It was he who invented and wrote much of their best material.

After a solid run of 20 years, the twosome began to go out of style in the late 1940s. They made their last picture together in 1949 – a completely unfunny French-Italian piece called *Atoll K,* which was released in 1950 and which played in the US first as *Robinson Crusoe-Land* and then *Utopia.* On retiring from films, Laurel and Hardy did a highly successful British music hall tour and then, when television gave their work a fresh and enthusiastic audience, began planning a new series of films. Their plans ended abruptly with Hardy's death of a stroke in 1957. Throughout their association, the two men had been the closest of friends and the loss of Hardy devastated Laurel. He

vowed never to work in films again. It was a promise that, except for some comedy writing, he kept to the end of his own days in 1965.

By the 1930s, filmed comedy had become a well developed and highly diverse genre. Comic offerings of every stripe were available for the price of a ticket at the box office. The decade saw:

• *The baby-faced comedy of Harry Langdon.* A veteran of vaudeville, burlesque and the circus, Langdon came to films in the mid-20s, making such a hit in two-reelers as a child-like creature enduring life's travails that he was taken on by Warners for feature work. His first features established him as a major talent, with some critics announcing that he was destined to be Chaplin's successor. But, too much impressed with his success, Langdon took full artistic control of his subsequent pictures, a move that proved to be a fatal mistake. As impractical in his life as he was infantile on the screen, he badly mishandled the films and they turned out to be critical and financial disasters. Langdon returned to short subjects and never regained his status as a major star.

• *The inspired buffoonery of the Marx Brothers.* As a foursome – Groucho, Chico, Harpo, and Zeppo – they made their film debut in 1929,

Harpo and Chico play a couple of the worst spies in history and Louis Calhern is the wily ambassador of Sylvania to Fredonia in *Duck Soup* (1933).

starring in Paramount's *The Cocoanuts,* an adaptation of their Broadway success. In the Marx's adroit mixture of slapstick and (sometimes risqué) sophistication, moviegoers found something new and unique, and the brothers went on to the further riotous successes in Paramount's *Animal Crackers* (1930), *Monkey Business* (1931), *Horse Feathers* (1932) and *Duck Soup* (1933). Then, with their number reduced to three by Zeppo's retirement to become an agent, they moved to MGM for *A Night at the Opera* (1935), with its memorable sequence in the jam-packed ship's stateroom, and *A Day at the Races* (1937). MGM, however, not knowing how best to handle the Marx's brand of humor, then proceeded to give them such faltering vehicles as *At the Circus* (1939), *Go West* (1940) and *The Big Store* (1941). They retired on completing *The Big Store,* returned briefly for *A Night in Casablanca* (1946) and *Love Happy* (1949) and then limited themselves to solo appearances in features and shorts. Groucho eventually made a new career for himself as a television quizmaster.

• *The blustery doings of W C Fields,* a comedian whose work was especially suited to the sound era because it depended as much on his raspy voice and verbal pyrotechnics as on his visual antics. Fields made a few silents from 1915 onward and then appeared in the feature-length *Sally of the Sawdust* (1925), the filmed version of his Broadway hit, *Polly*. But his greatest successes came in the 1930s and at the dawn of the 40s – *Million Dollar Legs* (1932), *International House* (1933), *Mississippi* (1935), *Poppy* (1936), *You Can't Cheat an Honest Man* (1939), *My Little Chickadee* and *The Bank Dick* (both 1940). A master at portraying the pompous, grandiloquent charlatan, Fields is regarded to have turned in his finest characterization not in a comedy but a drama, when he portrayed Micawber in MGM's 1935 production of *David Copperfield*.

• *The screwball comedies.* Launched by the overwhelming success of director Frank Capra's *It Happened One Night* (1934) and subsequently given their name by the studio publicity departments, these were light-hearted offerings that depicted the blossoming of romance for attractive young couples under the most unorthodox and, at times, implausible circumstances. In *It Happened One Night,* newspaperman

Opposite: W C Fields in *You Can't Cheat an Honest Man* (1930). He played Larson E Whipsnade, the owner of a bankrupt circus always just one jump ahead of its creditors.

Above: In *My Little Chickadee* (1940), Fields teamed with Mae West, who had made a career out of being a female W C Fields.

Left: Many say that *The Bank Dick* (1940) was Field's best. He played the role of Egbert Sousé, who had a nagging mother-in-law, an unsympathetic wife and a brat of a daughter.

Above: In *You Can't Take It with You* (1938), James Stewart played the son of Edward Arnold (center), the stuffy businessman who is converted to happiness by members of a happy-go-lucky family who do exactly what they want to in life.

Below: Barbra Streisand and Ryan O'Neal in *What's Up, Doc?* (1972). She was a co-ed and he was an absent-minded professor.

Opposite: The beginning of the hitch-hiking scene in *It Happened One Night* (1934) with Clark Gable and Claudette Colbert. The film raked in the Oscars: best picture, best screenplay (Robert Riskin), best direction (Frank Capra), best female lead (Colbert), best male lead (Gable).

Clark Gable took runaway heiress Claudette Colbert on a cross-country journey back to her family and fell in love with her in the process. Carole Lombard, in *Nothing Sacred* (1937), quested after national publicity by posing as a young woman about to die, only to find herself in love with newsman Fredric March, who was working the story of her coming demise for all it was worth. Jean Arthur and James Stewart somehow fell in love in the midst of her family's happy anarchy and his father's greedy connivances in *You Can't Take it With You* (1938). A poetry writing, tuba playing Gary Cooper, up against forces who wanted to grab his wealth by proving him mentally incompetent in *Mr Deeds Goes to Town* (1936), won out when he proved to the court that it was quite all right to be a 'pixalated' free spirit.

The screwball comedies provided a welcome escapist break from the continuing Depression and remained highly popular throughout the 1930s. That popularity began to fade in the 40s, though such films as Cary Grant's *My Favorite Wife* (1940) and *The Bachelor and the Bobby Soxer* (1947) fared well at the box office, in all likelihood because of his personal appeal. Efforts were made in the 1950s and 70s to return the screwball offerings to vogue, in 1956

Above: Mickey Rooney and June Preisser in *Judge Hardy & Son* (1939), one of the many Andy Hardy films.

Below: Donna Reed got her break with Mickey in *The Courtship of Andy Hardy* (1942).

with the Jack Lemmon-June Allyson vehicle, *You Can't Run Away from It* (a remake of *It Happened One Night*) and with director Peter Bogdanovich's *What's Up, Doc?* (1972), starring Barbra Streisand. Both efforts went in vain. Straight romantic comedies such as *The Awful Truth* (1937) and *Holiday* (1938), however, continued to thrive and please throughout the years.

• *The family comedies.* These pictures were usually offered as series fare. The most popular of their number concerned the Hardy Family and the misadventures of son Andy Hardy, an energetic, naive and girl-shy teenager. The Hardys were launched in 1937 with a well budgeted MGM second feature, *A Family Affair,* in which Lionel Barrymore played the head of the household, Judge Hardy. The film proved so popular that the family was given a series and made 14 more pictures in the next ten years. Mickey Rooney worked throughout as Andy Hardy, while Lewis Stone appeared as the Judge, Fay Holden as the mother, Cecilia Parker as the daughter, and Ann Rutherford as Polly, the girl next door. 'Niceness' was the keynote of the Hardys' lives, so much so that some moviegoers found the going pretty sticky at times. But most audiences enjoyed the idealized depiction of the US home. The Hardys received a special Academy Award in

1942 for 'furthering the American way of life.' All the niceness, however, wouldn't dovetail with the bleak attitudes of the post-World War II era and the series went out of business after its 1947 offering, *Love Laughs at Andy Hardy.* An attempt to revive the pleasures of old was tried in 1958 with *Andy Hardy Comes Home,* featuring an adult Mickey Rooney. It failed.

Though the Hardy Family was the most popular of the series comedies, it was not the oldest. That honor goes to the Jones Family at 20th Century Fox. Featuring Jed Prouty as Father and Spring Byington as Mother, the Joneses got their start in a 1936 B feature, *Every Saturday Night.* They then proceeded to do 16 more films before their final effort, a mere four years later.

The honor, however, of being the busiest of the series must go to the Bumstead Family, which was based on Chic Young's popular cartoon strip, 'Blondie.' The pretty young housewife, in the person of Penny Singleton, broke into the movies in 1938, in a Columbia second feature, *Blondie.* The picture was such a hit that it was graduated immediately to series status, with Columbia then cranking out two 'Blondie' films per year for the next decade. Miss Singleton (formerly Dorothy McNulty) played the title role throughout and for a time took the character to radio. Arthur Lake, who had been in films since his youth, worked as the bumbling Dagwood while Larry Simms did Baby Dumpling (later Alexander) and Jonathan Hale performed as Dagwood's fiery boss, Mr Dithers. One of the choice bit parts in the industry was to be found in the series. Remember the postman who was always being knocked down as Dagwood made his ritualistic dash out the front door to work each morning? He was played by Irving Bacon.

Adding to the variety of comedy entertainment available in the 1930s were such performers as: Mae West with her blatant satires on sex in *She Done Him Wrong* and *I'm No Angel* (both 1933 and both featuring newcomer Cary Grant); Broadway veteran Will Rogers with his homespun humor in *State Fair* (1933) and *David Harum* (1934); writer Robert Benchley with his hilarious short-subject lectures on such earth-shaking topics as *How to Sleep* (which won 1935's Academy Award for Best Short Subject) and *The Romance of Digestion* (1937); Marie Dressler and Wallace Beery with their earthy humanity in *Min and Bill* (1930) and *Tugboat Annie* (1933); Joe E Brown with his masterful clowning in *Fireman, Save My Child* (1932) and *Alibi Ike* (1935); and, with their crude but popular slapstick, The Three Stooges,

Danny Kaye starred with Virginia Mayo in *The Kid from Brooklyn* (1946). It was a comedy about a milkman accidentally turned into a prizefighter.

who, after beginning their film work in 1934, made no fewer than 49 shorts before the end of the decade.

Variety continued to be the keynote of the genre from the 1940s onward. Straight romantic comedies – perhaps best exemplified by such widely spaced offerings as Katherine Hepburn's *The Philadelphia Story* (1940), Judy Holliday's *Born Yesterday* (1950) and Glenda Jackson's *House Calls* (1979) – were on hand to please. So were the character comedies. Ranking high among them were the Walter Matthau-George Burns delight, *The Sunshine Boys* (1975) and those Matthau-Jack Lemmon treats, *The Fortune Cookie* (1966), *The Odd Couple* (1968) and the very off-beat *Buddy Buddy* (1981). All such films as these were perfomed by players who were not exclusively comedians but all-around actors who were equally adept at comedy and drama.

Whimsy was well represented by Danny Kaye's masterfully done *The Secret Life of Walter Mitty* (1947) and *On the Double* (1961), by James Stewart's *Harvey* (1950), by *The Russians are Coming, the Russians are Coming* (1966) and by George Burns' *Oh God!* (1977). Family comedy was handled by Doris Day and David Niven in *Please Don't Eat the Daisies* (1960), by Stewart in *Mr Hobbs Takes a Vacation* (1962)

and *Dear Brigette* (1965), by Lucille Ball and Henry Fonda in *Yours Mine and Ours* (1968) and, years earlier, by Claudette Colbert and Fred MacMurray in *The Egg and I* (1947), the film that introduced Percy Kilbride and Marjorie Main as Ma and Pa Kettle. In what was possibly the most unusual family series ever filmed, Kilbride and Main, between 1949 and 1958, did nine pictures together as the earthy, conniving leaders of the boisterous Kettle clan.

Pure clowning was handled by Red Skelton in a career that, extending from 1938 to 1965, saw such mugging masterpieces as *A Southern Yankee* (1948) and *The Yellow Cab Man* (1950). That premiere female clown, Lucille Ball, did *The Fuller Brush Girl* (1950) and *The Long Long Trailer* (1951) and then went on to her greatest successes on television. One-liner fun was provided by Bob Hope, who quickly established himself as the wisecracking and often frightened bumbler who somehow always

Above: Bing Crosby, Dorothy Lamour and Bob Hope in *The Road to Zanzibar* (1941). Bob and Bing are circus performers looking for a diamond mine in the jungle.

Below: In *The Road to Utopia* (1945), the trio are in the Klondike in search of an Alaskan gold mine. Dorothy Lamour sang the hit song 'Personality.'

manages to win the beautiful girl, and then played the character to the hilt in *The Cat and the Canary* (1939), *My Favorite Brunette* (1947), and *The Paleface* (1948). His most popular work, however, was done in the seven *Road* pictures with Bing Crosby, pictures that began with the *Road to Singapore* (1940) and ended more than two decades later with *Road to Hong Kong* (1962). All were spiced with singing, dancing and the pair's classic hand-clapping routine before starting to take punches at their screen adversaries. In his later years, becoming as much a national institution as Crosby, Hope turned to seriocomic work and earned critical praise for his *Seven Little Foys* (1955) and *Beau James* (1957).

Slapstick remained on the scene, so raucously done, on the one hand by Dean Martin and Jerry Lewis in *That's My Boy* (1951) and *Jumping Jacks* (1952), but so delicately offered, on the other, by France's Jacques Tati as he sat, dignified and helpless, while his canoe folded up in the middle in *Le Vacances de Monsieur Hulot/Monsieur Hulot's Holiday* (1953). Abbott and Costello, making the most of time-honored burlesque routines, got a fine start in *Buck Privates* (1941) and then bounced and slapped their way through a 15-year career that eventually saw them chased hither and yon by every odd screen creation from Frankenstein's Monster to the Keystone Kops. The Three Stooges continued to crank out their pratfall and poke-in-the-eye two-reelers, making, in all, 149 shorts from 1940 through their final year, 1959. Then there was the slapstick picture meant to end all slapstick pictures – director Stanley Kramer's *It's a Mad, Mad, Mad, Mad World* (1963). And, finally, the altogether crude and altogether funny *National Lampoon's Animal House* (1978).

Over the years, the familiar and traditional themes were joined by new ones or were approached in new ways that gave them an extra dimension. Katharine Hepburn and Spencer Tracy added a realistic touch to the age-old 'battle of the sexes' theme in *Woman of the Year* (1940), *Adam's Rib* (1949) and *The Desk Set* (1957). Romance was given a new twist when Miss Hepburn matched her spinster primness against an unshaven, slovenly Humphrey Bogart in *The African Queen* (1952). Political life came in for a kidding when she and Tracy did *State of the Union* (1949), as it did when William Powell cavorted through *The Senator was Indiscreet* (1947) and deadpan Bob Newhart greeted the White House in *The First Family* (1980). Westerns were roundly spoofed in *Cat Ballou* (1965) and *Blazing Saddles* (1974).

Even such a comically hazardous sub-

Above: The Three Stooges in one of their short comedies. Left to right: Jerry (Curly) Howard, Larry Fine, Moe Howard.

Below: Terry-Thomas prepares to fight Milton Berle in *It's a Mad, Mad, Mad, Mad World* (1963).

Above: John Belushi in *National Lampoon's Animal House* (1978). He played the ultimate slob.

ject as crime received its share of attention. Making light of unlawful shenanigans were such films as *Topkapi* (1964), *The Hot Rock* (1972) and *Murder by Death* (1976). But the best work in the area undoubtedly came from Britain. Over the years, British studios turned out *Kind Hearts and Coronets* (1949) and *The Lavender Hill Mob* (1951), both with excellent Alec Guinness performances; *Two-Way Stretch* (1960) and *The Wrong Arm of the Law* (1963), both starring Peter Sellers; and Terry-Thomas' *Make Mine Mink* (1960), And, of course, the list must include Peter Ustinov's *Hot Millions* (1968) with its hilarious sequence featuring a stylishly dressed Cesar Romero as a Brazilian customs inspector who, insulted to the core, refuses to allow a bottle of coffee crystals into his country but then joyously welcomes Ustinov and $1 million in absconded corporate funds.

For Americans, the most interesting of the new comic themes had to be sex. For years, while Europe had been tickled by the likes of Britain's *29 Acacia Avenue* (1945) and *Captain's Paradise* (1953), US audiences had, thanks to the Hays Production Code and the Legion of Decency, put up with some of the silliest prohibitions ever devised for sexually accented material. But the situation began to change in 1952 with the filmed version of the F Hugh Herbert play, *The Moon is Blue*. The producers defied the censors and had the nerve to leave in in the script such words as 'mistress,' 'virgin' and 'seduction' and then to make a thorough joke of them. In the light of much current film fare, *The Moon is Blue* ranks as pretty tame stuff, but, in its day, it created a national sensation, earning, in equal parts, public delight and shock. But the delight won out, with the picture doing such a box office business that the taboos of old were

Top: One of the great comedy teams, Spencer Tracy and Katharine Hepburn, in *Woman of the Year* (1941), a film about the marriage of a nonchalant sports writer and a charming international reporter.

Above: Hepburn with Humphrey Bogart in *The African Queen* (1952), the story of a romance between a rough and sloppy captain of an African river boat and a prim, refined lady.

Right: Gene Wilder (left) and Cleavon Little in *Blazing Saddles* (1974), Mel Brooks' wildly funny spoof of Western movies.

Above: Detective Peter Ustinov (center) and his friend David Niven question Bette Davis about what she might know concerning the murder of the richest girl in the world in Agatha Christie's *Death on the Nile* (1978).

Left: Peter Sellers (left) and Bernard Cribbins starred in *The Wrong Arm of the Law* (1962) – a crime film spoof about a very complicated robbery.

fated to be soon dropped. Welcoming such imports as Britain's *Only Two can Play* and Italy's *Divorce Italian Style* (both 1962), the US began to widen its own sexual horizons with *The Seven-Year Itch* (1955), *Wives and Lovers* (1963), *The Graduate* (1967), *Plaza Suite* (1971) and *Private Benjamin* (1980), and with a string of those sophomoric Doris Day features in which she so adroitly played the eternal virgin hoping for – and eventually getting – something better. The best of them were *Pillow Talk* (1959) and *That Touch of Mink* (1962).

From its very beginnings, filmed comedy has brought audiences new talents with each decade. The tradition was born in the teen years with Chaplin, Mabel Normand, Marie Dressler and Fatty Arbuckle. It continued in the 1920s with Keaton, Laurel and Hardy, Lloyd and Harry Langdon; in the 1930s with Fields, Burns and Allen, The Marx Brothers and Joe E Brown; in the 1940s with Hope, Skelton, Kaye and Abbott and Costello; and in the 1950s with Martin and Lewis, Ball, and the first work of that master comedian-character actor, Peter Sellers.

The tradition continues to this day. The 1960s and 70s have seen the arrival of such diverse talents as the innocent and sometimes befuddled Gene Wilder; the anything-from-frantic-to-gentle Dom DeLuise; the street-wise but still timid Richard Pryor; the brooding, satirical and self-effacing humor of Woody Allen; the outright comic madness of Mel Brooks; the crude presence of John Belushi in *1941* (1979) and *The Blues Brothers* (1980), but of such greater depth and refinement in the last film made before his death, *The Neighbors*

Opposite: Marilyn Monroe rehearses for the famous skirt-blowing scene in *The Seven Year Itch* (1955). She was cast as a sexy model who lived in the same apartment building as a married man (Tom Ewell) whose wife is on a summer vacation. Many say it was Monroe's best role.

Top: Goldie Hawn as *Private Benjamin* (1980).

Left: Margaret Rutherford as Miss Marple, Agatha Christie's aged lady detective, in *Murder Most Foul* (1965).

Above: Jerry Lewis (center) and Dean Martin (right), starred in *At War With the Army* (1950). Mike Kellin is at left. This film shot the team to fame.

Below: Martin and Lewis in *Sailor Beware* (1951). The picture was a vague remake of the 1942 Dorothy Lamour, William Holden, Betty Hutton film, *The Fleet's In*.

(1982). And, representing the distaff side, there is Goldie Hawn and her brilliant charcterizations of the free – but underneath it all, sensible – spirit.

There can be little argument that the major comic talents of the early 1980s belong to Woody Allen, Mel Brooks and Goldie Hawn. Had Belushi lived and had he continued to develop as his pictures indicated, he might have turned the trio into a foursome.

With a *Midsummer Night's Sex Dream* (1982), Allen continues to provide the ever-deepening sardonic, wildly funny, and yet thoughtful humor that was seen in *Play It Again, Sam* (1972), *Sleeper* (1973), *The Front* (1976), *Annie Hall* (1977), *Manhattan* (1979) and *Stardust Memories* (1980). More comedy as wild as *Blazing Saddles* (1974), *Silent Movie* (1976) and *High Anxiety* (1977) can be anticipated from the fertile imagination of Mel Brooks. And Miss Hawn, who has consistently broadened her scope with each film – steadily maturing her characterizations as she went from *Cactus Flower* (1969) to *The Girl from Petrovka* (1974) to *Foul Play* (1978) – can only be expected to surpass herself.

And who will join the threesome as the 1980s develop? Comedy being what it is, it can only be fun to sit and watch and wait for the answer.

THE NAVY NEEDS MEN

Above: Diane Keaton and Woody Allen in *Annie Hall* (1977). The film was directed and co-authored by Allen. In the picture he has been in analysis for 15 years when he falls in love with the beguiling Keaton.

Left: A romantic boat ride is unpleasantly interrupted for Isaac Davis (Woody Allen) and Mary Wilke (Diane Keaton) in *Manhattan* (1979).

OF NO LESSER IMPORTANCE

This chapter brings us to the secondary genre. In no way, however, is the designation meant to suggest a lack of quality in their work, the fact being that many of the films emerging from them over the years have been among the most impressive and significant ever produced. Rather, this book has been constructed to give the most space to the busiest and, therefore, the largest of the film categories and so the secondary genre are secondary only in that they have been less active. We'll consider them now in alphabetical order.

CRIME

Crime holds a dual position in film history. It is, first, a subject that can be, and is, employed in so many other categories – the good guy-bad guy arrangement in westerns obviously involves a crime much of the time, as do the mad doctor antics in so many science fiction pieces – and, second, as a genre itself, it is among the oldest in films. One of the earliest of its US examples dates back to 1913 – *Traffic in Souls*. Told here is the story of a young New York City woman who tracks down the leaders of the vice

ring that shanghaied her sister into white slavery.

The picture did a land office business in its day, principally because of public fascination with the investigations then being conducted by New York officials into enforced prostitution in their state. Any genre can take advantage of headline-grabbing circumstances, but crime, due to the nature of so much of the news in any era, has always been in the best postion to do so and has acted accordingly throughout the years. Germany's superb *M* (1931), directed by Fritz Lang and starring Peter Lorre, was inspired by a Düsseldorf murder. In the 1950s, the Brinks armored car hold-up in Boston resulted in such pictures as Tony Curtis' *Six Bridges to Cross* (1955). As late as 1979, Britain was still recalling the most daring of its railway robberies in Sean Connery's *The Great Train Robbery*. And, in the best known of all instances, the Prohibition years in the US, fostering the gangland element that they did, were responsible for the greatest popularity ever realized by the genre.

That popularity began to take shape in 1927 with director Josef von Sternberg's *Underworld* (British title: *Paying the Penalty*), starring George Bancroft as a Chicago mobster sent to

Pages 191-92: The helicopters come in in Francis Ford Coppola's *Apocalypse Now* (1979).

Above: Edward G Robinson (second from right) played a merciless killer in *Little Caesar* (1930).

prison for killing a rival. It was furthered by *Lights of New York* (1928), a crudish piece that is of historical note only for the fact that it was America's first all-talking picture, and furthered still by James Cagney's second film, *Doorway to Hell* and Edward G Robinson's *Outside the Law* (both 1930). Full public embrace came a year later, with Warners' 1931 release of *Little Caesar* and *The Public Enemy*. These films marked the start of the 'gangster cycle' that saw 1930s audiences become more than well acquainted with ruthless hoodlums and such underworld jargon (real or dreamed up in the writers' building) as 'gats,' 'typewriters,' 'tommy guns,' and 'molls.'

Starring Robinson and Cagney respectively, *Little Caesar* and *The Public Enemy* told the stories of the rise to power of two young hoodlums and then their fall. At base, both films were rather ordinary offerings, with the ascent to

power of each man taken in predictable steps. But both were compelling – and still are when seen today – in that they told their stories in straight-forward and economical manners and were marked by excellent performances from their two stars. Robinson fashioned in Cesare Bandello a cold, ignorant and merciless killer so driven by the desire for power that *The New York Times* likened the character to a figure in Greek tragedy. Cagney made of Tom Powers a cocky, vicious thug who nevertheless, at the core, was a troubled human being with a strong sense of personal honor.

In the light of the blood baths to be so lovingly staged in their every gory detail in such later productions as *Bonnie and Clyde* (1968) and *The Godfather* (1972), *The Public Enemy* is very interesting for its lack of visual violence. The film is punctuated by killings, but only one – the gunning down in the street of Cagney's best friend (Edward Woods) – is actually seen by the audience. An early killing takes place in the dark and is marked only by flashes of gunfire. In another sequence, Cagney draws a gun and prepares to kill a double-crossing friend while the friend desperately tries to distract him by playing the piano; in the instant before Cagney

Above: James Cagney demonstrates his disapproval of Mae Clarke, in a scene from *The Public Enemy* (1931) that no one ever forgot.

Below: Michael J Pollard doing some dirty work. He played one of the henchmen for Warren Beatty and Faye Dunaway in *Bonnie and Clyde* (1967).

The Corteleone family from *The Godfather* (1972). Left to right: Al Pacino, Marlon Brando (the Godfather), James Caan, John Cazale.

pulls the trigger, the camera moves across the room to where Edward Woods stands watching, with the shots then being heard by the audience while the death is reflected in Woods' face. Cagney's own end comes when, seeking revenge for Woods' murder, he slaughters a rival gang during a restaurant meeting. The camera watches him enter the restaurant and then remains out on the street while the audience listens to the rattle of gunfire inside. A moment later, the mortally wounded Cagney reappears and staggers along the street, at last collapsing in the gutter. In all, the picture's greatest visual violence comes in that now famous scene in which Cagney pushes a grapefruit into Mae Clarke's face.

Both *Little Caesar* and *The Public Enemy*, like their predecessors, outraged some US religious and civic groups, among them The Daughters of the American Revolution and The American Legion. But, despite being castigated for focusing on 'an American shame,' the studios nurtured the gangland cycle, knowing full well from box office receipts that the dissenters were in the minority. While Cagney turned to other roles for a time – wisecracking newsmen and race car drivers – Robinson went on to make the strange *The Hatchet Man* (1932), an underworld story centering on Chinese tong wars, and *The Little Giant* (1933). Paul Muni did *Scarface* in 1933; loosely based on the career of Chicago racketeer Al Capone, the film established George Raft's life-long image as an expressionless, coin-flipping thug. Raft himself did *Quick Millions* (1931) and *Limehouse Blues* (1934). Humphrey Bogart won critical acclaim for his re-creation of his stage role as escaped killer Duke Mantee in *The Petrified Forest* (1934) and then played supporting hoodlum roles until he won full stardom in 1941 as aging and doomed Roy Earle in *High Sierra* and hard-talking private detective Sam Spade in *The Maltese Falcon*.

By 1935, however, the cycle was beginning to die of over-exposure. Warners breathed new life into it – and simultaneously quieted some of the continuing pressure-group outcries – by shifting the accent from the criminal to the lawman. The studio turned Cagney into a racket-busting federal agent in *G-Men* (1935). Robinson became a law professor waging a one-man war against the underworld in *I am the Law* (1938). In turn, Paramount's Fred Mac-Murray played a heroic policeman in *Car 99* and a federal undercover agent in *Men Without Names* (both 1935).

These are some of the earliest examples of a very distinct branch sprouted by the crime genre, the police film. In them, the policeman was always pretty much visualized as an outright hero. Later years rendered him more human and brought his problems, fears and failings as an individual to the forefront. He became distinctly human in Britain's beautifully understated *The Blue Lamp* (1950), in Italy's *Indagine su un Cittadino al di sopra di orni Sospetto/ Investigation of a Citizen Above Suspicion* (1970) and in America's *Detective Story* (1951), *The Laughing Policeman* (1973) and the adaptation of the Joseph Wambaugh novels, *The New Centurians* (1972) and *The Onion Field* (1979).

Warners also tried, successfully, other measures to keep the 1930s cycle alive. It made light of gangland problems in such comedy fare as Edward G Robinson's *The Whole Town's Talking* (1935), *Bullets or Ballots* (1936) and *Brother Orchid* (1940). The first of the three cast him as a timid band clerk who is a mobster's double; the second, as a gangster trying his hand at politics; and the third, as a racketeer who, fleeing his enemies, takes refuge in a monastery and then proceeds to be touched by the peace and moral values found there. The studios also turned out two highly budgeted Cagney prison melodramas that emphasized how much crime doesn't pay – *Angels with Dirty Faces* (1938) and *Each Dawn I Die* (1939).

The mention of the two Cagney films brings us to yet another branch sprouted by the genre. Prison pictures enjoyed a cycle in the 1930s along with the gangster pieces, their chief representatives being *The Big House* (1930), *20,000 Years in Sing Sing* (1932), *The Last Mile* (1932), *San Quentin* (1938), *Invisible Stripes* (1939) and the Paul Muni classic that was as much a social comment as a drama, *I am a Fugitive from a Chain Gang* (1932). Prison material went out of fashion in the early 1940s, but returned late in the decade with Burt Lancaster's hard-bitten *Brute Force* (1947). Since then, each decade has seen a steady flow (but never a flood) of products from the category – *Riot in Cell Block 11* (1954), *Behind the High Wall* (1956), Lancaster's superior and factual *Bird Man of Alcatraz* (1962), the suspenseful US-Spanish production, *The Ceremony* (1964) and

Above: Left to right: Jerome Cowan, Mary Astor and Humphrey Bogart in *The Maltese Falcon* (1941).

Left: Burt Lancaster as the *Bird Man of Alcatraz* (1962) – the semi-true story of convict Robert Stroud, who became an expert on bird life while serving time for murder.

Clint Eastwood's taut *Escape from Alcatraz*. Like *Bird Man of Alcatraz*, which tells the story of convict ornithologist Robert Stroud, *Escape* is based in fact. It concerns a break from the San Francisco Bay facility in 1962, one that may have been successful because the prisoners were never located again. If so, it was the only successful escape in the history of the island prison.

The last gangster film of the 1930s was *The Roaring Twenties* (1939), a Cagney vehicle that drew a grim picture of the Prohibition era and that was far more visually violent than *The Public Enemy* eight years earlier. Tyrone Power followed with *Johnny Apollo* in 1940, but the cycle definitely ended on America's entry into World War II, with the real violence of warfare taking the place of the let's pretend violence of the screen gangsters. Alan Ladd won stardom in the well received *This Gun for Hire* (1942); it was not, however, a gangster film but a psychological study of professional killer. James Cagney, after working in a variety of other roles, returned in 1949 with one of his finest bad-guy portrayals, the psychopathic killer in *White Heat,* and then gave gangsterism a brief shot in the arm with *Kiss Tomorrow Goodbye* (1950).

Despite Cagney's efforts, gangsters received little attention in the 1950s. The decade concentrated on other areas

Above: Frank McHugh pours some bathtub gin for James Cagney in *The Roaring Twenties* (1939). It was a saga of the Prohibition Era, with its gang wars and speakeasies.

Right: James Cagney holds a gun on Edmond O'Brien in *White Heat* (1949) – a gangster drama with Cagney as a heartless killer.

of crime, following up on one of the best efforts ever made in this direction, Italy's 1948 triumph, *Ladri di Biciclette/Bicycle Thieves* (US title: *The Bicycle Thief*), a sensitive depiction of the effects that such a simple matter as a bicycle theft can have on a poverty-stricken family. *The Asphalt Jungle* (1950) looked at the subject of high stakes burglary and, in Sterling Hayden's character, drew a memorable portrait of a third-rate hoodlum. Japan's impressive *Rashomon* (1950), directed by Akira Kurosawa, dealt with a murder and rape as recalled by four people. *On the Waterfront* (1954) came close to gangsterism when it dealt with racketeering on New York's waterfront, but concentrated quite as much on the characterizations of its ill-fated people. France's *Rififi* (1954) centered on the tensions within a band of robbers.

The 1960s saw something of a return to the gangsterism of old. But the accent was now on specific criminals and specific incidents. Ray Danton opened the decade with the fast-paced *The Rise and Fall of Legs Diamond* (1960). Racketeer Arnold Rothstein was the subject of David Janssen's *King of the Roaring Twenties* (1961). Jason Robards and George Segal restaged *The Valentine's Day Massacre* (1967). Warren Beatty and Faye Dunaway joined forces for *Bonnie and Clyde* (1967), the most suc-

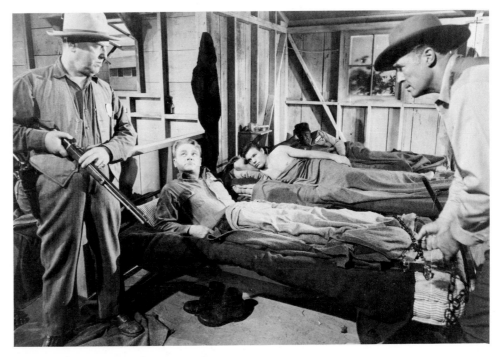

Above: Cagney played a convict in *Kiss Tomorrow Goodbye* (1950). At left is the warden, William Frawley. In the bunk next to Cagney is Neville Brand.

Below: *The Bicycle Thief* (1949). This was the tragic story of a poor man whose bicycle is stolen and his search through Rome with his small son to find the thief.

cessful crime film of the decade. The trend continued into the 1970s with *Dillinger* (1973) and *Capone* (1975), starring, respectively, Warren Oates and Ben Gazzara in the title roles.

The late 1960s and early 70s saw an interest in the doings of the Mafia, in Kirk Douglas' *The Brotherhood* (1968), in Charles Bronson's French-Italian *The Valachi Papers* (1972) and in what may be the two most successful gangland films ever made – director Francis Ford Coppola's *The Godfather* (1972) and *The Godfather, Part II* (1974). The 1970s also gave audiences Britain's moody *Get Carter* (1971), America's violent *The French Connection* (1971), and the French-Italian *Borsalino* (1970), a nostalgic return to the US gangland offerings of the 1930s. Great Britain opened the 1980s with the highly successful *The Long Good Friday*.

Above: Michael Caine (standing) was the star of *Get Carter* (1971). Caine is a cheap hood who returns home to investigate his brother's death. It was one of his best performances.

Right: A robbery scene from *Borsalino* (1970), a French tribute to the Hollywood gangster films of the 1930s.

Below: Detective Jimmy 'Popeye' Doyle (Gene Hackman) runs for cover after being shot at by a sniper in *The French Connection* (1971).

DISASTER

If we can exclude from it all the destruction done by the likes of Godzilla and his fellow science fiction creatures, we come here to what is certainly, in total number of films produced, the smallest of the genre. But, considering the audience response granted those few films, it is also one of the most profitable of all the film categories.

Disaster films, though Italy tried one as early as 1908 with its *Gli Ultima Giorni di Pompeii/The Last Days of Pompeii*, did not really get their start until the mid-1930s, when the state of the art in Hollywood's special effects departments made wholesale destruction at last possible. Then awed moviegoers were treated to one calamity per year for the remainder of the decade. Vesuvius erupted and buried everyone under tons of ash and collapsing buildings in *The Last Days of Pompeii* (1935). Earthquake and fire leveled *San Francisco* (1936). A monstrous storm swept a South Sea island paradise bare in *Hurricane* (1937). Mrs O'Leary's cow kicked over a lantern and triggered a city-wide conflagration in *In Old Chicago* (1938). A monsoon flooded an Indian province in *The Rains Came* (1939).

The genre went into a hiatus in the early 1940s when the world was treated to the genuine calamity of World War II. But disaster films were revived in the 1950s with two films centered on the most famous maritime tragedy in history – Hollywood's *Titanic* (1952) and Britain's far superior and almost documentary *A Night to Remember* (1958). The decade also produced Britain's thought-provoking *Seven Waves Away* (1957; US title: *Abandon Ship*). Starring Tyrone Power and based on a true incident, it told the story of a ship's officer who, after a luxury liner has gone to the bottom, is forced to decide which of the survivors must be sacrificed if an overcrowded lifeboat is not to sink. In theme alone, it stands as possibly the best disaster film ever made.

The 1960s were relatively quiet, their principal offerings being *The Last Voyage* (1961), *The Devil at 4 O'Clock* (1961) and *Krakatoa – East of Java* (1968). *The Last Voyage*, telling the story of a husband's desperate efforts to free his wife after a shipboard explosion has trapped her in their stateroom, was suspenseful throughout and was highlighted by superb climactic scenes of the ship sinking beneath them. Both *The Devil* and *Krakatoa* featured excellent volcanic eruptions, with the former also

The *Titanic* goes down in *A Night to Remember* (1958) – a documentarylike retelling of the fateful maiden voyage of the vessel.

receiving fine character performances from Spencer Tracy and Frank Sinatra. *Krakatoa*'s title caused a national laugh when, after all the film's publicity had been released, geographers pointed out that the island lay to the west of Java. Alfred Hitchcock's *The Birds* (1963), though primarily a suspense yarn, should likely be included among the decade's disaster offerings because of its excellent attack sequences, among them the one that ends with a dock area burning.

Due greatly to Irwin Allen, a television and documentary producer whose *Sea Around Us* had won a special Academy Award in 1953, the genre enjoyed its greatest popularity in the 70s. Allen started with *The Poseidon Adventure* (1972), fascinating moviegoers with the special effects of the ship capsizing (not to mention the spectacular stunt and crowd work in the overturn-

Right: A scene from *Krakatoa – East of Java* (1969), originally titled *Volcano*. Maximilian Schell (center) aboard his boat.

Below: Israeli commando Robert Shaw arrives at the launching pad too late to prevent a blimp from being hi-jacked by terrorists in *Black Sunday* (1977).

ing dining area) and with the subsequent scenes of the survivors working their way out of an upside-down world. Next came *The Towering Inferno* (1974), this time featuring exciting fire sequences and the hair-raising trip of an outside elevator down the face of the burning skyscraper. From there, Allen went to *Beyond the Poseidon Adventure* and *The Day the World Ended*. Both were done in 1979 and, though entertaining, did not match his previous work.

Other standout disaster films of the decade were Burt Lancaster's *Airport* (1970), Charlton Heston's *Earthquake* (1974), *Jaws* (1975), *The Hindenburg* (1975), Heston and David Jansen's *Two-Minute Warning* (1976) and Bruce Dern's *Black Sunday* (1977) with its implausible but nevertheless exciting plot of a blimp attacking the Super Bowl football game for the purpose of exploding and killing the President of the United States. The first of their number, *Airport*, featuring a fine cast that included Helen Hayes and Van Heflin, was a tense and highly entertaining picture that spawned two sequels – *Airport 1975* (1974) and *Airport 77* (1977). neither matched the story quality of the parent. *Airport 1975* dealt with an airliner left without a pilot when the captain is injured and saw Heston, in what was likely the most derring-do moment of his career, make a mid-air transfer to the troubled plane. *Airport 77*, which could not be faulted for its special effects, trapped Jack Lemmon and an all-star cast beneath the waves when their aircraft went down at sea.

But, thanks to the sequels, the decade ended on a happily insane note with *Airplane* (1979), an altogether funny spoof of the *Airport* films. The early 1980s brought a well deserved sequel, *Airplane II*.

Above: The most famous scene in *The Poseidon Adventure* (1972). The ship is upside-down, and a body crashes through the dining room skylight.

Left: Los Angeles is being destroyed in *Earthquake* (1974).

Audrey Hepburn played a terrified blind woman in *Wait Until Dark* (1967).

MYSTERY-SUSPENSE

The mystery-suspense genre has been with us since the earliest days of filmed story telling. In all that time, it has dealt with just two questions: If the villain is unknown, who is he and how will he be unmasked? And, whether he be known and unknown, how will the protagonists foil his dastardly plots and feed him his just desserts? Though only two, the questions have been more than enough on which to build a genre. When cleverly asked and answered – and when such assorted villains as murderers, master spies, arch fiends, unseen evil and malignant psychological forces are well used – they've never failed to please.

Mystery and suspense have worked together in many films, from such teen-years serials as *The Perils of Pauline* (1914) and such 20s features as *The Cat and the Canary* (1927) to Alfred Hitchcock's *The 39 Steps* (1935) and Audrey Hepburn's chilling *Wait Until Dark* (1967). But, over the years, their tendency has been more to divide themselves into separate categories, with the division based on the emphasis given the genre's two questions. The mystery

has concentrated primarily on the unknown villain and his unmasking while suspense has attended to getting the protagonists out of whatever mess the villain or circumstances have gotten them into. Let's look at each category in turn.

Though Sherlock Holmes appeared on the film scene as early as 1903 and was joined there by France's chivalrous Arsene Lupin in 1917, the mystery did not blossom as a full category until the coming of the 30s. Made available then was the sound needed for the voicing of the protagonist's deductions and for those slips of the tongue that let him identify 'whodunit' from among all the suspects. Strongly established at the time was a trend that has continued to this day. Detectives, amateur and professional, were needed to sniff out the murderer. They abounded in popular literature. Producers immediately hired them on.

Along with Holmes and Lupin, Charlie Chan was one of the first detectives to be transferred from literature to the screen. The creation of Earl Derr Biggers, the rotund Oriental sleuth, with his always more-than-adequate supply of wise sayings, made his film debut in 1926, in a serial starring George Kumo. In 1931, he was handed to Swedish actor Warner Oland, who then portrayed him

in 16 films over the seven-year period before Oland's death in 1938. The role then went, in turn, to Sidney Toler (1938-1947) and Roland Winters (1948-1952). Between them, Toler and Winters did 28 Chan films, all of them B products, before the character was finally dropped in 1952. Charlie, in his customary white suit and panama hat, was revived in 1957 for a 39-episode television series with J Carroll Naish.

Though always an audience pleaser – especially in the Oland period when the pictures were given their best budgets – Chan had to take a back seat to Dashiell Hammett's Nick and Nora Charles so far as popularity was concerned. The central characters in Hammett's 1934 novel, *The Thin Man,* they came to the screen that same year in the persons of William Powell and Myrna Loy. Perfectly matched and exuding a boozey worldliness, Powell and Loy gave the picture a touch of the then-popular screwball comedies and quite thoroughly charmed audiences everywhere. Publicized as the 'screen's perfect married couple' – and critically applauded for being the first acting team ever to portray a sophisticated and affectionate marriage on film – the two went on to five sequels: *After the Thin Man* (1937), *Another Thin Man* (1939), *Shadow of the Thin Man* (1942), *The Thin Man*

Below: William Powell (center) played Nick Charles in *The Thin Man* (1933).

Goes Home (1944) and *Song of the Thin Man* (1946). It's interesting to note that, though audiences always believed that the 'Thin Man' tag belonged to Powell, it actually referred to the murderer's victim in the novel.

Surrounding Mr and Mrs Charles in the 1930s and 40s were such other luminaries from the pages of crime fiction as: *Philo Vance,* played for a time by Powell himself and then taken over by Warren William; *Perry Mason,* handled by William after completing his Vance chores; *Bulldog Drummond,* Ronald Colman and then John Howard; *Ellery Queen,* Ralph Bellamy and William Gargan; *The Falcon,* George Sanders and his brother, Tom Conway; *Hildegarde Withers,* Edna May Oliver; *Nick Carter,* Walter Pidgeon; *Boston Blackie,* Chester Morris; *The Saint,* Louis Hayward; *Mike Shayne,* Lloyd Nolan; and *Sherlock Holmes,* Basil Rathbone.

Great Britain was quite as busy with its sleuths from literature. In 1931, Agatha Christie's Hercule Poirot made his film debut in *Alibi,* starring Austin Trevor as the little Belgian of the active 'gray cells.' The exploits of such characters as The Toff and Alastair Sim's Inspector Hornleigh soon followed. And, of course, Sherlock Holmes was quite busy, portrayed through the 1930s by Raymond Massey (*The Speckled Band,*

Right: Basil Rathbone – everyone's favorite Sherlock Holmes – in *The Adventures of Sherlock Holmes* (1939).

Opposite: Humphrey Bogart and Lauren Bacall in *The Big Sleep* (1946), one of the many Philip Marlowe detective dramas.

1931), Robert Rendel (*The Hound of the Baskervilles,* 1932), and the actor said to be the perfect embodiment of the character, Arthur Wontner. Wontner did five Holmes' films between 1931 and 1937.

Unquestionably, of all the fictional detectives, Sherlock Holmes has led the busiest screen life. Since his debut in a series of US one-reelers cranked out between 1903 and 1908, he has worked in approximately 100 films. The US, Great Britain, France, Germany and Denmark have all put him to use. Starting in 1908, Denmark produced upwards of 25 Holmes' one-reelers. France did six shorts in 1912. Britain gave him full-length treatment in 1914 and 1916, first with *A Study in Scarlet* and then with *Valley of Fear,* coming up later with a full-length version of *The Hound of the Baskervilles* (1922), after which Ellie Norwood spent several years portraying the sleuth in more than 25 two-reelers. With Wontner, Rendell, and Massey doing the acting honors, Britain kept Holmes steadily occupied throughout the 1930s. The nation then turned to other matters for close to two decades and did not use the character again un-

til 1959, in that year starring Peter Cushing in a remake of *The Hound of the Baskervilles,* with Andre Morell as Watson. In 1965, Britain tried Holmes (John Neville) in an original screenplay that involved him with Jack the Ripper, *A Study in Terror.* Since then, the British have employed the detective mainly in television.

After introducing him in 1903, US producers turned continually to Holmes through the years. Henry Benham starred in a two-reel version of *The Sign of Four* in 1913. Essanay had William Gillette transfer his stage success, *Sherlock Holmes,* to film three years later. John Barrymore, ably assisted by Roland Young as Watson, headed the cast in Goldwyn's adaptation of the play in 1922. Britisher Clive Brook, working in the US since the early 1920s, closed the decade with *The Return of Sherlock Holmes* (1929), one of the detective's first sound features, and then moved to *Sherlock Holmes* (1932). Reginald Owen played Watson in the latter production, after which he graduated to the starring role for the inferior *A Study in Scarlet* (1933). The 1930s hit a high note at their end when 20th Century Fox

paired Basil Rathbone's Holmes with Nigel Bruce's quirky Watson in yet another version of *The Hound of the Baskervilles* (1939). The team charmed audiences – with Rathbone challenging Arthur Wontner's reputation as the perfect Holmes – and a sequel followed within the year, a remake of the stage play, *Sherlock Holmes,* and titled *The Adventures of Sherlock Holmes.* Hastily done, the picture, though enjoyable, was not up to *Hound*'s standards.

In 1941 Rathbone and Bruce moved to Universal, where they did a series of 12 Holmes' films, all of them well produced but of B caliber. The pictures have the reputation of being the oddest ever concocted in the great detective's name. Most carried plots that Conan Doyle would never have recognized. All were given a modern-day setting, with Universal's wardrobe department cleverly providing the two principals with costumes that struck a compromise between 1890s and 1940s garb. And several story lines – among them *Sherlock Holmes and the Voice of Terror* (1941) and *Sherlock Holmes and the Secret Weapon* (1942) – were built around wartime themes. Film buffs remember them fondly for their traditional closing scenes in which Rathbone, aided by a stirring musical background, would tell Bruce of the fine new world that was to come when the Axis was at last defeated and all men were again free.

Rathbone and Bruce closed the series in 1946 with *Dressed to Kill* (British title: *Sherlock Holmes and the Secret Code*). The US then forgot about the master sleuth until 1969, when Billy Wilder directed the spoof, *The Private Life of Sherlock Holmes,* starring Robert Stephens. A year later, George C Scott played a daffy ex-jurist who thought he was Holmes, in a highly entertaining and, at times, moving and bewildering film with Joanne Woodward, *They Might be Giants.* Finally, in a 1976 filmed version of the novel, *The Seven Per Cent Solution,* Nicol Williamson did a Holmes being treated by Sigmund Freud.

But now back to the 1940s. They were the years that saw the fictional sleuths joined by the tough, hard-talking private investigator. Humphrey Bogart provided the quintessential Sam Spade in *The Maltese Falcon* (1941), a superb telling of the Dashiell Hammett novel. Bogart then went on to portray Raymond Chandler's Philip Marlowe in *The Big Sleep* (1946). He was not alone in doing the character. It was Marlowe who, in 1945's *Murder, My Sweet* (British title and the Chandler novel's actual title: *Farewell, My Lovely*), gave Dick Powell a second career by proving that he could be something other than a smiling, sweet-voiced singer; on the

basis of the film, Powell worked as a hard-bitten leading man until the mid-50s. And it was as Marlowe that Robert Montgomery made his interesting and experimental *Lady in the Lake* (1947), a film in which all the action was seen through Marlowe's eyes, with the camera serving as those eyes. In later years, the character was handled by James Garner in *Marlowe* (1969) and Robert Mitchum in *Farewell, My Lovely* (1975). Both men came through with effective portrayals.

All the space that has been devoted here to the fictional detectives and their series work is not to say that the years did not produce fine individual mysteries. They were seen in goodly number. Among them were the haunting adaptation of Vera Caspary's novel, *Laura* (1944); Agatha Christie's *And Then There Were None* (1945; British title: *Ten Little Niggers*); Glenn Ford's *The Gazebo* (1960); Paul Newman's *Harper* (1966), based on the Ross MacDonald novel, *The Moving Target*; and Britain's hilarious *Green for Danger* (1946) with Alastair Sim as the gawky, clumsy, but absolutely brilliant Inspector Cockrill. The character was so good and so splendidly done by Sim that no one has ever been able to figure out why a sequel – or an entire series – never materialized.

In recent years, the mystery has been seen mainly on television. But, though its theater appearances have been few, they've been grade-A products, both in production values and performances. The 1960s were graced with the wonderfully eccentric Margaret Rutherford doing four films as Agatha Christie's Miss Marple, among them *Murder at the Gallop* (1963) and *Murder Most Foul* (1964). 1972 brought Laurence Olivier and Michael Caine in a stylish version of the Anthony Shaffer play, *Sleuth*. Later years produced the taut *Chinatown* (1974), the all-round spoof, *Murder by Death* (1976) and the amusing *Who Is Killing the Great Chefs of Europe?* (1978). But the two best 'whodunits' of the decade were acknowledged to be *Murder on the Orient Express* (1977) and *Death on the Nile* (1978). Both featured Agatha Christie's Hercule Poirot, with the character being taken, in turn, by Albert Finney and Peter Ustinov. Neither man in the least resembled physically the diminutive and bald detective, but both, as is their bent, gave pleasing performances. Finney was fussily precise and pomaded, while Ustinov proved a rumpled and thoughtful fellow, quite human enough to be scared stiff by the venomous snake in his bathroom. Any failure to match Poirot physically mattered little in the long run. Both films – intricately and cleverly plotted, beautifully photo-

Opposite: Paul Newman as *Harper* (1966). He played a Bogart-type detective who gets beaten up as often as he dishes it out.

Below: Albert Finney as Hercule Poirot in *Murder on the Orient Express* (1977).

Above: Once again Margaret Rutherford played Agatha Christie's Miss Marple in *Murder Ahoy* (1964). Miss Marple was the geriatric set's answer to James Bond – an amateur detective in her 70s who solves murder mysteries.

graphed, and marked by solid performances from Lauren Bacall, Wendy Hiller and Ingrid Bergman *(Orient Express),* Bette Davis, David Niven and, especially, Angela Lansbury *(Nile)* – were delights to watch.

Suspense is a far more flexible category than the mystery and, as a result, has played a part in other of the genre, being present in films ranging from the Bob Hope comedy, *My Favorite Blonde,* to science fiction's grim *Panic in the Year Zero.* As a category unto itself, it has been responsible for some of the screen's most entertaining and compelling fare and has lent itself to a variety of themes. A listing of just a few of its better films proves both points.

• Joel McCrea becomes the quarry of demented hunter Leslie Banks in *The Most Dangerous Game* (1932; British title: *The Hounds of Zaroff).*

• An airliner crashes in a South American jungle in *Five Came Back* 1939) and the survivors muster their wits to make repairs and fly out again.

• A shy young woman, Joan Fontaine, is bewildered and threatened by her new husband's secret past in Alfred Hitchcock's *Rebecca* (1940).

• Four workers, stranded in South America, risk their lives for the money to be had by transporting a cargo of nitroglycerine over several hundred miles of treacherous roads in the French-Algerian masterpiece *La Salaire de la Peur/The Wages of Fear* (1953).

• An injured Robert Ryan struggles to survive and escape the desert after his wife and her lover leave him there to die in *Inferno* (1953).

• The body of a 'murdered' man keeps reappearing before the two women who supposedly killed him in

Above: Robert Donat in Hitchcock's *The 39 Steps* (1935). He played a young man who was accidentally thrown into a spy plot and races through England and Scotland with both the police and spies chasing him.

Right: A scene from another Hitchcock film *North By Northwest* (1959), in which Cary Grant is restrained by the police.

France's *Les Diaboliques* (1955).

• Samantha Egger is held prisoner by a psychopath in Britain's *The Collector* (1966).

As above, no listing of suspense films can be complete without mention of at least one Alfred Hitchcock work. His name is synonomous with the category. Though in his career he directed romantic comedies (*Mr and Mrs Smith*, 1941) and even musicals (*Elstree Calling*, 1930), Hitchcock early concentrated his talents on the thriller, in the 1930s doing such notable examples in the category as *The 39 Steps* (1935), *Secret Agent* (1936) and *The Lady Vanishes* (1939) and moving on to the 40s with *Rebecca*, *Lifeboat* (1944) and *Spellbound* (1948). He reached the zenith of his career in the 1950s, giving the decade a succession of spine-tingling wares that are perhaps best represented by *Strangers on a Train* (1950), *Rear Window* (1954), and *North by Northwest* (1959) with its dizzying climax on the stone faces of Mount Rushmore and the memorable sequence in which the crop dusting airplane pursues Cary Grant through a lonely stretch of farmland. The scene is undoubtedly one of the most implausible ever put on film (there were so many easier ways for the villains to dispose of Grant), but so well did Hitchcock build his way to it that no one thought about its implausibility until hours after leaving the theater. The 1960s brought *Psycho* (1960) and *The Birds* (1963), and the 70s, his final film, *The Family Plot* (1976), a search-for-a-lost-heir yarn in which he masterfully blended two separate stories – the first involving the hunt for the young heir, the second dealing with his efforts not to be found because he is in trouble with the law.

Hitchcock, who died in 1980, was periodically castigated by the intelligentsia, the accusation being that he was a fine artist who wasted his talents on sheer entertainment rather than directing them to serious drama and social issues. No creative talent can get through this life without criticism, but, for the millions who enjoyed his work, the charges were nonsense. Sheer entertainments his pictures may have been, but they were, even the weakest of their number, excellent, neither wastes of time to have made nor to have watched.

Listed above among Hitchcock's 1930s works is *Secret Agent*. The picture is a standout example of a specific type of suspense offering – the espionage film. Espionage films, which have been around since glamorously dressed spies lurked behind curtains in World War I two-reelers, have usually been handled over the years as melodramas

Claire Bloom in *The Spy Who Came in from the Cold* (1965), the story of betrayal and hypocrisy in the world of espionage.

or comedies, with their protagonists being anything from amateur to professional agents, and anything from the most frightened to the bravest of individuals. Melodramatic fare has been on hand in such films as *Secret Agent* itself, *Foreign Correspondent* (1940), *Hotel Reserve* (1944), *Cloak and Dagger* (1946) and *The Naked Runner* (1967). Comedy has been represented by Jack Benny's *To Be or Not To Be* (1942), Bob Hope's *They Got Me Covered* (1943) and Great Britain's *Top Secret* (1952; US title: *Mr Potts Goes to Moscow*) and *The Intelligence Men* (1964).

Periodically through the years, there have been attempts to treat spy activities seriously. Major examples here include *Five Fingers* (1952) and *The Man Who Never Was* (1956), both based on fact, and William Holden's *The Counterfeit Traitor* (1962); the reality has been downright grim in the filmed ver-

sion of John le Carre's novel, *The Spy Who Came in From the Cold* (1965). Since the early 1960s, however, the emphasis has been on treating espionage in a sophisticated, light-hearted and sexy manner. The trend started with the phenomenally successful James Bond films, starring first Sean Connery and then Roger Moore, and has continued to the present, being seen along the way in Cary Grant's *Charade* (1963), David Niven's *Where the Spies Are* (1966) and Dean Martin's *Matt Helm* series.

ROMANCE

At first glance, it may seem odd to designate romance a secondary type. It is, after all, the most widely used of all cinema topics. Romance has played a part in the films of every other genre and has been present to varying degrees in easily more than 90 percent of the industry's output. But, as a distinct type, it must be listed as secondary because, of the thousands of films that the passing years have seen, only a relative few have either dealt exclusively with love or have used it as their primary theme.

In those relatively few films, however, romance has presented a multi-faceted view of love. Love was a grand, all consuming passion – and often the prelude to disaster – in films such as *Wuthering Heights* (1939), *Anna Karenina* (1948), *An American Tragedy* (1931) and its 1951 remake, *A Place in the Sun*. It was comically depicted as the core contest in the so-called 'battle of the sexes' in such Tracy-Hepburn films as *Woman of the Year* (1941), and melodramatically in *Gone With the Wind* (1939). It marked the bewildering opening to adulthood in Britain's *Blue Lagoon* (1949; not the Brooke Shields' teenage kissy-kissy 1980 remake). It was, on the one hand, a neurotic compulsion in *Leave Her to Heaven* (1945) and, on the other, the emotion that knows no ethnic bounds in *Love is a Many Splendored Thing* (1955). It was a fragile and forbidden extra-marital adventure that at last had to be abandoned by two mature adults, the closing of the door on a future that could not be, in Britain's *Brief Encounter* (1945). And, if love meant the closing of a door for them, then it was the opening of a door to the future for the two gentle and lost people in *Marty* (1955).

Though the view has been multi-faceted, the screen treatments of love have usually fallen into two distinctly opposed camps, with one stressing innocence and the other sex. Only the most sensitive and mature of the genre's offerings – *Brief Encounter* is a superb case in point – have managed to walk a line between the two and have made genuine efforts to depict love as it might be felt and handled by ordinary men and women. When innocence has been stressed, love has been presented as the happy joining of two hearts noble and not tainted with a smidgen of lust. Such was the case in the Charles Ray rustic comedy-romances of the 1920s. Such was the case with Gary Cooper and Jean Arthur in *Mr Deeds Goes to Town* (1936), with Mickey Rooney in the throes of Andy Hardy's adolescence and

Above: Laurence Olivier and Geraldine Fitzgerald in *Wuthering Heights* (1939).

with the Lane sisters in the *Four Daughters* films of the late 1930s and early 40s. And such, indeed, was the case with Clark Gable and Claudette Colbert in *It Happened One Night* (1934). Remember how Gable, so blatantly virile minus his undershirt, honorably suspended that blanket – the 'walls of Jericho' – between the tourist cabin beds and how it didn't come 'tumbling down' until he and Colbert were wed?

As for sex, it has been on view since the very start of the industry. In 1896, Edison filmed what is now known as the *John Rice-May Irwin Kiss*; taken from a sequence in the two players' then popular Broadway production, *The Widow Jones,* it emerged as a somewhat protracted amount of amatory pleasure that was, by modern standards, pretty tame stuff but spicy enough in its day to

Opposite: Leslie Howard and Norma Shearer played the title roles in *Romeo and Juliet* (1936).

Above: Montgomery Clift and Elizabeth Taylor in *A Place in the Sun* (1951). Based upon a Theodore Dreiser novel, the film told the story of a factory worker (Clift) who loves a wealthy girl (Taylor), but has an affair with a working girl, with tragic results.

Right: Clift with Shelley Winters, who played the working girl in *A Place in the Sun*.

incite a burst of pressure-group outrage, with ministers dubbing it 'a lyric of the stockyards' and shocked families circulating petitions to have it banned from theaters. But, as love in its more torrid aspects has been doing ever since, the snippet of film drew record crowds. Knowing a good thing when they saw it, producers early began dishing out sex, blatantly in the teen-years 'vamp' films of Theda Bara, Virginia Pearson, and Barbara La Marr. They continued to do so in the 1920s with Rudolph Valentino's *The Sheik* (1921) and Clara Bow's 'flapper' pictures. Cecil B DeMille handed out sexually accented material throughout the decade in such fare as *Dynamite* (1929) with its bedroom sequences and titilatingly revealing bathroom scenes, and in the orgies that he staged for *Saturday Night* and *Manslaughter* (both 1922). Extra-marital entanglements served as themes for his *The Golden Bed* (1925) and *Why Change Your Wife?* (1920).

It was films such as these, plus Hollywood's well publicized assortment of scandals at the time, that led to the establishment of the US Production Code and the power of the Legion of Decency, with the result that chaste innocence came into full play for the next two decades. The industry was strapped with regulations that reduced the depiction of love to absurdity by insisting that not

Above: Brooke Shields and Christopher Atkins in the remake of *The Blue Lagoon* (1980).

Below: Rudolph Valentino steals away with Agnes Ayres in one of his most successful roles as *The Sheik* (1922).

Above: Leslie Howard and Bette Davis starred in
Of Human Bondage (1934) – the film adaptation
of W Somerset Maugham's novel about a doctor
and his strange infatuation with a vulgar
waitress. It made Davis a star.

Right: John Garfield and Lana Turner in *The
Postman Always Rings Twice* (1946) – the story of
two lovers who murder her husband.

even married couples could share the same mattress and that, should a man and a woman ever find themselves on the same bed, they must keep at least one foot on the floor. Not similarly fettered, Europe continued to use sex as a theme, presenting it boldly (for that day) in Czechoslovakia's *Extase/Ecstacy* (1933) with Hedwig Kiesler, later Hedy LaMarr. Europeans also enjoyed a dash of sex from the US, a Hollywood habit of the time being often to shoot two versions of love scenes – a properly innocent one for the domestic market and a steamy one for export. Yet, despite the strictures, US films still managed to handle sexual themes. Sexual enslavement was seen in *Of Human Bondage* (1934). An undercurrent of prostitution ran through *Waterloo Bridge* (1940). And plain unvarnished lust was the key to the Lana Turner-John Garfield and the Barbara Stanwyck-Fred MacMurray relationships in, respectively, *The Postman Always Rings Twice* (1946) and *Double Indemnity* (1944), both based on James M Cain novels.

And, of course, sex was unmistakably present in one of Hollywood's most memorable endeavors – David O Selznick's *Gone With the Wind* (1939). It ran throughout Scarlett's entanglements with both Rhett Butler and Ashley Wilkes and became about as explicit as the times would permit in the sequence

that ended with a drunken Clark Gable storming up a stairway with Vivient Leigh in his arms. The film, based on Margaret Mitchell's best selling novel and heavily publicized by Selznick's international search for an actress to portray Scarlett O'Hara, proved to be one of the industry's all-time money earners. It claimed for itself best picture honors at the 1939 Academy Awards presentation. Clark Gable was nominated for the best work of the year by an actor, but lost to Robert Donat in *Goodbye, Mr Chips*. Miss Leigh, however, was named for best actress honors. The award for best direction went to *GWTW*'s Victor Fleming, one of several directors who worked on the picture.

Hollywood's patience with censorship ran out in the early 1950s with *The Moon is Blue* (1952). Since then, America's treatment of sex has broadened (or deteriorated; it all depends on the individual's point of view) until, in the 1980s, such steamy offerings as *Body Heat* and the remake of *The Postman Always Rings Twice* are quite commonplace. At the same time, in an effort to permit the free handling of all themes while protecting the younger moviegoers, the US has established a rating system similar to that used in Britain, classifying its pictures from *G* (general viewing) to *X* (pornographic) and accordingly limiting attendance by

Double Indemnity, another film based upon a James M Cain (author of *Postman*) novel told of an insurance salesman (Fred MacMurray) who is coerced into a plot to kill her husband by Barbara Stanwyck.

age. The US trend towards the increasingly explicit filming of sex has gone hand in hand over the years with a national change in moral attitudes and has, as is true of any creative medium, been simultaneously a causal agent and a reflection of that change. But we may be seeing the end of the trend. Becoming increasingly apparent is a public tiredness of 'sexploitation,' perhaps caused by recent tendencies towards conservatism or perhaps simply from having seen just too much for too long. Whatever the case, the indications are strong that films with sexually accented material will no longer, except for the drive-in types, draw audiences on the basis of detailed eroticism alone. It may be that the pendulum of American tastes is swinging back to a bygone age. If so, then is it likely that we'll one day again see a Gable by some other name hang that 'walls of Jericho' blanket between the motel room beds and not let it come 'tumbling down' until the wedding night.

SOCIAL COMMENT

The motion picture, with its awesome ability to mold public opinion, has long been criticized for concentrating too much on sheer entertainment and not giving enough of itself to commenting on the social problems and injusties that plague the world. The criticism has merit, but it must not be accepted without reservation. It is true, granted, that most films are – and always have been – made for the purpose of entertaining. But it is quite as true to say that the cinema *does* have a social conscience and that thoughtful producers, sometimes effectively and sometimes not, have voiced it regularly through the years.

Not only is this true, but it is just as valid to say that they've voiced that conscience in a goodly number of different arenas. Olivia de Havilland's *The Snake Pit* (1948) asked for an understanding of the mentally unbalanced and their problems; more than a quarter of a century later *One Flew Over the Cuckoo's Nest* (1975) cried out against the poor and sometimes cruel practices followed in the institutional care of the

insane. Italy's *Umberto D* (1952) spoke movingly of the loneliness of the aged. At the opposite pole, *Dead End* (1937) and *The Blackboard Jungle* (1955) looked hard at juvenile delinquency. In *The Lost Weekend* (1945) Ray Milland etched an uncompromising portrait of the alcoholic, with Frank Sinatra then drawing an equally uncompromising picture of the drug addict in *The Man with the Golden Arm* (1955). *The Good Earth* (1937), based on Pearl Buck's novel of China, sought a sympathetic understanding for the poor of other nations while *The Grapes of Wrath* (1940) dealt with the poor and dispossessed of America's Depression. *The Best Years of Our Lives* (1946) took as its theme the trials faced by ex-soldiers and their families readjusting to peacetime life.

In one very specific area, director Fritz Lang, in *Fury* (1936), spoke out against the blind violence that can destroy an innocent man, in this instance a young service station attendant (Spencer Tracy) who is falsely accused of kidnapping and is then attacked by a lynch mob. The details achieved in Lang's depiction of the horror that is mob violence – the glimpses of hysteria, the moments of brutal enjoyment, the adolescent watching with moronic glee, the mother lifting her child high for a better view – were all unforgettable.

The same mob violence was criticized more than a decade later in an excellent but almost forgotten Lloyd Bridges film, *Try and Get Me* (1951). In a variation of the theme, the anger and prejudice that sent Sacco and Vanzetti to be executed in the US 1920s was reflected and denounced in *Winterset* (1936), as were the political prejudices and fears of the McCarthy era in *Advise and Consent* (1962).

Social comment began early in film history. It was voiced in such westerns as *An Indian Wife's Devotion* (1911) and *The Squaw Man* (1914), films that treated the Indian as a human being and were the advance guard of such later red man-white man treatises as *Broken Arrow* (1950). David Wark Griffith investigated the hardships of slum life in *A Child of the Ghetto* (1910) and *The Musketeers of Pig Alley* (1912), forerunners of such similar studies as *The Quiet One* (1948) and Britain's *Love on the Dole* (1941). The coming of World War I brought a trio of remarkable pacifist films – Thomas Ince's *Civilization*, Griffith's *Intolerance* and Lewis Selznick's *War Brides* (all 1916). The first centered on a submarine inventor who, when ill and delirious, envisions a trip through hell with the Spirit of Christ and then, on recovery, opposes his country's war aims and is sentenced to death

Right: Henry Fonda played Tom Joad and Jane Darwell was Ma Joad in *The Grapes of Wrath* (1940), based on John Steinbeck's novel of impoverished migratory workers during the Great Depression.

Left: Victor McLaglen (left) played a slow-witted traitor to the Irish rebels in the 1920s in *The Informer* (1935).

Right: Dustin Farnum in *The Squaw Man* (1913).

Opposite: The slaughter on the Odessa steps in *The Battleship Potemkin* (1925).

Right: Warren Beatty starred in *Reds* (1982) as a political activist.

Below: An unidentified soldier ogles Lillian Gish in *The Birth of a Nation* (1915).

Bottom: Carpetbaggers registering black voters in *The Birth of a Nation* (1915).

for his stand. *Intolerance,* as ambitious an undertaking for Griffith as *The Birth of a Nation* before it, divided itself into four stories, each set in a different historical period, and, through them, developed the themes of man's never-ending inhumanity to man and love's enduring struggle against brutality. *War Brides* dealt with the protests of a group of women against the promised battlefield slaughter of their future sons.

In 1915, with *The Birth of a Nation,* Griffith touched on the subject of race. The film, three hours long and superbly crafted, is considered a masterpiece, but Griffith's handling of the blacks in it earned him widespread criticism at the time and has tainted its memory ever since. Adapted from an obviously racist novel, *The Clansman,* and set in Civil War and Reconstruction years, *The Birth of a Nation,* in its famous rape sequence, depicted a black as the vicious attacker of a white woman and then represented the Ku Klux Klan as the South's rescuer from such outrages. On its release, the picture drew angry protests from various liberal groups and caused riots at New York, Chicago and Boston theaters. The question of whether Griffith, a Southerner whose family's wealth was lost in the Civil War, was simply filming the book or revealing his own feelings has never been answered. He was reportedly hurt and bewildered by the public reaction and a significance is seen in the fact that his next undertaking was the pacifistic *Intolerance.*

The films of the next three decades touched on racial themes, from time to time. King Vidor's musical, *Hallelujah* (1929), attempted to recapture the energies and passions of the blacks he had known in boyhood. George Arliss' *The House of Rothschild* (1934) provided an insight into European anti-Semitism. Humphrey Bogart's *The Black Legion* (1936) cried out against a mid-30s resurgence of the Ku Klux Klan. But, in general, any depiction of race was limited to characterizations, all of which were along 'ethnic joke' lines. Russians were dour or volatile in, respectively, the Mischa Auer and Gregory Ratoff images. Swedes were the happy El Brendel types. Jews were, in turn, jolly, hand-rubbing, and greedy. Blacks were dependent figures, faithful servants of the Louise Beavers mold or as shiftless and as tired and as shuffling as Stepin Fetchit; it must be said, though, that their strengths were well represented by Hattie McDaniel's Mammy and Everett Brown's Big Sam in *Gone With The Wind* (1939).

But then came the post-World War II years. In the aftermath of the First World War, a new creative force had been unloosed in Germany. Now, in the

Above: The Babylonian set from D W Griffith's *Intolerance* (1916).

Below: Ray Milland won an Oscar for his role as a drunk in *The Lost Weekend* (1945).

wake of the century's latest conflict, a new thematic force took shape in the US – the racial protest. It was heralded by *Gentleman's Agreement* and *Crossfire*, both made in 1947 and both strong indictments of anti-Semitism. They were followed by the modestly budgeted but powerfully done *Home of the Brave* (1949), the story of a black soldier (James Edwards) driven to mental unbalance by the hostility of his white companions during a dangerous jungle mission.

The years since have seen a succession of effective and ineffectual comments on the racial problem. *Pinky* (1949) dealt with a light-skinned black woman (Jeanne Crain) passing as a white; it had its good moments but was, at times, weakened by a melodramatic treatment. *No Way Out* (1950), with Richard Widmark and Sidney Poitier, spoke grippingly of the racial hatreds in a slum area. *Edge of the City* (1948) and *Sounder* (1972) won acclaim for dealing with the black as a human being, with the former praised as the first film ever really to do so. Britain's *To Sir with Love* (1967) saw a black teacher (Sidney Poitier) and his white students learning from each other. *In the Heat of the Night* (1967) established the angers on both sides of the color fence and saw the two protagonists – Poitier and Rod Steiger –

Above: Left to right: James Edwards, Lloyd Bridges, Frank Lovejoy in *Home of the Brave* (1949), in which a black soldier on a Pacific patrol is rendered a mental case by the intolerance of his comrades.

Below: Sidney Poitier (left) and Rod Steiger starred in *In the Heat of the Night* (1967). Steiger won an Oscar for his role as a bigoted small town sheriff, forced to use the services of Poitier, the big city detective.

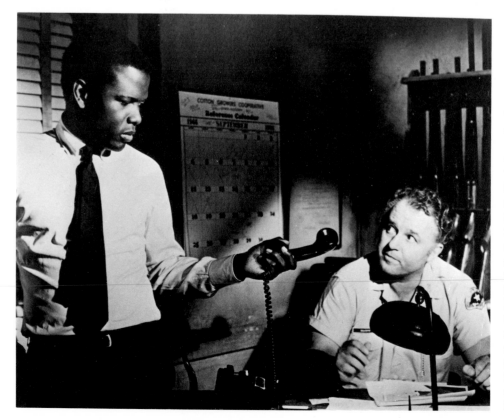

emerge with a greater understanding and appreciation of each other. One of the most controversial themes of all – miscegenation – was taken on by *Guess Who's Coming to Dinner* (1967). The film ended up being both praised and criticized, praised for its performances, its final speech by Spencer Tracy, and its sheer nerve for tackling the subject, but criticized for side-stepping some of the very ugly issues in an interracial marriage by treating the subject lightly and making all the characters a little too nice, too affluent, and ultimately too cooperative and understanding.

It may well be that the best racial film done to date is *The Defiant Ones* (1958), the story of a prison escape that sees Sidney Poitier and Tony Curtis physically chained together during their flight. In the minds of many critics, though it was judged too didactic in some parts, here was a picture that said as much as any dramatic work could say about prejudice, voicing the angers, frustrations, and suspicions that give it life, but, of greater importance, voicing even more strongly – in the oneness of mankind as symbolized by the pair's chains, in their growing recognition of each other's worth, and in their realization that they are dependent on each other for survival – the understandings fundamental to ending the problem.

Left: In *Guess Who's Coming to Dinner*, Spencer Tracy (in his final role) and Katharine Hepburn play the parents of a white girl who is engaged to a black man (Sidney Poitier).

Below: Poitier appeared again in *The Defiant Ones* (1958). He co-starred with Tony Curtis in this story of two chain gang escapees who are chained together.

WAR

Though it had played a part in some early European historical films, war did not emerge as a genre until the outbreak of World War I. At that time, the participating nations, each boasting the nobility and heroism of its own troops and damning the villainy of the enemy's, began turning out wares that were propagandist to the core. In the neutral United States of 1914-1917, the people, following the headlines and viewing these imported efforts, were soon dividing themselves into two camps, with one calling for preparedness against the day when the country would be drawn into the conflict, and the other pleading that involvement must be avoided altogether. Producers, their hands filled with the problems of a rapidly growing industry, at first failed to recognize the box office potential in the national preoccupation. But the success of Griffith's Civil War treatise, *The Birth of a Nation,* awoke them with a start.

Immediately, a public whose sym-

pathies lay predominantly with the Allies was introduced to a diet of war films that would not end until the 1918 Armistice. The initial wares reflected the nation's current division of opinion. Such films as *The Battle Cry of Peace* and *The Fall of a Nation* (both 1915) – the first depicting German soldiers as war-loving beasts and the second damning pacifists as sweet do-gooders who could take a nation to disaster – argued vehemently for preparedness. From the other side of the fence came, in 1916, the previously mentioned *Civilization, Intolerance,* and *War Brides.* America's entry into the war put an end to Hollywood's participation in the debate and the industry now cranked out a parade of films in which the Allied soldier and civilian were depicted as the courageous and noble-hearted foe of the sadistic, raping, and butchering 'Hun.' Mary Pickford stood up bravely to the brutal Prussian types who held her captive in *The Little American* (1917). Heroic spy Rita Jolivet faced an execution squad in *Lest We Forget* (1918). And Robert Harron was ready to shoot and kill his beloved Lillian Gish to save her from the lustful clutches of the enemy in

A scene from *Wings* (1927), perhaps the greatest of the early aviation epics.

Hearts of the World (1918). These and their fellow films of the day have long been acknowledged as some of the most venomous pieces of porpaganda ever produced.

With the Armistice, their flow ceased. Europe and the US took an understandable respite from war films. But the mid-20s saw a revival of the genre, however now with pictures of a different breed. The wartime work had been done by men who had never been near a battlefield, but home at last from overseas were the ones who had fought the war and they set out to tell audiences what it was like to have 'been there.' They did so, most effectively, in the next years. *The Big Parade* (1925) offered realistic battle sequences and sketched, in the comradeship of the soldiers and the love affair between a young American and a French girl, the humanity that somehow manages to survive in the midst of horror. *Wings* (1927) depicted the tensions of the men who fought in the air war. *What Price Glory?* (1926), though concentrating much on the amorous doings of its two principals, Captain Flagg and Sergeant Quirt, cried out unforgettably against the horrors of war in its depictions of battle and the injuries suffered. The US-UK adaptation of the R C Sheriff play, *Journey's End* (1930), spoke honestly of fear, dealt with the balance of tedium and terror found in trench warfare, and made heroism not a thing of derring-do but the selfless facing of one's day-to-day duties. *The Dawn Patrol* (1930 and remade in 1939) looked at the loneliness of command and the terrible burden of daily dispatching men to almost certain death. And *All Quiet on the Western Front* (1930), based on the Erich Maria Remarque novel, made US cinema history – and reflected a fading of American wartime passions – by viewing the conflict from the German side and presenting its young soldiers not as barbarian 'Huns' but as human beings, humorous, hopeful, loving, finally chilled into hard resignation by battle, and the ravaged victims of a tragedy that was of no more their making than it was of their counterparts across No Man's Land.

Memories of the war lingered throughout the 1930s. They were echoed dramatically in *The Road to Glory* (1936) and France's antiwar *La Grand Illusion/Grand Illusion* (1937). The first detailed the strains and misunderstandings between the men and commanders in a French regiment while the latter centered on the friendship of a Prussian prison camp commandant (Erich von Stroheim) and one of his French officer prisoners (Pierre Fresnay), both of whom shared the experience of having had the war destroy their aristocratic ways of life. For the most part, though, the war was now treated melodramatically, as exampled by *The Lost Squadron (1932) and The Fighting 69th* (1939). A later year, 1957, would bring an especially effective memory in Kirk Douglas' *Paths of Glory* and its story of the fates of the men selected for courts-martial after their French troop refuses a general's order to stand firm and be slaughtered by an enemy barrage.

World War II, as did its predecessor, brought its share of propagandist and morale-boosting films in which the Germans and Japanese were pictured as heartless brutes being resisted and ultimately defeated by Allied heroism. But the years of conflict, unlike those of World War I, also produced films that gave a genuine feel of the fighting and a

Above: Lew Ayres as the young German Army soldier in the stirring anti-war film, *All Quiet on the Western Front* (1930).

Below: Kirk Douglas played a French officer who treated his men in a humane manner in *Paths of Glory* (1957).

Above: George Murphy (left foreground) and Robert Taylor (right foreground) in *Bataan* (1942), a story of the heroes who endured one of the early US defeats in World War II.

Left: The great John Wayne in *The Longest Day* (1962), the story of the Normandy invasion in World War II.

Above: Noel Coward (in civilian clothing) wrote, co-directed, composed the music and starred in *In Which We Serve* (1942).

genuine, often sensitive, insight into the human spirits caught in it. Ranking high among the examples of such efforts were *Wake Island* (1942), *Guadalcanal Diary* (1943), *They Were Expendable* (1945) and, most especially, Britain's magnificent *In Which We Serve* (1942).

And, as was the case earlier, the postwar years have brought the most significant of the era's film depictions – *Command Decision* (1948) and *Twelve O'Clock High* (1950), both, as was *The Dawn Patrol* before them, studies of the strains and responsibilities of command; *A Walk in the Sun* (1948), *Battleground* (1949) and *The Naked and the Dead* (1958), each providing an infantryman's 'ground level' view of war; Italy's *Open City* (1945), a memorable portrait of the resistance movement in Rome; France's *Les Jeux Interdits/Forbidden Games* (1952), picturing the macabre obsession of two children for the rituals of death; *From Here to Eternity* (1953), a look at the professional soldier; *Mister Roberts* (1955), commenting on the boredom endured in the backwaters of the fighting; the US-UK triumph, *The Bridge on the River Kwai* (1957), that enigmatic study of an imprisoned British commander's cooperation with the enemy; *Catch 22* (1970), the wildly funny and yet touching statement that war is simply insanity; and *Das Boot* (1982), Germany's gripping

Above: Dana Andrews (left) and Herbert Rudley were in *A Walk in the Sun* (1945), the story of infantry men in Italy who must clear German soldiers out of a farmhouse.

Below: Alec Guinness (left) played a British officer who was a captive of the Japanese in *The Bridge on the River Kwai* (1957). He drives his men to build a bridge as therapy.

Above: The U-96 sails out of the occupied French port of La Rochelle to begin a daring patrol of the North Atlantic in *Das Boot* (1982).

Right: Robert Duvall (center) played an army officer with manic tendencies in *Apocalypse Now* (1979).

Opposite: George C Scott in his Academy Award winning role as *Patton* (1970).

drama of submarine warfare.

The passing years have also seen a number of fact-based and biographical films of World War II. They range from such excellent works as Britain's *Dam Busters* (1955) and *Reach for the Sky* (1956 – the story of double amputee flying ace Douglas Bader) and America's *The Longest Day* (1962) and *Patton* (1970) to the deservedly castigated *Inchon* (1982).

The Korean War produced relatively few films, among the best of which were *Retreat Hell!* (1952), *The Bridges at Toko-Ri* (1955) and *Pork Chop Hill* (1959). A Korean setting, however, was used in the Vietnam era's most potent anti-war offering, *M*A*S*H** (1970). As for Vietnam itself, it was responsible for John Wayne's embarrassingly militaristic and propagandist *The Green Berets* (1968); the superb *The Deer Hunter* (1978), with its haunting depiction of the horror of the unwanted conflict and its terrible psychological toll on the men who fought it; and Francis Ford Coppola's strange *Apocalypse Now* (1979), so brutal and telling in its battle sequences but so bewildering in some of its themes. Though Vietnam has already resulted in fine films, if the screen history of preceding wars is to be repeated, then the best is yet to come.

HONORS DESERVED

Each genre has produced its share of good and bad pictures. Each has experienced its financial successes and failures. Each has had some of its offerings critically praised and others damned. But how has each genre fared in the reception of awards and recognitions for works that are especially meritorious or that have marked a contribution to the development of the motion picture as an art form?

It's a question that we'll attempt to answer in this chapter. The answer is necessary to round out a study of what the genre have done because the awards and recognitions come from people within the industry and from judges expert in film-making and film criticism. While they often echo public reaction, these peers and judges just as often have more to say of a given picture's true quality than do the lines – or absence of lines – at the box office.

Following now is a listing of the awards and recognitions that have been bestowed on pictures within each genre by what are generally conceded to be the six most prestigious film honors groups in the world. In the order in which they were founded, they are: the US Academy of Motion Pictures Arts and Sciences (1928), the US National Board of Review (1930), the New York

Film Critics Circle (1935), the US Golden Globe Awards (1943), the Cannes Film Festival (1946) and the British Film Academy (1948), now the British Academy of Film and Television Arts.

Since we are concerned only with the films produced by the various genre, the listing is restricted to honors given to the pictures themselves. Individual awards for performance, direction, writing, musical and technical achievements are not included.

The Western

Cimarron (1931, USA) was the first western ever, to be honored with awards. It claimed two when both the American Academy Awards and the National Board of Review named it the best motion picture of the year.

Butch Cassidy and the Sundance Kid 1970 USA
British Academy Award: Best Film

High Noon 1952 USA
US Academy Award Nomination: Best Picture (Winner: *The Greatest Show on Earth*)
US National Board of Review: List of Ten Best American Films
New York Film Critics Award: Best Film

The Ox-Bow Incident 1943 USA
US Academy Award Nomination: Best Picture (Winner: *Casablanca*)

Pages 228-29: Scarlett O'Hara visits the army hospital in *Gone With the Wind* (1939).

Above: Al Pacino (in front of the bank) was the star of *Dog Day Afternoon* (1975).

US National Board of Review Award: Best English Language Film

Treasure of the Sierra Madre 1948 USA
US Academy Award Nomination: Best Picture (Winner: *Hamlet*)
US National Board of Review: List of Ten Best (including foreign) Films
New York Film Critics Award: Best Film
US Golden Globe Award: Best Film, Drama
British Academy Award Nomination, 1949: Best Film (Winners: *Bicycle Thief/Bicycle Thieves,* Italy, Best Film; *The Third Man,* Best British Film)
Note: While *The Treasure of Sierra Madre* is not strictly a western, it is included here because it is generally conceded to fit within the overall framework of the genre.

Shane 1953 USA
US Academy Award Nomination: Best Picture (Winner: *From Here to Eternity*)
US National Board of Review: List of Ten Best American Films
British Academy Award Nomination: Best Film (Winners: *Les Jeux Interdits,* France; Best Film: *Genevieve,* Best British Film)

Considering the size and activity of the genre, the western has claimed relatively few awards over the years. Its products, however, though losing out to other films, have done well so far as Best Picture nominations by the US Academy Awards are concerned. Earning nominations over the years have been: *In Old Arizona* (1928/29), *Viva Villa* (1934), *Ruggles of Red Gap* (1935), *The Alamo* (1960) and *How the West Was Won* (1963). *How the West Was Won* was also included on the national Board of Review's List of Ten Best Films for the year.

Science Fiction and Horror

Here we have the most ignored of all the genre. Completely overlooked by the awards groups then in existence, all of them American, were such landmark productions as *Frankenstein* (1931, USA), *Dracula* (1931, USA) and *Things to Come* (1936, UK). The exclusion of the first two (and especially of *Frankenstein*, which is generally considered the superior of the pair) suggests an early tendency not to take the genre seriously. The failure to acknowledge a production of the sheer excellence of Britain's *Things to Come* can only indicate a provincialism on the parts of the US groups at the time.

Of the two categories, horror is the far more ignored. Only one horror film, *The Exorcist* (1973, USA), has ever claimed any honors for itself. The American Academy Awards nominated *The Exorcist* as a Best Picture (it lost to *The Sting*) and the Golden Globe Awards named it the Best Film, Drama, for the year.

A Clockwork Orange 1971 UK
US Academy Award Nomination: Best Picture (Winner: *The French Connection*)
New York Critics Award: Best Film
British Academy Award Nomination, 1972: Best Film (Winner: *Cabaret*)

Close Encounters of the Third Kind 1977 USA
US National Board of Review: List of Ten Best English Language Films
British Academy Award Nomination, 1978: Best Film (Winner: *Julia*)

Dr Strangelove 1964 UK-USA
US Academy Award Nomination: Best Picture (Winner: *My Fair Lady*)
British Academy Award: Best Film and Best British Film
Note: So far as country of origin is concerned, *Dr Strangelove* presents a problem. Some authorities cite it as a British production while others list it as a United States work. Since it was directed by American-born Stanley Kubrick, boasted a British-American cast and was a Columbia release, it seems fair to see it as a combined effort, hence the UK-USA designation above.

Star Wars 1977 USA
US Academy Award Nomination: Best Picture (Winner: *Annie Hall*)
US National Board of Review: List of Ten Best English Films
British Academy Award Nomination, 1978: Best Film (Winner: *Julia*)

The Musical

The Broadway Melody (1929, USA) was the first musical to win Best Picture honors from the American Academy Awards. It was so named at the Academy's 1928/29 banquet. Another musical – *The Hollywood Revue of 1929* (1929, USA) – was included in the Academy's list of Best Picture nominations that year.

All That Jazz 1979 USA
US Academy Award Nomination: Best Picture (Winner: *Kramer Vs Kramer*)
Cannes Film Festival Award, 1980: Golden Palm

An American in Paris 1951 USA
US Academy Award: Best Picture
US National Board of Review: List of Ten Best American Films
US Golden Globe Award: Best Film, Musical/Comedy
British Academy Award Nomination: Best Film (Winners: *La Ronde*, France, Best Film; *The Lavender Hill Mob*, Best British Film)

Cabaret 1972 USA
US Academy Award Nomination: Best Picture (Winner: *The Godfather*)
US National Board of Review Award: Best English Language Film
US Golden Globe Award: Best Film, Musical/Comedy
British Academy Award: Best Film

Gigi 1958 USA
US Academy Award: Best Picture
US National Board of Review: List of Ten Best American Films
US Golden Globe Award: Best Film, Musical
British Academy Award Nomination, 1959: Best Film (Winners: *Ben Hur*, Best Film; *Sapphire*, Best British Film)

The Great Ziegfeld 1936 USA
US Academy Award: Best Picture

My Fair Lady 1964 USA
US Academy Award: Best Picture
US National Board of Review: List of Ten Best English Langue Films
New York Film Critics Award: Best Film
US Golden globe Award: Best Film, Musical/Comedy
British Academy Award, 1965: Best Film

Oliver! 1968 UK
US Academy Award: Best Picture
US National Board of Review: List of Ten Best English Language Films
US Golden Globe Award: Best Film, Musical/Comedy
British Academy Award Nomination: Best Film (Winner: *The Graduate*)

The Sound of Music 1965 USA
US Academy Award: Best Picture

US National Board of Review: List of Ten Best English Language Films
US Golden Award: Best Film, Musical/Comedy

The Umbrellas of Cherbourg 1964 France-West Germany
US Academy Award Nomination: Best Foreign Film (Winner: *Yesterday, Today, and Tomorrow*, Italy)
Cannes Film Festival Award: Golden Palm

West Side Story 1961 USA
US Academy Award: Best Picture
US National Board of Review: List of Ten Best American Films
New York Film Critics Award: Best Film
US Golden Globe Award: Best Film, Musical
British Academy Award Nomination, 1962: Best Film (Winner: *Lawrence of Arabia*)

US musicals have always done well for themselves in the American Academy Awards nominations for Best Picture honors, markedly so in their earliest days. Director Ernst Lubitsch's *One Hour with You* and *The Smiling Lieutenant* were both nominated in 1931/32; *Flirtation Walk* and *The Gay Divorcee* made the list in 1935 and *The Broadway Melody of 1936, Naughty Marietta* and *Top Hat* all found themselves nominated in 1935. Later nominees included *Alexander's Ragtime Band* (1938), *The Wizard of Oz* (1939), *Yankee Doodle Dandy* (1942), *Anchors Aweigh* (1945), *The King and I* (1956), *The Music Man* (1962), *Funny Lady* (1968) and *Fiddler on the Roof* (1971).

Comedy

It Happened One Night (1934, USA) was the first comedy to win a Best Picture American Academy Award. In fact, it swept the four principal awards given that year – Best Picture, Best Direction (Frank Capra), Best Actor (Clark Gable) and Best Actress (Claudette Colbert). The categories for Best Supporting Actor and Actress would not be added to the Academy roster until 1936. *It Happened One Night* was also named the year's Best American Film by the National Board of Review.

Annie Hall 1977 USA
US Academy Award: Best Picture
US National Board of Review: List of Ten Best English Language Films
New York Film Critics Award: Best Film
British Academy Award: Best Film

The Apartment 1960 USA
US Academy Award: Best Picture
US National Board of Review: List of Ten Best American Films
New York Film Critics Award: Best Film (Co-Winner: *Sons and Lovers*)
US Golden Globe Award: Best Film, Comedy
British Academy Award: Best Film

La Cage Aux Folles 1979 France-Italy
US National Board of Review Award: Best
Foreign Language Film
US Golden Globe Award: Best Foreign Film

Closely Observed Trains 1967 Czechoslovakia
US Academy Award: Best Foreign Language Film

The Graduate 1968 USA
British Academy Award: Best Film

Manhattan 1979 USA
US National Board of Review Award: Best
English Language Film
British Academy Award: Best Film

Mr Deeds Goes to Town 1936 USA
US Academy Award Nomination: Best Picture (Winner: *The Great Ziegfeld*)

Mon Oncle 1958 France-Italy
US Academy Award: Best Foreign Lan-
guage Film
US National Board of Review: List of Five
Best Foreign Films
New York Film Critics Award: Best Foreign
Film
Cannes Film Festival Award: Special Prize,
Jacques Tati

The Sting 1973 USA
US Academy Award: Best Film
US National Board of Review Award: Best
English Language Film

Tom Jones 1963 UK
US Academy Award: Best Picture
US National Board of Review Award: Best
English Language Film
New York Film Critics Award: Best Film

US Golden Globe Award: Best Film, Music-
al/Comedy
British Academy Award: Best Film

Yesterday, Today and Tomorrow 1964 Italy
US Academy Award: Best Foreign Lan-
guage Film
US National Board of Review: List of Five
Best Foreign Language Films

You Can't Take it With You 1938 USA
US Academy Award: Best Picture

Although losing the Oscar to others, a
series of fine US comedies have received
Best Picture nominations from the
Academy Awards. They include *The
Awful Truth* (1937), *Mr Smith Goes to
Washington* (1939), *Father of the Bride*
(1950), *Auntie Mame* (1958), *The Rus-
sians are Coming, the Russians are
Coming* (1966), *The Goodbye Girl*
(1977) and *Breaking Away* (1979). Pic-
tures nominated by the Academy for
Best Foreign Film awards have in-
cluded Spain's delightful black comedy
My Dearest Señorita (1972) and Italy's
Marriage, Italian Style (1964), *Scent of a
Woman* (1975) and *Viva Italia!* (1978).
Oddly, Charlie Chaplin's feature
work went virtually unnoticed by the
Academy until his special award in
1972. The only Chaplin picture to be
nominated for an Oscar was *The Great
Dictator* (1940). His *Monsieur Verdoux*,
however, was named the Best Film of
1947 by the National Board of Review.

Bruce, the mechanical shark
hero? of *Jaws* (1975), one of the
great box office hits of all time.

Crime

Ladri di Biciclette/Bicycle Thieves (US Title:
The Bicycle Thief) 1948 Italy
US Academy Award, 1949: Best Foreign
Language Film
US National Board of Review Award, 1949:
Best Film
New York Film Critics Award, 1949: Best
Foreign Language Film
British Academy Award, 1949: Best Film

The Big House 1930 USA
US Academy Award Nomination: Best Pic-
ture (Winner: *All Quiet on the Western
Front*)

The Blue Lamp 1950 UK
British Academy Award: Best British Film

Dog Day Afternoon 1975 USA
US Academy Award Nomination: Best Pic-
ture (Winner: *One Flew Over the Cuckoo's
Nest*)
US National Board of Review: List of Ten
Best English Language Films
British Academy Award Nomination: Best
Film (Winner: *Alice Doesn't Live Here
Anymore*)

The French Connection 1971 USA
US Academy Award: Best Picture

US National Board of Review: List of Ten
Best English Language Films
US Golden Globe Award: Best Film, Drama
British Academy Award Nomination, 1972:
Best Film (Winner: *Cabaret*)

The Godfather 1972 USA
US Academy Award: Best Picture
US National Board of Review: List of Ten
Best English Language Films
US Golden Globe Award: Best Film, Drama
British Academy Award Nomination: Best
Film (Winner: *Cabaret*)

The Godfather, Part II 1974 USA
US Academy Award: Best Picture

High Sierra 1941 USA
US National Board of Review: List of Ten
Best American Films

I Am a Fugitive From a Chain Gang 1932
USA
US Academy Award Nomination: Best Pic-
ture (Winner: *Cavalcade*)
US National Board of Review: Best Amer-
ican film

On the Waterfront 1954 USA
US Academy Award: Best Picture
New York Film Critics Award: Best Film
US National Board of Review Award: Best
American Film
US Golden Globe Award: Best Film, Drama
British Academy Award Nomination: Best
Film (Winners: *The Wages of Fear*,
France-Italy, Best Film; *Hobson's Choice*,
Best British Film)

Rashomon 1950 Japan
US Academy Award, 1951: Best Foreign
Language Film
US National Board of Review, 1951: Best
Foreign Film

Z 1969 France-Algeria
US Academy Award: Best Foreign Lan-
guage Film
New York Film Critics Award: Best Film
US Golden Globe Award: Best Foreign Lan-
guage Film
British Academy Award Nomination: Best
Film (Winner: *Midnight Cowboy*)

Above: Spencer Tracy and Anne
Francis in *Bad Day at Black Rock*
(1954).

Left: Ali MacGraw and Ryan
O'Neal in *Love Story* (1970).

Disaster

The disaster films have never managed
to do better for themselves than capture
Best Picture nominations from the US
Academy Awards. One, *Jaws* (1975,
USA), also received a Best Film
nomination from the British Academy
Awards.

Airport 1970 USA
US Academy Award Nomination: Best Picture (Winner: *Patton*)

In Old Chicago 1937 USA
US Academy Award Nomination: Best Picture (Winner: *The Life of Emile Zola*)

Jaws 1975 USA
US Academy Award Nomination: Best Pic-
ture (Winner: *One Flew Over the Cuckoo's
Nest*)
British Academy Award Nomination: Best
Film (Winner: *Alice Doesn't Live Here
Anymore*)

San Francisco 1936 USA
US Academy Award Nomination: Best Picture (Winner: *The Great Ziegfeld*)

The Towering Inferno 1974 USA
US Academy Award Nomination: Best Picture (Winner: *The Godfather, Part II*)

Mystery and Suspense

Bad Day at Black Rock 1955 USA
US National Board of Review: List of Ten
Best American films
British Academy Award Nomination: Best
Film (Winner: *Hamlet*, judged Best film
and Best British film)

Chinatown 1974 USA
US Academy Award Nomination: Best Pic-
ture (Winner: *The Godfather, Part II*)
US Golden Globe Award: Best Film, Drama
British Academy Award Nomination: Best
Film (Winner: *Lacombe Lucien*, France-
Italy-West Germany)

Les Diaboliques 1955 France
US National Board of Review: List of Five
Best Foreign Films
New York Film Critics Circle Award: Best
Foreign Language Film (Co-Winner with
Umberto D, Italy)

Gaslight 1944 USA
US Academy Award Nomination: Best Picture (Winner: *Going My Way*)

The Maltese Falcon 1941 USA
US Academy Award Nomination: Best Picture (Winner: *How Green Was My Valley*)

Rebecca 1940 USA
US Academy Award: Best Picture
US National Board of Review: List of Ten
Best American Films

Spellbound 1954 USA
US Academy Award Nomination: Best Picture (Winner: *The Lost Weekend*)

The Thin Man 1934 USA
US Academy Award Nomination: Best Picture (Winner: *It Happened One Night*)

US National Board of Review: List of Ten
  Best American Films

The Wages of Fear/La Salaire de la Peur
  1953 France-Algeria
Cannes Film Festival Award: Golden Palm
British Academy Award, 1954: Best Film

Romance

Brief Encounter 1946 UK
US National Board of Review: List of Ten
  Best (including foreign language) Films
Cannes Film Festival Award: Best Film
  (This award, presented in the Festival's
  initial year, was shared with seven other
  films)

The Go-Between 1971 UK
US National Board of Review: List of Ten
  English Language Films
Cannes Film Festival Award: Golden Palm
British Academy Award Nomination: Best
  Film (Winner: *Sunday, Bloody Sunday*)

Gone With the Wind 1939 USA
US Academy Award: Best Picture
US National Board of Review, 1940: List of
  Ten Best American Films

Love is a Many Splendored Thing 1955
  USA
US Academy Award Nomination: Best Pic-
  ture (Winner: *Marty*)
US Golden Globe Award: Film Best Promot-
  ing International Understanding

Love Story 1970 USA
US Academy Award Nomination: Best Pic-
  ture (Winner: *Patton*)
US National Board of Review: List of Ten
  Best English Language Films
US Golden Globe Award: Best Film

A Man and a Woman 1966 France
US Academy Award: Best Foreign Lan-
  guage Film
US National Board of Review: List of Five
  Best Foreign Language Films
US Golden Globe Award: Best Foreign Lan-
  guage Film
Cannes Film Festival Award: Golden Palm
  (Co-winner with *Signore e Signori*, Italy)

Marty 1955 USA
US Academy Award: Best Picture
US National Board of Review Award: Best
  American Film
New York Film Critics Award: Best Film
Cannes Film Festival Award: Golden Palm
British Academy Award Nomination: Best
  Film (Winner: *Richard III,* judged both
  Best Film and Best British Film)

A Place in the Sun 1951 USA
US Academy Award Nomination: Best Pic-
  ture (Winner: *An American in Paris*)
US National Board of Review: List of Ten
  Best American Films
US Golden Globe Award: Best Film, Drama

Roman Holiday 1953 USA
US Academy Award Nomination: Best Pic-
  ture (Winner: *From Here to Eternity*)
US National Board of Review: List of Ten
  Best American Films
British Academy Award Nomination: Best

Film (Winners: *Le Jeux Interdits,* France,
Best Film; *Genevieve,* Best British Film)

Romeo and Juliet 1968 UK-Italy
US Academy Award Nomination: Best Pic-
  ture (Winner: *Oliver!*)
US National Board of Review: List of Ten
  Best English Language Films
US Golden Globe Award: Best English Lan-
  guage Foreign Film

La Ronde 1950 France
British Academy Award, 1951: Best Film

A Streetcar Named Desire 1951 USA
US Academy Award Nomination: Best Pic-
  ture (Winner: *An American in Paris*)
US National Board of Review: List of Ten
  Best American Films
New York Film Critics Award: Best Film
British Academy Award Nomination: Best
  Film (Winner: *The Sound Barrier,* judged
  both Best Film and Best British Film. US
  title: *Breaking the Sound Barrier*)

Wuthering Heights 1939 USA
US Academy Award Nomination: Best Picture (Winner: *Gone With the Wind*)

Opposite: Rhett and Scarlett
(Clark Gable and Vivien Leigh)
at the cotillion, from *Gone With
the Wind* (1939).

Above: Olivia Hussey and
Leonard Whiting starred in
Franco Zeffirelli's *Romeo and
Juliet* (1968).

Left: Ernest Borngine and Betsy Blair in *Marty* (1955)

Right: Robert De Niro (left) and John Savage hang from a helicopter in *The Deer Hunter* (1978).

US National Board of Review: List of Ten Best English Language Films
New York Film Critics Award: Best Film

Social Comment

The Best Years of Our Lives 1946 USA
US Academy Award: Best Picture
US National Board of Review: List of Ten Best (including foreign) Films
New York Film Critics Award: Best Film
US Golden Globe Award: Best Film, Drama
British Academy Award, 1947: Best Film

Crossfire 1947 USA
US Academy Award Nomination: Best Picture (Winner: *Gentleman's Agreement*)
US National Board of Review: List of Ten Best (including foreign) Films
Cannes Film Festival: Best Film (Honor shared with four other films)
British Academy Award Nomination, 1947: Best Film (Winners: *Hamlet,* UK, Best Film; *The Fallen Idol,* Best British Film)

The Defiant Ones 1958 USA
US Academy Award Nomination: Best Picture (Winner: *Gigi*)
New York Film Critics Award: Best Film
Golden Globe Award: Best Film, Drama
British Academy Award Nomination: Best Film (Winner: *Room at the Top* judged both Best Film and Best British Film)

Gentleman's Agreement 1974 USA
US Academy Award: Best Picture
US National Board of Review: List of Ten Best (including foreign) Films

New York Film Critics Award: Best Film
US Golden Globe Award: Best Film, Drama

The Grapes of Wrath 1940 USA
US Academy Award Nomination: Best Picture (Winner: *Rebbecca*)
US National Board of Review: List of Ten Best American Films
New York Critics Award: Best Film

Guess Who's Coming to Dinner 1967 USA
US Academy Award Nomination: Best Picture (Winner: *In the Heat of the Night*)

In the Heat of the Night 1967 USA
US Academy Award: Best Picture
New York Film Critics Award: Best Film
US Golden Globe Award: Best Film, Drama
British Academy Award Nomination: Best Film (Winner: *A Man for all Seasons,* judged both Best Film and Best British Film)

The Lost Weekend 1945 USA
US Academy Award: Best Picture
US National Board of Review: List of Ten Best (including foreign) Films
New York Film Critics Award: Best Film
US Golden Globe Award: Best Film, Drama
Cannes Film Festival Award: Best Film (Shared honor with six other films)

Of Mice and Men 1939 USA
US Academy Award Nomination: Best Picture (Winner: *Gone With the Wind*)

One Flew Over the Cuckoo's Nest 1975 USA
US Academy Award: Best Picture
US National Board of Review: List of Ten Best English Language Films
US Golden Globe Award: Best Film, Drama

The Snake Pit 1948 USA
US Academy Award Nomination: Best Picture (Winner: *Hamlet*)
US National Board of Review: List of Ten Best (including foreign) Films

Umberto D 1952 Italy
New York Film Critics Award: Best Foreign Language Film (Co-winner: *Les Diaboliques,* France)

War

Two war offerings hold the distinction of being the first films ever to be named best pictures by America's two oldest awards groups. *Wings* (1927, USA) was presented with Best Picture honors for 1927/28 at the first Academy Awards banquet. To *All Quiet on the Western Front* (1930, USA) went a spot on the first list of Ten Best Films issued by the National Board of Review. The film was also designated Best Picture of 1929/30 by the Academy Awards.

Apocalypse Now 1979 USA
US Academy Award Nomination: Best Picture (Winner: *Kramer Vs Kramer*)
US National Board of Review: List of Ten Best English Language Films
British Academy Award Nomination: Best Film (Winner: *Manhattan*)
Cannes Film Festival Award: Golden Palm

Ballad of a Soldier 1961 USSR
British Academy Award: Best Film (Co-winner: *The Hustler*)

Black and White in Color 1976 France-Switzerland-Ivory Coast
US Academy Award: Best Foreign Language Film

The Bridge 1961 West Germany
US National Board of Review: Best Foreign Film

The Bridge on the River Kwai 1957 UK-USA
US Academy Award: Best Picture
US National Board of Review: Best American Film
New York Critics Award: Best Film
US Golden Globe Award: Best Film, Drama
British Academy Award: Best Film and Best British Film

The Deer Hunter 1978 USA
US Academy Award: Best Picture
New York Film Critics Award: Best Film

From Here to Eternity 1953 USA
US Academy Award: Best Picture
US National Board of Review: List of Ten Best American Films
New York Film Critics Award: Best Film
British Academy Award Nomination: Best Film (Winners: *Genevieve*, Best British Film; *Les Jeux Interdits*, France, Best Film)

La Grande Illusion 1937 France
US Academy Award Nomination, 1938: Best Picture (Winner: *You Can't Take it With You*)
US National Board of Review, 1938: Best Foreign Film
New York Film Critics Award, 1938: Best Foreign Language Film

In Which We Serve 1942 UK
US Academy Award Nomination, 1943: Best Picture (Winner: *Casablanca*)
US National Board of Review Award: Best English Language Film
New York Critics Award, 1942: Best Film

Les Jeux Interdits 1952 France
US Academy Award: Best Foreign Language Film
US National Board of Review: List of Five Best Foreign Films
New York Film Critics Award: Best Foreign Language Film

M*A*S*H 1970 USA
US Academy Award Nomination: Best Picture (Winner: *Patton*)
US Golden Globe Award: Best Film, Musical/Comedy
British Academy Award Nomination: Best Film (Winner: *Butch Cassidy and the Sundance Kid*)
British Academy Award: United Nations Award
Cannes Film Festival Award: Golden Palm

Patton 1970 USA
US Academy Award: Best Picture
US National Board of Review Award: Best English Language film

Other war films that have won recognition include *Sergeant York* (1941, USA), *Wake Island* (1942, USA), *Mr Roberts* (1955, USA) and *The Longest Day* (1926, USA), all of which earned Academy Award Best Picture nominations. *Open City* (1946, Italy) received the Best Foreign Language film award from the New York Film Critics and was included in the National Board of Review's list of Ten Best Films.

The list of honors and recognitions is an impressive one. But, in one way, it is an unfair one. It does not – obviously cannot – include the names of the many fine and ambitious films that were made in the years before there were such things as awards organizations. The pictures themselves have been mentioned in the course of this book and so, as we close, let us at least give a very deserved and respectful nod in their direction by mentioning just several of their most distinguished respresentatives – *The Covered Wagon*, *La Voyage dans le Lune/A Trip to the Moon*, *Das Kabinett des Dr Caligari/The Cabinet of Dr Caligari*, *The Kid*, *A Study in Scarlet*, *Intolerance* and *The Big Parade*.

In all, hundreds of films were made over the world before the coming of the awards organizations. Though never recognized with an Oscar or a Golden Palm, they were admired in their day, as they are when seen today, and they led the way to the present, just as today's films are leading to tomorrow.

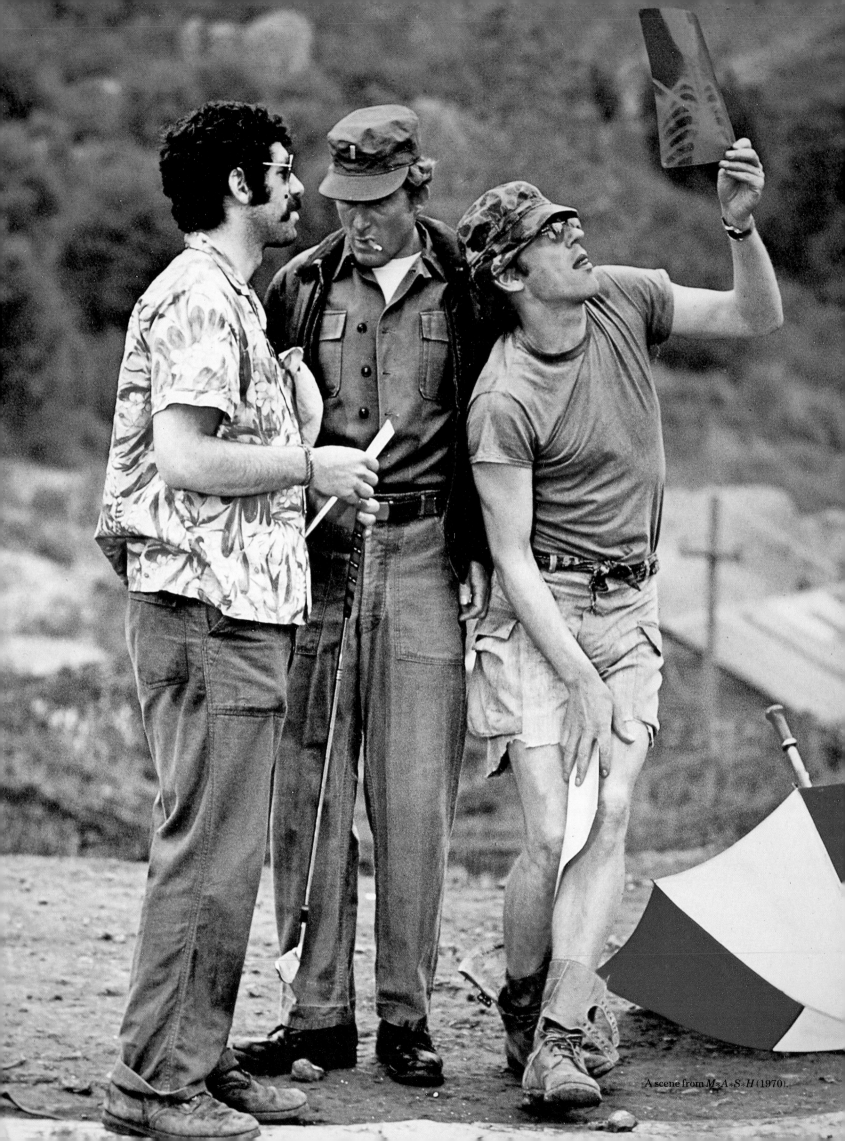

A scene from *M*A*S*H* (1970).

FILMOGRAPHY

The Western

Across the Wide Missouri 1951 (USA, MGM). D: William A Wellman. S: Clark Gable, Ricardo Montalban, John Hodiak, Adolphe Menjou.

Alamo, The 1960 (USA, Batjac/United Artists). D: John Wayne. S: John Wayne, Richard Widmark, Laurence Harvey.

Ambush 1950 (USA, MGM). D: Sam Wood. S: Robert Taylor, Arlene Dahl, John Hodiak.

Apache 1954 (USA, Hecht-Lancaster). D: Robert Aldrich. S: Burt Lancaster, Jean Peters.

Apple Dumpling Gang, The 1975 (USA, Buena Vista). D: Norman Tokar. S: Bill Bixby, Susan Clark.

Arizona 1940 (USA, Par). D: Wesley Ruggles. S: William Holden, Jean Arthur.

Bandit Makes Good, The 1907 (USA, Essanay). D: G A (Broncho Billy) Anderson. S: G A (Broncho Billy) Anderson.

Bargain, The 1914 (USA, New York Motion Picture Corp/Par). D: Reginald Barker. S: William S Hart, J Frank Burke, Clara Williams, J Barney Sherry.

Belle Starr 1941 (USA, 20th). D: Irving Cummings. S: Gene Tierney, Randolph Scott, Dana Andrews.

Billy the Kid 1941 (USA, MGM). D: David Miller. S: Robert Taylor, Brian Donlevy.

Blazing Saddles 1974 (USA, Warners). D: Mel Brooks. S: Mel Brooks, Gene Wilder, Cleavon Little, Madeleine Kahn.

Breakheart Pass 1976 (USA, United Artists). D: Tom Gries. S: Charles Bronson, Ben Johnson, Richard Crenna, Jill Ireland.

Butch Cassidy and the Sundance Kid 1969 (USA, 20th). D: George Roy Hill. S: Paul Newman, Robert Redford, Katharine Ross.

Cahill, United States Marshal 1973 (USA, Warners). D: Andrew V McLaglen. S: John Wayne, George Kennedy, Garry Grimes.

Cat Ballou 1965 (USA, Col). D: Elliot Silverstein. S: Jane Fonda, Lee Marvin, Michael Callan.

Cheyenne Autumn 1964 (USA, 20th). D: John Ford. S: Richard Widmark, Carroll Baker, Karl Malden, James Stewart, Edward G Robinson, Dolores Del Rio.

Cimarron 1931 (USA, RKO). D: Wesley Ruggles. S: Richard Dix, Irene Dunne, Edna May Oliver, Estelle Taylor.

Commanche Station 1960 (USA, Ranown). D: Budd Boetticher. S: Randolph Scott.

Covered Wagon, The 1923 (USA, Famous Players-Lasky/Par). D: James Cruze. S: Ernest Torrence, Tully Marshall, J Warren Kerrigan, Lois Wilson, Ethel Wales, Alan Hale (Sr.).

Cowboy 1958 (USA, Col). D: Delmar Daves. S: Glenn Ford, Jack Lemmon.

Death of a Gunfighter 1969 (USA, Universal). D: Allen Smithee. S: Richard Widmark, Lena Horne, Carroll O'Connor, John Saxon.

Decision at Sundown 1957 (USA, Ranown). D: Budd Boetticher. S: Randolph Scott, John Carroll, Karen Steele.

Destry Rides Again 1939 (USA, Universal). D: George Marshall. S: James Stewart, Marlene Dietrich, Brian Donlevy.

Dodge City 1940 (USA, Warners). D: Michael Curtiz. S: Errol Flynn, Ann Sheridan, Olivia de Havilland.

Duel in the Sun 1947 (USA, Selznick). D: King Vidor. S: Gregory Peck, Jennifer Jones, Lionel Barrymore, Joseph Cotten, Lillian Gish, Charles Bickford, Walter Huston, Harry Carey (Sr.).

Electric Horseman, The 1979 (USA, Col). D: Sydney Pollack. S: Robert Redford, Jane Fonda, Valerie Perrine, Willie Nelson.

Fistful of Dollars, A 1964 (Italy-Spain-West Germany). D: Sergio Leone. S: Clint Eastwood, Marianne Koch, Gian Maria Volonte.

For a Few Dollars More 1967 (Italy). D: Sergio Leone. S: Clint Eastwood, Lee Van Cleef.

Fort Apache 1948 (USA, 20th). D: John Ford. S: John Wayne, Henry Fonda, Pedro Armendariz, Ward Bond.

Frontier Marshal 1939 (USA, 20th). D: Allan Dwan. S: Randolph Scott, Nancy Kelly, Cesar Romero.

Good, the Bad and the Ugly, The 1966 (Italy). D: Sergio Leone. S: Clint Eastwood, Eli Wallach, Lee Van Cleef.

Great Train Robbery, The 1903 (USA, Edison). D: Edwin S Porter. S: G A (Broncho Billy) Anderson, Marie Murray, George Barnes, Frank Hanaway.

Gunfight at the OK Corral 1957 (USA, Par). D: John Sturges. S: Burt Lancaster, Kirk Douglas, Jo Van Fleet, Rhonda Fleming.

Gunfighter, The 1950 (USA, Goldwyn). D: Henry King. S: Gregory Peck, Karl Malden, Jean Parker, Skip Homeier.

Hang 'Em High 1968 (USA, United Artists). D: Ted Post. S: Clint Eastwood, Inger Stevens, Ed Begley.

High Noon 1952 (USA, Kramer/United Artists). D: Fred Zinnemann. S: Gary Cooper, Grace Kelly, Thomas Mitchell, Lloyd Bridges, Lon Chaney, Jr.

Hondo 1954 (USA, Warners). D: John Farrow. S: John Wayne, Geraldine Page, Ward Bond.

How the West was Won 1962 (USA, MGM). D: John Ford, Henry Hathaway, George Marshall. S: James Stewart, Henry Fonda, Gregory Peck, John Wayne, Richard Widmark, Carroll Baker.

Hud 1963 (USA, Par). D: Martin Ritt. S: Paul Newman, Patricia Neal, Melvyn Douglas.

In Old Arizona 1929 (USA, Fox). D: Irving Cummings. S: Warner Baxter.

Jeremiah Johnson 1972 (USA, Warners). D: Sydney Pollack. S: Robert Redford, Will Geer.

Jesse James 1939 (USA, 20th). D: Henry King. S: Tyrone Power, Henry Fonda, Nancy Kelly.

Johnny Guitar 1954 (USA, Republic). D: Nicholas Ray. S: Joan Crawford, Sterling Hayden, Ernest Borgnine.

Left-Handed Gun, The 1958 (USA, Warners). D: Arthur Penn. S: Paul Newman, John Dehner, Hurd Hatfield.

Little Big Man 1970 (USA, Warners). D: Arthur Penn. S: Dustin Hoffman, Faye Dunaway, Chief Dan George, Richard Mulligan.

Lone Star 1952 (USA, MGM). D: Vincent Sherman. S: Clark Gable, Ava Gardner, Lionel Barrymore.

Man of Conquest 1939 (USA, Republic). D: George Nicholls. S: Richard Dix, Joan Fontaine, Gail Patrick, C. Henry Gordon.

Man of the West 1958 (USA, United Artists). D: Anthony Mann. S: Gary Cooper, Julie London, Lee J Cobb.

Mark of Zorro, The 1920 (USA, United Artists). D: Fred Niblo. S: Douglas Fairbanks (Sr.), Marguerite de la Motte, Claire McDowell, Noah Berry.

Mark of Zorro, The 1940 (USA, 20th). D: Rouben Mamoulian. S: Tyrone Power, Linda Darnell, Basil Rathbone.

My Darling Clementine 1946 (USA, 20th). D: John Ford. S: Henry Fonda, Linda Darnell, Victor Mature.

Nevada Smith 1966 (USA, Embassy). D: Henry Hathaway. S: Steve McQueen, Suzanne Pleshette, Karl Malden, Brian Keith.

Oklahoma Kid, The 1939 (USA, Warners). D: Lloyd Bacon. S: James Cagney, Humphrey Bogart, Rosemary Lane.

One-Eyed Jacks 1961 (USA, Par). D: Marlon Brando. S: Marlon Brando, Karl Malden, Katy Jurado.

Outlaw, The 1943 (USA, RKO). D: Howard Hughes. S: Jane Russell, Jack Beutel, Walter Huston, Thomas Mitchell.

Outlaw Josey Wales, The 1976 (USA, Warners). D: Clint Eastwood. S: Clint Eastwood, Sondra Locke, Chief Dan George.

Ox-Bow Incident, The 1943 (USA, 20th). D: William A Wellman. S: Henry Fonda, Dana Andrews, Anthony Quinn, Henry (Harry) Morgan, Jane Darwell.

Paleface, The 1948 (USA, Par). D: Norman Z McLeod. S: Bob Hope, Jane Russell.

Plainsman, The 1936 (USA, Par). D: Cecil B DeMille. S: Gary Cooper, Jean Arthur, James Ellison, Anthony Quinn.

Rangers of Fortune 1940 (USA, Par). D: Sam Wood. S: Fred MacMurray, Patricia Morrison, Albert Dekker.

Red River 1948 (USA, United Artists). D: Howard Hawks. S: John Wayne, Montgomery Clift, Joanne Dru, Walter Brennan.

Ride Lonesome 1959 (USA, Ranown). D: Budd Boetticher. S: Randolph Scott, Karen Steele, Pernell Roberts.

Ride the High Country 1962 (USA, MGM). D: Sam Peckinpah. S: Randolph Scott, Joel McCrea, Mariette Hartley.

Rio Bravo 1959 (USA, Warners). D: Howard Hawks. S: John Wayne, Dean Martin, Ricky Nelson, Walter Brennan, Angie Dickinson.

San Antonio 1945 (USA, Warners). D: Raoul Walsh. S: Errol Flynn, Alexis Smith.

Santa Fe Trail 1940 (USA, Warners). D: Michael Curtiz. S: Errol Flynn, Olivia de Havilland, Ronald Reagan, Van Heflin, Raymond Massey.

Searchers, The 1956 (USA, Warners). D: John Ford. S: John Wayne, Jeffrey Hunter, Vera Miles, Ward Bond, Natalie Wood.

Seven Men from Now 1956 (USA, Warners). D: Budd Boetticher. S: Randolph Scott, Gail Russell, Lee Marvin.

Shane 1953 (USA, Par). D: George Stevens. S: Alan Ladd, Jean Arthur, Van Heflin,

Brandon de Wilde, Jack Palance.

Son of Paleface 1952 (USA, Par). D: Frank Tashlin. S: Bob Hope, Jane Russell, Roy Rogers.

Spoilers, The 1914 (USA, Selig). D: William N Selig. S: William Farnum, Tom Santschi, Bessie Eyton, Kathlyn Williams.

Spoilers, The 1942 (USA, Universal). D: Ray Enright. S: John Wayne, Randolph Scott, Marlene Dietrich, Richard Barthelmess.

Squaw Man, The 1914 (USA, Jesse Lasky Feature Play Co.). D: Cecil B DeMille. S: Dustin Farnum.

Stagecoach 1936 (USA, Wanger/United Artists). D: John Ford. S: John Wayne, Claire Trevor, Thomas Mitchell, John Carradine, Louise Platt, George Bancroft, Andy Devine, Berton Churchill, Donald Meek.

Tall T, The 1957 (USA, Warners). D: Budd Boetticher. S: Randolph Scott, Richard Boone, Maureen O'Sullivan.

Texas 1941 (USA, Par). D: George Marshall. S: William Holden, Glenn Ford, Claire Trevor.

They Died With Their Boots On 1941 (USA, Warners). D: Raoul Walsh. S: Errol Flynn, Olivia de Havilland, Arthur Kennedy.

3:10 to Yuma 1957 (USA, Col). D: Delmar Daves. S: Glenn Ford, Van Heflin, Felicia Farr, Leora Dana.

Treasure of Sierra Madre, The 1947 (USA, Warners). D: John Huston. S: Humphrey Bogart, Walter Huston, Tim Holt, Alfonso Bedaya.

True Grit 1969 (USA, Par). D: Henry Hathaway. S: John Wayne, Kim Darby, Glen Campbell, Robert Duvall.

Union Pacific (British title: *Pacific Express*) 1939 (USA, Par). D: Cecil B DeMille. S: Joel McCrea, Barbara Stanwyck, Robert Preston, Brian Donlevy.

Virginia City 1940 (USA, Warners). D: Michael Curtiz. S: Errol Flynn, Humphrey Bogart, Miriam Hopkins, Randolph Scott.

Virginian, The 1929 (USA, Par). D: Victor Fleming. S: Gary Cooper, Richard Arlen, Walter Huston, Mary Brian.

Viva Villa 1934 (USA, MGM). D: Howard Hawks, Jack Conway. S: Wallace Beery, Stuart Erwin, Leo Carillo.

Way Out West 1936 (USA, Roach/MGM). D: James W. Horne. S: Laurel and Hardy.

Western Union 1941 (USA, 20th). D: Fritz Lang. S: Randolph Scott, Robert Young, Dean Jagger.

Westerner, The 1940 (USA, Goldwyn). D: William Wyler. S: Gary Cooper, Walter Brennan, Doris Davenport.

Westward the Women 1951 (USA, MGM). D: William A Wellman. S: Robert Taylor, Denise Darcel.

Wild Bunch, The 1969 (USA, Warners). D: Sam Peckinpah. S: William Holden, Robert Ryan, Ernest Borgnine.

Yellow Sky 1948 (USA, 20th). D: William A Wellman. S: Gregory Peck, Richard Widmark, Anne Baxter.

Chapter 3
Fantasy I: Science Fiction

Abbott and Costello Meet Frankenstein 1948 (USA, Universal). D: Charles Barton. S: Bud Abbott, Lou Costello, Lon Chaney, Bela Lugosi.

Abbott and Costello Go to Mars 1953 (USA, Universal). D: Charles Lamont. S: Bud Abbott, Lou Costello, Martha Hyer, Horace McMahan.

Abbott and Costello Meet the Invisible Man 1951 (USA, Universal). D: Charles Lamont. S: Bud Abbott, Lou Costello, Nancy Guild.

Aelita 1924 (USSR). D: Yakov Protazanov. S: Yulia Solntseva, Nikolai Batalov, Igor Illinsky.

Alien 1979 (USA, 20th). D: Ridley Scott. S: Sigourney Weaver, Ian Holm, Tom Skerritt, Yaphet Kotto, Veronica Cartwright.

Alligator People, The 1959 (USA, 20th). D: Roy Del Ruth. S: Beverly Garland, Lon Chaney, Bruce Bennett.

Alphaville 1965 (France). D: Jean-Luc Godard. S: Eddie Constantine, Akim Tamiroff, Anna Karina.

Andromeda Strain, The 1971 (USA, Universal). D: Robert Wise. S: Arthur Hill, James Olson, David Wayne, Katie Reid.

Angry Red Planet, The 1959 (USA, American International). D: Ib Melchier. S: Gerald Mohr, Les Tremayne, Nora Hayden.

Attack of the Crab Monsters 1957 (USA, Allied Artists). D: Roger Corman. S: Richard Garland, Russell Johnson, Pamela Duncan.

Battle for the Planet of the Apes 1973 (USA, 20th). D: J. Lee Thompson. S: Roddy McDowall, Claude Akins, John Huston, Natalie Trundy.

Beast from 20,000 Fathoms, The 1953 (USA, Warners). D: Eugene Lourie. S: Kenneth Tobey, Paul Christian, Paula Raymond.

Beneath the Planet of the Apes 1970 (USA, 20th). D: Ted Post. S: Charlton Heston, James Franciscus, Roddy McDowall, Kim Hunter.

Black Cat, The 1934 (USA, Universal). D: Edgar G Ulmer. S: Boris Karloff, Bela Lugosi, David Manners.

Black Scorpion 1957 (USA, Warners). D: Edward Ludwig. S: Richard Denning, Mara Corday.

Blob, The 1958 (USA, Par). D: Irvin Yeaworth. S: Steve McQueen, Aneta Corseaut, Earl Rowe.

Brain from Planet Arous, The 1957 (USA, Howco International). D: Nathan Juran. S: John Agar, Robert Fuller, Joyce Meader.

Bride of Frankenstein, The 1935 (USA, Universal). D: James Whale. S: Boris Karloff, Colin Clive, Elsa Lanchester, Ernest Thesiger, Valerie Hobson, Dwight Frye.

Buck Rogers (serial) 1939 (USA, Universal). D: Ford Beebe, Saul Goodkind. S: Buster Crabbe, Constance Moore, Henry Branden.

Clockwork Orange, A 1971 (UK). D: Stanley Kubrick. S: Malcolm McDowell, Patrick Magee, Adrienne Corri.

Close Encounters of the Third Kind 1977 (USA, Col). D: Stephen Spielberg. S: Richard Dreyfuss, Melinda Dillion, Teri Garr, Francois Truffaut.

Colossus of New York 1958 (USA, Par). D: Eugene Lourie. S: John Baragrey, Otto Kruger, Mala Powers.

Conquest of Space 1955 (USA, Par). D: Byron Haskin. S: Eric Fleming, Walter Brooke, Phil Foster.

Conquest of the Planet of the Apes 1972 (USA, Fox). D: J Lee Thompson. S: Roddy McDowall, Ricardo Montalban, Don Murray, Natalie Trundy.

Crack in the World 1965 (USA, Par). D: Andrew Marton. S: Dana Andrews, Janette Scott, Kieron Moore.

Creature from the Black Lagoon 1954 (USA, Universal). D: Jack Arnold. S: Richard Carlson, Julia Adams, Richard Denning.

Creeping Unknown, The (British title: *The Quatermass Experiment*) 1956 (UK) D: Val Guest. S: Brian Donlevy, Jack Warner, Margia Dean.

Curse of Frankenstein, The 1957 (UK). D: Freddie Francis. S: Peter Cushing, Christopher Lee.

Day of the Triffids 1963 (UK). D: Steve Sekely. S: Howard Keel, Janette Scott, Nicole Maurey, Kieron Moore.

Day the Earth Caught Fire, The 1962 (UK). D: Val Guest. S: Leo McKern, Janet Munro, Edward Judd.

Day the Earth Stood Still, The 1951 (USA, 20th). D: Robert Wise. S: Michael Rennie, Patricia Neal, Hugh Marlowe.

Destination Moon 1950 (USA, United Artists). D: Irving Pichel. S: Warner Anderson, John Archer, Tom Powers.

Destroy All Monsters 1969 (Japan). D: Inoshiro Honda. S: Akira Kubo, Jun Tazaki.

Dr. Cyclops 1940 (USA, Par). D: Ernest Schoedsack. S: Albert Dekker, Janice Logan.

Dr. Strangelove – or How I Learned to Stop Worrying and Love the Bomb 1964 (UK). D: Stanley Kubrick. S: Peter Sellers, George C Scott, Sterling Hayden, Keenan Wynn.

Empire Strikes Back, The 1980 (USA, 20th). D: Irvin Kershner. S: Mark Hamill, Carrie Fisher, Harrison Ford, Alec Guinness.

Enemy from Space 1957 (UK). D: Val Guest. S: Brian Donlevy, Vera Day, Sidney James.

Escape from the Planet of the Apes 1971 (USA, 20th). D: Don Taylor. S: Roddy McDowall, Kim Hunter, Bradford Dillman, Sal Mineo.

E.T. – The Extra-Terrestrial 1982 (USA, Universal). D: Stephen Spielberg. S: Henry Thomas, Robert McNaughton, Drew Barrymore, Dee Wallace.

Flash Gordon (Serial) 1936 (USA, Universal). D: Frederick Stephani. S: Buster Crabbe, Jean Rogers, Charles Middleton, Frank Shannon.

Flash Gordon Conquers the World (Serial) 1940 (USA, Universal). D: Ford Beebe, Ray Taylor. S: Buster Crabbe, Carol Hughes, Charles Middleton, Frank Shannon.

Flash Gordon's Trip to Mars (Serial) 1938 (USA, Universal). D: Ford Beebe, Robert Hill. S: Buster Crabbe, Jean Rogers, Charles Middleton, Frank Shannon.

Fly, The 1958 (USA, 20th). D: Kurt Neumann. S: Vincent Price, Al (David) Hedison, Herbert Marshall, Patricia Owens.

Forbidden Planet 1956 (USA, MGM). D: Fred M Wilcox. S: Walter Pidgeon, Anne Francis, Leslie Nielsen, Warren Stevens.

Evil of Frankenstein, The 1964 (UK). D: Freddie Francis. S: Peter Cushing, Duncan Lamont, Peter Woodthorpe.

Fahrenheit 451 1966 (UK). D: Francois Truffaut. S: Oskar Werner, Julie Christie, Anton Diffring.

Fail Safe 1964 (USA, Col). D: Sidney Lumet. S: Henry Fonda, Walter Matthau, Dan O'Herlihy, Larry Hagman.

Fantastic Voyage 1966 (USA, 20th). D: Richard Fleischer. S: Stephen Boyd, Raquel Welch, Edmond O'Brien, Arthur Kennedy.

First Men in the Moon, The 1964 (UK). D: Nathan Juran. S: Lionel Jeffries, Martha Hyer, Edward Judd.

First Spaceship on Venus (East Germany-Poland). D: Kurt Maetzig. S: Yoko Tani, Oldrich Lukes, Ignacy Machowski.

Five 1951 (USA, Col). D: Arch Oboler. S: James Anderson, Charles Lampkin, William Phipps.

Five Million Years to Earth 1967 (UK). D: Roy Baker. S: James Donald, Andrew Keir, Barbara Shelley.

Forbin Project, The (Alternate title: *Colossus: The Forbin Project*) 1970 (USA. Universal). D: Joseph Sargent. S: Eric Braeden, Susan Clark, William Schallert.

Frankenstein 1931 (USA, Universal). D: James Whale. S: Boris Karloff, Colin Clive, John Boles, Mae Clarke, Dwight Frye.

Frankenstein Conquers the World 1966 (Japan). D: Inoshiro Honda. S: Nick Adams, Tadao Takashima.

Frankenstein Created Woman 1967 (UK), D: Terence Fisher. S: Peter Cushing, Susan Denberg.

Frankenstein Meets the Wolf Man 1943 (USA, Universal). D: Roy William Neill. S: Lon Chaney, Jr., Bela Lugosi.

Frankenstein Must be Destroyed 1969 (UK). D: Terence Fisher. S: Peter Cushing, Simon Ward, Veronica Carlson.

Frankenstein 1970 1978 (USA, Allied Artists). D: Howard W Koch. S: Boris Karloff, Charlotte Austin.

From the Earth to the Moon 1958 (USA, Warners/RKO). D: Byron Haskin. S: Joseph Cotten, George Sanders, Debra Paget.

Ghidrah, the Three-Headed Monster 1965 (Japan). D: Inoshiro Honda. S: Yosuke Natsuki, Emi Ito, Uuriko Hoshi.

Giant Behemoth, The 1959 (UK). D: Eugene Lourie. S: Gene Evans, Andre Morell, Leigh Madison.

Girl in the Moon 1929 (Germany). D: Fritz Lang. S: Gerda Maurus, Fritz Rasp, Willy Fritsch.

Godzilla, King of the Monsters 1955 (Japan). D: Inoshiro Honda. S: Raymond Burr, Momoko Kochi, Takashi Shimura.

Godzilla vs the Sea Monster 1966 (Japan). D: Jun Fukuda. S: Akira Takarada, Toru Watanabe.

Gorgo 1961 (UK). D: Eugene Lourie. S: Bill Travers, William Sylvester, Vincent Winter.

Have Rocket Will Travel 1959 (USA, Col). D: David Lowell Rich. S: The Three Stooges, Jerome Cowen.

I Married a Monster from Outer Space 1958 (USA, Par). D: Gene Fowler, Jr. S: Tom Tryon, Gloria Talbott, Ken Lynch.

Incredible Shrinking Man, The 1957 (USA, Universal). D: Jack Arnold. S: Grant Williams, Paul Langdon, Randy Stuart.

Invaders from Mars 1958 (USA, 20th). D:

The Bride of Frankenstein (1935), Elsa Lanchester.

William Cameron Menzies. S: Arthur Franz, Helena Carter, Jimmy Hunt.

Invasion of the Body Snatchers 1956 (USA, Allied Artists). D: Don Siegel. S: Kevin McCarthy, Dana Wynter, Larry Gates.

Invisible Man, The 1933 (USA, Universal). D: James Whale. S: Claude Rains, Gloria Stuart, Henry Travers, Una O'Connor.

Invisible Man Returns, The 1940 (USA, Universal). D: Joe May. S: Vincent Price, Cedric Hardwicke, Nan Grey.

Invisible Man's Revenge, The 1944 (USA, Universal). D: Ford Beebe. S: John Carradine, Jon Hall.

Invisible Ray, The 1936 (USA, Universal). D: Lambert Hillyer. S: Boris Karloff, Bela Lugosi.

Island of Lost Souls 1932 (USA, Par). D: Erle C Kenton. S: Charles Laughton, Richard Arlen, Leila Hyams.

It Came from Beneath the Sea 1955 (USA, Col). D: Robert Gordon. S: Kenneth Robey, Donald Curtis, Faith Domergue.

Journey to the Center of the Earth 1959 (USA, 20th). D: Henry Levin. S: James Mason, Pat Boone, Diane Baker, Arlene Dahl.

Journey to the Far Side of the Sun 1969 (UK). D: Robert Parrish. S: Roy Thinnes, Herbert Lom, Lynn Loring.

Journey to the Seventh Planet 1962 (USA, American International). D: Sidney Pink. S: John Agar, Greta Thyssen.

Just Imagine 1930 (USA, MGM). D: David Butler. S: John Garrick, Maureen O'Sullivan, El Brendel, Hobart Bosworth.

King Kong 1933 (USA, RKO). D: Merian C Cooper, Ernest B Schoedsack. S: Robert Armstrong, Bruce Cabot, Fay Wray.

Konga 1961 (UK). D: John Lemont. S: Michael Gough, Margo Johns, Jess Conrad.

Man Made Monster 1941 (USA, Universal). D: George Waggner. S: Lon Chaney, Jr., Lionel Atwill, Anne Nagel.

Marooned 1970 (USA, Col). D: John Sturges. S: Gregory Peck, David Janssen, Gene Hackman, James Franciscus.

Metropolis/Metropolis – Das Schicksal einer

Menscheit im Jahre 2000 1926 (Germany). D: Fritz Lang. S: Brigette Helm, Alfred Abel, Gustav Frohlich.

Mothra 1962 (Japan). D: Inoshiro Honda. S: Franky Sakai, Hiroshi Koizumi, Hyoko Hagawa.

1984 1955 (UK). D: Michael Anderson. S: Edmond O'Brien, Michael Redgrave, Jan Sterling.

Omega Man, The 1971 (USA, Warners). D: Boris Sagal. S: Charlton Heston, Anthony Zerbe, Rosalind Clark.

On the Beach 1959 (USA, United Artists). D: Stanley Kramer. S: Gregory Peck, Ava Gardner, Fred Astaire, Anthony Perkins.

Panic in the Year Zero! 1962 (USA, American International/Alta Vista). D: Ray Milland. S: Ray Milland, Jean Hagen, Frankie Avalon.

Plan Nine from Outer Space (UK Title: *Grave Robbers from Outer Space*) 1959 (USA, DCA). D: Edward Wood, Jr. S: Bela Lugosi, Lyle Talbot, Gregory Walcott.

Planet of the Apes 1968 (USA, 20th). D: Franklin J Schaffner. S: Charlton Heston, Roddy McDowall, Kim Hunter, Maurice Evans.

Red Planet Mars 1952 (USA, United Artists). D: Harry Horner. S: Peter Graves, Andrea King, Marvin Miller.

Return of the Fly 1959 (USA, 20th). D: Edward L Bernds. S: Vincent Price, Brett Halsey.

Rocketship XM 1950 (USA, Lippert). D: Kurt Neumann. S: Lloyd Bridges, Hugh O'Brian, Osa Massen.

Rodan, the Flying Monster 1957 (Japan). D: Inoshiro Honda. S: Kenji Sawara, Yumi Shirakawa, Arihiko Hirato.

Silent Running 1972 (USA, Universal). D: Douglas Trumbull. S: Bruce Dern, Cliff Potts, Ron Rivkin.

Son of Frankenstein 1939 (USA, Universal). D: Rowland V Lee. S: Boris Karloff, Basil Rathbone, Bela Lugosi, Lionel Atwill.

Soylent Green 1973 (USA, MGM). D: Richard Fleischer. S: Charlton Heston, Edward G Robinson, Leigh Taylor-Young, Joseph Cotten, Chuck Connors.

Star Trek – The Motion Picture 1979 (USA, Par). D: Robert Wise. S: William Shatner, Leonard Nimoy, DeForest Kelley.

Star Trek II: The Wrath of Khan 1982 (USA, Par). D: Nicholas Meyer. S: William Shatner, Leonard Nimoy, DeForest Kelley, Ricardo Montalban.

Star Wars 1977 (USA, 20th). D: George Lucas. S: Mark Hamill, Carrie Fisher, Harrison Ford, Alec Guinness.

Teenagers from Outer Space 1959 (USA, Warners). D: Tom Graeff. S: David Lowe, Dawn Anderson.

Them! 1954 (USA, Warners). D: Gordon Douglas. S: James Whitmore, Edmund Gwenn, James Arness, Joan Weldon.

The Thing from Another World 1951 (USA, RKO). D: Christian Nyby. S: Kenneth Tobey, James Arness, Margaret Sheridan.

Things to Come 1936 (UK). D: William Cameron Menzies. S: Raymond Massey, Ralph Richardson, Ann Todd, Cedric Hardwicke.

This Island Earth 1955 (USA, Universal). D: Joseph M Neumann. S: Jeff Morrow, Rex Reason, Faith Domergue.

Three Stooges in Orbit, The 1962 (USA, Col).

D: Edward L Bernds. S: The Three Stooges, Carol Christensen.

THX 1138 1971 (USA, Warners). D: George Lucas. S: Robert Duvall, Donald Pleasence, Ian Wolfe.

Time Machine, The 1960 (USA, MGM). D: Goerge Pal. S: Rod Taylor, Yvette Mimieux, Sebastian Cabot, Alan Young.

Trip to the Moon, A/Le Voyage dans la Lune 1903 (France). D: Georges Méliès. S: Georges Melies, Victor Andre, Depierre Farjoux.

20,000 Leagues Under the Sea 1954 (USA, Disney). D: Richard Fleischer. S: Kirk Douglas, James Mason, Peter Lorre.

2001: A Space Odyssey 1968 (UK-USA). D: Stanley Kubrick. S: Keir Dullea, Gary Lockwood, William Sylvester.

Voyage to the Bottom of the Sea 1961 (USA, 20th). D: Irwin Allen. S: Walter Pidgeon, Joan Fontaine, Peter Lorre, Barbara Eden, Frankie Avalon, Robert Sterling.

War of the Worlds 1953 (USA, Par). D: Byron Haskin. S: Gene Barry, Ann Robinson, Les Tremayne.

When Worlds Collide 1951 (USA, Par). D: Rudolph Mate. S: Richard Derr, Barbara Rush, John Hoyt.

World, the Flesh and the Devil, The 1959 (USA, MGM). D: Ranald MacDougall. S: Harry Belafonte, Mel Ferrer, Inger Stevens.

World Without End 1956 (USA, Allied Artists). D: Edward L Bernds. S: Hugh Marlowe, Rod Taylor, Nancy Gates.

Chapter 4
Fantasy II: Horror

Abbott and Costello Meet Dr. Jekyll and Mr. Hyde 1953 (USA, Universal). D: Charles Lamont. S: Bud Abbott, Lou Costello, Boris Karloff.

Abbott and Costello Meet the Mummy 1955 (USA, Universal). D: Charles Lamont. S: Bud Abbott, Lou Costello, Marie Windsor.

Amityville Horror, The 1979 (USA, Filmways/American International). D: Stuart Rosenberg. S: James Brolin, Margot Kidder, Rod Steiger.

Billy the Kid vs. Dracula 1966 (USA, Embassy). D: William Beaudine. S: John Carradine, Chuck Courtney, Melinda Plowman.

Blacula 1972 (USA, American International). D: William Crain. S: William Marshall, Vonetta McGee, Emily Yancy.

Black Sunday/Mashera del Demonia (UK title: *Revenge of the Vampire*) 1961 (Italy). D: Mario Bava. S: Barbara Steele, John Richardson.

Blood and Roses/El Mourier de Plaiser 1960 (France). D: Roger Vadim. S: Mel Ferrer, Elsa Martinelli, Annette Vadim.

Brides of Dracula, The 1960 (UK). D: Terence Fisher. S: Peter Cushing, David Peel.

Burn, Witch Burn 1962 (UK). D: Sidney Hayers. S: Janet Blair, Peter Wyngarde.

Cabinet of Dr. Caligari, The/Das Kabinett des Dr. Caligari 1919 (Germany). D: Robert Wiene. S: Werner Krauss, Conrad Veidt, Lil Dagover, Friedrich Feher.

Carrie 1976 (USA, United Artists). D: Brian De Palma. S: Sissy Spacek, Piper Laurie, John Travolta.

Cat People, The 1942 (USA, RKO). D: Jacques Tourneur. S: Simone Simon, Kent Smith, Jane Randolph, Tom Conway.

Count Yorga, the Vampire 1970 (USA, American International). D: Robert Kelljan. S: Robert Quarry, Roger Perry.

Countess Dracula 1970 (UK). D: Peter Sandy. S: Ingrid Pitt.

Curse of the Cat People, The 1944 (USA, RKO). D: Robert Wise. S: Simone Simon, Kent Smith, Jane Randolph.

Curse of the Mummy's Tomb 1964 (UK). D: Michael Carreras. S: Terence Morgan, Ronald Howard.

Curse of the Werewolf 1961 (UK). D: Terence Fisher. S: Oliver Reed, Clifford Evans.

Dead of Night 1945 (UK). D: Alberto Cavalcanti, Basil Deardon, Charles Crichton, Robert Hamer. S: Michael Redgrave, Mervyn Johns, Googie Withers, Ralph Michael, Sally Anne Howes, Basil Radford, Naunton Wayne.

Death Line 1972 (UK). D: Garry Sherman. S: Christopher Lee, Donald Pleasence, Norman Rossington.

Devil Doll, The 1936 (USA, MGM). D: Tod Browning. S: Lionel Barrymore, Maureen O'Sullivan, Frank Lawton, Henry B Wathall.

Dracula 1931 (USA, Universal). D: Tod Browning. S: Bela Lugosi, Helen Chandler, Edward Van Sloan, David Manners, Dwight Frye.

Dracula A.D. 1972 (UK). D: Alan Gibson. S: Christopher Lee, Peter Cushing, Stephanie Beacham.

Dracula's Daughter 1936 (USA, Universal). D: Lambert Hillyer. S: Gloria Holden, Otto Kruger, Edward Van Sloan, Irving Pichel.

Dracula Has Risen from the Grave 1969 (UK). D: Freddie Francis. S: Peter Cushing.

Dracula Prince of Darkness 1968 (UK). D: Terence Fisher. S: Christopher Lee, Barbara Shelley.

Dr. Jekyll and Mr. Hyde 1920 (USA, Par). D: John S Robertson. S: John Barrymore, Martha Mansfield, Brandon Hurst, Charles Lane, Louis Wolheim.

Dr. Jekyll and Mr. Hyde 1932 (USA, Par). D: Rouben Mamoulian. S: Fredric March, Miriam Hopkins, Rose Hobart.

Dr. Jekyll and Mr. Hyde. 1941 (USA, MGM). D: Victor Fleming. S: Spencer Tracy, Ingrid Bergman, Lana Turner, Donald Crisp.

Dr. Terror's House of Horrors (Alternate title: *The Blood Suckers*) 1965 (UK-USA). D: Freddie Francis. S: Peter Cushing, Christopher Lee, Donald Sutherland.

Exorcist, The 1973 (USA, Warners). D: William Friedkin. S: Ellen Burstyn, Linda Blair, Lee J Cobb, Jason Miller.

Frankenstein Meets the Wolf Man 1943 (USA, Universal). D: Roy William Neill. S: Lon Chaney, Jr., Bela Lugosi.

Friday the 13th 1980 (USA, United Artists). D: Sean S. Cunningham. S: Betsy Palmer, Harry Crosby, Adrienne King.

Ghost and Mrs. Muir, The 1947 (USA, 20th). D: Joseph L Mankiewicz. S: Gene Tierney, Rex Harrison, George Sanders.

Ghost Breakers, The 1940 (USA, Par). D: George Marshall. S: Bob Hope, Paulette Goddard.

Ghost Goes West, The 1935 (UK). D: Rene Clair. S: Robert Donat, Jean Parker, Eugene Pallette.

Ghosts of Rome 1961 (Italy). D: Antonio Pietrangeli. S: Marcello Mastroianni, Sandro Milo, Vittorio Gassman.

Golem, Der/The Monster of Fate 1914 (Germany). D: Henrick Galeen, Paul Wegener. S: Paul Wegener, Lyda Salmonova, Henrik Galeen.

Golem und die Tanzerin, Der/The Golem and the Dancing Girl 1917 (Germany). D: Paul Wegener. S: Paul Wegener.

Golem: Wie er in die Welt kam, Der/The Golem How He Came into the World 1920 (Germany) D: Paul Wegener, S: Paul Wegener, Lyda Salmonova, Albert Steinruck.

Golem, Le/The Legend of Prague 1935 (Czechoslovakia). D: Julien Duvivier. S: Harry Baur, Roger Karl, Charles Dorat, Marcel Dalio.

Halloween 1978 (USA, Compass). D: John Carpenter. S: Jamie Lee Curtis, Donald Pleasence, Nancy Loomis.

Hands of Orlac, The/Orlacs Hände 1925 (Austria). D: Robert Wiene. S: Conrad Veidt, Werner Krauss.

Haunted Palace, The 1963 (USA, American International). D: Roger Corman. S: Vincent Price, Lon Chaney, Jr.

Haunting, The 1963 (UK). D: Robert Wise. S: Claire Bloom, Julie Harris, Richard Johnson.

Horror of Dracula 1958 (UK). D: Terence Fisher. S: Christopher Lee, Peter Cushing, Michael Gough.

House of Dracula 1945 (USA, Universal). D: Erle C Kenton. S: Lon Chaney, Jr., John Carradine, Lionel Atwill.

I Walked with a Zombie 1943 (USA, RKO). D: Jacques Tourneur. S: Frances Dee, Tom Conway.

I Was a Teenage Werewolf 1957 (USA, American International). D: Gene Fowler, Jr. S: Michael Landon, Whit Bissell, Yvonne Lime.

Innocents, The 1961 (UK-USA). D: Jack Clayton. S: Deborah Kerr, Pamela Franklin, Martin Stevens.

In Search of Dracula 1975 (Sweden). D: Calvin Floyd. S: Christopher Lee.

Isle of the Dead 1945 (USA, RKO). D: Mark Robson. S: Boris Karloff, Ellen Drew.

Kiss of the Vampire (Alternate title: *Kiss of Evil*) 1963 (UK). D: Don Sharp. S: Noel Willman, Clifford Evans.

Lady and the Monster, The 1944 (USA, Republic). D: George Sherman. S: Erich von Stroheim, Vera Hruba Ralston, Richard Arlen.

Legend of Hell House, The 1973 (UK). D: John Hough. S: Roddy McDowall, Pamela Franklin, Clive Revell.

Life Without a Soul 1915 (USA). D: Joseph W Smiley. S: Perry Darrel Standing.

London After Midnight 1927 (USA, MGM). D: Tod Browning. S: Lon Chaney, Marceline Day, Henry B Walthall.

Love at First Bite 1979 (USA, American International/Filmways). D: Stan Dragoti. S: George Hamilton, Susan Saint James, Richard Benjamin.

Mad Love 1935 (USA, MGM). D: Karl Freund. S: Peter Lorre, Frances Drake,

Colin Clive, Ted Healy.

Magician, The 1926 (USA, MGM). D: Rex Ingram. S: Paul Wegener, Alice Terry.

Manoir Diable, Le (US title: *The Haunted Castle*; UK title: *The Devil's Castle*) 1896 (France). D: George Méliès.

Mark of the Vampire 1935 (USA, MGM). D: Tod Browning. S: Lionel Barrymore, Bela Lugosi, Elizabeth Allen.

Miracle Man, The 1919 (USA, Artcraft/Par). D: George Loane Tucker. S: Lon Chaney, Thomas Meighan, Betty Compson.

Mother Riley Meets the Vampire (US titles: *My Son the Vampire; Vampire over London*) 1952 (UK). D: John Gilling. S: Bela Lugosi, Arthur Lucan.

Mummy, The 1932 (USA, Universal). D: Karl Freund. S: Boris Karloff, David Manners, Zita Johann, Edward Van Sloan.

Mummy, The 1959 (UK). D: Terence Fisher. S: Christopher Lee, Peter Cushing.

Mummy's Ghost, The 1944 (USA, Universal). D: Reginald Le Borg. S: Lon Chaney, Jr., John Carradine.

Mummy's Shroud, The 1967 (UK). D: John Gilling. S: Andre Morell, John Phillips, Elizabeth Sellers.

Mummy's Tomb, The 1942 (USA, Universal). D: Harold Young. S: Lon Chaney, Jr., Dick Foran.

Mystery of the Wax Museum, The 1933 (USA, Warners). D: Michael Curtiz. S: Lionel Atwill, Fay Wray, Glenda Farrell, Frank McHugh.

Nosferatu – Eine Symphonie des Grauns (English titles: *Nosferatu, the Vampire; Nosferatu: A Symphony of Horror*) 1922 (Germany). D: F W Murnau. S: Max Schreck, Gustav von Wangenheim, Greta Schroeder.

Omen, The 1976 (USA, 20th). D: Richard Donner. S: Gregory Peck, Lee Remick, David Warner, Billie Whitelaw.

Phantom of the Opera, The 1925 (USA, Universal). D: Rupert Julian. S: Lon Chaney, Mary Philbin, Norman Kerry.

Poltergeist 1982 (USA, Col). D: Stephen Spielberg. S: Craig T Nelson, Jobeth Williams, Oliver Robbins, Heather O'Rourke.

Premature Burial, The 1962 (USA, American International). D: Roger Corman. S: Ray Milland, Hazel Court, Heather Angel.

Pyscho 1960 (USA, Par). D: Alfred Hitchcock. S: Anthony Perkins, Vera Miles, Janet Leigh, Martin Balsam, John Gavin.

Return of Count Yorga, The 1971 (USA, American International). D: Robert Kelljan. S: Robert Quarry.

Return of Dracula, The (UK title: *Fantastic Disappearing Man*) 1958 (USA, United Artists). D: Paul Landres. S: Francis Lederer, Norma Eberhardt.

Scared Stiff 1953 (USA, Par). D: George Marshall. S: Jerry Lewis, Dean Martin, Lizabeth Scott.

Scars of Dracula, The 1970 (UK). D: Roy Ward Baker. S: Christopher Lee, Dennis Waterman, Jenny Hanley.

Scream, Blacula, Scream 1973 (USA, American International). D: Robert Kelljan. S: William Marshall, Pam Grier, Don Mitchell.

Shining, The 1980 (USA, Warners). D: Stanley Kubrick. S: Jack Nicholson, Shelley Duval, Anne Jackson, Danny Lloyd.

Son of Dracula 1943 (USA, Universal). D: Robert Siodmak. S: Lon Chaney, Jr., Louise Albritton.

Svengali 1931 (USA, Warners). D: Archie Mayo. S: John Barrymore, Marion Marsh.

Svengali 1954 (UK). D: Noel Langley. S: Donald Wolfit, Hildegarde Neff.

Teenage Zombies 1960 (USA, American International). D: Jerry Warren. S: Don Sullivan, Katherine Victor.

Theater of Blood 1973 (UK). D: Douglas Hickox. S: Vincent Price, Diana Rigg.

Theatre of Death 1966 (UK). D: Samuel Gallu. S: Christopher Lee, Lelia Godoni, Julian Glover.

Two Faces of Dr. Jekyll, The 1960 (UK). D: Terence Fisher. S: Christopher Lee, Paul Massie.

Undying Monster, The 1942 (US, Fox). D: John Brahm. S: John Howard, Heather Thatcher, Dudley Digges.

Uninvited, The 1944 (USA, Par). D: Lewis Allen. S: Ray Milland, Ruth Hussey, Gail Russell, Donald Crisp.

Vampyr (Alternate title: *The Strange Adventures of David Gray*; US title; *Castle of Doom*) 1932 (Germany-France). D: Carl Theodor Dreyer. S: Julian West, Sybille Schmitz, Henriette Gerard.

Walking Dead, The 1936 (Warners). D: Michael Curtiz. S: Boris Karloff, Edmund Gwenn, Ricardo Cortez, Marguerite Churchill.

Werewolf of London, The 1935 (USA, Universal). D: Stuart Walker. S: Henry Hull, Warner Oland, Valerie Hobson, Spring Byington.

Werewolf in a Girl's Dormitory 1962 (Italy). D: Richard Benson. S: Carl Schell, Barbara Lass.

White Zombie 1932 (USA, United Artists). D: Victor Halperin. S: Bela Lugosi, Madge Bellamy, Joseph Cawthorne.

Wolf Man, The 1941 (USA, Universal). D: George Waggner. S: Lon Chaney, Jr., Claude Rains, Ralph Bellamy, Maria Ouspenskaya, Bela Lugosi, Evelyn Ankers.

Chapter 5
The Musical

Alexander's Ragtime Band 1938 (USA, 20th). D: Henry King. S: Tyrone Power, Alice Faye, Don Ameche, Jack Haley, Ethel Merman.

All That Jazz 1979 (USA, 20th). D: Bob Fosse. S: Roy Scheider, Ann Reinking, Leland Palmer, Jessica Lange, Ben Vereen.

An American in Paris 1951 (USA, MGM). D: Vincente Minnelli. S: Gene Kelly, Leslie Caron, Georges Guetary, Oscar Levant.

Anchor's Aweigh 1945 (USA, MGM). D: George Sidney. S: Gene Kelly, Frank Sinatra, Kathryn Grayson, Jose Iturbi.

Annie 1982 (USA). D: John Huston. S: Albert Finney, Carol Burnett, Aileen Quinn.

Annie Get Your Gun 1950 (USA, MGM). D: George Sidney. S: Betty Hutton, Howard Keel, Louis Calhern, Edward Arnold, J. Carrol Naish.

Applause 1929 (USA, Par). D: Rouben Mamoulian. S: Helen Morgan, Joan Peers, Joe King.

Babes in Arms 1939 (USA, MGM). D: Busby Berkeley. S: Judy Garland, Mickey Rooney, Charles Winninger, Guy Kibbee, June Preisser.

Babes on Broadway 1941 (USA, MGM). D: Busby Berkeley. S: Judy Garland, Mickey Rooney, Fay Bainter, Virginia Weidler, Ray McDonald.

Barkleys of Broadway, The 1949 (USA, MGM). D: Charles Walters. S: Fred Astaire, Ginger Rogers, Billie Burke, Oscar Levant.

Bathing Beauty 1944 (USA, MGM). D: George Sidney. S: Esther Williams, Red Skelton, Basil Rathbone, Ethel Smith, Harry James and orchestra.

Bells Are Ringing 1960 (USA, MGM). D: Vincente Minnelli. S: Judy Holliday, Dean Martin, Fred Clark, Eddie Foy, Jr., Frank Gorshin.

Benny Goodman Story, The 1956 (USA, Universal). D: Valentine Davies. S: Steve Allen, Donna Reed, Sammy Davis, Jr., Harry James, Gene Krupa, Lionel Hampton.

Big Broadcast, The 1932 (USA, Par). D: Frank Tuttle. S: Bing Crosby, Stuart Erwin, Kate Smith, Boswell Sisters, George Burns, Gracie Allen.

Big Broadcast of 1937, The 1936 (USA, Par). D: Mitchell Leisen. S: Jack Benny, George Burns, Gracie Allen, Martha Raye, Shirley Ross, Ray Milland.

Big Broadcast of 1938, The 1938 (USA, Par). D: Mitchell Leisen. S: W C Fields, Bob Hope, Martha Raye, Shirley Ross, Kirsten Flagstad.

Billy Rose's Jumbo 1962 (USA, MGM). D: Charles Walters. S: Doris Day, Stephen Boyd, Martha Raye, Jimmy Durante.

Bitter Sweet 1940 (USA, MGM). D: W S Van Dyke. S: Jeanette MacDonald, Nelson Eddy, Ian Hunter, George Sanders.

Blue Skies 1946 (USA, Par). D: Stuart Heisler. S: Bing Crosby, Fred Astaire, Joan Caulfield.

Born to Dance 1936 (USA, MGM). D: Roy Del Ruth. S: Eleanor Powell, James Stewart, Virginia Bruce, Buddy Ebsen.

Brigadoon 1954 (USA, MGM). D: Vincente Minnelli. S: Gene Kelly, Cyd Charisse, Van Johnson.

Broadway Melody, The 1929 (USA, MGM). D: Harry Beaumont. S: Charles King, Bessie Love, Anita Page, Jed Prouty.

Broadway Melody of 1936 1935 (USA, MGM). D: Roy Del Ruth. S: Eleanor Powell, Robert Taylor, Jack Benny, Buddy Ebsen.

Broadway Melody of 1938 1937 (USA, MGM). D: Roy Del Ruth. S: Eleanor Powell, Robert Taylor, George Murphy, Sophie Tucker, Judy Garland, Buddy Ebsen.

Broadway Melody of 1940 1940 (USA, MGM). D: Norman Taurog. S: Fred Astaire, Eleanor Powell, George Murphy.

Buddy Holly Story, The 1978 (USA, Col). D: Steve Rash. S: Gary Busey, Don Stroud, Charles Martin Smith.

Bye Bye Birdie 1963 (USA, Col). D: George Sidney. S: Dick Van Dyke, Janet Leigh, Ann-Margret, Paul Lynde, Bobby Rydell.

Cabaret 1971 (USA, Allied Artists). D: Bob Fosse. S: Liza Minnelli, Michael York, Joel Grey.

Cabin in the Sky 1943 (USA, MGM). D:

Vincente Minnelli. S: Ethel Waters, Eddie Anderson, Lena Horne, Rex Ingram.

Calamity Jane 1953 (USA, Warners). D: David Butler. S: Doris Day, Howard Keel, Allyn McLerie, Dick Wesson.

Call Me Madam 1953 (USA, 20th). D: Walter Lang. S: Ethel Merman, Donald O'Connor, George Sanders, Vera-Ellen, Billy De Wolfe.

Camelot 1967 (USA, Warners). D: Joshua Logan. S: Richard Harris, Vanessa Redgrave, Franco Nero, David Hemmings, Lionel Jeffries.

Can-Can 1960 (USA, 20th). D: Walter Lang. S: Frank Sinatra, Shirley MacLaine, Maurice Chevalier, Louise Jourdan, Juliet Prowse.

Captain January 1936 (USA, 20th). D: David Butler. S: Shirley Temple, Buddy Ebsen, Guy Kibbee, Slim Summerville, June Lang.

Carefree 1938 (USA, RKO). D: Mark Sandrich. S: Fred Astaire, Ginger Rogers, Ralph Bellamy, Jack Carson, Luella Gear.

Carmen Jones 1954 (USA, 20th). D: Otto Preminger. S: Harry Belafonte, Dorothy Dandridge, Pearl Bailey, Diahann Carroll.

Carousel 1956 (USA, 20th). D: Henry King. S: Shirley Jones, Gordon MacRae, Cameron Mitchell, Barbara Ruick.

College Humor 1933 (USA, Par). D: Wesley Ruggles. S: Bing Crosby, Jack Oakie, Mary Carlisle, Richard Arlen, George Burns, Gracie Allen.

Coney Island 1943 (USA, 20th). D: Walter Lang. S: Betty Grable, George Montgomery, Cesar Romero, Phil Silvers, Charles Winninger.

Cover Girl 1944 (USA, Col). D: Charles Vidor. S: Rita Hayworth, Gene Kelly, Phil Silvers, Eve Arden.

Curly Top 1935 (USA, 20th). D: Irving Cummings. S: Shirley Temple, John Boles, Rochelle Hudson, Arthur Treacher.

Dames 1934 (USA, Warners). D: Ray Enright, Busby Berkeley. S: Dick Powell, Ruby Keeler, Joan Blondell, ZaSu Pitts, Hugh Herbert, Guy Kibbee.

Damn Yankees 1958 (USA, Warners). D: George Abbott, Stanley Donen. S: Gwen Verdon, Tab Hunter, Ray Walston, Jean Stapleton.

Damsel in Distress, A 1937 (USA, RKO). D: George Stevens. S: Fred Astaire, Joan Fontaine, George Burns, Gracie Allen, Reginald Gardiner.

Dancing Lady 1933 (USA, MGM). D: Robert Z Leonard. S: Joan Crawford, Clark Gable, Fred Astaire, Franchot Tone.

Desert Song, The 1929 (USA, Warners). D: Roy Del Ruth. S: John Boles, Myrna Loy, Carlotta King, Louise Fazenda.

Doctor Doolittle 1967 (USA, 20th). D: Richard Fleischer. S: Rex Harrison, Samantha Egger, Anthony Newley, Richard Attenborough.

Dolly Sisters, The 1945 (USA, 20th). D: Irving Cummings. S: Betty Grable, June Haver, John Payne, Reginald Gardiner.

Down Argentine Way 1940 (USA, 20th). D: Irving Cummings. S: Don Ameche, Betty Grable, Carmen Miranda, Charlotte Greenwood.

Down to Earth 1947 (USA, Col). D: Alexander Hall. S: Rita Hayworth, Larry Parks,

Marc Platt, Roland Culver, Edward Everett Horton.

Du Barry Was a Lady 1943 (USA, MGM). D: Roy Del Ruth. S: Lucille Ball, Red Skelton, Gene Kelly, Virginia O'Brien, Rags Ragland, Zero Mostel.

Easter Parade 1948 (USA, MGM). D: Charles Walters. S: Judy Garland, Fred Astaire, Peter Lawford, Ann Miller, Keenan Wynn.

Eddy Duchin Story, The 1966 (USA, Col). D: George Sidney. S: Tyrone Power, Kim Novak, James Whitmore, Victoria Shaw, Sheppard Strudwick.

Espresso Bongo 1960 (UK). D: Val Guest. S: Laurence Harvey, Cliff Richard, Sylvia Syms.

Fiddler on the Roof 1971 (USA, United Artists). D: Norman Jewison. S: Topol, Norma Crane, Leonard Frey, Molly Picon.

Finian's Rainbow 1968 (USA, Warners). D: Francis Ford Coppola. S: Fred Astaire, Petula Clark, Tommy Steele.

Firefly, The 1937 (USA, MGM). D: Robert Z Leonard. S: Jeanette MacDonald, Allan Jones, Warren William, Billy Gilbert.

Fleet's In, The 1942 (USA, Par). D: Victor Schertzinger. S: Betty Hutton, Dorothy Lamour, William Holden, Eddie Bracken.

Flirtation Walk 1934 (USA, Warners). D: Frank Borzage. S: Dick Powell, Ruby Keeler, Pat O'Brien, Ross Alexander.

Flower Drum Song 1961 (USA, Universal-International). D: Henry Koster. S: Nancy Kwan, James Shigeta, Miyoshi Umeki, Juanita Hall, Jack Soo.

Flying Down to Rio 1933 (USA, RKO). D: Thornton Freeland. S: Gene Raymond, Dolores Del Rio, Fred Astaire, Ginger Rogers.

Follow the Fleet 1936 (USA, RKO). D: Mark Sandrich. S: Fred Astaire, Ginger Rogers, Harriet Hilliard, Randolph Scott.

Footlight Parade 1933 (USA, Warners). D: Lloyd Bacon. S: James Cagney, Dick Powell, Ruby Keeler, Joan Blondell.

For Me and My Gal 1942 (USA, MGM). D: Busby Berkeley. S: Judy Garland, Gene Kelly, George Murphy, Ben Blue, Keenan Wynn.

42nd Street 1933 (USA, Warners). D: Lloyd Bacon. S: Warner Baxter, Bebe Daniels, Dick Powell, Ruby Keeler, George Brent.

Funny Girl 1968 (USA, Col). D: William Wyler. S: Barbra Streisand, Omar Sharif, Walter Pidgeon, Anne Francis, Kay Medford.

Funny Lady 1975 (USA, Col). D: Herbert Ross. S: Barbra Streisand, Omar Sharif, James Caan, Roddy McDowall.

Funny Thing Happened on the Way to the Forum, A 1966 (USA, United Artists). D: Richard Lester. S: Zero Mostel, Jack Gilford, Michael Crawford, Phil Silvers, Buster Keaton.

Gay Divorcee, The 1934 (USA, RKO). D: Mark Sandrich. S: Fred Astaire, Ginger Rogers, Edward Everett Horton, Eric Blore, Erik Rhodes, Alice Brady.

Gentlemen Prefer Blondes 1953 (USA, 20th). D: Howard Hawks. S: Marilyn Monroe, Jane Russell, Charles Coburn, Elliott Reid.

George White's Scandals 1934 (USA, 20th). D: Howard Hawks. S: Rudy Vallee, Alice Faye, Adrienne Ames, Gregory Ratoff, Dixie Dunbar, Cliff Edwards.

Gigi 1958 (USA, MGM). D: Vincente Minnelli. S: Leslie Caron, Maurice Chevalier, Louis Jourdan, Hermione Gingold.

Girl Crazy 1943 (USA, MGM). D: Norman Taurog. S: Judy Garland, Mickey Rooney, Nancy Walker, June Allyson, Gil Stratton, Tommy Dorsey and orchestra.

Girl of the Golden West, The 1938 (USA, MGM). D: Robert Z Leonard. S: Jeanette MacDonald, Nelson Eddy, Walter Pidgeon, Leo Carillo, Buddy Ebsen.

Glenn Miller Story, The 1954 (USA, Universal). D: Anthony Mann. S: James Stewart, June Allyson, Charles Drake, George Tobias, Phil Harris.

Go Into Your Dance 1935 (USA, Warners). D: Archie Mayo. S: Al Jolson, Ruby Keeler, Helen Morgan, Phil Regan.

Gold Diggers of 1933 1933 (USA, Warners). D: Mervyn LeRoy. S: Dick Powell, Ruby Keeler, Joan Blondell, Warren William, Ginger Rogers.

Gold Diggers of 1935 1935 (USA, Warners). D: Busby Berkeley. S: Dick Powell, Gloria Stuart, Adolphe Menjou, Alice Brady, Glenda Farrell.

Gold Diggers of 1937 1936 (USA, Warners). D: Lloyd Bacon. S: Dick Powell, Joan Blondell, Victor Moore, Lee Dixon.

Goldwyn Follies, The 1938 (USA, Goldwyn). D: George Marshall. S: Adolphe Menjou, Andrea Leeds, Vera Zorina, Bobby Clark, Ella Logan, Edgar Bergen and Charlie McCarthy.

Grease 1978 (USA, Par). D: Randal Kleiser. S: John Travolta, Olivia Newton-John, Stockard Channing, Eve Arden, Jeff Conaway, Didi Conn, Frankie Avalon.

Great Caruso, The 1951 (USA, MGM). D: Richard Thorpe. S: Mario Lanza, Ann Blyth, Kirsten Flagstad, Jarmila Novotna.

Great Ziegfeld, The 1936 (USA, MGM). D: Robert Z Leonard. S: William Powell, Myrna Loy, Luise Rainer, Virginia Bruce, Frank Morgan, Ray Bolger.

Guys and Dolls 1955 (USA, Goldwyn/MGM). D: Joseph L. Mankiewicz. S: Marlon Brando, Frank Sinatra, Jean Simmons, Vivian Blaine.

Gypsy 1962 (USA, Warners). D: Mervyn LeRoy. S: Rosalind Russell, Natalie Wood, Karl Malden.

Hair 1979 (USA, United Artists). D: Milos Forman. S: John Savage, Treat Williams, Beverly D'Angelo.

Half a Sixpence 1967 (US-UK). D: George Sidney. S: Tommy Steele, Cyril Ritchard, Julia Foster, Penelope Horner.

Harvey Girls, The 1946 (USA, MGM). D: George Sidney. S: Judy Garland, John Hodiak, Angela Lansbury, Ray Bolger, Cyd Charisse, Virginia O'Brien.

Hello, Dolly! 1969 (USA, 20th). D: Gene Kelly. S: Barbra Streisand, Walter Matthau, Michael Crawford.

Hello Frisco, Hello 1943 (USA, 20th). D: Bruce Humberstone. S: Alice Faye, John Payne, Jack Oakie, Lynn Bari.

High Society 1956 (USA, MGM). D: Charles Walters. S: Bing Crosby, Grace Kelly, Frank Sinatra, Celeste Holm.

Holiday Inn 1942 (USA, Par). D: Mark Sandrich. S: Bing Crosby, Fred Astaire, Marjorie Reynolds, Virginia Dale.

Hollywood Revue of 1929, The 1929 (USA, MGM). D: Charles F Reisner, S: Jack

Grace Kelly and Bing Crosby in
High Society (1956).

Benny, Conrad Nagel, Marion Davies, Joan Crawford, Marie Dressler, Buster Keaton, Norma Shearer, John Gilbert.

How to Succeed in Business Without Really Trying 1967 (USA, United Artists). D: David Swift. S: Robert Morse, Michele Lee, Rudy Vallee.

I'll Cry Tomorrow 1955 (USA, MGM). D: Daniel Mann, S: Susan Hayward, Richard Conte, Eddie Albert, Jo Van Fleet.

I Married an Angel 1942 (USA, MGM). D: W S Van Dyke. S: Jeanette MacDonald, Nelson Eddy, Edward Everett Horton, Binnie Barnes.

In the Good Old Summertime 1949 (USA, MGM). D: Robert Z Leonard. S: Judy Garland, Van Johnson, Buster Keaton.

Jailhouse Rock 1957 (USA, MGM). D: Richard Thorpe. S: Elvis Presley, Judy Tyler, Mickey Shaughnessy.

Jazz Singer, The 1927 (USA, Warners). D: Alan Crosland. S: Al Jolson, Warner Oland, May McAvoy, Eugenie Besserer.

Jesus Christ, Superstar 1973 (USA, Universal). D: Norman Jewison. S: Ted Neeley, Carl Anderson, Yvonne Ellman.

Jolson Story, The 1946 (USA, Col). D: Alfred E Green. S: Larry Parks, Evelyn Keyes, Ludwig Donath, William Demarest.

King and I, The 1956 (USA, 20th). D: Walter Lang. S: Yul Brynner, Deborah Kerr, Rita Moreno, Martin Benson, Terry Saunders.

Kismet 1955 (USA, MGM). D: Vincente Minnelli. S: Howard Keel, Ann Blyth, Dolores Del Rio, Vic Damone.

Kiss Me, Kate 1953 (USA, MGM). D: George Sidney. S: Kathryn Grayson, Howard Keel, Ann Miller, Bob Fosse, Bobby Van.

Lady in the Dark 1944 (USA, Par). D: Mitchell Leisen. S: Ginger Rogers, Ray Milland, Warner Baxter, Jon Hall, Barry Sullivan.

Lili 1953 (USA, MGM). D: Charles Walters. S: Leslie Caron, Mel Ferrer, Jean Pierre Aumont, Zsa Zsa Gabor.

Lillian Russell 1940 (USA, 20th). D: Irving Cummings. S: Alice Faye, Don Ameche, Henry Fonda, Warren William, Edward Arnold.

Little Night Music, A 1977 (UK). D: Harold Prince. S: Elizabeth Taylor, Diana Rigg, Len Cariou, Lesley-Anne Down, Hermione Gingold.

London Town 1946 (UK). D: Westley Ruggles. S: Sid Field, Kay Kendall, Greta Gynt, Petula Clark.

Love Parade, The 1929 (USA, Par). D: Ernst Lubitsch. S: Maurice Chevalier, Jeanette MacDonald, Lupino Lane, Lillian Roth.

Mame 1974 (USA, Warners). D: Gene Saks. S: Lucille Ball, Robert Preston, Bea Arthur.

Man of La Mancha 1972 (USA, United Artists). D: Arthur Hiller. S: Peter O'Toole, Sophia Loren, James Coco, Harry Andrews.

Mary Poppins 1964 (USA, Disney). D: Robert Stevenson. S: Julie Andrews, Dick Van Dyke, David Tomlinson, Glynis Johns, Ed Wynn.

My Fair Lady 1964 (USA, Warners). D: George Cukor. S: Rex Harrison, Audrey Hepburn, Stanley Holloway, Wilfrid Hyde-White, Gladys Cooper, Jeremy Brett, Theodore Bikel.

Naughty Marietta 1935 (USA, MGM). D: W S Van Dyke. S: Jeanette MacDonald Nelson Eddy, Frank Morgan, Elsa Lanchester.

New Moon 1940 (USA, MGM). D: Robert Z Leonard. S: Jeanette MacDonald, Nelson Eddy, George Zucco, Mary Boland.

Night and Day 1946 (USA, Warners). D: Michael Curtiz. S: Cary Grant, Alexis Smith, Monty Wooley, Jane Wyman, Ginny Simms.

Oklahoma! 1955 (USA, Arthur Hornblow/Magna). D: Fred Zinnemann. S: Gordon MacRae, Shirley Jones, Rod Steiger, Charlotte Greenwood, Eddie Albert, Gloria Grahame, Gene Nelson.

Oliver! 1968 (UK). D: Carol Reed. S: Ron Moody, Mark Lester, Oliver Reed, Shani Wallis, Harry Secombe.

On a Clear Day You Can See Forever 1970 (USA, Par). D: Vincente Minnelli. S: Barbra Streisand, Yves Montand, Larry Blyden, Jack Nicholson, Bob Newhart.

Maytime 1937 (USA, MGM). D: Robert Z Leonard. S: Jeanette MacDonald, Nelson Eddy, John Barrymore, Herman Bing.

Meet Me in St. Louis 1944 (USA, MGM). D: Vincente Minnelli. S: Judy Garland, Margaret O'Brien, Leon Ames, Tom Drake, Joan Carroll.

Merry Widow, The 1934 (USA,MGM). D: Ernst Lubitsch. S: Jeanette MacDonald, Maurice Chevalier, Edward Everett Horton, Una Merkel.

Merry Widow, The 1952 (USA, MGM). D: Curtis Bernhardt. S: Lana Turner, Fernando Lamas, Richard Haydn, Una Merkel.

Mississippi 1935 (USA, Par). D: Edward A. Sutherland. S: Bing Crosby, W C Fields, Joan Bennett, Gail Patrick.

Monte Carlo 1930 (USA, Par). D: Ernst Lubitsch. S: Jeanette MacDonald, Jack Buchanan, ZaSu Pitts.

Moon Over Miami 1941 (USA, 20th). D: Walter Lang. S: Betty Grable, Don Ameche, Carole Landis, Robert Cummings, Charlotte Greenwood, Jack Haley.

Mother Wore Tights 1947 (USA, 20th). D: Walter Lang. S: Betty Grable, Dan Dailey, Mona Freeman, Connie Marshall.

Music Man, The 1962 (USA, Warners). D: Morton Da Costa. S: Robert Preston, Shirley Jones, Paul Ford, Buddy Hackett, Hermione Gingold.

One Hour with You 1932 (USA, Par). D: Ernst Lubitsch. S: Maurice Chevalier, Jeanette MacDonald, Genevieve Tobin, Roland Young, Charles Ruggles.

One in a Million 1936 (USA, 20th). D: Sidney Lanfield. S: Sonja Henie, Don Ameche, Adolphe Menjou, Ned Sparks.

On the Town 1949 (USA, MGM). D: Stanley Donen, Gene Kelly. S: Gene Kelly, Frank Sinatra, Jules Munshin, Vera-Ellen, Betty Garrett, Ann Miller.

Paint Your Wagon 1969 (USA, Par). D: Joshua Logan. S: Lee Marvin, Clint Eastwood, Harve Presnell, Jean Seberg, Ray Walston.

Pajama Game, The 1957 (USA, Warners). D: George Abbott, Stanley Donen. S: Doris Day, John Raitt, Carol Haney, Eddie Foy, Jr.

Pal Joey 1957 (USA, Col). D: George Sidney. S: Frank Sinatra, Kim Novak, Rita Hayworth, Barbara Nichols, Hank Henry, Bobby Sherwood.

Paramount on Parade 1930 (USA, Par). D: Various directors. S: Maurice Chevalier, Clara Bow, Fredric March, Gary Cooper, Jack Oakie, Nancy Carroll, Jean Arthur, Phillips Holmes, Virginia Bruce, Ruth Chatterton.

Pennies from Heaven 1936 (USA, Col). D: Norman Z McLeod. S: Bing Crosby, Edith Fellows, Madge Evans, Donald Meek, Louis Armstrong and orchestra.

Porgy and Bess 1959 (USA, Goldwyn/Col). D: Otto Preminger. S: Sidney Poitier, Dorothy Dandridge, Sammy Davis, Jr., Diahann Carroll, Pearl Bailey, Brock Peters

Red Garters 1954 (USA, Par). D: George Marshall. S: Jack Carson, Rosemary Clooney, Guy Mitchell, Pat Crowley, Buddy Ebsen.

Rhapsody in Blue 1945 (USA, Warners). D: Irving Rapper. S: Robert Alda, Alexis Smith, Joan Leslie, Oscar Levant, Charles Coburn.

Rhythm on the Range 1936 (USA, Par). D: Norman Taurog. S: Bing Crosby, Frances Farmer, Martha Raye, Bob Burns.

Rio Rita 1929 (USA, RKO). D: Luther Reed. S: John Boles, Bebe Daniels, Bert Wheeler, Robert Woolsey.

Roberta 1935 (USA, RKO). D: William A Seiter. S: Fred Astaire, Ginger Rogers, Irene Dunne, Randolph Scott.

Roman Scandals 1933 (USA, Goldwyn). D: Frank Tuttle. S: Eddie Cantor, Gloria Stuart, Ruth Etting, David Manners, Edward Arnold.

Rosalie 1937 (USA, MGM). D: W S Van Dyke. S: Eleanor Powell, Nelson Eddy, Frank Morgan, Ilona Massey, Edna May Oliver, Billy Gilbert, Reginald Owen.

Rose, The 1979 (USA, 20th). D: Mark Rydell. S: Bette Midler, Alan Bates, Harry Dean Stanton, Frederic Forrest, Barry Primus.

Rose Marie 1936 (USA, MGM). D: W S Van Dyke. S: Jeanette MacDonald, Nelson Eddy, James Stewart, Reginald Owen, Allan Jones.

Rose Marie 1954 (USA, MGM). D: Mervyn LeRoy. S: Howard Keel, Ann Blyth, Fernando Lamas, Bert Lahr.

Rose of Washington Square 1939 (USA, 20th). D: Gregory Ratoff. S: Alice Faye, Tyrone Power, Al Jolson, Joyce Compton, William Frawley.

Sailing Along 1938 (UK). D: Sonnie Hale. S: Jessie Matthews, Jack Whiting, Roland Young.

Sally 11929 (USA, Warners). D: John Francis Dillon. S: Marilyn Miller, Joe E Brown, Alexander Gray, Pert Kelton.

Scrooge 1970 (UK). D: Ronald Neame. S: Albert Finney, Alec Guinness, Edith Evans.

Seven Brides for Seven Brothers 1954 (USA, MGM). D: Stanley Donen. S: Howard Keel, Jane Powell, Julie Newmar, Tommy Rall, Russ Tamblyn.

1776 1972 (USA, Jack Warner/Col). D: Peter Hunt. S: Howard da Silva, William Daniels, Ken Howard, Blythe Danner.

Shall We Dance 1937 (USA, RKO). D: Mark Sandrich. S: Fred Astaire, Ginger Rogers, Edward Everett Horton, Eric Blore.

Shocking Miss Pilgrim, The 1947 (USA, Fox). D: George Seaton. S: Betty Grable, Dick Haymes, Allyn Joslyn, Anne Revere.

Show Boat 1936 (USA, Universal). D: James Whale. S: Irene Dunne, Allan Jones, Charles Winninger, Paul Robeson, Helen Morgan, Helen Westley.

Show Boat 1951 (USA, MGM). D: George Sidney. S: Kathryn Grayson, Howard Keel, Ava Gardner, Joe E Brown, William Warfield, Marge and Gower Champion, Agnes Moorehead.

Show of Shows 1929 (USA, Warners). D: John Adolfi. S: Beatrice Lillie, Frank Fay, Loretta Young, John Barrymore, Louise Fazenda, Chester Morris, Harriette Lake (Ann Sothern), Ted Lewis and orchestra.

Silk Stockings 1957 (USA, MGM). D: Rouben Mamoulian. S: Fred Astaire, Cyd Charisse, Peter Lorre, Janis Paige, Jules Munshin.

Singing Fool, The 1928 (USA, Warners). D: Lloyd Bacon. S: Al Jolson, Betty Bronson, Davy Lee, Josephine Dunn.

Sing You Sinners 1938 (USA, Par). D: Wesley Ruggles. S: Bing Crosby, Fred MacMurray, Donald O'Connor, Ellen Drew.

Smiling Lieutenant, The 1931 (USA, Par). D: Ernst Lubitsch. S: Maurice Chevalier, Miriam Hopkins, Claudette Colbert, Charles Ruggles.

Sound of Music, The 1965 (USA, 20th). D: Robert Wise. S: Julie Andrews, Christopher Plummer, Eleanor Parker, Richard Haydn.

South Pacific 1958 (USA, 20th). D: Joshua Logan. S: Mitzi Gaynor, Rossano Brazzi, France Nuyen, Juanita Hall, Ray Walston, John Kerr.

Stand Up and Cheer 1934 (USA, 20th). D: Hamilton McFadden. S: Shirley Temple, Warner Baxter, Madge Evans, James Dunn, John Boles.

Star! 1968 (USA, 20th). D: Robert Wise. S: Julie Andrews, Daniel Massey, Richard Crenna, Robert Reed.

Star is Born, A 1954 (USA, Warners). D: George Cukor. S: Judy Garland, James Mason, Jack Carson, Charles Bickford.

Star is Born, A 1976 (USA, Warners). D: Frank Pierson. S: Barbra Streisand, Kris Kristofferson, Paul Mazursky, Gary Busey.

Story of Vernon and Irene Castle, The 1939 (USA, RKO). D: H C Potter. S: Fred Astaire, Ginger Rogers, Walter Brennan, Edna May Oliver.

Strike Up the Band 1940 (USA, MGM). D: Busby Berkeley. S: Judy Garland, Mickey Rooney, June Preisser, William Tracy, Paul Whiteman.

Sunny Side Up 1929 (USA, 20th). D: David Butler, S: Janet Gaynor, Charles Farrell, El Brendel, Frank Albertson.

Sun Valley Serenade 1941 (USA, 20th). D: Bruce Humberstone. S: Sonja Henie, John Payne, Milton Berle, Glenn Miller.

Sweet Charity 1969 (USA, Universal). D: Bob Fosse. S: Shirley MacLaine, Ricardo Montalban, Sammy Davis, Jr., John McMartin.

Sweethearts 1938 (USA, MGM). D: W S Van Dyke. S: Jeanette MacDonald, Nelson Eddy, Ray Bolger, Florence Rice, Frank Morgan.

Sweet Rosie O'Grady 1943 (USA, 20th). D: Irving Cummings. S: Betty Grable, Robert Young, Adolphe Menjou, Reginald Gardiner.

Swing Time 1936 (USA, RKO). D: George Stevens. S: Fred Astaire, Ginger Rogers, Helen Broderick. Victor Moore, Eric Blore.

That Night in Rio 1941 (USA, 20th). D: Irving Cummings. S: Alice Faye, Don Ameche, Carmen Miranda, S Z Sakall.

There's No Business Like Show Business 1954 (USA, 20th). D: Walter Lang. S: Ethel Merman, Mitzi Gaynor, Dan Dailey, Donald O'Connor, Marilyn Monroe.

Thoroughly Modern Millie 1967 (USA, Universal). D: George Roy Hill. S: Julie Andrews, Carol Channing, Mary Tyler Moore, Beatrice Lillie, James Fox.

Thousands Cheer 1943 (USA, MGM). D: George Sidney. S: Gene Kelly, Kathryn Grayson, John Boles, Judy Garland, Eleanor Powell, Red Skelton, Ann Sothern, Lucille Ball, Lena Horne, June Allyson, Jose Iturbi.

Three Little Words 1950 (USA, MGM). D: Richard Thorpe. S: Fred Astaire, Red Skelton, Vera-Ellen, Arlene Dahl, Gloria De Haven, Debbie Reynolds.

Till The Clouds Roll By 1946 (USA, MGM). D: Richard Whorf. S: Judy Garland, Robert Walker, Van Heflin, June Allyson, Van Johnson, Lena Horne, Kathryn Grayson, Frank Sinatra.

Top Hat 1935 (USA, RKO). D: Mark Sandrich. S: Fred Astaire, Ginger Rogers, Helen Broderick, Edward Everett Horton, Erik Rhodes, Eric Blore.

Unsinkable Molly Brown, The 1964 (USA, MGM). D: Charles Walters. S: Debbie Reynolds, Harve Presnell, Ed Begley, Hermione Baddeley, Martita Hunt.

Up in Arms 1944 (USA, Goldwyn/RKO). D: Elliott Nugent. S: Danny Kaye, Dinah Shore, Dana Andrews, Louis Calhern, Constance Dowling.

Variety Girl 1947 (USA, Par). D: George Marshall. S: Bing Crosby, Bob Hope, and variety of stars.

West Side Story 1961 (USA, United Artists). D: Robert Wise. S: Natalie Wood, Rita Moreno, Richard Beymer, George Chakiris, Russ Tamblyn.

White Christmas 1954 (USA, Par). D: Michael Curtiz. S: Bing Crosby, Danny Kaye, Vera-Ellen, Rosemary Clooney.

Whoopee 1931 (USA, Goldwyn/United Artists). D: Thornton Freeland. S: Eddie Cantor, Eleanor Hunt, Paul Gregory, Betty Grable.

Wiz, The 1978 (USA, Universal). D: Sidney Lumet. S: Diana Ross, Nipsey Russell, Ted Ross, Richard Pryor, Lena Horne.

Wizard of Oz, The 1939 (USA, MGM). D: Victor Fleming. S: Judy Garland, Ray Bolger, Bert Lahr, Jack Haley, Frank Morgan, Margaret Hamilton, Billie Burke.

Wonder Bar 1934 (USA, Warners). D: Lloyd Bacon. S: Al Jolson, Dick Powell, Kay Francis, Dolores Del Rio.

Yankee Doodle Dandy 1942 (USA, Warners). D: Michael Curtiz. S: James Cagney, Joan Leslie, Walter Huston, Rosemary DeCamp.

Yolanda and the Thief 1945 (USA, MGM). D: Norman Taurog. S: Fred Astaire, Lucille Bremer, Mildred Natwick, Frank Morgan.

You'll Never Get Rich 1941 (USA, Col). D: Sidney Lanfield. S: Fred Astaire, Rita Hayworth, Robert Benchley, John Hubbard.

You Were Never Lovelier 1942 (USA, Col). D: William A Seiter. S: Fred Astaire, Rita Hayworth, Adolphe Menjou, Xavier Cugat.

Ziegfeld Follies 1946 (USA, MGM). D: Lemuel Ayres, Robert Lewis, Vincente Minnelli, George Sidney. S: Judy Garland, Gene Kelly, Fred Astaire, William Powell, Esther Williams, Lena Horne, Lucille Ball.

Ziegfeld Girl 1941 (USA, MGM). D: Robert Z Leonard. S: James Stewart, Lana Turner, Judy Garland, Hedy Lamarr, Tony Martin, Dan Dailey, Jackie Cooper, Ian Hunter.

Chapter 6
Comedy

In its early years, filmed comedy produced so many memorable shorts that this filmography must be divided into two sections – one for feature-length material and the other for the shorts. The section on the one- and two-reel pictures follows the listing of the features.

Features

Adam's Rib 1955 (USA, MGM). D: George Cukor. S: Spencer Tracy, Katharine Hepburn, Judy Holliday.

Andy Hardy Comes Home 1958 (USA, MGM). D: Howard Koch. S: Mickey Rooney, Fay Holden, Pat Breslin.

Animal Crackers 1930 (USA, Par). D: Victor Heerman. S: Groucho, Chico, Harpo, and Zeppo Marx, Lillian Roth, Margaret Dumont.

Annie Hall 1977 (USA, United Artists) D: Woody Allen. S: Woody Allen, Diane Keaton, Shelley Duvall.

Apartment, The 1960 (USA, Mirisch-United Artists). D: Billy Wilder. S: Jack Lemmon,

Shirley MacLaine, Fred MacMurray.

At the Circus 1939 (USA, MGM). D: Edward Buzzell. S: Groucho, Chico, and Harpo Marx, Florence Rice, Kenny Baker, Margaret Dumont.

Atoll K (Alternate titles: *Robinson Crusoe-Land/Utopia*) 1950 (France-Italy). D: John Berry, Leo Joannon. S: Stan Laurel, Oliver Hardy, Suzy Delair.

Awful Truth, The 1937 (USA, Col). D: Leo MaCarey. S: Cary Grant, Irene Dunne, Ralph Bellamy.

Bank Dick, The 1940 (USA, Universal). D: Edward Cline. S: W C Fields, Grady Sutton, Franklin Pangborn..

Belle du Jour 1967 (France-Italy). D: Luis Bunuel. S: Catherine Deneuve, Jean Sorel, Michel Piccoli.

Big Store, The 1941 (USA, MGM). D: Charles Reisner. S: Groucho, Chico, and Harpo Marx, Tony Martin, Douglas Dumbrille.

Birds, the Bees and the Italians, The 1966 (France-Italy). D: Pietro Germi. S: Virna Lisi, Gastone Moschin.

Blazing Saddles 1974 (USA, Warners). D: Mel Brooks. S: Mel Brooks, Gene Wilder, Cleavon Little, Madeline Kahn.

Blondie 1938 (USA, Col). D: Frank R Strayer. S: Penny Singleton, Arthur Lake, Larry Simms, Jonathan Hale.

Blues Brothers, The 1980 (USA, Univ). D: John Landis. S: John Belushi, Dan Ackroyd, Aretha Franklin.

Bread and Chocolate 1974 (Italy). D: Franco Brusati. S: Nino Manfredi, Anna Karina.

Buck Privates 1941 (USA, Universal). D: Arthur Lubin. S: Bud Abbott, Lou Costello, the Andrews Sisters.

Caddy, The 1953 (USA, Par). D: Norman Taurog. S: Dean Martin, Jerry Lewis, Donna Reed.

Cage aux Folles, La 1978 (France-Italy). D: Edouard Molinaro. S: Michel Serrault, Ugo Tognazzi, Michel Galabru.

Captain's Paradise, The 1953 (UK). D: Anthony Kimmins. S: Alec Guinness, Celia Johnson, Yvonne DeCarlo.

Casanova's Big Night 1954 (USA, Par). D: Norman Z McLeod. S: Bob Hope, Joan Fontaine, Basil Rathbone.

Caught in the Draft 1941 (USA, Par). D: David Butler. S: Bob Hope, Dorothy Lamour.

Circus, The 1928 (USA, United Artists). D: Charles Chaplin. S: Charles Chaplin, Allan Garcia, Merna Kennedy.

City Lights 1931 (USA, United Artists). D: Charles Chaplin. S: Charles Chaplin, Virginia Cherrill, Florence Lee.

Coconuts, The 1929 (USA, Par). D: Joseph Santley, Robert Florey. S: Groucho, Chico, Harpo, and Zeppo Marx, Kay Francis, Margaret Dumont.

Countess from Hong Kong, A 1967 (UK). D: Charles Chaplin. S: Marlon Brando, Sophia Loren, Margaret Rutherford.

Court Jester, The 1956 (USA, Par). D: Norman Panama. S: Danny Kaye, Glynis Johns, Basil Rathbone.

Day at the Races, A 1937 (USA, MGM). D: Sam Wood. S: Groucho, Chico, and Harpo Marx, Maureen O'Sullivan, Allan Jones.

Day for Night 1972 (France). D: Francois Truffaut. S: Francois Truffaut, Jacqueline Bisset, Jean-Pierre Leaud.

Desk Set, The 1957 (USA, 20th). D: Walter

Claudette Colbert in *It Happened One Night.*

Lang. S: Spencer Tracy, Katharine Hepburn, Gig Young.

Duck Soup 1933 (USA, Par). D: Leo McCarey. S: Groucho, Chico, and Harpo Marx, Louis Calhern, Margaret Dumont.

Eight on the Lam 1967 (USA, United Artists). D: George Marshall. S: Bob Hope, Jonathan Winters, Jill St. John.

Everything You Always Wanted to Know About Sex But Were Afraid to Ask 1972 (USA, United Artists). D: Woody Allen. S: Woody Allen, Lou Jacobi, Gene Wilder.

Excuse My Dust 1951 (USA, MGM). D: Roy Rowland. S: Red Skelton, McDonald Carey, Sally Forrest.

Facts of Life, The 1960 (USA, United Artists). D: Melvin Frank. S: Lucille Ball, Bob Hope.

Family Affair, A 1937 (USA, MGM). D: George B Seitz. S: Mickey Rooney, Lionel Barrymore, Spring Byington.

Flying Deuces, The 1939 (USA, Morros-RKO). D: Edward A Sutherland. S: Stan Laurel, Oliver Hardy, Reginald Gardiner, Jean Parker.

Foul Play 1978 (USA, Par). D: Colin Higgins. S: Goldie Hawn, Chevy Chase, Dudley Moore

Freshman, The 1925 (USA, Lloyd-Pathe). D: Sam Taylor. S: Harold Lloyd, Jobyna Ralston.

Fuller Brush Girl, The 1950 (USA, Col). D: Lloyd Bacon. S: Lucille Ball, Eddie Albert, Lee Patrick, Red Skelton (guest appearance).

Fuller Brush Man, The 1948 (USA, Col). D: S Sylvan Simon. S: Red Skelton, Janet Blair.

Geisha Boy, The 1958 (USA, Par). D: Frank Tashlin. S: Jerry Lewis, Marie McDonald, Suzanne Pleshette.

General, The 1926 (USA, Keaton-Schenck-United Artists). D: Buster Keaton, Clyde Bruckman. S: Buster Keaton, Marion Mack, Glen Cavander.

Go West 1925 (USA, Keaton-Schenck-Metro) D: Buster Keaton. S: Buster Keaton, Howard Truesdale, Kathleen Myers.

Go West 1940 (USA, MGM). D: Edward

Buzzell. S: Groucho, Chico, and Harpo Marx, John Carroll, Robert Barrat.

Go West, Young Man 1936 (USA, Par). D: Henry Hathaway. S: Mae West, Warren William, Randolph Scott.

Gold Rush, The 1925 (USA, United Artists). D: Charles Chaplin. S: Charles Chaplin, Mack Swain, Tom Murray.

Graduate, The 1968 (USA, Turman-Avemb). D: Mike Nichols. S: Dustin Hoffman, Anne Bancroft, Katharine Ross.

Great Dictator, The 1940 (USA, United Artists). D: Charles Chaplin. S: Charles Chaplin, Paulette Goddard, Jack Oakie.

Great Lover, The 1949 (USA, Par). D: Alexander Hall. S: Bob Hope, Rhonda Fleming, Roland Young.

Half a Hero 1953 (USA, MGM). D: Don Weis. S: Red Skelton, Jean Hagen.

Hobson's Choice 1954 (UK). D: David Lean. S: Charles Laughton, John Mills, Brenda de Banzie.

Hook, Line and Sinker 1969 (USA, Col). D: George Marshall. S: Jerry Lewis, Anne Francis, Peter Lawford.

Horse Feathers 1932 (USA, Par). D: Norman Z McLeod. S: Groucho, Chico, Harpo, and Zeppo Marx.

If I Had a Million 1932 (USA, Par). D: Ernst Lubitsch, Norman Taurog, James Cruze, H Bruce Humberstone, William A Seiter, Stephen Roberts. S: W C Fields, George Raft, Gary Cooper, Charles Laughton, Allison Skipworth, Jack Oakie.

International House 1933 (USA, Par). D: Edward Sutherland. S: W C Fields, Stuart Erwin, George Burns, Gracie Allen.

It Happened One Night 1934 (USA, Col). D: Frank Capra. S: Clark Gable, Claudette Colbert, Walter Connolly.

It's a Gift 1934 (USA, Par). D: Norman Z McLeod. S: W C Fields.

It's a Mad, Mad, Mad, Mad World 1963 (USA, United Artists). D: Stanley Kramer. S: Spencer Tracy, Milton Berle, Sid Caesar, Ethel Merman, Dorothy Provine, Jimmy Durante, Buddy Hackett, Buster Keaton, Phil Silvers.

Judge Priest 1934 (USA, 20th). D: John Ford. S: Will Rogers, Anita Louise, Stepin Fetchit.

Jumping Jacks 1952 (USA, Par). D: Norman Taurog. S: Jerry Lewis, Dean Martin, Mona Freeman.

Keep 'em Flying 1941 (USA, Universal). D: Arthur Lubin. S: Bud Abbott, Lou Costello, Martha Raye.

Kid, The 1921 (USA, First National). D: Charles Chaplin. S: Charles Chaplin, Jackie Coogan, Edna Purviance.

Kid from Brooklyn, The 1946 (USA, Goldwyn-RKO). D: Leo McCarey. S: Danny Kaye, Virginia Mayo, Vera-Ellen.

Kind Hearts and Coronets 1949 (UK). D: Robert Hamer. S: Alec Guinness, Dennis Price, Joan Greenwood.

King in New York, A 1957 (UK). D: Charles Chaplin. S: Charles Chaplin, Dawn Addams, Maxine Audley.

Klondike Annie 1936 (USA, Par). D: Raoul Walsh. S: Mae West, Victor McLaglen, Gene Austin.

Knock on Wood 1954 (USA, Par). D: Norman Panama. S: Danny Kaye, Mai Zetterling.

Ladykillers, The 1955 (UK). D: Alexander MacKendrick. S: Alec Guinness, Cecil Parker, Peter Sellers, Herbert Lom.

Lavender Hill Mob, The 1951 (UK). D: Charles Crichton. S: Alec Guinness, Stanley Holloway, Audrey Hepburn.

Lemon Drop Kid, The 1951 (USA, Par). D: Sidney Lanfield. S: Bob Hope, Marilyn Maxwell.

Limelight 1952 (USA, United Artists). D: Charles Chaplin. S: Charles Chaplin, Claire Bloom, Nigel Bruce, Buster Keaton.

Love Crazy 1941 (USA, MGM). D: Jack Conway. S: William Powell, Myrna Loy, Jack Carson, Gail Patrick.

Love Happy 1949 (USA, Cowan-United Artists). D: David Miller. S: Groucho, Chico, and Harpo Marx, Ilona Massey, Vera-Ellen, Marilyn Monroe.

Milky Way, The 1936 (USA, Par). D: Leo McCarey. S: Harold Lloyd, Adolphe Menjou, Helen Mack.

Million Dollar Legs 1932 (USA, Par). D: Edward Cline. S: W C Fields, Jack Oakie, Susan Fleming, Lyda Roberti, Ben Turpin.

Mr. Deeds Goes to Town 1936 (USA, Col). D: Frank Capra. S: Gary Cooper, Jean Arthur, George Bancroft.

Modern Times 1936 (USA, United Artists). D: Charles Chaplin. S: Charles Chaplin, Paulette Goddard.

Monkey Business 1931 (USA, Par). D: Norman Z McLeod. S: Groucho, Chico, Harpo and Zeppo Marx, Thelma Todd, Ruth Hall.

Mon Oncle/My Uncle 1958 (France-Italy). D: Jacques Tati. S: Jacques Tati, Jean-Pierre Zola, Alain Becourt.

Monsieur Hulot's Holiday/Les Vacances de Monsieur Hulot 1953 (France). D: Jacques Tati. S: Jacques Tati.

Monsieur Verdoux 1947 (USA, United Artists). D: Charles Chaplin. S: Charles Chaplin, Martha Raye, Marilyn Nash.

More the Merrier, The 1943 (USA, Col). D: George Stevens. S: Jean Arthur, Joel McCrea, Charles Coburn.

My Little Chickadee 1940 (USA, Universal). D: Edward Cline. S: W C Fields, Mae West, Joseph Calleia, Margaret Hamilton.

National Lampoon's Animal House 1978 (USA, Universal). D: John Landis. S: John Belushi, Tim Matheson, John Vernon.

Navigator, The 1924 (USA, Keaton-Schenck-Metro). D: Donald Crisp. S: Buster Keaton, Kathryn McGuire.

Never Give a Sucker an Even Break 1941 (USA, Universal). D: Edward Cline. S: W C Fields, Gloria Jean, Margaret Dumont.

Night at the Opera, A 1935 (USA, MGM). D: Sam Wood. S: Groucho, Chico, and Harpo Marx, Kitty Carlisle, Allan Jones.

Night in Casablanca, A 1946 (USA, Loew-United Artists). D: Archie Mayo. S: Groucho, Chico, and Harpo Marx.

1941 1979 (USA, Universal). D: Steven Spielberg. S: John Belushi, Dan Ackroyd, Ned Beatty, Lorraine Gary.

Nothing Sacred 1937 (USA, Selznick). D: William A Wellman. S: Carole Lombard, Fredric March, Walter Connolly.

Odd Couple, The 1968 (USA, Par). D: Gene Saks. S: Jack Lemmon, Walter Matthau, Herb Edelman.

Oh God! 1977 (USA, Warners). D: Carl Reiner. S: George Burns, John Denver, Paul Sorvino, Terri Garr.

Oh God! Book Two 1980 (USA, Warners). D: Gilbert Cates. S: George Burns, Susan Pleshette, David Birney.

Old Fashioned Way, The 1934 (USA, Par). D: William Beaudine. S: W C Fields.

On the Double 1961 (USA, Par). D: Melville Shavelson. S: Danny Kaye, Dana Wynter, Margaret Rutherford.

On the Riviera 1951 (USA, 20th). D: Walter Lang. S: Danny Kaye, Gene Tierney, Corinne Calvet.

One of Our Dinosaurs is Missing 1975 (UK). D: Robert Stevenson. S: Helen Hayes, Peter Ustinov, Clive Revill.

Only Two Can Play 1962 (UK). D: Sidney Gilliat. S: Peter Sellers, Mai Zetterling, Richard Attenborough.

Paleface, The 1948 (USA, Par). D: Norman Z McLeod. S:. Bob Hope, Jane Russell.

Pardners 1956 (USA, Par). D: Norman Taurog. S: Dean Martin, Jerry Lewis, Agnes Moorehead.

Pardon My Sarong 1942 (USA, Universal). D: Erle C Kenton. S: Bud Abbott, Lou Costello, Virginia Bruce.

Parlor, Bedroom and Bath 1931 (USA, MGM). D: Edward Sedgwick. S: Buster Keaton, Charlotte Greenwood, Reginald Denny, Cliff Edwards.

Passport to Pimlico 1949 (UK). D: Henry Cornelius. S: Stanley Holloway, Margaret Rutherford, Basil Radford.

Phffft 1954 (USA, Col). D: Mark Robson. S: Jack Lemmon, Judy Holliday, Kim Novak, Jack Carson.

Pillow Talk 1959 (USA, Universal). D: Michael Gordon. S: Doris Day, Rock Hudson, Tony Randall.

Pink Panther 1964 (UK). D: Blake Edwards. S: Peter Sellers, David Niven, Capucine.

Poppy 1936 (USA, Par). D: Edward Sutherland. S: W C Fields, Rochelle Hudson, Richard Cromwell.

Private Benjamin 1980 (USA, Warners). D: Howard Zieff. S: Goldie Hawn, Eileen Brennan, Armand Assante.

Professor Beware 1938 (USA, Par). D: Elliott Nugent. S: Harold Lloyd, Phyllis Welch, Lionel Stander.

Quiet Wedding 1941 (UK). D: Anthony Asquith. S: Margaret Lockwood, Derek Farr.

Return of the Pink Panther 1975 (UK). D: Blake Edwards. S: Peter Sellers, Herbert Lom, Christopher Plummer, Catherine Schell.

Ride 'em Cowboy 1942 (USA, Universal). D: Arthur Lubin. S: Bud Abbott, Lou Costello, Dick Foran, Anne Gwynne.

Road to Hong Kong 1961 (USA, United Artists). D: Norman Panama. S: Bob Hope, Bing Crosby, Joan Collins.

Road to Morocco 1942 (USA, Par). D: David Butler. S: Bob Hope, Bing Crosby, Dorothy Lamour.

Road to Rio 1948 (USA, Par). D: Norman Z McLeod. S: Bob Hope, Bing Crosby, Dorothy Lamour.

Road to Singapore 1940 (USA, Par). D: Victor Schertzinger. S: Bob Hope, Bing Crosby, Dorothy Lamour, Anthony Quinn.

Road to Utopia 1945 (USA, Par). D: Hal Walker. S: Bob Hope, Bing Crosby, Dorothy Lamour, Hillary Brooke.

Road to Zanzibar 1941 (USA, Par). D: Victor Schertzinger. S: Bob Hope, Bing Crosby, Dorothy Lamour, Una Merkel.

Room Service 1938 (USA, RKO). D: William A Seiter. S: Groucho, Chico, and Harpo Marx, Lucille Ball, Ann Miller.

Russians are Coming, The Russians are Coming, The 1966 (USA, United Artists). D: Norman Jewison. S: Alan Arkin, Paul Ford, Carl Reiner, Eva Marie Saint.

Sad Sack, The 1957 (USA, Par). D: George Marshall. S: Jerry Lewis, David Wayne, Phyllis Kirk.

Safety Last 1923 (USA, Roach-Pathe). D: Fred Newmeyer. S: Harold Lloyd, Mildred Davis.

Secret Life of Walter Mitty, The 1947 (USA, Goldwyn-RKO). D: Norman Z McLeod. S: Danny Kaye, Virginia Mayo.

Seven Year Itch, The 1955 (USA, 20th). D: Billy Wilder. S: Marilyn Monroe, Tom Ewell, Evelyn Keyes.

Sherlock Jr 1924 (USA, Metro). D: Buster Keaton and, unconfirmed, Roscoe Arbuckle. S: Buster Keaton, Kathryn McGuire.

Silent Movie 1976 (USA, 20th). D: Mel Brooks. S: Mel Brooks Marty Feldman, Dom DeLuise.

Sins of Harold Diddlebock, The (Alternate title: *Mad Wednesday*) 1947 (USA, California-United Artists). D: Preston Sturges. S: Harold Lloyd, Frances Ramsden, Ruddy Vallee.

Some Like It Hot 1959 (USA, United Artists). D: Billy Wilder. S: Jack Lemmon, Tony Curtis, Marilyn Monroe, Joe E Brown.

Son of Paleface 1952 (USA, Par). D: Frank Tashlin. S: Bob Hope, Jane Russell, Roy Rogers.

Steamboat Bill, Jr 1928 (USA, Keaton-Schenck-United Artists). D: Charles F Reisner. S: Buster Keaton, Ernest Torrence, Marion Byron.

Sting, The 1973 (USA, Univ). D: George Roy Hill. S: Robert Redford, Paul Newman, Robert Shaw.

State of the Union 1948 (USA, MGM). D:

Bing Crosby in *The Road to Bali* (1953).

Frank Capra. S: Spencer Tracy, Katharine Hepburn, Van Johnson, Angela Lansbury.

Strange Bedfellows 1964 (USA, Universal). D: Melvin Frank. S: Rock Hudson, Gina Lollobridgida, Gig Young.

Take the Money And Run 1969 (USA, Cinerama). D: Woody Allen. S: Woody Allen, Janet Margolin, Lonny Chapman.

There's a Girl in My Soup 1970 (UK). D: Roy Boulting. S: Peter Sellers, Goldie Hawn, Tony Britton.

Those Magnificent Men in Their Flying Machines 1965 (UK). D: Ken Annakin. S: Stuart Whitman, Sarah Miles, Terry-Thomas.

Tight Little Island (Alternate title: *Whisky Galore*). 1949 (UK). D: Alexander MacKendrick. S: Basil Radford, Joan Greenwood.

Topper 1937 (USA, Roach). D: Norman Z McLeod. S: Cary Grant, Constance Bennett, Roland Young, Billie Burke.

Touch of Class, A 1972 (UK). D: Melvin Frank. S: George Segal, Glenda Jackson.

Tugboat Annie 1933 (USA, MGM). D: Mervyn LeRoy. S: Marie Dressler, Wallace Beery, Robert Young, Maureen O'Sullivan.

Two-Way Stretch 1960 (UK). D: Robert Day. S: Peter Sellers, Lionel Jeffries, Wilfrid Hyde White.

Up in Smoke 1978 (USA, Par). D: Lou Adler. S: Cheech and Chong, Tom Skerritt, Stacy Keach.

What's New, Pussycat? 1965 (USA, United Artists). D: Clive Donner, Richard Talmadge. S: Peter Sellers, Peter O'Toole, Romy Schneider, Woody Allen.

What's Up, Doc? 1972 (USA, Warners). D: Peter Bogdanovich. S: Barbra Streisand, Ryan O'Neal.

Woman of the Year 1942 (USA, MGM). D: George Stevens. S: Spencer Tracy, Katharine Hepburn, Fay Bainter, William Bendix.

Wonder Man 1945 (USA, Goldwyn-RKO). D: H Bruce Humberstone. S: Danny Kaye, Vera-Ellen, Steve Cochran, Virginia Mayo.

Wrong Arm of the Law, The 1961 (UK). D: Cliff Owen. S: Peter Sellers, Bernard Cribbins, Lionel Jeffries.

You Can't Cheat an Honest Man 1939 (USA, Universal). D: George Marshall. S: W C Fields, Edgar Bergen and Charlie McCarthy.

You Can't Take it with You. 1938 (USA, Col). D: Frank Capra. S: James Stewart, Jean Arthur, Lionel Barrymore, Edward Arnold.

Short Subjects

The following is a representative listing of the one- and two-reel films made by the great comedians of the silent era.

Charlie Chaplin

For Mack Sennett (All 1914)
Making a Living (First film appearance)
Kid Auto Races at Venice
Caught in a Cabaret (First co-directorial assignment, with Mabel Normand)
Caught in the Rain (First solo directorial assignment)

Laughing Gas
The Face on the Barroom Floor
His Musical Career
Tillie's Punctured Romance

For Essanay (All 1915)
His New Job (First Essanay film)
A Night Out
The Champion
The Tramp (Said to be Chaplin's first masterwork)
By the Sea
Work
Shanghaied

For Mutual (1916 and 1917)
The Floorwalker
The Fireman
The Vagabond
One A.M.
The Count
The Pawnshop
Behind the Screen
Easy Street 1917
The Cure
The Immigrant
The Adventurer

For First National (1918-1923)
A Dog's Life
Shoulder Arms
Sunnyside 1919
The Idle Class 1921
Pay Day 1922
The Pilgrim 1923 (Chaplin's final short subject)

Buster Keaton

For Comique (1917-1920)
The Butcher Boy
His Wedding Night
Oh, Doctor!
Out West 1918
The Bell Boy
The Cook
Backstage 1919
The Hayseed
The Garage 1920

For the Keaton Production Unit (1920-1923)
The High Sign
One Week
The Scarecrow
Neighbors 1921
The Haunted House
The Boat
The Paleface 1922
My Wife's Relations
The Electric House
The Balloonatic 1923
The Love Nest

Harold Lloyd

For Hal Roach (1915-1921)
Just Nuts
Lonesome Luke
A Mix-up for Maizie
Lonesome Luke, Social Gangster
Luke Lugs Luggage 1916
Luke Foils the Villain
Luke's Last Laugh
Luke Joins the Navy
Luke's Movie Muddle
Luke's Lost Liberty 1917

Luke's Trolley Troubles
Lonesome Luke's Honeymoon
Lonesome Luke, Plumber
We Never Sleep (The final Lonesome Luke film)
The Tip
The Lamb 1918
A Gasoline Wedding
The Non-Stop Kid
Kicking the Germ out of Germany
Nothing But Trouble
Ask Father 1919
Crack Your Heels
Just Neighbors
Don't Shove
The Rajah
His Royal Slyness 1920
Haunted Spooks
Get Out and Get Under
Number Please
Now or Never 1921
Among Those Present
I Do
Never Weaken

Laurel and Hardy

For Hal Roach (The silent shorts; 1926-1929)
45 Minutes from Hollywood
Duck Soup 1927
Sugar Daddies
Sailors Beware
Putting Pants on Philip
Leave 'Em Laughing 1928
Flying Elephants
From Soup to Nuts
Early to Bed
Two Tars
Liberty 1929
Wrong Again
Big Business
Bacon Grabbers
Angora Love

For Hal Roach (The sound shorts; 1929-1935)
Unaccustomed as We Are
Berth Marks
Perfect Day
The Hoose-Gow
Night Owls 1930
Blotto
Brats
The Laurel-Hardy Murder Case
Another Fine Mess
Be Big 1931
Laughing Gravy
Our Wife
Come Clean
Beau Hunks
Helpmates 1932
The Music Box (Academy Award for Best Short Subject, Comedy)
The Chimp
County Hospital
Their First Mistake
Twice Two 1933
Me and My Pal
Busy Bodies
Oliver the Eighth 1934
Them Thar Hills
The Live Ghost
Tit for Tat 1935
The Fixer Uppers
Thicker Than Water

Chapter 7
Crime

Angels with Dirty Faces 1938 (USA, Warners). D: Michael Curtiz. S: James Cagney, Pat O'Brien, Humphrey Bogart, Ann Sheridan, the Dead End Kids.

Asphalt Jungle, The 1950 (USA, MGM). D: John Huston. S: Sterling Hayden, Sam Jaffe, Louis Calhern, Jean Hagen, Marilyn Monroe.

Bicycle Thieves (U.S. title: *The Bicycle Thief*) 1948 (Italy). D: Vittorio De Sica. S: Lamberto Maggiorani, Enzo Staiola, Lianella Carell.

Big House, The 1930 (USA, MGM). D: George Hill. S: Chester Morris, Wallace Beery, Lewis Stone.

Birdman of Alcatraz 1962 (USA, United Artists). D: John Frankenheimer. S: Burt Lancaster, Karl Malden.

Blue Lamp, The 1950 (UK). D: Basil Dearden. S: Jack Warner, Dirk Bogarde.

Bonnie and Clyde 1967 (USA, Warners). D: Arthur Penn. S: Warren Beatty, Faye Dunaway, Michael J Pollard, Estelle Parsons.

Brother Orchid 1940 (USA, Warners). D: Lloyd Bacon. S: Edward G Robinson, Ann Sothern, Humphrey Bogart.

Bullets or Ballots 1936 (USA, Warners). D: William Keighley. S: Edward G Robinson, Joan Blondell, Humphrey Bogart.

Capone 1975 (USA, 20th). D: Steve Carver. S: Ben Gazzara, Susan Blakely, John Cassavetes.

Detective Story 1951 (USA, Par). D: William Wyler. S: Kirk Douglas, Eleanor Parker, William Bendix.

Dog Day Afternoon 1975 (USA, Warners). D: Sidney Lumet. S: Al Pacino, James Broderick, John Cazale, Charles Durning.

Each Dawn I Die 1939 (USA, Warners). D: William Keighley. S: James Cagney, George Raft, Jane Bryan.

Escape from Alcatraz 1979 (USA, Par). D: Don Siegel. S: Clint Eastwood, Patrick McGoohan.

French Connection, The 1971 (USA, 20th). D: William Friedkin. S: Gene Hackman, Fernando Rey, Roy Scheider.

French Connection II, The 1975 (USA, 20th). D: John Frankenheimer. S: Gene Hackman, Fernando Rey.

G-Men 1935 (USA, Warners). D: William Keighley. S: James Cagney, Lloyd Nolan

Get Carter 1971(UK). D: Michael Hodges. S: Michael Caine, Britt Ekland.

Godfather, The 1972 (USA, Par). D: Francis Ford Coppola. S: Marlon Brando, Al Pacino, Diane Keaton, James Caan, Robert Duvall.

Godfather, Part II, The 1974 (USA). D: Francis Ford Coppola. S: Al Pacino, Robert De Niro, Robert Duvall.

Great Train Robbery, The 1979 (UK). D: Michael Crichton. S: Sean Connery, Donald Sutherland, Lesley Anne Down.

Hatchet Man, The 1932 (USA, Warners). D: William A Wellman. S: Edward G Robinson, Loretta Young.

High Sierra 1941 (USA, Warners). D: Raoul Walsh. S: Humphrey Bogart, Ida Lupino, Joan Leslie.

I am a Fugitive from a Chain Gang 1932 (USA, Warners). D: Mervyn LeRoy. S: Paul Muni, Glenda Farrell, Preston Foster.

Investigation of à Citizen Above Suspicion 1970 (Italy). D: Elio Petri. S: Gian Maria Volonte, Florinda Bolkan.

Johnny Apollo 1940 (USA, 20th). D: Henry Hathaway. S: Tyrone Power, Dorothy Lamour, Lloyd Nolan.

Little Caesar 1931 (USA, Warners). D: Mervyn LeRoy. S: Edward G Robinson, Douglas Fairbanks, Jr., Glenda Farrell, Thomas Jackson.

The New Centurians 1972 (USA, Col). D: Richard Fleischer. S: George C Scott, Stacy Keach, Jane Alexander, Scott Wilson.

On the Waterfront 1954 (USA, Horizon/Col). D: Elia Kazan. S: Marlon Brando, Karl Malden, Rod Steiger, Eva Marie Saint.

Petrified Forest, The 1936 (USA, Warners). D: Archie Mayo. S: Leslie Howard, Bette Davis, Humphrey Bogart, Dick Foran.

Public Enemy, The 1931 (USA), Warners. D: William A Wellman. S: James Cagney, Edward Woods, Donald Cook, Jean Harlow.

Rashomon 1951 (Japan). D: Akira Kurosawa. S: Toshiro Mifune, Masayuki Mori.

Rififi 1954 (France). D: Jules Dassin. S: Jean Servais, Carl Mohner, Jules Dassin.

Roaring Twenties, The 1939 (USA, Warners). D: Raoul Walsh. S: James Cagney, Priscilla Lane, Humphrey Bogart.

Scarface 1932 (USA, United Artists). D: Howard Hawks. S: Paul Muni, George Raft, Boris Karloff, Ann Dvorak.

This Gun for Hire 1942 (USA, Par). D: Frank Tuttle. S: Alan Ladd, Veronica Lake, Laird Cregar.

Traffic in Souls 1913 (USA, Universal). D: George Loane Tucker. S: Jane Gail, Ethel Grandin, Fred Turner.

Underworld (British title: *Paying the Penalty*) 1927 (USA, Par). D: Josef von Sternberg. S: George Bancroft, Evelyn Brent, Clive Brook.

Disaster

Abandon Ship (British title: *Seven Waves Away*) 1957 (UK). D: Richard Sale. S: Tyrone Power, Mai Zetterling, Lloyd Nolan.

Airplane 1979 (USA, Par). D: J Abrahams, D Zucker, J Zucker. S: Leslie Nielsen, Lloyd Bridges, Robert Stack.

Airport 1975 (USA, Universal). D: George Seaton. S: Burt Lancaster, Dean Martin, Helen Hayes, Van Heflin.

Airport 1975 1974 (USA, Universal). D: Jack Smight. S: Charlton Heston, Karen Black, George Kennedy, Efram Zimbalist, Jr.

Airport 77 1977 (USA, Universal). D: Jerry Jameson. S: Jack Lemmon, Lee Grant, James Stewart, Olivia de Havilland, Joseph Cotten.

Beyond the Poseidon Adventure 1979 (USA, 20th). D: Irwin Allen. S: Michael Caine, Sally Field, Telly Savalas.

Birds, The 1963 (USA, Universal). D: Alfred Hitchcock. S: Rod Taylor, Tippi Hedren, Suzanne Pleshette.

Devil at 4 O'Clock, The 1961 (USA, Col). D: Mervyn LeRoy. S: Spencer Tracy, Frank Sinatra, Jean-Pierre Aumont.

Earthquake 1974 (USA, Universal). D: Mark Robson. S: Charlton Heston, Ava Gardner, Richard Roundtree, Anthony Perkins.

Hindenburg, The 1975 (USA, Universal). D: Robert Wise. S: George C Scott, Anne Bancroft, Burgess Meredith, Charles Durning.

Hurricane, The 1937 (USA, Goldwyn). D: John Ford. S: Dorothy Lamour, Jon Hall, Thoms Mitchell, Raymond Massey.

In Old Chicago 1938 (USA, 20th). D: Henry King. S: Tyrone Power, Alice Faye, Don Ameche, Alice Brady.

Jaws 1975 (USA, Universal). D: Steven Spielberg. S: Robert Shaw, Roy Scheider, Richard Dreyfuss.

Jaws II 1978 (USA, Universal). D: Jeannot Szwarc. S: Roy Scheider, Lorraine Gary, Murray Hamilton.

Last Voyage, The 1960 (USA, Universal). D: Andrew L Stone. S: Robert Stack, Edmond O'Brien, Dorothy Malone, George Sanders.

Night to Remember, A 1958 (UK). D: Roy Baker. S: Kenneth More, David McCallum, Honor Blackman.

Rains Came, The 1939 (USA, 20th). D: Clarence Brown. S: Tyrone Power, Myrna Loy, George Brent.

San Francisco 1936 (USA, MGM). D: W S Van Dyke, S: Clark Gable, Spencer Tracy, Jeanette MacDonald, Jack Holt.

Towering Inferno, The 1974 (USA, 20th/Warners). D: Irwin Allen. S: Paul Newman, Steve McQueen, Faye Dunaway, Jennifer Jones, Fred Astaire, Robert Wagner.

Mystery and Suspense

Ace in the Hole (British title: *The Big Carnival*) 1951 (USA, Par). D: Billy Wilder. S: Kirk Douglas, Jan Sterling, Richard Benedict.

Adventures of Sherlock Holmes, The 1939 (USA, 20th). D: Alfred Werker. S: Basil Rathbone, Nigel Bruce, Ida Lupino.

After the Thin Man 1936 (USA, MGM). D: W S Van Dyke. S: William Powell, Myrna Loy, James Stewart, Joseph Calleia.

And Then There Were None (British title: *Ten Little Niggers*) 1945 (USA, Wanger). D: Rene Clair. S: Louis Hayward, Walter Huston, Barry Fitzgerald, Judith Anderson.

Another Thin Man 1939 (USA, MGM). D: W S Van Dyke. S: William Powell, Myrna Loy.

Bad Day at Black Rock 1955 (USA, MGM). D: John Sturges. S: Spencer Tracy, Robert Ryan, Anne Francis, Ernest Borgnine.

Big Sleep, The 1946 (USA, Warners). D: Howard Hawks. S: Humphrey Bogart, Lauren Bacall, Martha Vickers, John Ridgeley.

Big Sleep, The 1978 (UK). D: Michael Winner. S: Robert Mitchum, Sarah Miles, James Stewart.

Blackmail 1929 (UK). D: Alfred Hitchcock. S: Anny Ondra, John Longden, Sara Allgood.

Robert Mitchum (left) and Simon Turner in *The Big Sleep* (1978).

Cat and the Canary, The 1939 (USA, Par). D: Elliot Nugent. S: Bob Hope, Paulette Goddard, John Beal, Gale Sondergaard.

Cat Creeps, The 1930 (USA, Universal). D: Rupert Julian. S: Helen Twelvetrees, Raymond Hackett.

Charlie Chan at the Opera 1936 (USA, 20th) D: Bruce Humberstone. S: Warner Oland, Boris Karloff.

China Syndrome, The 1979 (USA, Col). D: James Bridges, S: Jack Lemmon, Jane Fonda.

Chinatown 1974 (USA, Par). D: Roman Polanski. S: Jack Nicholson, Faye Dunaway.

Crime Without Passion 1934 (USA, Par). D: Ben Hecht, Charles MacArthur. S: Claude Rains, Margo.

Deadly Affair 1967 (UK). D: Sidney Lumet. S: James Mason, Simone Signoret, Maximilian Schell.

Dear Detective 1978 (France). D: Philippe De Broca. S: Philippe Noiret, Annie Giradot.

Diaboliques, Les 1955 (France). D: Henri-Georges Clouzet. S: Simone Signoret, Vera Clouzet, Paul Meurisse.

Falcon Out West, The 1944 (USA, RKO). D: William Clemens. S: Tom Conway, Barbara Hale.

Falcon Takes Over, The 1942 (USA, RKO). D: Irving Reis. S: George Sanders, Lynn Bari.

Five Came Back 1939 (USA, RKO). D: John Farrow. S: Chester Morris, Wendy Barrie, Kent Taylor, C Aubrey Smith.

From Russia With Love 1963 (UK). D: Terence Young. S: Sean Connery, Daniel Biancha, Lotte Lenya.

Gaslight (British title: *Murder in Thornton Square*) 1944 (USA, MGM). D: George Cukor. S: Charles Boyer, Ingrid Bergman, Joseph Cotten.

Gaslight (U.S. title: *Angel Street*) 1940 (UK). D: Thorold Dickinson. S: Anton Walbrook, Diana Wynyard.

Goldfinger 1964 (USA, United Artists). D: Guy Hamilton. S: Sean Connery, Honor Blackman, Gert Frobe.

Green for Danger 1946 (UK). D: Sidney Gilliat. S: Alastair Sim, Sally Gray, Leo Genn.

Green Man, The 1957 (UK). D: Robert Day. S: Alastair Sim, George Cole, Terry-Thomas.

Hound of the Baskervilles, The 1939 (USA, 20th). D: Sidney Lanfield. S: Basil Rathbone, Nigel Bruce, Richard Greene.

Hound of the Baskervilles, The 1959 (UK). D: Terence Fisher. S: Peter Cushing, Andre Morell, Christopher Lee.

Inferno 1953 (USA, 20th). D: Roy Baker. S: Robert Ryan, Rhonda Fleming, William Lundigan.

Kennel Club Murder Case, The 1933 (USA, Warners). D: Michael Curtiz. S: William Powell, Mary Astor, Eugene Pallette.

Kiss Me Deadly 1955 (USA, United Artists). D: Robert Aldrich. S: Ralph Meeker, Paul Stewart.

Lady in the Car with Glasses and a Gun, The 1970 (US-France). D: Anatole Litvak. S: Samantha Egger, Oliver Reed.

Lady in the Lake 1946 (USA, MGM). D: Robert Montgomery. S: Robert Montgomery, Audrey Totter, Lloyd Nolan.

Laura 1944 (USA, 20th) D: Otto Preminger. S: Gene Tierney, Dana Andrews, Clifton Webb, Vincent Price.

Maltese Falcon, The (British title: *Dangerous Female*) 1931 (USA, Warners). D: Roy Del Ruth. S: Ricardo Cortez, Bebe Daniels, J Farrell MacDonald.

Maltese Falcon, The 1941 (USA, Warners). D: John Huston. S: Humphrey Bogart, Mary Astor, Peter Lorre, Sidney Greenstreet.

Man Who Knew Too Much, The 1934 (UK). D: Alfred Hitchcock. S: Leslie Banks, Edna Best, Peter Lorre.

Man Who Knew Too Much, The 1955 (USA, Par). D: Alfred Hitchcock. S: James Stewart, Doris Day, Bernard Miles.

Most Dangerous Game, The 1932 (USA, RKO). D: Ernest B Schoedsack, Irving Pichel. S: Leslie Banks, Fay Wray, Joel McCrea.

Murder at a Gallop 1963 (UK). D: George Pollock. S: Margaret Rutherford, Robert Morley.

Murder by Death 1976 (USA, Col). D: Robert Moore. S: Alec Guinness, Peter Sellers, Peter Falk, Maggie Smith.

Murder Most Foul 1964 (UK). D: George Pollock. S: Margaret Rutherford, Ron Moody.

Murder, My Sweet (British title: *Farewell, My Lovely*) 1944 (USA, RKO). D: Edward Dmytryk. S: Dick Powell, Claire Trevor, Anne Shirley.

Murder on the Orient Express 1974 (UK). D: Sidney Lumet. S: Albert Finney, Lauren Bacall, Ingrid Bergman, Sean Connery, John Gielgud, Wendy Hiller, Anthony Perkins.

Notorious 1946 (USA, RKO). D: Alfred Hitchcock. S: Cary Grant, Ingrid Bergman, Claude Rains.

North by Northwest 1959 (USA, MGM). D: Alfred Hitchcock. S: Cary Grant, Eva Marie Saint, James Mason.

Rebecca 1940 (USA, Selznick). D: Alfred Hitchcock. S: Laurence Olivier, Joan Fontaine, Judith Anderson, George Sanders.

Return of the Pink Panther 1978 (UK). D: Blake Edwards. S: Peter Sellers, Dyan Cannon, Herbert Lom.

Sherlock Holmes 1932 (USA). D: William K Howard. S: Clive Brook, Reginald Owen, Ernest Torrence.

Sherlock Holmes and the Deadly Necklace 1964 (UK-West Germany). D: Terence Fisher. S: Christopher Lee, Senta Berger, Thorley Walters.

Sherlock Holmes in Washington 1943 (USA, Universal). D: Roy William Neill. S: Basil Rathbone, Nigel Bruce.

Sherlock Holmes and the Secret Weapon 1943 (USA, Universal). D: Roy William Neill. S: Basil Rathbone, Nigel Bruce, Dennis Hoey.

Silver Streak 1976 (USA, 20th). D: Arthur Hiller. S: Gene Wilder, Jill Clayburgh, Richard Pryor.

Spellbound 1945 (USA, Selznick). D: Alfred Hitchcock. S: Gregory Peck, Ingrid Bergman, Leo G Carroll.

Strangers on a Train 1951 (USA, Warners). D: Alfred Hitchcock. S: Robert Walker, Farley Granger, Ruth Roman.

Thin Man, The 1934 (USA, MGM). D: W S Van Dyke. S: William Powell, Myrna Loy, Maureen O'Sullivan, Edward Ellis.

39 Steps, The 1935 (UK). D: Alfred Hitchcock. S: Robert Donat, Madeleine Carroll.

39 Steps, The 1959 (UK). D: Ralph Thomas. S: Kenneth More, Taina Elg.

39 Steps, The 1978 (UK). D: Don Sharp. S: Robert Powell, John Mills, Karen Dotrice.

Wages of Fear, The (*La Salaire de la Peur*) 1953 (France-Algeria). D: Henri-Georges Clouzot. S: Yves Montand, Charles Vanel, Vera Clouzot.

Romance

American Tragedy, An 1931 (USA, Par). D: Josef von Sternberg. S: Phillips Holmes, Sylvia Sidney, Frances Dee.

Anna Karenina 1935 (USA, MGM). D: Clarence Brown. S: Greta Garbo, Fredric March, Basil Rathbone.

Anna Karenina 1948 (UK). D: Julien Duvivier. S: Vivien Leigh, Ralph Richardson.

Barretts of Wimpole Street, The 1934 (USA, MGM). D: Sidney Franklin. S: Norma Shearer, Fredric March, Charles Laughton.

Barrets of Wimpole Street, The 1957 (UK). D: Sidney Franklin. S: Jennifer Jones, William Travers, John Gielgud.

Bishop's Wife, The 1947 (USA, Goldwyn). D: Henry Koster. S: Cary Grant, Loretta Young, David Niven.

Blue Lagoon, The 1948 (UK). D: Frank Launder. S: Jean Simmons, Donald Houston, Noel Purcell.

Blue Lagoon, The 1980 (USA, Col). D: Randal Kleiser. S: Brooke Shields, Christopher Atkins, Leo McKern.

Born Yesterday 1950 (USA, Col). D: George Cukor. S: Judy Holliday, William Holden, Broderick Crawford.

Brief Encounter 1946 (UK). D: David Lean. S: Celia Johnson, Trevor Howard, Stanley Holloway.

Camille 1936 (USA, MGM). D: George Cukor. S: Greta Garbo, Robert Taylor, Lionel Barrymore.

Chapter Two 1980 (USA, Col). D: Ray Stark. S: James Caan, Marsha Mason.

Claire's Knee 1970 (France) D: Eric Rohmer. S: Jean-Claude Brialy, Aurora Cornu, Beatrice Romand.

David and Lisa 1962 (USA, Continental). D: Frank Perry. S: Keir Dullea, Janet Margolin.

Devil is a Woman 1935 (USA, Par). D: Josef von Sternberg. S: Marlene Dietrich, Lionel Atwill, Cesar Romero.

Elvira Madigan 1967 (Sweden). D: Bo Widerberg. S: Pia Degermark, Thommy Berggren.

Extase/Ecstacy 1932 (Czechoslovakia). D: Gustav Machaty. S: Hedwig Kiesler (later Hedy Lamarr), Aribert Mog.

Far From the Madding Crowd 1967 (UK). D: John Schlessinger. S: Julie Christie, Alan Bates, Terence Stamp, Peter Finch.

Farewell to Arms, A 1932 (USA, Par). D: Frank Borsage. S: Helen Hayes, Gary Cooper, Adolphe Menjou.

Go-Between, The 1971 (UK). D: Joseph Losey. S: Julie Christie, Alan Bates, Dominic Guard.

Gone With the Wind 1939 (USA, Selznick). D: Victor Fleming. S: Vivien Leigh, Clark Gable, Leslie Howard, Olivia de Havilland.

Goodbye Girl, The 1977 (USA, Raster-Warners). D: Herbert Ross. S: Richard Dreyfuss, Marsha Mason, Quinn Cummings.

Hiroshima Mon Amour 1959 (France-Japan). D: Alain Resnais. S: Emmanuelle Riva, Eiji Okada.

Hold Back the Dawn 1941 (USA, Par). D: Mitchell Leisen. S: Charles Boyer, Olivia de Havilland, Paulette Goddard.

Holiday 1938 (USA, Col). D: George Cukor. S: Katharine Hepburn, Cary Grant, Lew Ayres.

I Married an Angel 1942 (USA, Par). D: Rene Clair. S: Fredric March, Veronica Lake, Susan Hayward.

Indiscreet 1958 (UK). D: Stanley Donen. S: Ingrid Bergman, Cary Grant, Cecil Parker, Phyllis Calvert.

It Should Happen to You 1954 (USA, Col). D: George Cukor. S: Judy Holliday, Jack Lemmon, Peter Lawford.

Leave Her to Heaven 1945 (USA, 20th). D: John M Stahl. S: Gene Tierney, Cornel Wilde, Jeanne Crain.

Letter to Three Wives, A 1948 (USA, 20th). D: Joseph L Mankiewicz. S: Jeanne Crain, Linda Darnell, Ann Sothern, Kirk Douglas.

Love and Marriage 1964 (Italy). D: Gianni Puccini, Mino Guerrini. S: Lando Buzzanca, Maria Grazia Buccella, Renato Tagliani.

Love and the Frenchman 1960 (France). D: Henri Decoin, Jean Delannoy, Michel Boisrond, Reni Clair, Henri Verneuil, Christian-Jaque, Jean Paul Le Chanois. S: Jean-Paul Belmondo, Annie Girardot, Martine Carol.

Love is a Many-Splendored Thing 1955 (USA, 20th). D: Henry King. S: Jennifer Jones, William Holden.

Love Story 1946 (UK). D: Maurice Ostrer. S: Margaret Lockwood, Stewart Granger, Patricia Roc.

Love Story 1970 (USA, Par). D: Arthur Hiller. S: Ali MacGraw, Ryan O'Neal, Ray Milland.

Man and a Woman, A 1966 (France). D: Claude Lelouch. S: Anouk Aimee, Jean-Louis Trintignant.

Marty 1955 (USA, Hecht-Lancaster-United Artists). D: Delbert Mann. S: Ernest Borgnine, Betsy Blair, Joe Mantell.

Mayerling 1936 (France). D: Anatole Litvak. S: Charles Boyer, Danielle Darrieux, Suzy Prim.

Ninotchka 1939 (USA, MGM). D: Ernst Lubitsch. S: Greta Garbo, Melvyn Douglas, Ina Claire.

Of Human Bondage 1934 (USA, Warners). D: John Cromwell. S: Leslie Howard, Bette Davis, Kay Johnson.

Of Human Bondage 1964 (UK). D: Ken Hughes. S: Kim Novak, Laurence Harvey.

Picnic 1955 (USA, Col). D: Joshua Logan. S: Kim Novak, William Holden, Rosalind Russell, Arthur O'Connell.

Place in the Sun, A 1951 (USA, Par). D: George Stevens. S: Montgomery Clift, Elizabeth Taylor, Shelley Winters.

Roman Holiday 1953 (USA, Par). D: William Wyler. S: Gregory Peck, Audrey Hepburn, Eddie Albert.

Romeo and Juliet 1936 (USA, MGM). D: George Cukor. S: Norma Shearer, Leslie Howard, John Barrymore, Basil Rathbone.

Romeo and Juliet 1968 (UK-Italy). D: Franco Zeffirelli. S: Leonard Whiting, Olivia Hussey, Michael York, Milo O'Shea.

Ronde, La 1950 (France). D: Max Ophuls. S: Anton Walbrook, Simone Signoret, Simone Simon, Danielle Darrieux.

Sabrina 1954 (USA, Par). D: Billy Wilder. S: William Holden, Audrey Hepburn, Humphrey Bogart.

H Bogart and Lauren Bacall in *To Have and Have Not* (1944).

Sheik, The 1921 (USA, Famous Players-Lasky). D: George Melford. S: Rudolph Valentino, Agnes Ayres, Adolphe Menjou.

10 1979 (USA, Orion). D: Blake Edwards. S: Dudley Moore, Bo Derek.

Three Coins in the Fountain 1954 (USA, 20th). D: Jean Negulesco. S: Dorothy Maguire, Clifton Webb, Louis Jourdan, Jean Peters.

Way We Were, The 1973 (USA, Col). D: Sidney Pollack. S: Robert Redford, Barbra Streisand, Bradford Dillman.

Wuthering Heights 1939 (USA, Goldwyn). D: William Wyler. S: Merle Oberon, Laurence Olivier, David Niven.

Yesterday, Today and Tomorrow 1963 (Italy). D: Vittorio De Sica. S: Sophia Loren, Marcello Mastroianni, Aldo Giuffre.

Social Comment

Accused, The (Alternate title: *The Defendant*) 1964 (Czechoslovakia). D: Jan Kadar, Elmar Klos. S: Vlado Muller, Juroslav Blazek.

Best Years of Our Lives, The 1946 (USA, Goldwyn). D: William Wyler. S: Fredric March, Dana Andrews, Teresa Wright, Virginia Mayo.

Birth of a Nation, The (Original title: *The Clansman*) 1915 (USA, Epoch). D: David Wark Griffith. S: Henry B Walthall, Mae Marsh, Miriam Cooper, Lillian Gish, Donald Crisp.

Blackboard Jungle, The 1955 (USA, MGM). D: Richard Brooks. S: Glenn Ford, Anne Francis, Sidney Poitier, Louis Calhern.

Black Legion 1936 (USA, Warners). D: Archie Mayo. S: Humphrey Bogart, Ann Sheridan, Dick Foran.

Civilization: Or He Who Returned 1916 (USA, Triangle). D: Thomas H Ince. S: Enid Markey, Howard Hickman, J Barney Sherry.

Corner In Wheat 1909 (USA, Biograph). D: David Wark Griffith. S: Frank Powell, W Christie Miller, Kate Bruce.

Criminal, The (US title: *Concrete Jungle*) 1960 (UK). D: Joseph Losey. S: Stanley Baker, Sam Wanamaker, Margit Saad.

Crossfire 1947 (USA, RKO). D: Edward Dmytryk. S: Robert Young, Robert Mitchum, Robert Ryan.

Crowd, The 1928 (USA, MGM). D: King Vidor. S: James Murray, Eleanor Boardman.

Dead End 1937 (USA, United Artists). D: William Wyler. S: Joel McCrea, Sylvia Sidney, Humphrey Bogart, the Dead End Kids.

Defiant Ones, The 1958 (USA, United Artists). D: Stanley Kramer. S: Tony Curtis, Sidney Poitier, Theodore Bikel.

Edge of the City (British title: *A Man is Ten Feet Tall*) 1956 (USA, MGM). D: Martin Ritt. S: John Cassavetes, Sidney Poitier.

Fury 1936 (USA, MGM). D: Fritz Lang. S: Spencer Tracy, Sylvia Sidney, Walter Abel, Walter Brennan.

Gentleman's Agreement 1947 (USA, 20th). D: Elia Kazan. S: Gregory Peck, Dorothy McGuire, John Garfield, Celeste Holm.

Good Earth, The 1937 (USA, MGM). D: Sidney Franklin. S: Paul Muni, Luise Rainer, Walter Connolly.

Grapes of Wrath, The 1940 (USA, 20th). D: John Ford. S: Henry Fonda, Jane Darwell, John Carradine, Russell Simpson.

Guess Who's Coming to Dinner? 1967 (USA). D: Stanley Kramer. S: Spencer Tracy, Katharine Hepburn, Sidney Poitier, Katharine Houghton.

Home of the Brave 1949 (USA). D: Mark Robson. S: Lloyd Bridges, James Edwards, Frank Lovejoy.

In the Heat of the Night 1967 (USA, Mirisch-Universal). D: Norman Jewison. S: Sidney Poitier, Rod Steiger, Lee Grant.

Intolerance 1916 (USA, Wark). D: David Wark Grififth. S: Lillian Gish, Robert Harron, Sam de Grasse, Vera Lewis.

Lost Weekend, The 1945 (USA, Par). D: Billy Wilder. S: Ray Milland, Jane Wyman, Phillip Terry, Howard Da Silva.

Man with the Golden Arm, The 1955 (USA, United Artists). D: Otto Preminger. S: Frank Sinatra, Kim Novak, Eleanor Parker.

Musketeers of Pig Alley, The 1912 (USA, Biograph). D: David Wark Griffith. S: Lillian Gish.

Neighbors 1952 (Canada). D: Norman McLaren. S: Jean-Paul Ladouceur, Grant Munro.

Of Mice and Men 1939 (USA, Roach-United Artists). D: Lewis Milestone. S: Burgess Meredith, Lon Chaney, Jr., Betty Field, Charles Bickford.

Our Daily Bread 1934 (USA, United Artists). D: King Vidor. S: Karen Morley, Tom Keene, John Qualen.

Pinky 1949 (USA, 20th). D: Elia Kazan. S: Jeanne Crain, Ethel Barrymore, Ethel Waters.

Quiet One, The 1948 (USA, Film Documents). D: Sidney Meyers. S: Donald Thompson, Sadie Stockton.

Snake Pit, The 1948 (USA, 20th). D: Anatole Litvak. S: Olivia de Havilland, Leo Genn, Mark Stevens.

Sounder 1972 (USA, Radnitz-Mattel). D: Martin Ritt. S: Cicely Tyson, Paul Winfield, Kevin Hooks.

Tobacco Road 1941 (USA, 20th). D: John Ford. S: Charlie Grapewin, Gene Tierney, Dana Andrews, Marjorie Rambeau.

Umberto D 1952 (Italy). D: Vittorio De Sica. S: Carlo Battisti, Maria Pia Casilio.

War Brides 1916 (USA, Selznick). D: Herbert Brenon. S: Nazimova, Charles Hutchinson, Charles Bryant.

War

Air Force 1943 (USA, Warners). D: Howard Hawks. S: John Garfield, Gig Young, Harry Carey.

All Quiet on the Western Front 1930 (USA, Universal). D: Lewis Milestone. S: Lew Ayres, Louis Wolheim, John Wray.

Apocalypse Now 1979 (USA, United Artists). D: Francis Ford Coppola. S: Martin Sheen, Marlon Brando, Robert Duvall.

Arsenal 1929 (USSR). D: Ed Alexander Dovzhenko. S: S Svashenko, A Buchma.

Ballad of a Soldier/Ballada O Soldate 1959 (USSR). D: Grigori Chukrai. S: Vladimir Ivanshov, Shanna Prokhorenko.

Bataan 1943 (USA, MGM). D: Tay Garnett. S: Robert Taylor, Thomas Mitchell, Robert Walker.

Battle of Britain 1969 (UK). D: Guy Hamilton. S: Michael Caine, Laurence Olivier, Trevor Howard.

Battleground 1949 (USA, MGM). D: William A Wellman. S: Van Johnson, John Hodiak, James Whitmore.

Big Parade, The 1925 (USA, MGM). D: King Vidor. S: John Gilbert, Renee Adoree, Karl Dane.

Bridge, The 1959 (West Germany). D: Bernhard Wicki. S: Volker Bohnet, Fritz Wepper, Michael Hinz.

Bridge on the River Kwai, The 1957 (USA, Col). D: David Lean. S: Alec Guinness, William Holden, Jack Hawkins, Sessue Hayakawa.

Bridge Too Far, A 1977 (USA, United Artists). D: Richard Attenborough. S: Robert Redford, Ryan O'Neal, Gene Hackman, Laurence Olivier.

Bridges at Toko-Ri, The 1954 (USA). D: Mark Robson. S: William Holden, Grace Kelly, Fredric March, Mickey Rooney.

Caine Mutiny, The 1954 (USA, Col). D: Edward Dmytryk. S: Humphrey Bogart, Van Johnson, Fred MacMurray, Jose Ferrer, Robert Francis.

Catch 22 1970 (USA, Par). D: Mike Nichols. S: Alan Arkin, Martin Balsam, Richard Benjamin.

Cry Havoc 1943 (USA, MGM). D: Richard Thorpe. S: Margaret Sullivan, Ann Sothern.

Dam Busters, The 1955 (UK). D: Michael Anderson. S: Richard Todd, Michael Redgrave.

Dawn Patrol, The (British title: *The Flight Commander*) 1930 (USA, First National). D: Howard Hawks. S: Richard Barthelmess, Douglas Fairbanks, Jr., Neil Hamilton.

Dawn Patrol, The 1939 (USA, Warners). D: Edmund Goulding. S: Errol Flynn, David Niven, Donald Crisp.

Deer Hunter, The 1978 (USA, Universal). D: Michael Cimino. S: Robert De Niro, John Cazale, John Savage.

Eroica 1957 (Poland). D: Andrzej Munk. S: Barbara Polemska, Roman Klosowski.

49th Parallel, The (US title: *The Invaders*) 1941 (UK). D: Michael Powell. S: Laurence Olivier, Raymond Massey, Leslie Howard, Eric Portman.

Four Horsemen of the Apocalypse, The 1921 (USA, Metro). D: Rex Ingram. S: Rudolph Valentino, Alice Terry, Nigel de Brulier.

Four Horsemen of the Apocalypse, The 1961 (USA, MGM). D: Vicente Minnelli. S: Glenn Ford, Ingrid Thulin, Charles Boyer.

From Here to Eternity 1953 (USA, Col). D: Fred Zinnemann. S: Burt Lancaster, Montgomery Clift, Frank Sinatra, Deborah Kerr.

Grande Illusion, La/Grand Illusion 1937 (France). D: Jean Renior. S: Jean Gabin, Pierre Fresnay, Erich von Stroheim

Guadalcanal Diary 1943 (USA, 20th). D: Lewis Seiler. S: William Bendix, Lloyd Nolan, Preston Foster.

Hearts of the World 1918 (USA, Griffith). D: David Wark Griffith. S: Lillian Gish, Dorothy Gish, Robert Harran.

Hell's Angels 1930 (USA, United Artists). D: Howard Hughes. S: Ben Lyon, James Hall, Jean Harlow (Greta Nissen: silent version).

In Which We Serve 1942 (UK). D: Noel Coward. S: Noel Coward, John Mills, Celia Johnson.

Jeux Interdits, Les/Forbidden Games 1952 (France). D: Rene Clement. S: Brigitte Fosey, Georges Poujouly.

Long Voyage Home, The 1940 (USA, Wanger-United Artists). D: John Ford. S: John Wayne, Thomas Mitchell, Ian Hunter, Barry Fitzgerald.

Longest Day, The 1962 (USA, 20th). D: Ken Annakin, Andrew Marton, Bernhard Wicki. S: John Wayne, Rod Steiger, Robert Ryan, Robert Mitchum.

*M*A*S*H* 1970 (USA, 20th). D: Robert Altman. S: Elliott Gould, Donald Sutherland, Sally Kellerman, Tom Skerritt.

Midway 1976 (USA, Universal). D: Jack Smight. S: Charlton Heston, Henry Fonda, James Coburn, Glenn Ford.

Mister Roberts 1955 (USA, Warners). D: Mervyn LeRoy, John Ford. S: Henry Fonda, James Cagney, Jack Lemmon, William Powell.

No Greater Glory 1934 (USA, Col). D: Frank Borsage. S: George Breakston, Jimmy Butler, Jackie Searl.

One of Our Aircraft is Missing 1941 (UK). D: Michael Powell. S: Godfrey Tearle, Eric Portman, Hugh Williams.

Open City 1945 (Italy). D: Roberto Rossellini. S: Anna Magnani, Aldo Fabrizi, Marcello Pagliero.

Paths of Glory 1957 (USA, Col). D: Stanley Kubrick. S: Kirk Douglas, Ralph Meeker, Adolphe Menjou, George Macready.

Patton 1970 (USA, 20th). D: Franklin J Shaffner. S: George C Scott, Karl Malden, Michael Bates, Stephen Young.

Reach for the Sky 1956 (UK). D: Lewis Gilbert. S: Kenneth More, Muriel Pavlow, Alexander Knox.

Road to Glory, The 1936 (USA, 20th) D: Howard Hawks. S: Fredric March, Lionel Barrymore, Warner Baxter.

Sergeant York 1941 (USA, Warners). D: Howard Hawks. S: Gary Cooper, Joan Leslie, Walter Brennan.

Stalag 17 1953 (USA, Par). D: Billy Wilder. S: William Holden, Robert Strauss, Harvey Lembeck.

They Were Expendable 1945 (USA, MGM). D: John Ford. S: John Wayne, Robert Montgomery, Donna Reed.

Thirty Seconds Over Tokyo 1944 (USA, MGM). D: Mervyn LeRoy. S: Spencer Tracy, Van Johnson, Robert Walker, Phyllis Thaxter.

Wake Island 1942 (USA, Par). D: John Farrow. S: Brian Donlevy, William Bendix, Robert Preston.

What Price Glory? 1926 (USA). D: Raoul Walsh. S: Victor McLaglen, Edmund Lowe, Dolores Del Rio.

Wings 1927 (USA, Par). D: William A Wellman. S: Charles 'Buddy' Rogers, Richard Arlen, Clara Bow, Gary Cooper.

Yank in the RAF, A 1941 (USA, 20th). D: Henry King. S: Tyrone Power, Betty Grable, John Sutton.

INDEX